# Acknowledgements

I wish to express my sincere appreciation to Tom Sigafoos of SDRC, Inc. Tom has provided I-DEAS software and other assistance for us to develop the book. My thanks also extend to Donna Russell who constantly encourages me to start and complete the project.

Thanks are given to Scholars staff, including Mei-shan Lin. Karen Sterzik edited the manuscript and prepared page layout. Joshua Chen created the cover design. My current and former students at Eastern Michigan University who contributed to the project include Yi-Pin Chen and his wife, Bryan Adams, Sai Vummethala, Twishampati Dattgupta, Samba Chanamolu and others. Their contribution to the book is greatly appreciated.

I am greatly indebted to my dear wife, Grace, for her continuous support. I am also grateful to my son, Andrew, and daughter, Carol, for their understanding and appreciation. Their endurance through 14 books is greatly appreciated.

# Table of Contents

**Table of Contents**

## Chapter 12. Analyzing and Animating Assemblies

## Chapter 13. Creating Surfaces

## Chapter 14. Editing Surfaces

# Chapter

# Introduction to I-DEAS

## Highlights of the Chapter
- Entering and exiting I-DEAS
- I-DEAS interfaces and windows
- Using the 3-button mouse
- Using dynamic views
- View orientations, layouts and display options
- Managing and saving files

## Overview

I-DEAS is a very powerful parametric, feature-based design software. It is actually a tightly integrated system with a part modeler as its nucleus. Many programs are interfaced with the solid part modeler to perform specific tasks such as modeling, design, drafting, analysis, and manufacturing functions. I-DEAS uses multiple windows as its user-interface layout. It has a main window with many sub-windows. Many separate sub-windows will appear as the modeling process proceeds. I-DEAS uses a three-button mouse to interact with the system. The left mouse button is used for selecting entities and commands, the middle mouse button for action completion (done) and accepting inputs, and the right mouse button for opening options.

I-DEAS uses a number of function keys to work with the mouse for manipulating the graphics views. A part model can be dynamically moved, rotated, and scaled using the function keys in combination with mouse movement. You can simultaneously show multiple views of the part model. There are four view layouts to choose from; one viewport, two viewports, three viewports, and four viewports. I-DEAS provides two commands to assign the view type to each viewport; view workplane and work viewport.

The units system for specifying length and force is very important in modeling a part. I-DEAS provides commonly used English and metric unit systems. They include meter-newton, meter-kilogram, millimeter-newton, centimeter-newton, millimeter-kilogram, foot-pound, foot-poundal, and inch-pound.

There are two file managing methods in I-DEAS; regular Windows NT file functions and library functions. The regular mode uses the Windows NT or Unix file management functions to save, open, export, and import part files. The Library mode is unique to I-DEAS. This approach allows more flexibility and control to manage a part model.

# 1.1 Introduction to Parametric Design

I-DEAS is a feature-based, parametric solid modeling software. Feature-based means that a part model consists of several distinct features, rather than unrelated geometric entities. A part can be regarded as a basic shape with features. The basic shape defines the primitive configuration of the part. Typical shapes are the channel, I-beam, cylinder, block, and others (Figure 1.1). Basic shapes are also referred to as base features.

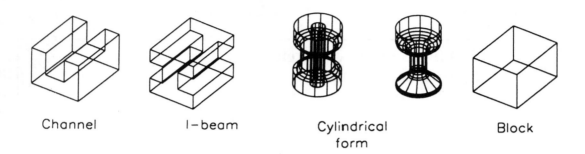

| Channel | I-beam | Cylindrical form | Block |

Figure 1.1

A **feature** is any geometry that augments a basic shape and makes it distinguishable from other parts that could be derived from the same basic shape. In other words, features are used to define the detail of the part. Those features that describe the details of the part are also referred to as added features or construction features. Figure 1.2 shows a number of parts that are created from the same base feature.

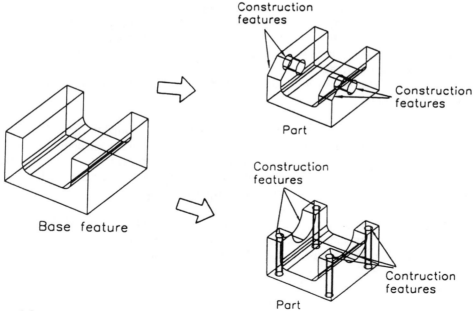

Figure 1.2

Mastering I-DEAS,
Scholars International Publishing Corp., 1999

# Introduction to I-DEAS

The term **parametric** means that parameters instead of simple dimensions are used to fully define the part model. Any change in numerical value of a parameter results in the change of shape and size of the model (Figure 1.3). Relations can be applied to parameters. The change in a parameter automatically causes the change in other parameters that are related by relation equations (Figure 1.4).

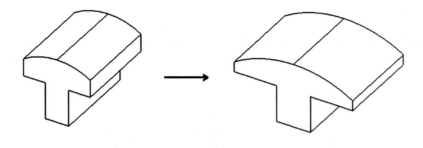

Figure 1.3

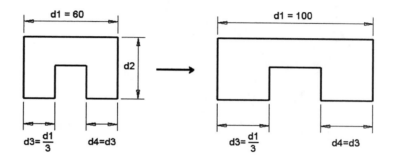

Figure 1.4

A **Family table** is another way to make use the parametric feature. A family of similar parts can be easily created from a family table (Figure 1.5). This can greatly reduce the time and improve accuracy in the creation of parts that are similar in shape.

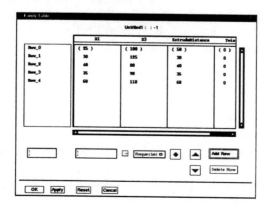

Figure 1.5

# 1.2 I-DEAS Product Family

I-DEAS is a feature-based, parametric solid modeling software. It actually is a tightly integrated software of many programs that center around the Master Modeler (Figure 1.6). I-DEAS programs are organized in two levels; applications and tasks. There are **seven applications** including **Design, Drafting, Simulation, Manufacturing, Management, Test,** and **Open Data/PCB**. Each application has several tasks. Table 1.1 on the next page describes the functionality of each application program in I-DEAS.

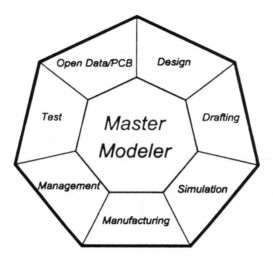

Figure 1.6

# 1.3 I-DEAS User Interface Layout

I-DEAS is a parametric, feature-based CAD system that can be used to easily create simple or complex parts for your applications. It can run under UNIX and Windows NT operation systems. This section covers the user interface of I-DEAS. Although the Windows NT operating system is used, most of the book's concepts can be used when running under the UNIX operation system.

## Entering I-DEAS

Follow these commands to enter I-DEAS:
- Click on the **Start** icon from the Window NT screen
- Select **Programs → I-DEAS Master Series 7 → I-DEAS Master Series OpenGL (or X3D)**

The I-DEAS Start window should appear as in Figure 1.7. It consists of the following four major items:

| | |
|---|---|
| **Project:** | specifies the project name to store the part model. |
| **Model file name:** | specifies the name of part model. |
| **Application:** | selects the application type. |
| **Task:** | selects the task type. |

Mastering I-DEAS,
Scholars International Publishing Corp., 1999

## Table 1.1  Functions of I-DEAS's programs

| Application | Task | Function |
|---|---|---|
| Design | Master Modeler | Creating solid models. |
| | Master Assembly | Creating sub-assemblies and assemblies from parts. |
| | Mechanism Design | Creating mechanisms for animation and analysis of motions and forces of assemblies. |
| | Harness Design | Creating path-based entity such as cables, tubes and flexible hoses. |
| | Drafting Setup | Creating various drawing views, dimensions, and annotations of parts. |
| | Relational Data Manager | Creating relational data for part models. |
| Drafting | | Creating drafting features, GD & T symbols, etc. |
| Simulation | | Performing engineering analysis such as finite element analysis. |
| Test | | Performing dynamic analysis of the modeling systems. |
| Manufacturing | | Generating NC toolpaths for the part models. |
| Management | | Managing project files. |
| Open Data/PCB | | Interfacing with user-developed programs. |

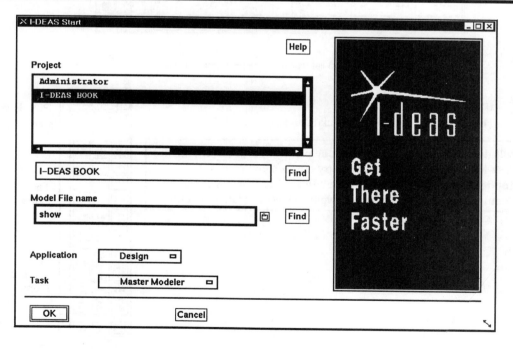

Figure 1.7

# Introduction to I-DEAS

Type in the proper name or selection for each of these four items, then select **OK** to enter I-DEAS Master Series. If the project name or file name is a new one, the system will prompt "New project file will be created or new model file will be created". Select **OK** to continue.

The initial main working window should appear as in Figure 1.8. It consists of the following five areas:

| | |
|---|---|
| **Icon panel:** | groups of command icons. |
| **Graphics window:** | part display area. |
| **I-DEAS list:** | I-DEAS message area. |
| **I-DEAS prompt:** | User-input to I-DEAS prompt area. |
| **Command line:** | numerical data input area. |

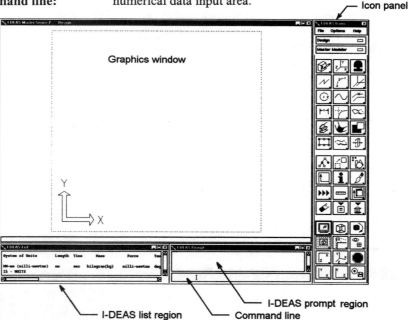

Figure 1.8

## Icon Panel

The icon panel has these four main areas (Figure 1.9):

| | |
|---|---|
| **Pull-down menus:** | file, options, help and applications sub-menus. |
| **Task icons:** | main geometry creation commands. |
| **Application icons:** | geometry modification and library functions. |
| **Common icons:** | display, viewport, view orientation functions. |

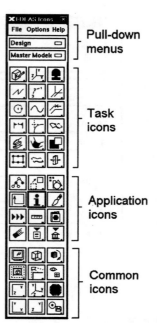

Figure 1.9

Mastering I-DEAS,
Scholars International Publishing Corp., 1999

## Graphics window

Use the graphics window to create, select, and modify graphical entities, and do most of your work. Cascading menus and pop-up menus, when displayed, appear in this window.

## I-DEAS list

The list window displays important data about the process or the data entities you created. It provides a lot of information about the process of building the model. Warning messages are also issued in this window. Figure 1.10 shows the partial list of model information.

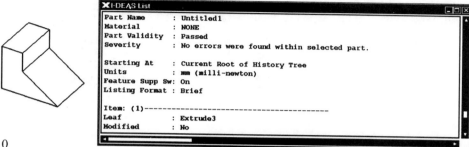

Figure 1.10

## I-DEAS prompt / Command line

The prompt window displays information that tells you what to do to complete a process or task. You can respond to the prompt by entering data on the command line (Figure 1.11).

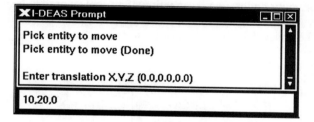

Figure 1.11

# Using a 3-Button Mouse

I-DEAS uses a three-button mouse to interact with the system. These three buttons are termed left button, middle button, and right button (Figure 1.12).

| Button | Function | Illustration |
|--------|----------|--------------|
| Left button | It is the pick button for selecting icons, menus, and graphic entities. | |
| Middle button | It is the accept/done button to accept the default option of a command, or ends a process. | 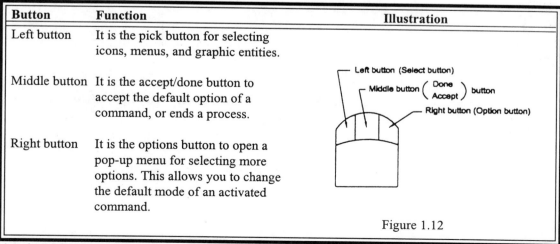 |
| Right button | It is the options button to open a pop-up menu for selecting more options. This allows you to change the default mode of an activated command. | |

Figure 1.12

**The procedure for picking modeling entities using the mouse is:**

1. Just place your pointer on the entity
2. The entity will be highlighted in white to show that it may be selected, then press the left mouse button to select it.
3. To pick more than one entity at a time, hold the Shift key while picking, or drag a box around several nearby entities (Figure 1.13).

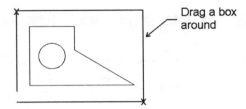

Figure 1.13

# 1.4 Creating a Simple Part

This section guides you through the creation of a simple extruded feature that can be used later in this chapter to show various display functions. The part consists of an extrude feature with a hole (Figure 1.14). Do not be concerned about the exact size of the part.

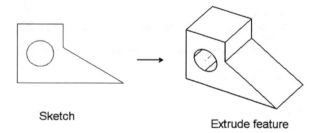

Figure 1.14

**Step 1. Entering I-DEAS.**

If I-DEAS is not open yet, follow this procedure to open it:

Click the **Start** icon from the Windows NT screen

Select **Programs** → I-DEAS Master Series7 → **I-DEAS Master Series OpenGL (or X3D)**

# Introduction to I-DEAS

Set the I-DEAS starting menu as below.

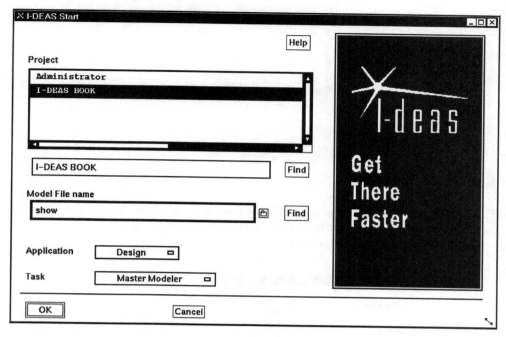

Select **OK** to enter I-DEAS

**Step 2.  Create a sketch. Use Figure 1.15 as reference.**

 Select the **Polylines** icon,
then use the left mouse button to consecutively pick **P1 – P5**,
and then pick **P1** again to create a sketch as shown
Click the middle mouse button to terminate the polyline creation

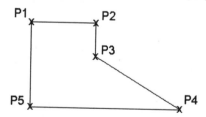

Figure 1.15

**Step 3.  Add a circle to the sketch. Use Figure 1.16 as reference.**

 Select the **Circle – Center-Edge** icon
Pick **P1** and **P2** to add a circle as shown

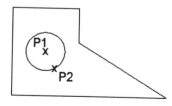

Figure 1.16

**Step 4. Change to isometric view.**

 Select the **Isometric view** icon to change to isometric view as in Figure 1.17

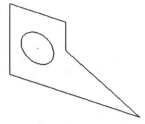

Figure 1.17

**Step 5. Create an extrude feature.**

 Select the **Extrude** icon

Pick any entity on the outer sketch and then select the circle

Press the middle mouse button to complete the curves selection

Define the Extrude parameters as below.

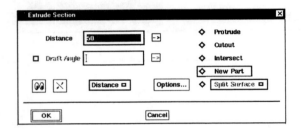

Select **OK** to complete the extrude feature

The extrude feature is shown in Figure 1.18.

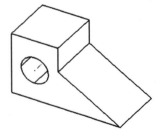

Figure 1.18

**Step 6. Save the part as "show".**

Select **File → Save As**

File name to save: **show**

Mastering I-DEAS,
Scholars International Publishing Corp., 1999

# 1.5 Dynamic Viewing

I-DEAS uses F#-function keys and the mouse to change the size, orientation, and location of your view of the part. Press and hold down a function key and move the mouse to dynamically change the view. Table 1.2 summarizes the dynamic view functions. Use the part you have created ("show") in the previous section to performing dynamic viewing functions listed in Table 1.2.

## Table 1.2 Dynamic viewing functions

| Function | Key | Description |
|----------|-----|-------------|
| **Pan** | **F1** | Move the view to a new location in the direction of mouse movement. |

| Function | Key | Description |
|----------|-----|-------------|
| **Zoom** | **F2** | Zoom in (enlarge) the view while the mouse moving downward (-Y direction) |

and zoom out (reduce) the view while the mouse moving upward (+Y direction).

**Table 1.2 continued**

**Rotate**    **F3**  Rotate the view about X, Y, or Z axis.

    (1) Rotate about X axis:  place the pointer in the center of the screen, then press F3 and move the pointer to left or right.

    (2) Rotate about Y axis: place the pointer in the center of the screen, then press F3 and move the pointer up and down.

    (3) Rotate about Z axis: place the pointer near the edge of screen, then press F3 and move the pointer up and down.

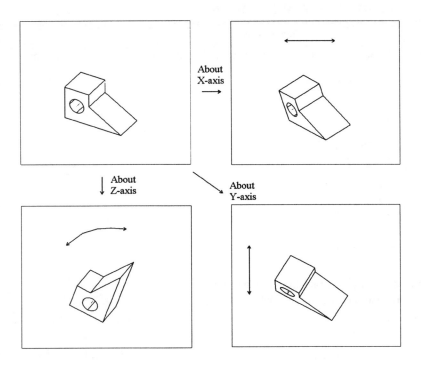

**Reset**    **F5**  Reset the view back to isometric, top, front, or side view.

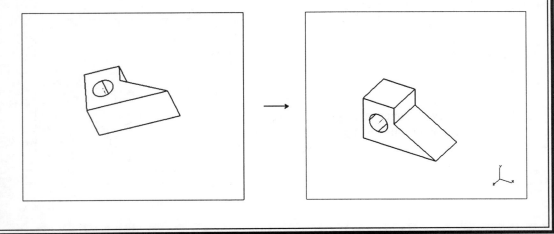

Mastering I-DEAS,
Scholars International Publishing Corp., 1999

**Table 1.2 continued**

| | | |
|---|---|---|
| **Rotate Triad Only** | **F4** | Press F4 to rotate the triad to proper orientation. During the rotation, geometry entities temporarily disappear from the screen. Move the mouse to orient the triad to proper orientation. The geometry view will resume when F4 is released. |

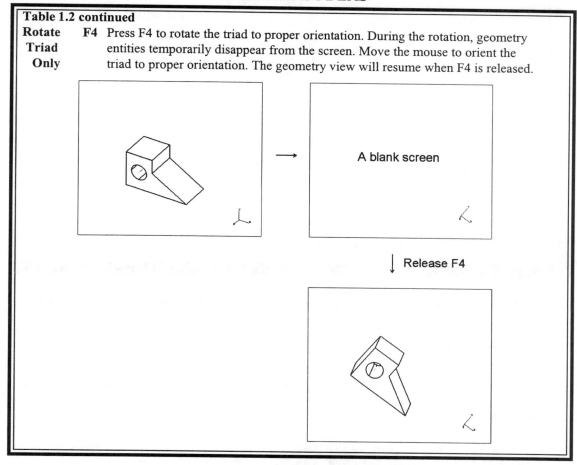

# 1.6   View Orientations

I-DEAS provides a variety of view options to change the view of the model for better visualization, to verify a feature creation direction, or to zoom in a small edge for selection. There are four view configurations you can choose to display your model. They are:

**Isometric view:**   display the isometric view of your object (Figure 1.19).
**Top view:**   display the top view of your object (Figure 1.20).
**Front view:**   display the front view of your object (Figure 1.21).
**Side view:**   display the side view of your object (Figure 1.22).

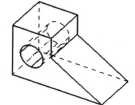

Figure 1.19 Isometric view

Figure 1.20 Top view

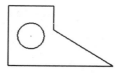

Figure 1.21 Front view                    Figure 1.22 Side view

# 1.7   Model Display Options

I-DEAS allows you to display the model in two modes, **shaded mode** and **wireframe mode**.

## Shaded Mode

In the shaded mode, the object is displayed as a shaded image. Two shade modes are available; **shaded hardware** and **shaded software**. Some systems only are capable of the shaded software mode. In the shaded mode, Select the "Shaded software" icon to shade the object (Figure 1.23).

Figure 1.23

## Wireframe Mode

In the wireframe mode, the object is displayed as a series of lines. It has three options; **line mode, hidden hardware**, and **hidden software**.

## Line mode

In the line mode, the system displays the wireframe representation of geometry (Figure 1.24). The edges and surfaces of the object are shown in the line mode. An object displayed in the line mode may appear somewhat confusing because it not only shows the edges, but also surfaces and sketch planes and feature termination planes.

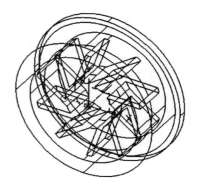

Figure 1.24

## Hidden hardware mode

This mode displays the surfaces with curve meshes as shown in Figure 1.25.

## Hidden software mode

This mode displays surfaces and edges of the object based on user perspective (Figure 1.26).

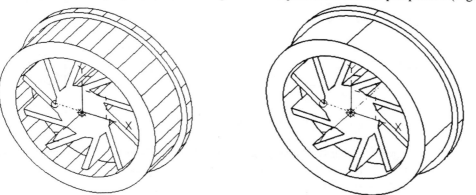

Figure 1.25                               Figure 1.26

I-DEAS provides an options menu to allow you to handle hidden lines. Select the Options icon to open the "Line & Hidden Line Options" menu as below.

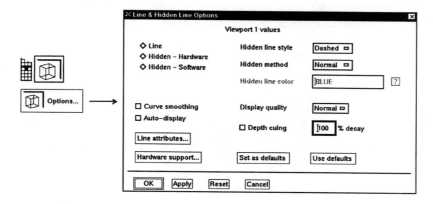

**Line attributes:** This parameter is used to select line, hidden line, or edge attribute options. Select "Line attributes" button to open the "Line Attributes" menu as below.

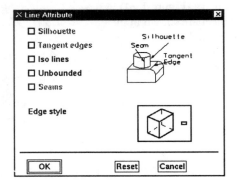

**Display entity selection:** can include silhouettes, tangent edges, iso lines, unbounded lines and seams(Figure 1.27).

Figure 1.27                                Figure 1.28

**Edge style:** select the thickness of display lines. Click the box to open four different thickness options as shown in Figure 1.28. Select the desired option, then click "OK" to return to "Line & Hidden Line Options" menu.

**Hidden line style:** This parameter controls how the hidden lines are shown. It has the following three options:

| |
|---|
| **Visible:** hidden lines are shown in solid lines (Figure 1.29). |
| **Invisible:** hidden lines are not shown in the model (Figure 1.30). |
| **Dashed:** hidden lines are shown in dashed lines (Figure 1.31). |

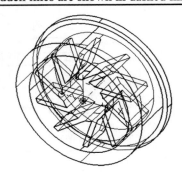

Figure 1.29 Visible mode

1-16

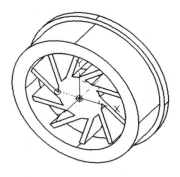

Figure 1.30 Invisible mode

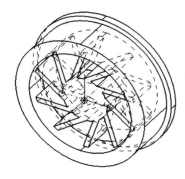

Figure 1.31Dashed mode

**Hidden method:** specifies how the color of hidden lines appears in the view. It has the following three options:

**Normal:** select the color of hidden lines as the same as the visible lines.
**Fixed:** select the color of hidden lines using the "hidden line color" parameter.
**Faded:** select the color of hidden lines as the same as the visible lines, yet shown in faded fashion.

**Display quality:** control the smoothness of the display of curves. It has four options; quick, coarse, normal, and fine.

# 1.8   View Layout

The I-DEAS graphics window can be configured to show multiple views of an object. It has the following four configurations:

**One viewport:**   creates one viewport using the entire graphics window (Figure 1.32).
**Two viewports:** creates two viewports side-by-side (Figure 1.33).
**Three viewports:** creates three viewports; one large on left two small on right (Figure 1.34).
**Four viewports:** creates four equal size viewports (Figure 1.35).

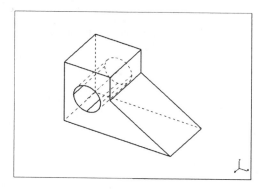

Figure 1.32

Figure 1.33

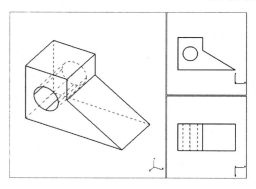

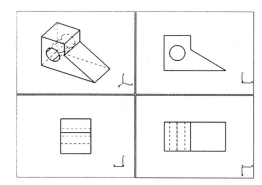

Figure 1.34                     Figure 1.35

The following two functions allow you to assign a view type to a viewport:

> **View workplane:** aligns your view to the workplane.
> **Work viewport:** selects the viewport in which work occurs (to make a viewport active).

 **These instructions show how to configurate and assign a view type to a viewport:**

1. Select a **Four Viewports** icon to make a four-viewport configuration as in Figure 1.36.

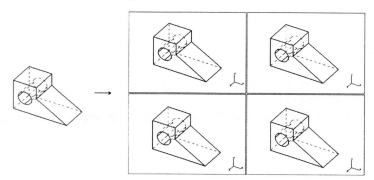

Figure 1.36

2. Make the Upper-left viewport become the top view.
    Select the **Work viewport** icon, then click the upper-left viewport to make it active

   Select the **Top view** icon
    The top view of the part should appear in the upper-left viewport as in Figure 1.37.

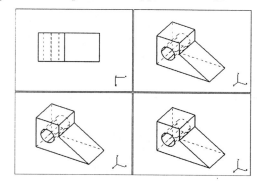

Figure 1.37

Mastering I-DEAS,
Scholars International Publishing Corp., 1999

3.  Make the lower-left viewport become the front view.

    Select the **Work viewport** icon, then click the lower-left viewport to make it active

    Select the **Front view** icon

    The front view of the part should appear in the lower-left viewport as in Figure 1.38.

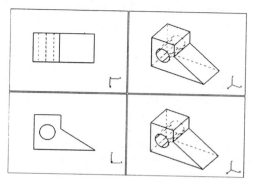

Figure 1.38

4.  Make the lower-right viewport display the right-side view.

    Select the **Work viewport** icon, then click the lower-right viewport to make it active

    Select the **Right view** icon

    The right-side view of the part should appear in the lower-right viewport as shown in Figure 1.39.

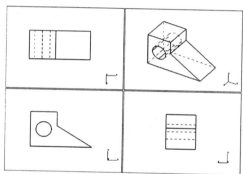

Figure 1.39

5.  Make the upper-right viewport as the isometric view.

    Select the **Work viewport** icon, then click the upper-right viewport to make it active

    Select the **Isometric view** icon

    The isometric view of the part should appear in the upper-right viewport as shown in Figure 1.40.

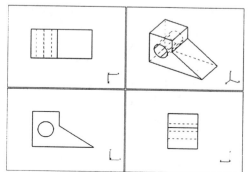

Figure 1.40

# 1.9 Zooming and Rotating Models

I-DEAS' dynamic viewing functions allow you to **zoom**, **rotate**, and **scale** the views of the part model using the function keys and mouse. It also provides a group of commands to perform similar functions. They are summarized below.

| | |
|---|---|
| **Zoom:** | enlarges a selected rectangular area to fit the graphics window (Figure 1.41). |
| **Magnify:** | scales the entities by the given magnification fraction value ( > 1 to increasing size and < 1 to reducing size) (Figure 1.42). |
| **Center of rotation:** | uses two points, target point and eye location, to define the center of rotation (Figure 1.43). |
| **Dynamic clip:** | no available in some hardware configurations. |
| **Rotate model:** | rotates the display by three given degree values about the X, Y, and Z axes (Figure 1.44). |
| **Zoom All:** | scales the display to fit the entire model on the screen (Figure 1.45). |

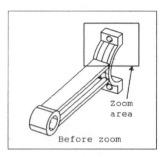

Figure 1.41a

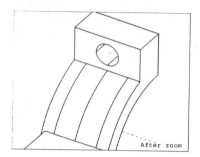

Figure 1.41b

Figure 1.42a

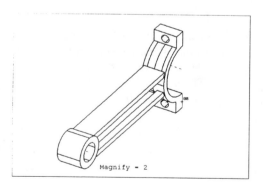

Figure 1.42b

Mastering I-DEAS,
Scholars International Publishing Corp., 1999

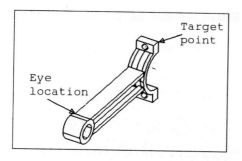

Figure 1.43a

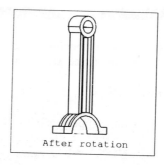

Figure 1.43b

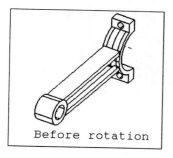

Figure 1.44a

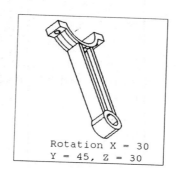

Figure 1.44b

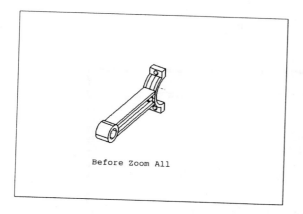

Figure 1.45a

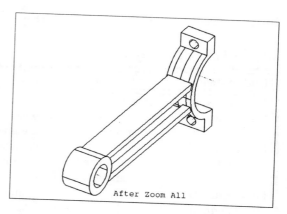

Figure 1.45b

# 1.10   Units System

The unit system used in modeling affects the size of the part features and the engineering analyses in the areas of **motion**, **force**, **stress**, **strain**, etc.

Select **Options** → **Units**

The units menu should appear as below.

```
Meter (newton)

Foot (pound f)

Meter (kilogram f)

Foot (poundal)

mm (milli newton)

cm (centi newton)

Inch (pound f)

mm (kilogram f)

User Defined

Units Help

Backup

Cancel
```

There are nine unit systems you can select. They are listed in Table 1.3.

## Table 1.3   Units system

| Unit System | Length | Force |
|---|---|---|
| Meter (newton) | meter | newton |
| Foot (pound f) | foot | pound |
| Meter (kilogram f) | meter | kilogram |
| Foot (poundal) | foot | poundal |
| mm (milli newton) | millimeter | newton |
| cm (centi newton) | centimeter | newton |
| Inch (pound f) | inch | pound |
| mm (kilogram f) | millimeter | kilogram |
| User Defined | define the length, force, and temperature units for the model | |

The units system must be specified <u>before</u> creating a part model. The default unit is **mm** (milli newton).

Mastering I-DEAS,
Scholars International Publishing Corp., 1999

# 1.11 Managing and Saving Files

I-DEAS uses a very sophisticated file management system to handle part files. It uses two ways to provide file management; **regular mode** and **library mode**. File management in library mode is a very powerful way for saving parts to library to share with other project users. It can be retrieved for further modifications or use. The file structure and a detailed discussion of saving and retrieving files to/from libraries are presented in chapter 9.

In **regular mode**, you save, open, import or export a file using Windows NT's file functions. These file functions include:

| | |
|---|---|
| **Save:** | write out the current model file using the current file name. |
| **Save As:** | write out the current model file using a new file name. |
| **Open:** | open a new model file or a new project to the workstation. |
| **Export:** | write data for use in another data installation or program. |
| **Import:** | get exported, archived, or universal data into a project. |
| **Program Files:** | access the macro and program file commands. |
| **Picture Files:** | capture graphic images to an external file. |
| **Plot:** | display jobs waiting to be queued. |
| **Exit:** | exit from I-DEAS software. |

## Save

The command to save a part model in the regular save mode is:

**Select File → Save**

The file is saved under the current file name in the specified drive.

## Save As

Use this command to save a part under a new name or a new drive.

Select the **Save As** command to open the **File Name Input** menu as below.

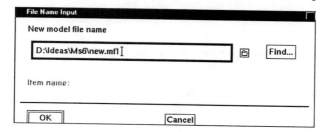

Enter the drive and file name for the part to save, then select OK

## Open

If a current part exists in the graphic window, the system will prompt "Save changes to file "file name" before switching model files?". You have the following three selections:

| | |
|---|---|
| **Yes:** | The current model will be saved in the current file name and removed from the workstation. |
| **No:** | The current model will be removed from the workstation without saving to the current file name. |
| **Cancel:** | No action will be taken. Abort the open command. |

The Open Model File menu should appear as below for you to select the file to open.

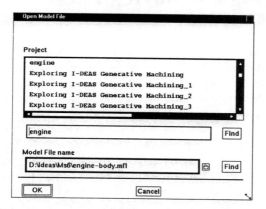

Select project and model file name from the menu, then select **OK** to open a file.
The part model should appear on the graphic window as shown in Figure 1.46.

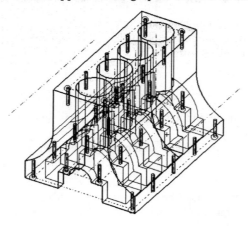

Figure 1.46

## Export

This function will export a selected part model and save to one of file formats.
Select the **Export** command to open the "Export Selections" menu as below.

Select one of file format option (ex. IGES), then select **OK**

The system prompts you to select an entity for exporting.
The "IGES export" menu appears as below.

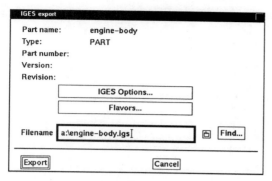

Specify the drive and file name to export, then select **Export**
Select **OK** to "New IGES file will be created"

## Import

The Import function gets a selected data file into a project.
Select **Import** to open the "Import Selections" menu as below.

Select file type from the list (ex. IGES), then select **OK** to open "IGES import" menu as below.

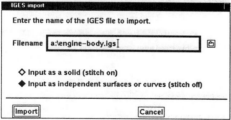

Enter the filename for import, then select the Import button. The system will prompt for specifying tolerances.

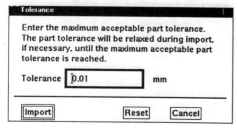

Select the **Import** button.  The part is retrieved as in Figure 1.47.

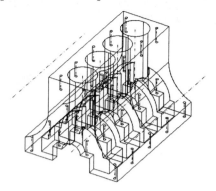

Figure 1.47

## Picture File

This function creates the picture file for selected entity.
Select the **Picture File** command to open the picture files menu as below.

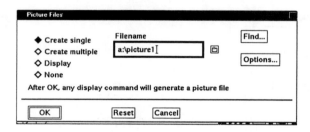

| | |
|---|---|
| **Create single:** | create a single picture file. |
| **Create multiple:** | create multiple picture files. |
| **Display:** | display the picture file to the graphic window. |
| **None:** | create no picture file. |

## Options

Click the **Options** button to open
the options menu which is shown here.

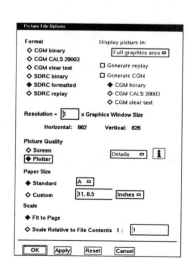

## Plot

Enter the name of an existing picture file to plot.

Mastering I-DEAS,
Scholars International Publishing Corp., 1999

# Chapter 1. Review Questions

1. What is feature-based modeling?

2. What is a feature?

3. What are base features?

4. What are added features?

5. What is parametric?

6. Explain how relation equations can be used in changing the shape and size of part models.

7. Explain the purpose of a family table.

8. List the two organization levels of I-DEAS programs.

9. List the seven applications of I-DEAS.

10. What are the five areas of I-DEAS initial main working window? Briefly describe what they are.

11. What are the four main areas of the icon panel? Briefly describe each area.

12. List the function of each button in I-DEAS for the three-button mouse.

13. Describe the function of these function keys:
    F1
    F2
    F3
    F4
    F5

14. What are the four view options to display a model?

15. What are the two display modes?

16. What are the three options of the wireframe display mode?

17. List and describe the four view layouts in the I-DEAS graphic window.

18. List the nine units systems available in I-DEAS.

19. What are the two ways to provide file management in I-DEAS? Describe their differences.

# Chapter 2

# I-DEAS Design Process Overview

**Highlights of the Chapter**
- Modeling processes for parts and assembly with I-DEAS
- Modeling parts
- Creating an assembly

## Overview

The intent of this chapter is to provide a bird's-eye view of the part modeling process using I-DEAS. The feature-based modeling concept is introduced. The first feature created is called the base feature. It defines the basic shape of a part, while the added features describe the details of a part. We will use a project to present an overview of the modeling and assembly process in I-DEAS. This project consists of two components, a cap and a body. These two components are put together to form an assembly. Step-by-step tutorials are provided to guide you through the modeling and assembling processes.

# 2.1  I-DEAS Design Procedure

A part can be regarded as a basic shape with features. The basic shape defines the primitive configuration of the part. Typical shapes are block, channel, I-beam, cylinder, and other basic forms (Figure 2.1). Basic shapes are also referred to as the base features.

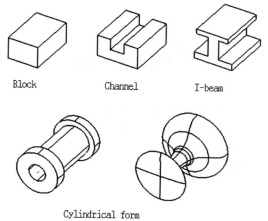

Figure 2.1 Basic shapes

A **feature** is any geometry that augments a basic shape and makes it distinguishable from other parts that could be derived from the same basic shape. In other words, a feature is used to define the details of the part. Those features that describe the details of the part are also referred to as added features. Figure 2.2 shows an example of two parts with different added features which were derived from the same base feature.

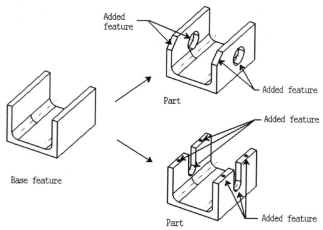

Figure 2.2 Two parts with different added features

Since a variety of parts can be developed from a base shape by adding different features, a logical, generic, four-step modeling approach should be followed to model parts. The four steps are listed here. They are followed by Figure 2.3 which illustrates the steps with sample parts.

Mastering I-DEAS,
Scholars International Publishing Corp., 1999

## The four-step part modeling procedure:

1. **Analyze the part**
   - Identify the constituent features of a part including the base shape and added features.

2. **Create a sketch (or cross section) of the base shape**
   - Keep the sketch of the base shape as simple as possible.
   - Use added features to define the details of the part.

3. **Create the base feature**
   - Use extrude or revolve function to make the sketch into a solid shape.

4. **Apply added features to the base shape**
   - One or more added features can be applied to the base shape to define the details of the part.

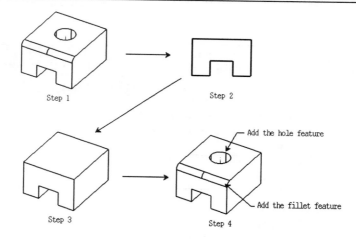

Step 1 → Step 2

Step 3 → Step 4

Add the hole feature

Add the fillet feature

Figure 2.3  Four-step part modeling procedure

## 2.2  I-DEAS Design Process Overview

We use a simple two-component assembly to show how to use I-DEAS to create part models, and put parts into an assembly. This section consists of three projects. The first two projects provide tutorial instructions to create two part models; cap and body. The third project shows how to assemble these two components to form an assembly. Figure 2.4 shows the exploded view of the assembly of the two parts.

Figure 2.4

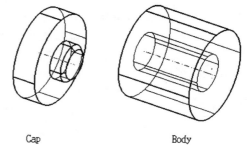

Cap        Body

# Project 1.
# Creating the cap model

This tutorial guides you through the process of creating the cap model of the assembly. Figure 2.5 shows the drawing views of the cap. This part consists of two features, **revolved** feature and **chamfer** feature. Save the part name as CAP. In this process, we create a closed section, then revolve this section about the bottom horizontal line to complete the base feature. A chamfer is added to the end edge of the smaller step.

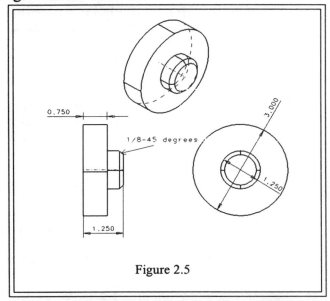

Figure 2.5

| **Note:** | The following abbreviations are used in this tutorial and other projects to simplify the text explanation of mouse clicking actions: | LMB - Left mouse button<br>MMB - Middle mouse button<br>RMB - Right mouse button |
| --- | --- | --- |

**Step 1.  Enter I-DEAS and create a model file name "CAP".**
Click **Start → programs → I-DEAS Master Series-7 → I-DEAS Master Series OpenGL**
Set your I-DEAS <u>start menu</u> as:

| Project name: | **overview** | Model file name: **cap** |
| --- | --- | --- |
| Application: | **Design** | Task: **Master Modeler** |

**Step 2.  Set the units to Inch-Pound.**
Click and hold the **"Options"** button at the top of the icon panel, select **"Units"** from the list
Select **"Inch (pound f)"** from the options list

**Step 3.  Set the workplane size.**
The workplane appearance icon actually is a "Stack" of icons. Hold your left mouse button to "pull down" the stack, and slide the cursor down to the **Workplane Appearance** icon and release the mouse button. Notice that while the command is activated, the corresponding icon is highlighted in a higher (darker) color background. Only one icon can be activated at a time.  Press the middle mouse button (MMB) to cancel an icon command.

Select **Workplane Appearance** to open the "Workplane Attributes" menu
Set the four border size parameters as below.

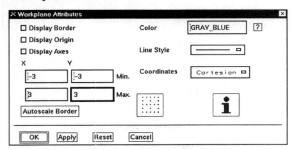

Mastering I-DEAS,
Scholars International Publishing Corp., 1999

Select **OK** to exit the menu
Select **Zoom All** to scale the display to fit the workplane limits

**Step 4.** **Set the automatic save reminder to 15 minutes.**

This setting will remind you to save your work at specified time intervals of 15 minutes.

Select **Options** → **Preferences** → **Data Management**
The "Data Management Preferences" menu appears as below.

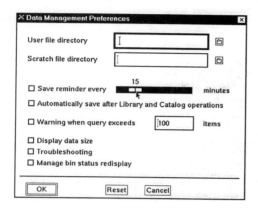

Use the left mouse button (LMB) to drag the time bar to **15**
Select **OK** → **OK** to return to graphic mode

| **Tip:** | At every 15- minute interval I-DEAS will prompt "Last save was more than 15 minutes ago. Save changes before continuing?". Press Yes to save all of your recent changes. |

**Step 5.** **Set to display three decimal places.**

Select **Appearance**
Click the right mouse button (RMB) to open the options list
Select **Defaults** → **Annotation** to open the "Dimensions/Notes/GD&T" menu
Select **Units/Decimal Places** from the menu to open the "Units & Decimal Places" menu
Enter "3" to the Decimal Places field as shown below.

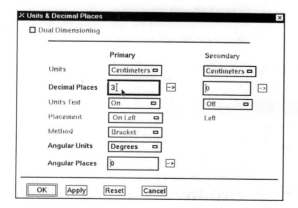

Select **OK** → **OK** to return back to graphic mode

**Step 6. Sketch a six-line section. Use Figure 2.6 as reference.**

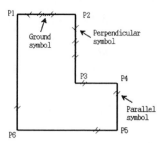

Figure 2.6

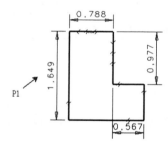

Select **Polylines**

| | |
|---|---|
| Locate start: | pick **P1** |
| Locate end: | pick **P2** (make sure that ground symbol appears to make the line horizontal) to create the first line |
| Locate end: | sequentially pick **P2 - P6** and **P1 again** to create the remaining five lines |

**Note:** The perpendicular symbol or parallel symbol appears for each line to ensure they are either perpendicular or parallel. The pick point P6 must be picked at a location to make the "H" symbol appear on the fifth line and has a cross "x" symbol at the pick location. This ensure that the X-coordinate of this point is same as the start point of first line.

Click the **MMB** to end the polylines function
The final section appears as in Figure 2.7.

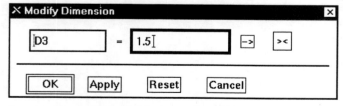

Figure 2.7

**Step 7. Modify the dimensions of the sketch. Use Figure 2.7 as reference.**

Select the "**Modify Entity**" icon
Pick an entity to modify: pick the left vertical dimension (P1 in Figure 2.7) to modify
The Modify Dimension menu appears as below.

Enter **1.5** to the input field, then select **OK**

Repeat the same procedure to change the value of the remaining three dimensions as shown in Figure 2.8.

Mastering I-DEAS,
Scholars International Publishing Corp., 1999

# I-DEAS Design Process Overview

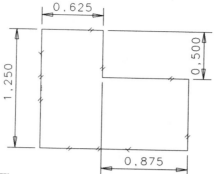

Figure 2.8

## Step 8. Zoom the graphic view.

Press the "**F2**" key, then move the mouse in the vertical direction to enlarge the section
Figure 2.9 shows the enlarged view of the section.

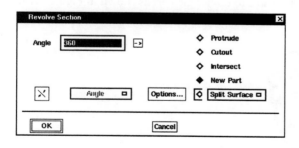

Figure 2.9

## Step 9. Create a revolved feature. Use the pick points in Figure 2.9.

Select **Revolve**
Pick a curve or section:   pick **P1** to select the section,
                then click the MMB to end curve selection
Pick axis to revolve about:   pick **P2**
Set the revolve section parameters as below.

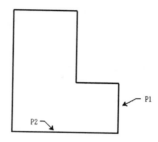

Select **OK** to complete the revolve feature

The front view of the revolved feature should
look like Figure 2.10.

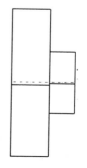

Figure 2.10

**Step 10.  Change to isometric view.**

 Select the **Isometric View** to display the model in isometric view as in Figure 2.11.

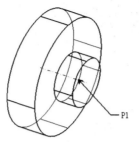

Figure 2.11

**Step 11.  Create a chamfer at the right edge of the cap. Use the pick point in Figure 2.11.**

 Select **Chamfer**

Pick edges, vertices or surfaces to chamfer:  pick  **P1** to select the right end edge
Pick edges, vertices or surfaces to chamfer (Done):  press MMB
Enter offset for selected edges (0.065):  **0.125**
Pick edges, vertices or surfaces to chamfer:  press MMB
The chamfer is added to the model as in Figure 2.12.

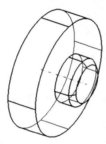

Figure 2.12

**Step 12.  Render the part model.**

 Select **Shade Software** or **Shade Hardware** to render the part as shown in Figure 2.13.

Figure 2.13

> *Note:* Shaded Hardware is disabled in certain workstations which are equipped with X3D display
> only. In this case, dynamic shading and rendering are not available. However, you can still
> see the dynamic wireframe rotation using the F3 function key.

Mastering I-DEAS,
Scholars International Publishing Corp., 1999

## Step 13. Name the part "cap".

 Select **Name Parts**

Pick the part to name:  pick any place on the part

Set the name parameters as below.

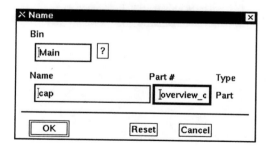

Select **OK** to complete the naming of the part

## Step 14. Check the part into library "overview".

 Select **Check In**

Pick part to check in:  pick anywhere on the part

Set Check-In parameters as below.

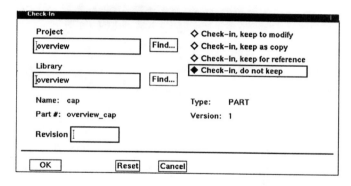

Select **OK** to "New Library will be created"

Select **OK** to check the part into the library

# Project 2.
# Creating the body part

This project shows how to create the body part which consists of two features, cylinder and hole (Figure 2.14). The cylinder feature is the base feature. It is created by extruding a circle by a given distance. The hole feature is the added feature created also by the extrude function.

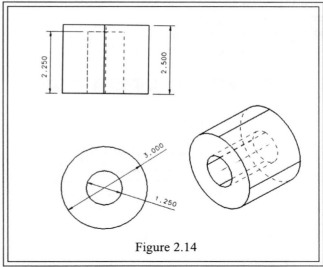

Figure 2.14

**Step 1. Change to the front view and select zoom all to fit workplane limit to the screen.**

  Select **Front View**

  Select **Zoom All**

**Step 2. Create a circle.**

  Select **Center Edge**

Pick two points **P1** and **P2** to create a circle as shown in Figure 2.15.

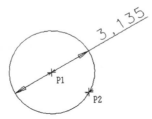

Figure 2.15

**Step 3. Modify the diameter of circle.**

  Select **Modify Entity**, then pick the diameter dimension

Enter "**3**" on the Modify Dimension menu, then select **OK**

The circle with the new dimension appears as in Figure 2.16.

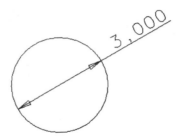

Figure 2.16

Mastering I-DEAS,
Scholars International Publishing Corp., 1999

**Step 4.  Create an extrude feature.**

Select **Extrude**

Pick curve or section: pick the circle,  then click MMB

Set the extrude section parameters as below.

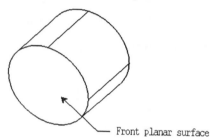

Select **OK** to complete the extrude feature

Select **Isometric View** to show the part in isometric view as in Figure 2.17.

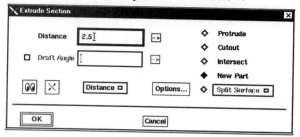

Figure 2.17                                                    — Front planar surface

**Step 5.  Select the front planar face as the sketch plane.**

Select **Sketch in plane**

Pick plane to sketch on:  pick the front planar face of the extrude feature (Figure 2.17)

**Note:** The front planar face will be highlighted in blue to indicate it is the current sketch plane. There will also be a cross added to the planar surface.

**Step 6.  Create a concentric circle.**

Select **Center Edge**

Pick two points to create a circle as shown in Figure 2.18.

**Note:** The center point must be trapped to the center point of the cylinder

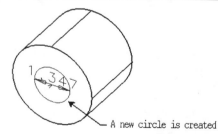

Figure 2.18                                          — A new circle is created

**Step 7.  Modify the diameter of the circle.**

Select **Modify Entity**

Pick the diameter dimension

Enter "**1.25**" to the dimension field in Modify Dimension menu

Select **OK**

The circle with the correct diameter value appears as in Figure 2.19.

Figure 2.19

**Step 8. Create an extrude feature.**

Select **Extrude**

Pick the circle as the section, then press MMB

Set the extrude section parameters as below. (The direction arrow must point inward.)

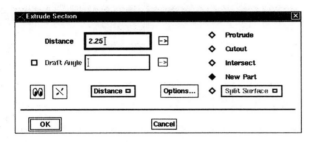

Select **OK** to complete the feature as in Figure 2.20.

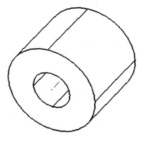

Figure 2.20

**Step 9. Render the model.**

Select **Shade Software or Hardware** to shade the model as shown in Figure 2.21.

Figure 2.21

Mastering I-DEAS,
Scholars International Publishing Corp., 1999

### Step 10.  Name the part "cylinder".

Select **Name Parts**
Pick part to name:  pick anywhere on the part
Set the name parameters as below.

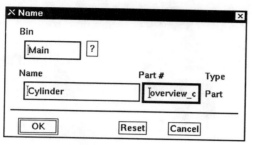

Select **OK**

### Step 11.  Check the part into the library.

Select **Check In**
Pick part to check in:  pick anywhere on the part
Set the check-in parameters as below.

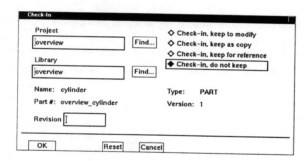

Select **OK** to check in the part

# Project 3.
# Creating an assembly

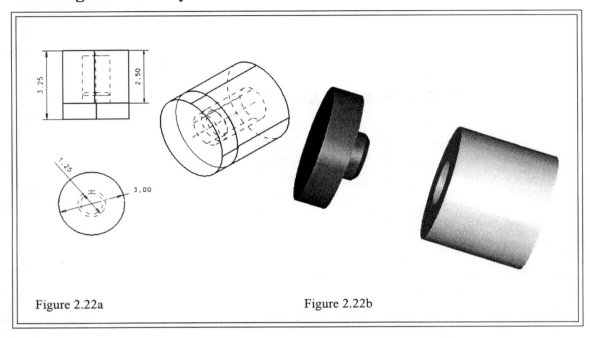

Figure 2.22a                     Figure 2.22b

This tutorial project provides instructions for putting together the two parts created in the two previous projects to form an assembly. Figure 2.22 shows the assembly drawing and its exploded drawing. Creating an assembly involves (1) getting parts from library, (2) creating assembly hierarchy, (3) adding parts to the assembly, (4) constraining parts, and (5) exploding assembly view.

**Step 1.   Enter I-DEAS's Master Assembly program.**
    Click the **Task bar** on the third row of the icon panel,
      then select **Master Assembly** from the list
      to enter the Assembly mode
    A partial assembly icon panel will appear.
    It is shown here for reference.

**Step 2.   Get two parts from library.**

    Select **Get** from the Library to
      open the "Get from Project Library" menu as shown next.

Mastering I-DEAS,
Scholars International Publishing Corp., 1999

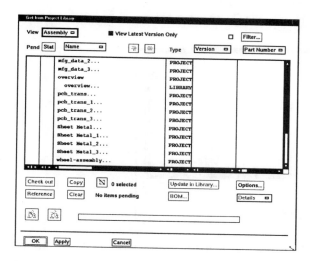

Click the **View button** appearing on the top of the menu
Select **Part**
Double click on **"overview..."** library under the "overview" project to list two parts
under this library as shown below.

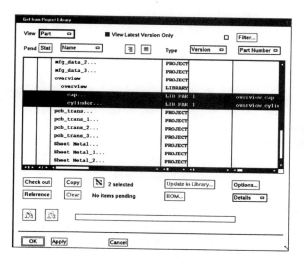

**Step 3. Copy these two parts out.**

Press the **Shift** key, then click on the **"cap"** and **"cylinder"** parts to highlight them
Select the **"Copy"** button near the bottom of the menu
Select **OK** to copy these two parts out

## Step 4.  Get these two parts from the bin.

Select **Get** to open the Get menu as below.

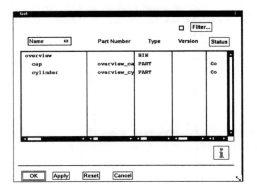

Press the **Shift** key, then pick both **"cap"** and **"cylinder"** parts from the menu
Select **OK** to exit the Get menu
The parts are shown in graphic view as in Figure 2.23.

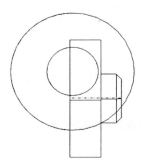

Figure 2.23

## Step 5.  Change to isometric view.

Select **Isometric View** to display the parts in isometric view as in Figure 2.24.

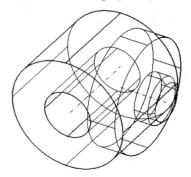

Figure 2.24

## Step 6. Create an assembly hierarchy.

Select **Hierarchy** to open the Hierarchy menu as shown below.

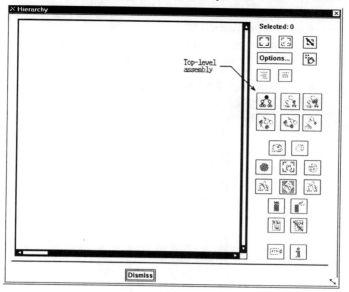

Select the **Top-level assembly** icon to open the Name menu as below.

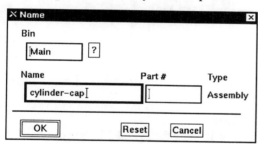

Enter "**cylinder-cap**" into the Name field as shown above
Select **OK** to return to the Hierarchy menu as below.

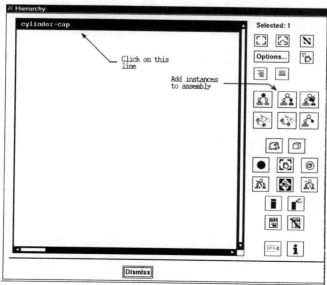

**Step 7. Add two instances.**

Click "**cylinder-cap**" from the menu to activate many assembly options

 Select the **Add instances to assembly** icon shown on the previous page

The system will return back to graphic mode

The system will prompt "Pick part or assembly to add": pick the cylinder and cap to add

Press the **Enter** key to return back to the Hierarchy menu as below.

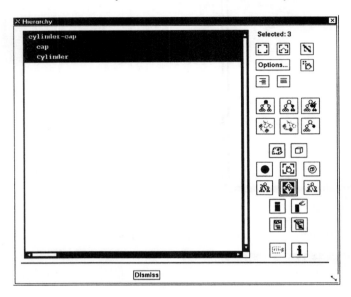

Select **Dismiss** to return to graphic mode

**Step 8. Lock the cylinder instance.**

 Select **Constrain & Dimension → Lock**

Pick the first part or instance to constrain: pick the cylinder instance

Pick the second part or instance to constrain: Click the right mouse button

and select **Hierarchy** from the list to open the Hierarchy Selection menu

Click "**cylinder-cap**" from the list to highlight the entire list

Select **OK** to return back to graphic mode

The lock is added as in Figure 2.25.

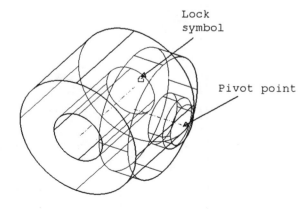

Figure 2.25

Mastering I-DEAS,
Scholars International Publishing Corp., 1999

**Step 9.** **Rotate the cap part 90 degrees about Y axis. Use Figure 2.25 as reference.**

Select **Rotate** and pick the cap as the entity to rotate
Pivot the center point at the right end face of the cap instance as the pivot point
Select **About Y** from the list

Enter angle about Y: **90**
The new drawing becomes Figure 2.26.

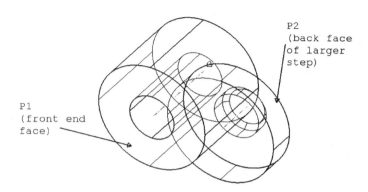

P2
(back face
of larger
step)

P1
(front end
face)

Figure 2.26

**Step 10.** **Apply Coincident & Collinear constraint to two surfaces. Use Figure 1.26 as reference.**

Select **Constrain & Dimension** → **Coincident & Collinear**
Pick the first entity to constrain:  Pick the front surface (**P1**) at cylinder part
Pick the second entity to constrain:  Pick the back surface (**P2**) of the cap part
The cap instance is moved to a new location as in Figure 2.27.

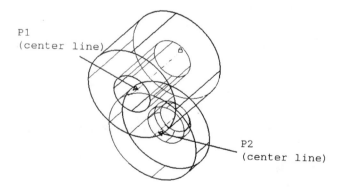

P1
(center line)

P2
(center line)

Figure 2.27

**Step 11.** **Apply Coincident & Collinear constraint to two center lines. Use Figure 2.27 as reference.**

Pick the first entity to constrain:  Pick the center line (**P1**) of cylinder
Pick the second entity to constrain:  pick the center line (**P2**) of cap

The two parts are assembled as in Figure 2.28.

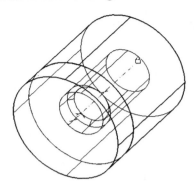

Figure 2.28

### Step 12.  Explode the assembly.

 Select **Explode Linearly**
Pick the assembly to explode
Select the **Z Direction** from the list
Enter the minimum distance between entities:  **2**
The explode assemble should resemble Figure 2.29.

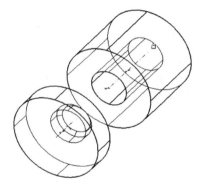

Figure 2.29

### Step 13.  Render the explode view.

 Select **Shade Hardware** or Shade Software to render the exploded assembly as in Figure 2.30.

Figure 2.30

Mastering I-DEAS,
Scholars International Publishing Corp., 1999

**Step 14. Change to Line display mode and unexplode the assembly.**

Select the **Line** icon

Select **Undo Orient** to return to assembly view as in Figure 2.31.

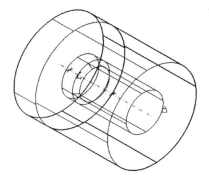

Figure 2.31

**Step 15. Check the assembly into library.**

Select **Check In** and pick the assembly
Set the check-in parameters as below.

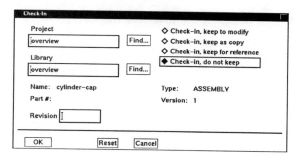

Select **OK** to check the part in

# Chapter 2.  Review Questions

1. What is a feature?

2. How is apart defined in I-DEAS.

3. What are base features?

4. What are typical basic features?

5. What are added features?

6. List the four steps of the part modeling procedure.

# Chapter 3

# Sketching and Constraints

## Highlights of the Chapter

■ Using sketch commands: line, arc, circle, rectangle, spline, and ellipse
   to create geometry
■ Creating geometry with the dynamic navigator
■ Applying dynamic dimensioning to geometry
■ Modifying dimensions to adjust geometry

## Overview

Sketches are the starting place for designing a part using parametric CAD software. A sketch is the rough shape and size of a section which is to be extruded or revolved for producing a part feature. After a sketch is created, you then add dimensional and geometric constraints to fully define the section. I-DEAS allows you to create basic geometric entities such as points, lines, rectangles, arcs, and splines. The relationships among geometric elements in a sketch can be automatically constrained. Dimensions can be modified in one of two ways; the modify entity method and the part equations method, to constrain the wireframe sections to exact size. I-DEAS provides various editing and transform functions to modify wireframe entities. Typical editing functions include trim/extend, dividing, merging, and offset. Five transform functions are move, rotate, drag, reflect, and scale. This chapter presents essential concepts and techniques required to create wireframe sections.

## 3.1 Sketch and Section

Sketching is a drawing operation which constructs wireframe entities such as lines, arcs, and curves. A sketch is the rough shape of a section profile that is to be constrained becoming a section. A sketch consists of a set of connected entities that do not necessarily have the true shape and true size. Eventually, the sketch will be constrained by permanent constraints and dimensions to become a section (Figure 3.1).

# Sketching and Constraints

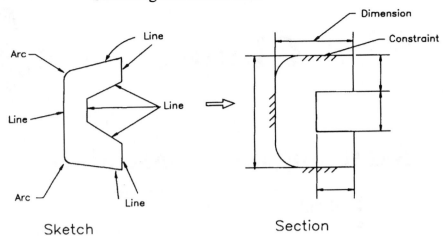

Figure 3.1

Sketch                         Section

Sketches are drawn on a 2-D sketching plane. The main benefit of using sketches is to make creating geometry easy and to convert sketches into sections. A section is a group of geometry entities that are constrained into a single unit. A section is used to define the shape profile of a solid feature. A section can be regarded as the section profile of a feature (Figure 3.2).

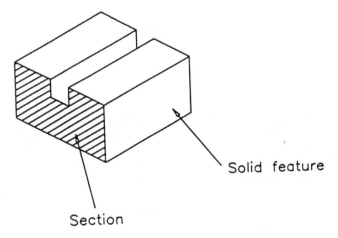

Figure 3.2                  Section

## Section Type

There are two types of sections; **closed sections** and **open sections**. A closed section has the starting point of the first entity and the ending point of the last entity join together (Figure 3.3). For an open section, the starting point and ending point are not located at the same point (Figure 3.4).

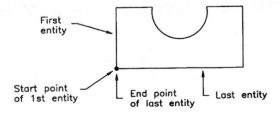

Figure 3.3 Closed section

3-2

Figure 3.4 Open section

# Section Loops

I-DEAS allows the use of multiple sections in creating features. As shown in Figure 3.5, sections can be arranged in a variety of configurations; **single section, multiple section-single loop, single section-multiple loop,** and **multiple section-multiple loop.**

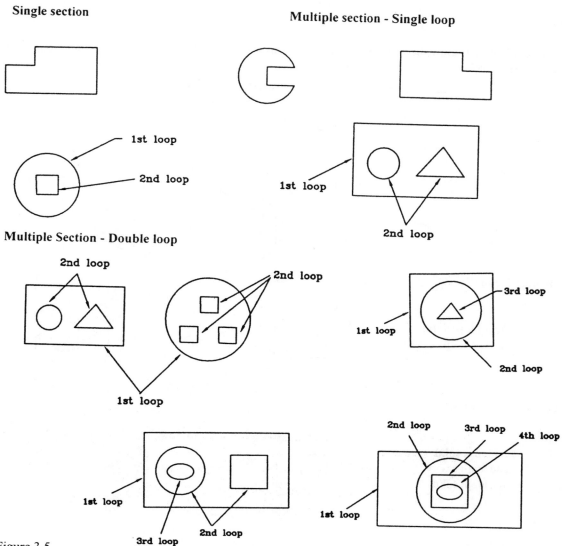

Figure 3.5

# Sketching and Constraints

When **multiple loops** are used, I-DEAS will produce solids and cavities according to the order of looping. The **rule of thumb** is that an odd number of loops produces solids and an even number of loops creates cavities. The loop number is counted from the outside toward the inside (Figure 3.6).

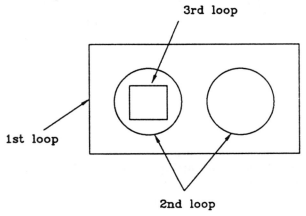

Figure 3.6

Figures 3.7 to 3.10 show the feature types created from single-loop, two-loop, three-loop, and four-loop cases, respectively.

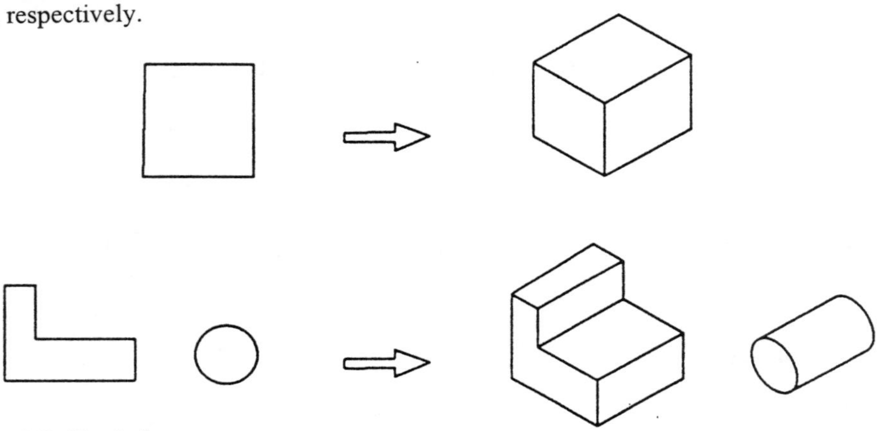

Figure 3.7  Single loop

**First loop: solid**
**Second loop: cavity**

Figure 3.8  Two-loop

**1st loop: solid**
**2nd loop: cavity**
**3rd loop: solid**

Figure 3.9  Three-loop

Mastering I-DEAS,
Scholars International Publishing Corp., 1999

**1st loop: solid**
**2nd loop: cavity**
**3rd loop: solid**
**4th loop: cavity**

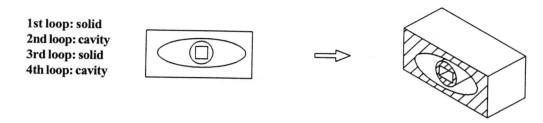

Figure 3.10  Four-loop

# Valid Section Requirements

A valid section can have the following characteristics:

    1. It can be a closed loop or open loop of curves (Figure 3.11).

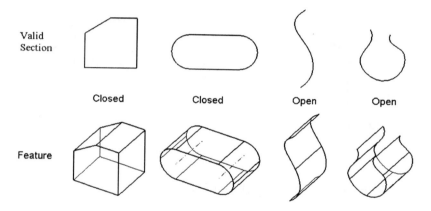

Figure 3.11

    2. It can be composed of multiple loops (Figure 3.12).

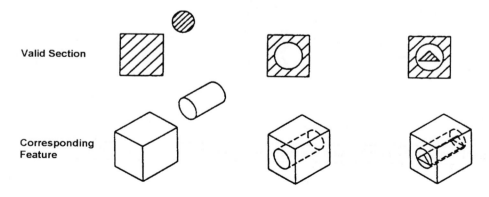

Figure 3.12

3. It can be 2-D (planar) or 3-D (non-planar) (Figure 3.13).

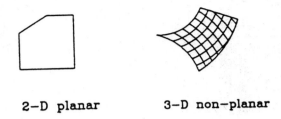

**2-D planar**       **3-D non-planar**

Figure 3.13

The following conditions cause the sections to be invalid:

1. It has self-intersecting curves (Figure 3.14).

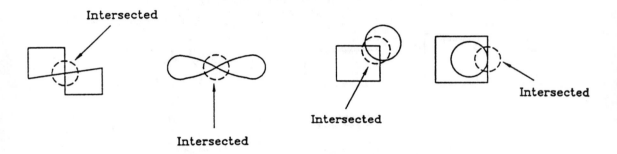

Figure 3.14

2. It has an invalid entity to form the section (Figure 3.15).

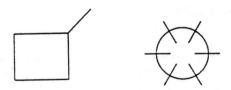

Figure 3.15

| Note: | I-DEAS has a built-in verification process to warn you if the section is invalid. |
|---|---|

Mastering I-DEAS,
Scholars International Publishing Corp., 1999

# 3.2 Creating Sketches

Sketches can be created by using the following I-DEAS geometric creation commands:

| | | |
|---|---|---|
| Line | Arc | Circle |
| Rectangle | Spline | Ellipse |

Figure 3.16 shows all geometric creation commands and their options. They can be classified into two groups; **2-D sketch commands** and **3-D sketch commands**. All sketch commands are stack-icon commands. This means that there are more icon command options behind each individual icon. Press and hold the **left** mouse button to display the rest of icons in the same stack.

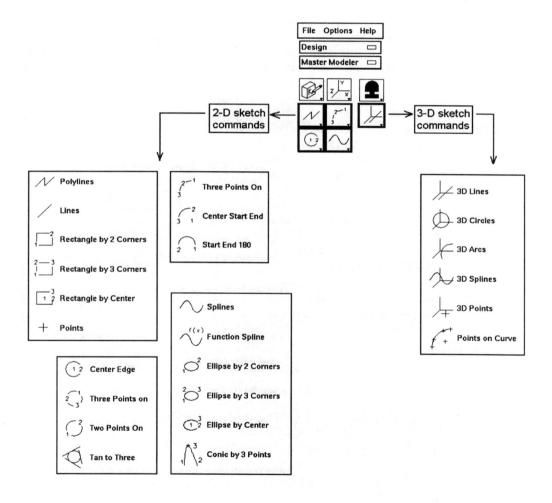

Figure 3.16

# Creating Lines, Polylines, Rectangles, and Points

Table 3.1 summarizes those functions used for creating various lines, polylines, rectangles, and points.

## Table 3.1  Creating lines, polylines, rectangles, and points

| Line Entity | Description | Illustration |
|---|---|---|
| Line | Use two points (start and end) to create a line. | |
| Polylines | Create a series of continuous line segments by specifying the start point of first line, and a set of end points of consecutive lines. | |
| Rectangle by 2-Corners | Use two points to define the two corners of a rectangle. This option is used to create rectangles whose **lines are parallel with X and Y axes.** | |
| Rectangle by 3-Corners | Use three points to define a boundary box for creating a rectangle. This option can be used to create rectangles in any orientation. The first two points define the orientation and distance of one side. **The third point defines the distance of the other side.** | |
| Rectangle by Center | Use three points to define the boundary box of the rectangle. This option can be used to create rectangles in any orientation. The first point is the rectangle center. The second point specifies the orientation and distance of one side. The third point specifies the distance of the other side. | |
| Point | Create a point at specified location. | |

Mastering I-DEAS,
Scholars International Publishing Corp., 1999

# Creating Arcs and Circles

Table 3.2 summarizes the available options for creating arcs and circles.

## Table 3.2  Creating arcs and circles

| Option | Description | Illustration |
|---|---|---|
| **For Creating Arcs** | | |
| Three Points On | Creates an arc that connects three points. These three points are termed start point, through point, and end point. | |
| Center Start End | Creates an arc by specifying its center, start point and end point. | |
| Start End 180 | Creates a 180-degree arc by specifying its start point and end point. The arc runs in the counterclockwise direction. | |
| **For Creating Circles** | | |
| Center Edge | Creates a circle by specifying its center point and a point on its edge. | |
| Three Points On | Creates a circle that passes through three given points. | |
| Two Points On | Creates a circle that passes two points. The distance of these two points is the diameter of the circle. | |
| Tan to Three | Creates a circle tangent to three entities. Valid entities include points, lines, arcs, and circles. Ellipses, splines, and conics can not be used as tangent entities. | |

# Adding Fillets and Corners

Fillets are often added between two intersected entities to smooth out transitions at corners. Fillets can be added to a section, a corner, or an intersection between entities. Fillets can be automatically added to all corners in a section in one operation (Figure 3.17).

Figure 3.17

If two entities are connected at one point to form a corner (Figure 3.18), we can pick the corner point to add a fillet between these two entities. If two entities are intersecting each other (Figure 3.19), we need to pick these two entities individually to define which corner to add fillet. There are four possible fillets that can be added between two intersecting entities (Figure 3.20). The fillet is added between two picked segments (Figure 3.21).

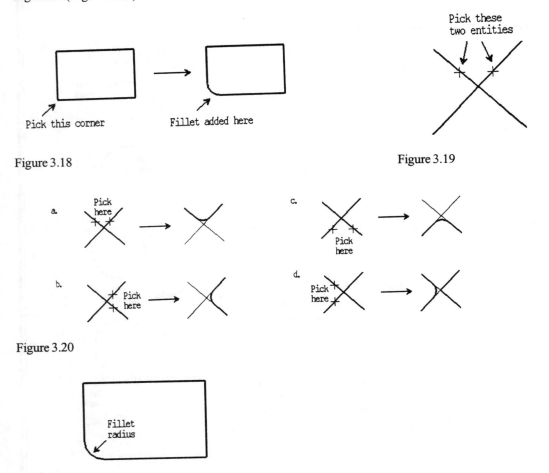

Figure 3.18

Figure 3.19

Figure 3.20

Figure 3.21

Mastering I-DEAS,
Scholars International Publishing Corp., 1999

The fillet parameters are shown below.

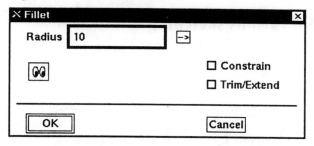

| Radius: | specifies the fillet radius. |
|---|---|
| **Constrain:** | automatically creates constraints for each fillet when it is toggled to ON. |
| **Trim/Extend:** | automatically trims or extends entities to the fillet (Figure 3.22). |

Figure 3.22

## Creating Corners

The **Make Corner** function trims or extends two entities to make a corner (Figure 3.23). This is a very useful function to make two entities connect at a point (Figure 3.24). Making a corner between a spline or arc with another entity requires the spline or arc to be intersected with the other entity (Figure 3.25).

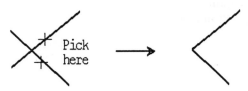

Figure 3.23

Figure 3.24

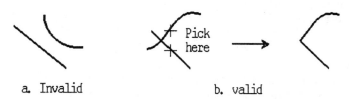

Figure 3.25

# Project 1.
# Creating a rough sketch using various sketching commands

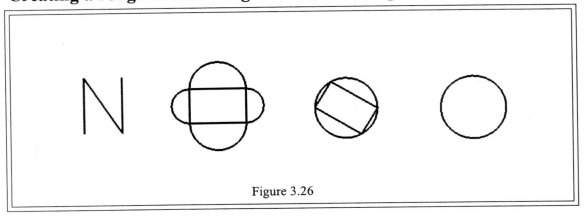

Figure 3.26

This project shows how to use line, rectangle, arc and circle to create a metric sketch as shown in Figure 3.26. Do not save the file since it will not be used in any other project in this book. Do not worry about the exact sizes, but do try to make them look like these drawings as much as possible.

**Step 1.  Set I-DEAS start menu.**
Set the I-DEAS start menu parameters as below.

> Project file name: **your initials** (or your account name)
> Model file name: **sketch1**
> Application:        **Design**
> Task:               **Master Modeler**

**Step 2.  Set the drawing unit and drawing limits.**

 Select **Options** → **Units** → **mm (milli-newton)**
Select **Workplane Attributes**

Set the workplane limits as below.

| X | Y | |
|------|------|------|
| -100 | -100 | min. |
| 100 | 100 | max. |

Select **OK** to exit the menu

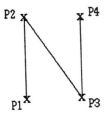

Figure 3.27

 Select **Zoom All** to fit the limits to the screen

**Step 3.  Create the letter N using polylines command.**
**Use the pick points in Figure 3.27.**

 Select **Polylines**
Locate Start:  pick **P1**
Locate End:    sequentially pick **P2 - P4** to complete a three-line sketch
Press middle mouse button (**MMB**) to terminate the polylines command

Mastering I-DEAS,
Scholars International Publishing Corp., 1999

**Step 4.** **Create a rectangle using 2 corners command.**
**Use the pick points in Figure 3.28.**

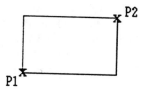

Figure 3.28

 Select **Rectangle by 2 Corners**
Locate first corner: pick **P1**
Locate second corner: pick **P2** to complete the rectangle
Press **MMB** to terminate the command

**Step 5.** **Create four 180 degrees arcs.**
**Use the pick points in Figure 3.29.**

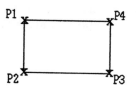

Figure 3.29

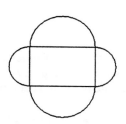 Select **Arc (Start-End-180)**
Pick **P1** and **P2** to create the first arc
Pick **P2** and **P3** to create the second arc
Pick **P3** and **P4** to create the third arc
Pick **P4** and **P1** to create the fourth arc
The rectangle with four arcs is shown in Figure 3.30.

Figure 3.30

**Step 6.** **Create a rotated rectangle using Rectangle by Center command.**
**Use the pick points in Figure 3.31.**

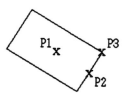

Figure 3.31

 Select **Rectangle by Center**
Locate center:     pick **P1**
Locate side:       pick **P2**
Locate corner:     pick **P3** to complete a rectangle
                   as in Figure 3.32
Locate center:     press **MMB** to terminate
                   this command

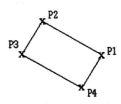

Figure 3.32

**Step 7.  Add two arcs using three points-on command. Use the pick points in Figure 3.32.**

 Select **Arc - Three Point On**
Sequentially pick **P1, P2** and **P3** to create the first arc
Sequentially pick **P3, P4** and **P1** to create the second arc
The two arcs are added as in Figure 3.33.

Figure 3.33

**Step 8.  Create a circle using Center Edge command.
Use the pick points in Figure 3.34.**

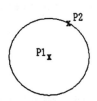

Figure 3.34

 Select **Circle - Center Edge**
Locate center:  pick **P1**
Locate point on edge:  pick **P2** to complete the circle

**Step 9.  Create a circle using Circle-3 Point on command.
Use the pick points in Figure 3.35.**

Figure 3.35

 Select **Circle - Three Point On**
Locate first point on edge:  pick **P1**
Locate second point on edge:  pick **P2**
Locate third point on edge:  pick **P3** to complete the circle
Press **MMB** to terminate this command

Mastering I-DEAS,
Scholars International Publishing Corp., 1999

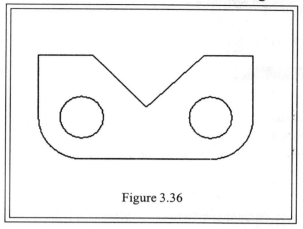

Figure 3.36

## Project 2.
## Creating a section using input exact coordinate values

This project creates a section consisting of lines, fillets, and circles (Figure 3.36). Metric units are used. All geometries are defined by inputting their exact coordinate values.

**Step 1. Set the unit to metric.**

 Select **Options → Units → mm (newton)**
Select **Workplace Appearance**
Set the workplane limits as below:

| X | Y | |
|------|------|------|
| -100 | -100 | min. |
| 100 | 100 | max. |

 Select **Zoom All** to fit the workplane limits to the screen

**Step 2. Create a seven-line section. Use Figure 3.37 as reference.**

 Select **Polylines**
Click the right mouse button (**RMB**),
then select **Options** from the list to open the Line Creation Options menu
Enter the following sets of point coordinate values for creating seven lines:

| Start: | X0 | Y0 | | |
|--------|------|------|-----------------|-------------------|
| End: | X100 | Y0 | (select Apply) | for the 1st line |
| End: | X100 | Y50 | (select Apply) | for the 2nd line |
| End: | X75 | Y50 | (select Apply) | for the 3rd line |
| End: | X50 | Y25 | (select Apply) | for the 4th line |
| End: | X25 | Y50 | (select Apply) | for the 5th line |
| End: | X0 | Y50 | (select Apply) | for the 6th line |
| End: | X0 | Y0 | (select OK) | for the 7th line |

Click the middle mouse button (**MMB**) to terminate the polyline creation
The seven-line section as shown in Figure 3.37.

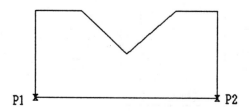

Figure 3.37

**Step 3. Add two fillets. Use the pick points in Figure 3.37.**

Select **Fillet**
Pick **P1** to select the left-front corner to add a fillet
Set the fillet parameters as below.

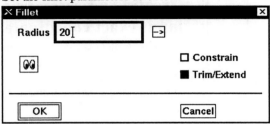

Select **OK** to add the first fillet
Pick **P2**
Select **OK** from the Fillet menu to add the second fillet
The two fillets are added as in Figure 3.38.

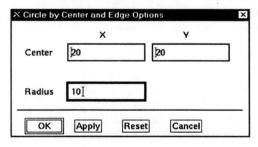

Figure 3.38

**Step 4. Add two concentric circles.**

Select **Circle by Center Edge**
Click the right mouse button to open circle by center and edge options menu
Set the center and radius values of the first circle as below.

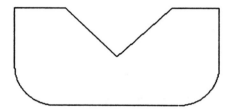

Select **Apply** to create the first circle
Set the center and radius values as below for the second circle, then select **OK**

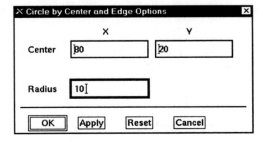

Mastering I-DEAS,
Scholars International Publishing Corp., 1999

The two circles are added as in Figure 3.39.

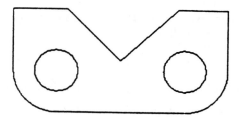

Figure 3.39

## Step 5.  Name the part.

 Select **Name Parts**
Pick the section just created
Define the name parameters as below.

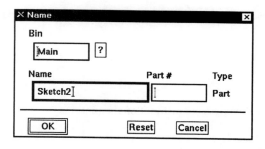

Select **OK**

## Step 6.  Put the part away.

 Select **Put Away**
Pick the part just created to put away
The part disappears from the display window

# 3.3 Creating Splines, Ellipses, and Conics

## Creating Splines

A spline is a smooth curve that blends through given points. There are two ways to create a spline in I-DEAS; **spline through points** and **spline by a function**.

### Spline through Points

This spline option specifies the control points of a spline by manually entering a set of points.

**The procedure for creating a spline through points is:**

1. Select **Splines**
2. Use mouse to locate a series of points for the spline to pass through
3. Click the middle mouse button to terminate the point input

The spline appears as in Figure 3.40.

Figure 3.40

### Spline by a Function

A spline can be mathematically defined using a set of functional equations.

**The procedure for creating a spline by a function:**

1. Select Function Spline to open "Function Manager" menu as below.

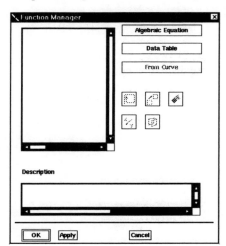

2. Select Algebraic Equation button to open Algebraic Equation Editor menu.

3. Define the algebraic equation parameters as next.

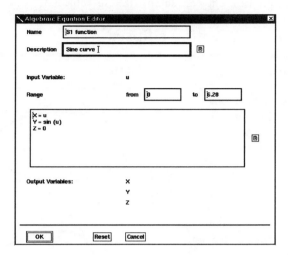

4. Select **OK** to exit Algebraic Equation Editor

The S1 function is added to the Function Manager menu as below.

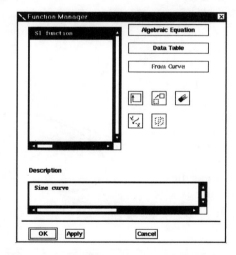

5. Select **OK** to create a sine curve as shown in Figure 3.41.

Figure 3.41

6. Select **Cancel** to exit Function Manager menu

## Creating Ellipses

I-DEAS provides three ways to create ellipses. They are summarized in Table 3.3.

## Table 3.3   Three methods for creating ellipses

| Ellipse Method | Description | Illustration |
|---|---|---|
| By 2 Corners | Use two corners as the bounding box for the ellipse. This option is used to create ellipses whose axes are aligned with X and Y axes. | Corner point / Corner point |
| By 3 Corners | Use three points to define a bounding box for creating an ellipse. This option can be used to create ellipses in any orientation. The first two points define the orientation and distance of one major axis. The third point defines the distance of the other major axis. | 1st point / 2nd point / 3rd point |
| By Center | Use three points to define the bounding box of the ellipse. This option can be used to create ellipses in any orientation. The first point is the ellipse center. The second point specifies the orientation and distance of one major axis. The third point specifies the distance of the other major axis. | 3rd point / 2nd point / center (1st) point |

## Creating Conics

A conic curve can be defined by three points; start point, end point, and shoulder point (Figure 3.42). The system automatically creates a smooth curve that passes through these three points.

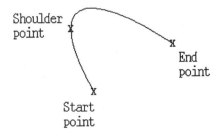

Figure 3.42

Mastering I-DEAS,
Scholars International Publishing Corp., 1999

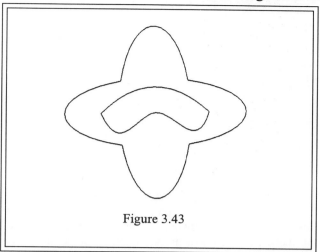

Figure 3.43

## Project 3.
## Creating splines, ellipses, and conics

This project practices creating ellipses, conics and splines. We input exact coordinate values of control points for defining curves. Figure 3.43 shows the wireframe sections to create in this project.

**Step 1. Create a horizontal ellipse using By 2 Corners method.**

Select **Ellipse by 2 Corners icon**
Click the right mouse button (**RMB**) to open the Options menu, then select **Options**
Enter coordinate values for two corner points as below.

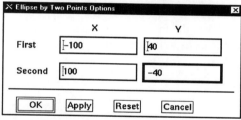

Select **OK** to create the first ellipse as in Figure 3.44.

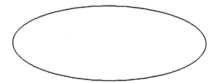

Figure 3.44

**Step 2. Create the second ellipse using Ellipse by Center method.**

Click **Ellipse by Center icon**
Click the right mouse button (**RMB**) to open the Options menu, then select **Options**
Set the coordinate values of three control points as below.

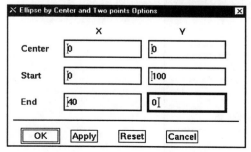

Select **OK** to complete the second ellipse as in Figure 3.45.

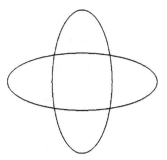

Figure 3.45

## Step 3. Divide two ellipses at their intersecting points.

 Select **Divide At** icon

Sequentially pick the horizontal ellipse as the curve to divide, and the vertical ellipse as the dividing curve for each of the four intersecting points (near their intersecting point)

The horizontal ellipse should be divided into five segments.

Sequentially pick the vertical ellipse as the curve to divide, and the horizontal ellipse as the dividing curve for each of the four intersecting points

The vertical ellipse should also be divided into five segments.

## Step 4. Delete four redundant segments.

 Select the **Delete** icon, then delete the four inside segments

The section after deleting appears as in Figure 3.46.

Figure 3.46

## Step 5. Create a conic curve.

 Select the **Conic by 3 Points** icon

Click the **RMB**, then select **Options**

Set the coordinate values of three control points as below.

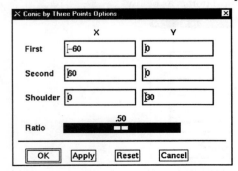

Select **OK** to complete the conic curve as in Figure 3.47.

Mastering I-DEAS,
Scholars International Publishing Corp., 1999

Figure 3.47

**Step 6. Add a spline curve.**

 Select the **Splines** icon
Pick five points to define a spline
(the start and end points should coincide with the conic curve)
The final drawing should resemble Figure 3.48.

Figure 3.48

# 3.4 Constraints and Dimensions

A sketch is the rough shape of a feature profile. It must be constrained to a definite shape and size. I-DEAS uses two types of constraints to define a sketch: **geometric constraints** and **dimensional constraints** (Figure 3.49). The purpose of constraining a sketch is to reduce the sketch's degrees of freedom (DOF).

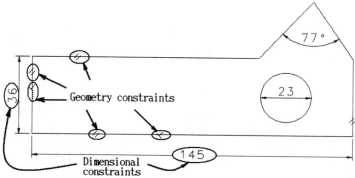

Figure 3.49

## Sketching and Constraints

A sketch having multiple elements requires a certain number of constraints to fully define the sketch. The sketch shown in Figure 3.50 requires eight constraints to fully define it including four geometric constraints and four dimensional constraints.

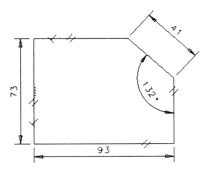

Figure 3.50

Depending on the number of constraints imposed on the sketch, a sketch may be under-constrained, fully constrained, or over-constrained. Table 3.4 summarizes the characteristics of these three constraint conditions.

## Table 3.4  Three Constraint Conditions

| Constraint Type | Constraint Condition | Illustration |
|---|---|---|
| Fully constrained | The number of applied constraints is equal to the number of degrees of freedom. | |
| Under-constrained | The number of applied constraints is less than the number of degrees of freedom. | |
| Over-constrained | The number of applied constraints is greater than the number of degrees of freedom. | |

Mastering I-DEAS,
Scholars International Publishing Corp., 1999

# Sketching and Constraints

## Geometry Constraints

Geometry constraints specify the following three relationships:

> 1. Between adjacent entities such as tangent, perpendicular, etc (Figure 3.51).
> 2. Between two non-connected entities such as collinear and parallel (Figure 3.52).
> 3. An entity with the X- or Y-axis such as horizontal and vertical (Figure 3.53).

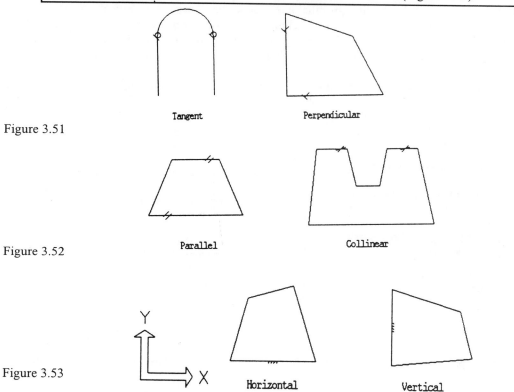

Figure 3.51

Tangent  Perpendicular

Figure 3.52

Parallel  Collinear

Figure 3.53

Horizontal  Vertical

## Dimensional constraints

Dimensional constraints specify the position and size of entities. There are three types of dimensional constraints (Figure 3.54): Linear dimension, Radial/Diametral dimension, and Angular dimension. Geometry constraints are recognized by geometric symbols and dimensional constraints are identified by numerical numbers with dimensional symbols.

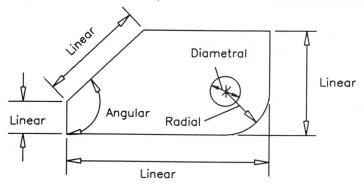

Figure 3.54

I-DEAS uses two ways to apply constraints: **pre-assigned constraints** and **variational constraints**. The pre-assigned constraints in I-DEAS are controlled by Dynamic Navigator, and variational constraints are applied by constraint and dimension commands. They are presented in the next two sections.

# 3.5 Dynamic Navigator Pre-Assigned Constraints

When you are sketching, the Dynamic Navigator is active to help you make logical choices and to capture your design intent. The logical choices include the recognition of existing end points, line centers, circle centers, perpendicular lines, parallel lines, tangencies, horizontal, vertical, etc. This minimizes the drawing time and saves you from picking a menu to filter point option. The Dynamic Navigator also captures your design intent by placing permanent constraints where they are recognized. To speed up your sketch process, it is important to recognize the graphical feedback symbols.

Figure 3.55 shows some of the symbols commonly used by the Dynamic Navigator. The pre-assigned constraints are summarized in Table 3.5.

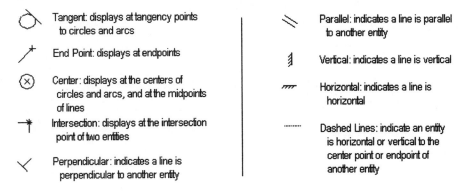

Tangent: displays at tangency points to circles and arcs

End Point: displays at endpoints

Center: displays at the centers of circles and arcs, and at the midpoints of lines

Intersection: displays at the intersection point of two entities

Perpendicular: indicates a line is perpendicular to another entity

Parallel: indicates a line is parallel to another entity

Vertical: indicates a line is vertical

Horizontal: indicates a line is horizontal

Dashed Lines: indicate an entity is horizontal or vertical to the center point or endpoint of another entity

Figure 3.55

I-DEAS organizes pre-assigned constraints in the Navigator Controls menu as shown in Figure 3.56.

### The procedure for using Navigator controls:

1. To access the Navigation Controls dialog box, press the right mouse button to open an options menu during the entity construction processes. These processes include creating line, arc, circle, rectangle, spline and ellipse. Select the Navigator option to open its dialog box.

2. Use the left mouse button to pick the toggle box to either activate or deactivate the control. Any constraint highlighted in the box automatically will be applied to the sketches while they are created. The recognize check boxes allow the system to show what constraints have been applied to the sketches on the screen.

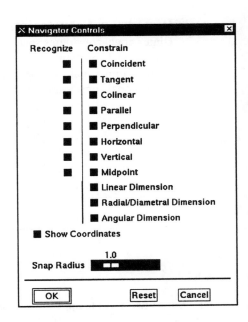

Figure 3.56

Mastering I-DEAS,
Scholars International Publishing Corp., 1999

## Table 3.5  Pre-assigned constraints used by Dynamic Navigator

| Constraint Type | Geometry Symbol | Description | Illustration |
|---|---|---|---|
| Coincident | | Circles or arcs that have their center roughly located at the same point are assigned to be exactly so. | |
| Tangent | | Elements that are roughly tangent to arcs or circles are assigned to be exactly so. | |
| Colinear | | Line segments that are roughly collinear are assigned to be exactly so. | |
| Parallel | | Lines that are roughly parallel are assigned to be exactly so. | |
| Perpendicular | | Lines that are roughly perpendicular are assigned to be exactly so. | |
| Horizontal | | Lines that are roughly horizontal are assigned to be exactly so. | |
| Vertical | | Lines that are roughly vertical are assigned to be exactly so. | |
| Midpoint | | Points that are roughly around the centers of circles and arcs, or close to the midpoints of a lines are assigned to be exactly so. | |

# 3.6 Variational Constraints

After sketches have been created, you may need to add or remove constraints to ensure your design intent. Figure 3.58 shows the influence of the shape after two variational constraints are added.

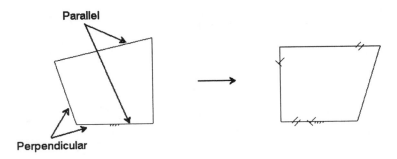

Figure 3.58

Variational constraints are useful to manipulate the final shape of the wireframe. To access the variational constraints commands, select the Constraint and Dimension icon to open the options menu (Figure 3.59) and use the left mouse button to choose and apply the constraints. Note that this constraint panel stays active unless you select the Close option in the panel.

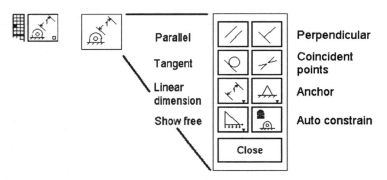

Figure 3.59

 **The procedure for adding geometrical constraints (Figure 3.60):**

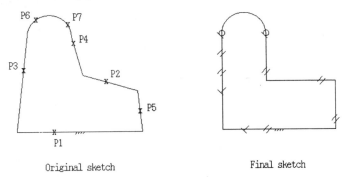

Original sketch         Final sketch

Figure 3.60

Mastering I-DEAS,
Scholars International Publishing Corp., 1999

# Sketching and Constraints

Step 1. Select **Dimension → Constraint & Dimension** to open its menu.

Step 2. Select **Parallel**, then pick **P1** and **P2** to make these two lines parallel.

Step 3. Select **Perpendicular**, then pick **P1** and **P3** to make these two lines perpendicular.

Step 4. Select **Parallel**, then pick **P3** and **P4**, as well as **P3** and **P5** to make them parallel.

Step 5. Select **Tangent**, then pick **P3** and **P6** to make the arc tangent to the left vertical line.

Step 6. Continue to pick **P4** and **P7** to make the arc being tangent to the middle vertical line.

The final sketch after applying the above constraints appears at the right side of Figure 3.60.

## Showing Constraints

The constraints applied to geometric entities in a section can be evaluated. I-DEAS provides the following five functions to display the constraint conditions of selected entities (Table 3.6).

## Table 3.6  Show constraints

| Display Function | Description | Illustration |
|---|---|---|
| Show Free | Show free geometry and direction of selected entities. | |
| Show Causes | Indicate constraints that affect selected entities. | |
| Show Effects | Indicate effects of selected constraints. | |
| Show Constraints | List and display constraints on selected on wireframe entities. | |
| Animate | Move a sketched dimension within a given range. | |

## Sketching and Constraints

Use the **Show Free** command in the constraint menu to discover what lines or curves have not yet been fully constrained. After you select an under constrained wireframe, the system animates the wireframe in the direction of its degrees of freedom. For an under constrained wireframe, arrows indicate the direction of movement. Levels of constraint are indicated by the following colors:

> Green is unconstrained
> Red is partially constrained
> Blue is fully constrained

**The procedure for showing constraints:**

Step 1.   Select **Constrain & Dimension** to open the constrain panel.

Step 2.   Select **Show Free** from the constrain panel.
Notice that the color change in the wireframe to reflect its level of constraint.

Step 3.   At the "Pick point, curve, section, or dimension" prompt, pick P1 (Figure 3.61).

The arrows to show free rotation should appear as in the figure on the right in Figure 3.61.

Arrows show the degrees of freedom

Figure 3.61

## 3.7   Dimensional Constraints

I-DEAS automatically gives initial dimensions to sketches while they are created. These initial dimensions are based on the initial shape. In many cases, you may want to add more dimensions or modify existing dimensions to fully define the size of the part feature. There are three dimension types I-DEAS uses to constrain sketches; **linear dimension**, **radial/diametral dimension**, and **angular dimension** (Figure 3.62).

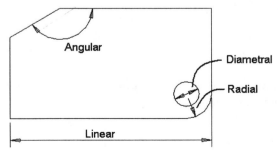

Figure 3.62

**The procedure to automatically give initial dimensions to sketches:**

Step 1.   Select any entity creation function, then click the right mouse button to open the **Options** menu. Then select **Navigator** to Open the Navigation Controls dialog box as below.

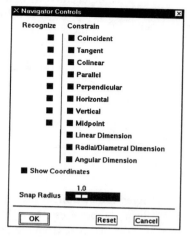

Step 2.   Make sure the following three dimension toggle boxes are activated:
Linear Dimension
Radial/Diametral Dimension
Angular Dimension

**Adding a linear dimension between two parallel lines (Figure 3.63):**
Pick two parallel entities (P1 and P2) to dimension,
then place the dimensions at proper location (P3).

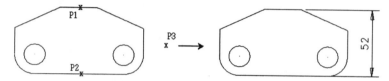

Figure 3.63

**Creating a slope dimensions (Figure 3.64):**
Pick two end points (P1 and P2) of the slope line, then place the dimension (P3).

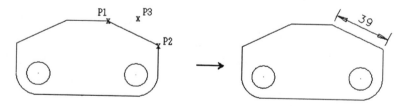

Figure 3.64

**Creating the vertical dimension of a slope line (Figure 3.65):**
Pick the adjacent horizontal line (P1) as the first entity to dimension
Pick the end point of the slope line at the other end (P2) as the second entity to dimension
Place the dimension (P3)

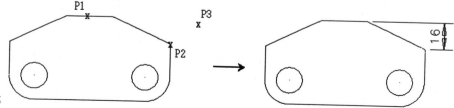

Figure 3.65

# Sketching and Constraints

**Creating the horizontal dimension of a slope line (Figure 3.66):**
Pick the adjacent vertical line (P1) as the first entity to dimension
Pick the end point of.the slope end at the other end (P2) as the second entity to dimension
Place the dimension (P3)

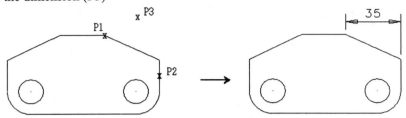

Figure 3.66

**Selection option:** If the initial dimension type is not what you want, you can change it to the desired type. Press the right mouse button to open the Options list as shown below. Then pick the desired type from the list. Figure 3.67 shows an initial dimension is slope.

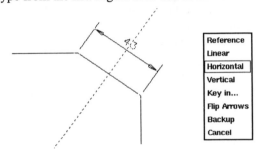

Figure 3.67

**Creating angular dimensions (Figure 3.67):**
Pick the two adjacent entities as the first entity (P1) and second entity (P2) to dimension
Place the dimension (P3)

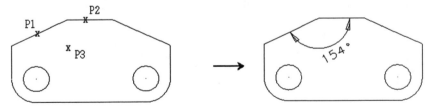

Figure 3.67

## Creating Radius and Diametral Dimensions
I-DEAS specifies circles by their diametral dimension and arcs by their radial dimension (Figure 3.68).
Pick the circle (P1) or arc (P3) to dimension, then pick a location (P2 or P4) to place the dimension.

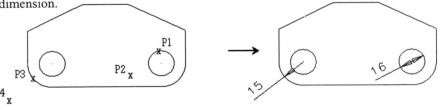

Figure 3.68

3-32

## Modifying Dimensions

Basic geometry can be created without concern about exact dimensional values. A rough sketch is what you need to start. In other words, what you are sketching is only the shape of the section. The exact dimensions will be assigned and modified to finalize the design intent.

Dimensions can be modified using the following two methods:

| | |
|---|---|
| Modify entity method: | modifies a selected dimension. |
| Part equations method: | modifies all dimensions. |

### Modify Entity Method
This method allows to modify dimension values one by one.

 **The procedure is (Figure 3.70):**

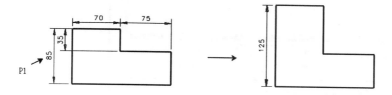

Figure 3.70

 1. Select the "**Modify Entity**" icon
2. Pick a dimension to modify (P1),
    the system will prompt a "Modify Dimension" menu as below.

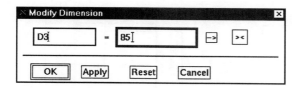

3. Enter new dimension value (125) to the menu, then select OK
    The system automatically updates the section based on the new dimension as shown in Figure 3.70 above.

## Part Equations Method

This method provides a menu showing all dimensions of a selected part or wireframe section. We can modify all dimensions in one operation.

**The procedure is:**

1. Select the **Part Equations** icon
2. Pick any dimension to open Equations menu as below.

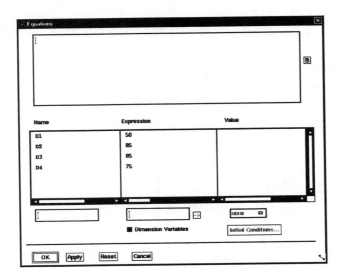

3. Click a dimension (ex. D1) to modify in Equations menu, the system highlights the selected dimension in white in the drawing.
4. Enter the new dimension value (ex. D1 = 50, D2 = 85, D4 = 75)
5. Select OK to exit modify mode

The new wireframe section becomes Figure 3.71.

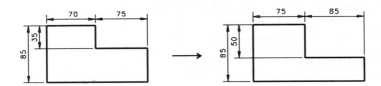

Figure 3.71

Mastering I-DEAS,
Scholars International Publishing Corp., 1999

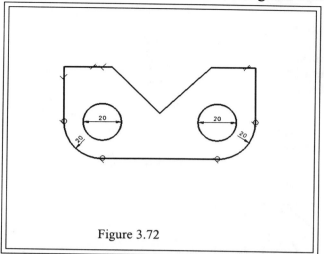

# Project 4.
# Adding dimensions and modifying dimensions

This project uses the sketch created in project 2 to practice adding and modifying dimensions.

Figure 3.72

**Step 1. Get the sketch "sketch2".**

Select **Get** to open the Get menu as shown below
(Your Get menu may appear different from what shown here.)

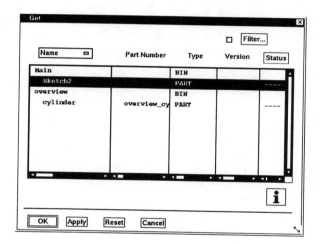

Select **sketch2** from Main bin, then select **OK**
The sketch2 appears on screen as shown in Figure 3.73.

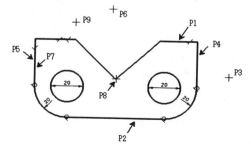

Figure 3.73

**Step 2. Add three linear dimensions. Use Figure 3.73 as reference.**

Select **Dimension**
Pick **P1** and **P2** to select two horizontal entities
Pick **P3** to place the dimension text
Pick **P4** and **P5** to select two vertical entities
Pick **P6** to place the dimension text
Pick **P7** and **P8** to select two entities
Pick **P9** to place the dimension text
The three dimensions are added as in Figure 3.74.

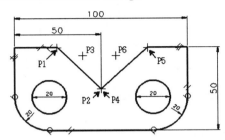

Figure 3.74

**Step 3. Add the dimensions of two slope lines. Use Figure 3.74 as reference.**

Pick two end points (**P1** and **P2**) of the left slope line, then pick **P3** to place the dimension text
Pick two end points (**P4** and **P5**) of the right slope line, then pick **P6** to place the dimension text
The two dimensions for slope lines are added as in Figure 3.75.

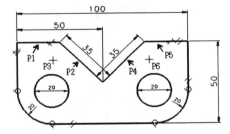

Figure 3.75

**Step 4. Add two angular dimensions. Use Figure 3.75 as reference.**

Pick **P1** and **P2** to select two entities, then pick **P3** to place the dimension text
Pick **P4** and **P5** to select two entities, then pick **P6** to place the dimension text
The two angular dimensions are added as in Figure 3.76.

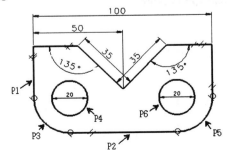

Figure 3.76

3-36

**Step 5. Apply a vertical constraint and two concentric constraints. Use Figure 3.76 as reference.**

Select the **Constrain & Dimension** icon to open the Constrain panel

Select **Perpendicular**, then pick **P1** and **P2** to make these two entities perpendicular

Select **Coincident & Collinear**, then pick **P3** and **P4** to make the arc and circle concentric

Pick **P5** and **P6** to make another pair of arc and circle concentric

A perpendicular symbol and two coincident symbols are added to the drawing as in Figure 3.77.

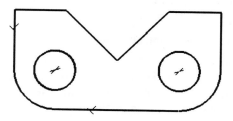

Figure 3.77

**Step 6. Modify the dimensions of two circles.**

Select the **Modify Entity** icon

Pick two circles and change their values to **15**

The new drawing after modifying becomes Figure 3.78.

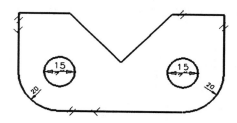

Figure 3.78

**Step 7. Modify two linear dimensions in horizontal direction.**

Change the two horizontal dimensions to **150** and **75** as shown in Figure 3.79, respectively. The new drawing becomes Figure 3.79.

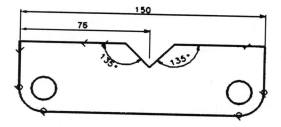

Figure 3.79

# 3.8  Deleting Entities

The Delete function is used for removing a single entity or group of entities from the screen and the system's database. Select **Delete** from the icon panel, and you will be prompted to:

> 1. Pick entity to delete:  Pick the entity
> 2. Press the middle mouse button to accept the selection

**The procedure for deleting multiple entities (Figure 3.80):**

1. Select the **Delete** icon
2. Hold the **Shift** key to pick multiple entities (P1 and P2)
3. Press the middle mouse button to terminate the entity selection
4. Select **Yes** to confirm the entities selection for deleting

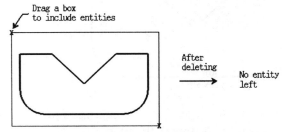

Figure 3.80

The other way to delete multiple entities is to drag a rectangular box to include all the entities to be deleted (Figure 3.81).

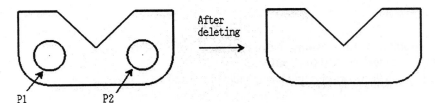

Figure 3.81

Press the right mouse button to access the extra option menu to choose either the entity type or all entities to be deleted (Figure 3.82).

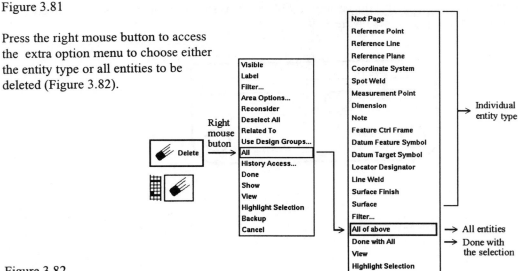

Figure 3.82

3-38

# 3.9   Editing Geometries

I-DEAS provides the following three functions to edit entities:

| | |
|---|---|
| **Trim/Extend:** | trims or extends an entity to a specified boundary. |
| **Divide At:** | divides an entity into two entities at a selected point. |
| **Merge Curve:** | merges two curve/line entities into one single entity. |

## Trim/Extend entities

The Trim/Extend function trims an entity to a specified intersection point. It may trim or extend the entity depending on the relation between the entity to trim and the entity to trim to.

**The procedure for trim/extend (Figure 3.83):**

Step 1.  Select **Trim/Extend** from the icon panel
Step 2.  Pick curve to trim:  pick P1
Step 3.  Pick curve to trim to:  pick P2

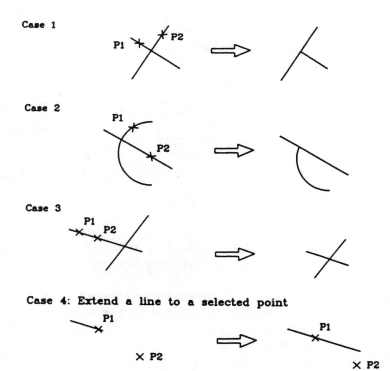

Figure 3.83

When trimming entities, you do not have to pick another line to trim to. Instead, you can pick a point on the selected entity you are trimming. I-DEAS will trim the selected entity up to that point as shown in Case 3 in Figure 3.83.  In Case 4, you can extend an entity beyond an intersecting line. Simply press the right mouse button, then select Point — Screen location, and then pick an existing point to which you want to extend your entity.

## Dividing Entities

The Divide At function divides a selected entity into two entities at the selected point. Figure 3.84 shows three possible cases of using the Divide At function to break an entity into two.

**The procedure for dividing entities (Figure 3.84):**

Step 1. Select **Divide At** icon from the icon panel
Step 2. Pick curve to divide: pick P1
Step 3. Pick dividing curve: pick P2

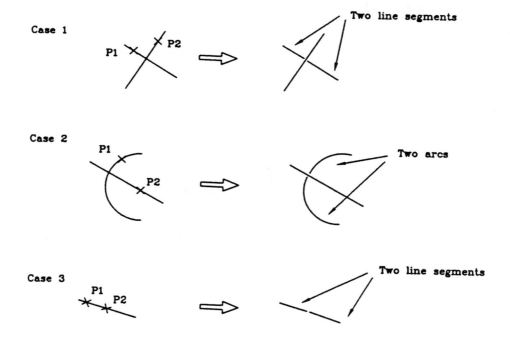

Figure 3.84

When dividing entities, you do not have to pick the dividing curve. Instead, you can pick a point on the selected entity. The system will divide the entity at that point as shown in Case 3 of Figure 3.84.

## Merging Curves

The Merge Curves function combines a line or curve with another entity. The two entities to be merged must share a common endpoint. Two merging entities can be of different types. For example, an arc can be merged with a line as long as they share a common endpoint. Two entities after merged become a single entity, yet their shape and size do not changed. Figure 3.85 shows two cases of using Merge Curves function.

**The procedure for merging curves (Figure 3.85):**

Step 1. Select the **Merge Curves** icon from the icon panel.
Step 2. Pick first curve to merge: pick P1
Step 3. Pick second curve: pick P2

Mastering I-DEAS,
Scholars International Publishing Corp., 1999

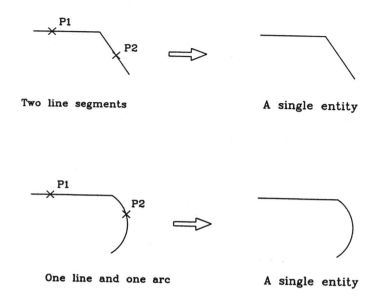

Figure 3.85

# 3.10   Build Section and Offset

The Offset function is used to create one or more entity by offsetting a selected entity to the specified side by a given distance. It can only offset one entity at a time. Often a group of entities should be built as a section before it can be used by the Offset function to offset them together. This section covers how to build sections and use the Offset function to create sections.

## Build Section

Sections are used in I-DEAS to create solids or surfaces. They can be created from existing wireframe geometry. The sections are shown in a thick color-line. There are two ways to build sections; **section with simple geometry** and **section with haystacking.**

### Creating a section from a simple geometry

The Build Section function is used to build a section with simple connected wireframe geometry. All connected entities are built as a section simply by picking a point on any entity. The section is then regarded as a single entity.

**The procedure for creating simple geometry (Figure 3.86):**

Step 1.  Select the **Build Section** icon from the icon panel

Step 2.  pick curve or section:  pick P1

Step 3.  Pick curve to add or remove (Done):  press middle mouse button to terminate the entity selection

Figure 3.86 shows three cases of converting geometry into section.

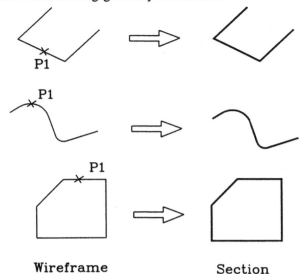

Figure 3.86       Wireframe       Section

You can build a section that consists of multiple unconnected entities (Figure 3.87). They are still treated as a single section. The features created from the section with multiple unconnected entities are still regarded as a single feature.

Figure 3.87       3 entities       A single section

### Creating a section using haystacking

For a complicated wireframe as the one shown in Figure 3.88, trimming may become necessary to create a section. I-DEAS provides a haystacking function to eliminate these trimming processes. It is a grouping function that allows you to pick only the wireframe you wish to include in the section. The advantages of haystacking include:

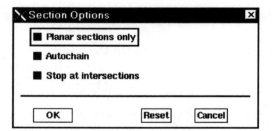

1. Provide flexibility to maintain design intent by leaving untrimmed curves.
2. Encourage engineering content over drafting technique.
3. Save time for trimming.

Haystacking is made possible when the section options "Stop at intersection" is toggled to ON. While using the Extrude or Revolve command, click the right mouse button and select "Section..." to open the sections menu as shown below. Toggle "Stop at intersections" to ON. Figure 3.88 shows and example of using haystacking for defining a section. Sequentially pick at points P1 through P4 to define a section as shown. We also can use the "Make Selection" command to define a section.

Mastering I-DEAS,
Scholars International Publishing Corp., 1999

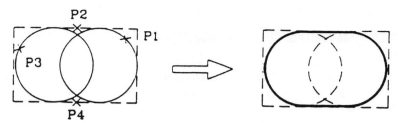

Figure 3.88

## Offset function

The Offset function offsets and duplicates wireframe geometry and sections by a given distance in the specified side. The valid entities to be offset include lines, arcs, circles, splines, and sections. The offset parameters are shown below.

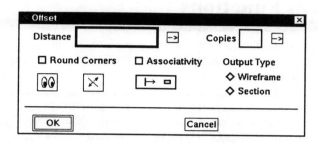

| | |
|---|---|
| Distance: | sets the offset distance. |
| Copies: | specifies the number of duplications of the selected offset geometry. |
| Round corners: | adds fillets to angular intersections on cross sections. |
| Associativity: | constrains offset wireframe geometry to its original geometry. |
| Output Type: | sets the offset to section or wireframe if a section is selected. |
| Flip Direction: | flips preview geometry to opposite side. |
| Opposite: | offsets wireframe or section in 1, or 2 opposing, directions. |

 **The procedure for offsetting geometry (Figure 3.89):**

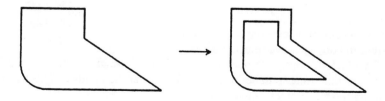

Figure 3.89

 1. Select **Offset** icon
2. Pick section or curve to offset: pick the section,
   then click the middle mouse button to accept the section

A tentative offset section should appear with the Offset menu as below.

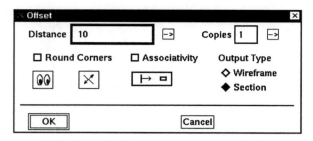

3. Set the offset parameters as above, then select **OK** to complete the offsetting

# 3.11 Transform Functions

I-DEAS provides useful transform functions to change the position, orientation, and size of existing geometry entities. These functions are Move, Rotate, Drag, Reflect and Scale. These five transform functions are summarized in below:

| | |
|---|---|
| **Move:** | moves or copies one or more selected entities to a new position. |
| **Rotate:** | moves or copies one or more selected entities by rotating about a selected point. |
| **Drag:** | simultaneously moves and changes the size of the selected entities. |
| **Reflect:** | moves or copies one or more selected entities by mirroring about a selected plane. |
| **Scale:** | enlarges and shrinks selected entities by a given scale factor about a selected point. |

## Moving Entities

The Move function moves entities from one location to another with a specific distance in a specific direction. Valid entity types to be moved include solids, wireframe geometry, surface, dimensions, and GD & T symbols. Table 3.7 summarizes the four move options available in I-DEAS.

The Translation Values option is the default option. The other three options will automatically appear in the graphic area for you to choose from. The Options menu should appear as here.

| Move To |
|---|
| Move Along |
| Slide On Screen |
| Copy sw |
| Measure |
| Backup |
| Cancel |

The "Copy sw" in the options menu is the copy toggle switch for you to decide whether to copy or move selected entities and by how many copies. Click this option to open the options menu which consists of "On" and "Off" options. The system will prompt "Enter number of copies (1)". Enter the number of desired copies to this prompt. Figure 3.90 shows three examples of using copy option.

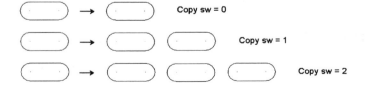

Figure 3.90

3-44

## Table 3.7  Four move options

| Move Option | Description | Illustration |
|---|---|---|
| Translation Values | This is the default option. Enter the translation values for X, Y, and Z axes, respectively to move entities to new location. | |
| Move To | The translation distance is determined by two points; point to move from and point to move to. | |
| Move Along | Move the selected entities along a vector by a given distance. The along vector can be specified by an existing line, an angle, vector values, point-to-point, or other options. | |
| Slide On Screen | This option allows dynamically dragging selected entities to any new location. Hold the left mouse button and drag it to a new location. | |

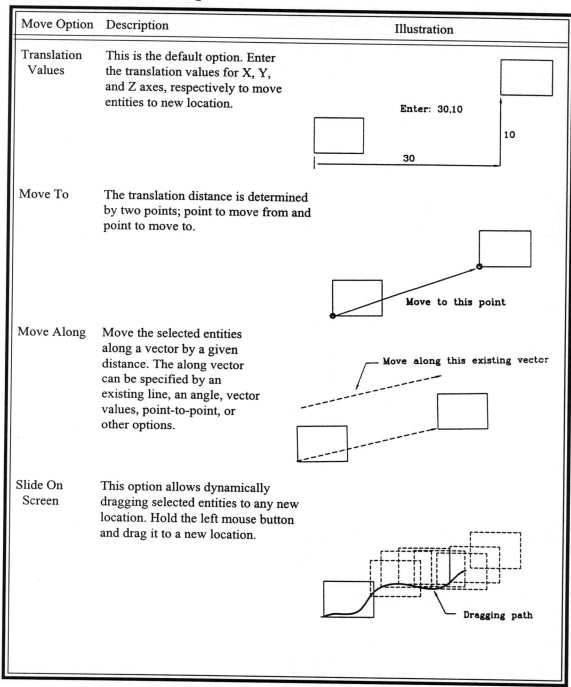

## Rotating Entities

The Rotate function rotates selected entities around a pivot point by given angles around X, Y, and Z axes. There are six options for defining rotation angles for rotate operation. They are summarized in Table 3.8.

## Table 3.8  Six options for specifying rotation angles

| Option | Description | Illustration |
|--------|-------------|--------------|
| Three Rotation Angles | This is the default option. Specify three rotation angle values with respect to three principal axes, respectively. | $x = 80°$ $y = -30°$ $z = 10°$ |
| About X | Rotate the selected entities about the X axis by a given angle value. | $x = 80°$ |
| About Y | Rotate the selected entities about the Y axis by a given angle value. | $y = 60°$ |
| About Z | Rotate the selected entities about the Z axis by a given angle value. | $z = 120°$ |
| About Vector | Rotate the entities about a selected line vector by a given angle value. The vector can be an entity of the wireframe or a workplane axis. | Selected vector as a part of wireframe |
| Align Vectors | Use two vectors to determine the rotation direction and angle. The first is the vector to rotate from and the second is the vector to rotate to. The system will prompt you to select the vector direction. | Vector 2, Arc angle, Vector 1, Pivot point |

Mastering I-DEAS,
Scholars International Publishing Corp., 1999

# Dragging Entities

The Drag function can be used to simultaneously move and resize the selected wireframe geometry and its associated dimensions. You can select a single entity or multiple entities to drag. However, the entire section will be affected if even a single entity is selected. Table 3.9 summarizes several typical cases of using Drag function.

## Table 3.9  Using Drag function

| Action | Description | Illustration |
|---|---|---|
| Drag entire geometry | The entire geometry will be dragged with reference to a default line. | |
| Drag an entity | The entire geometry will be dragged with reference to the selected entity. | |
| Drag a dimension text | Move the dimension text to a new location. No size and position change will be found. | |
| Drag a dimension | Resize the wireframe geometry arrow based on the new location of the dimension arrow. Extend or shorten its associated entity in the dimension direction. | |
| Drag a unconstrained geometry | Resize the unconstrained entity. | |

## Reflecting Entities

The Reflect function can be used to move or copy selected entities about a plane using the mirroring principle (Figure 3.91). The key to successfully reflecting entities is to specify the reflecting plane. I-DEAS provides a variety of ways to define a plane. Table 3.10 shows the seven plane definition options and their effect on the reflecting entities.

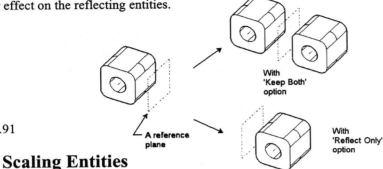

Figure 3.91

## Scaling Entities

The Scale function is used to scale selected entities about a point by a given scale value. There are two types of scale; **uniform** and **non-uniform**. The uniform scale mode applies the same scale value to dimensions in all three axes. Non-uniform mode allows the scale value in each axis to be independently specified. A scale value greater than one enlarges the geometry, while a scale value less than one reduces the geometry. Figure 3.92 shows an example of using uniform scale (2). Figure 3.93 illustrates the effect of scaling using non-uniform mode.

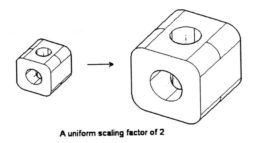

A uniform scaling factor of 2

Figure 3.92

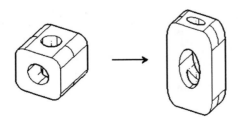

A non-uniform scaling factor of 1, 2, 0.5

Figure 3.93

Mastering I-DEAS,
Scholars International Publishing Corp., 1999

# Table 3.10  Plane definition options and effect on the reflecting entities

| Plane Option | Description | Illustration |
|---|---|---|
| Key In | Use four coefficients in the plane equation to define a plane. The plane equation is in the form of Plane = C1*X + C2*Y + C3*Z + D. | |
| Three Point | Use three points to define a plane. | |
| Point Normal | Use a vector and a point to define a plane. The plane is normal to the selected vector and passes through the selected point. | |
| Offset Surface | Define a new plane that is parallel to an existing plane and offset by a given distance from it. The existing plane can be the workplane or any planar face of the solid features. | |
| Axis Planes | Select one of three principal planes as the reflecting plane. The three principal planes are XY plane, YZ plane, and ZX plane. The system will prompt to enter the offset distance from the selected principal plane. | |
| On Curve | Define a plane that is tangent to a curve at a selected point on the curve. The orientation of the plane is determined by the selected point on the curve. | |
| Surface Tangent | Define a plane that is tangent to a planar surface. | |

# Project 5.
# Editing and transforming entities

The part shown in Figure 3.94 involves using various editing and transforming functions to create sections for creating an extrude feature.

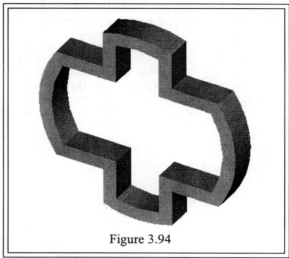

Figure 3.94

**Step 1. Create an arc and two lines. Use Figure 3.95 as reference.**

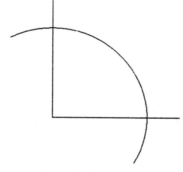

Figure 3.95

 Select the **Arc - Center Start End** icon
Pick three points to create an arc that spans greater than 90 degrees as shown in Figure 3.95

 Select **Lines**
Create a horizontal line starting at the arc center
Create a vertical line starting at the arc center

**Step 2. Add a rectangle. Use Figure 3.96 as reference.**

 Select the **Rectangle by 2 Corners** icon
Pick at two corner points to add a rectangle as in Figure 3.96.

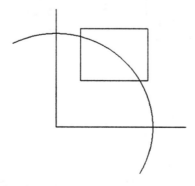

Figure 3.96

3-50

**Step 3. Add dimensions. Use Figure 3.97 as reference.**

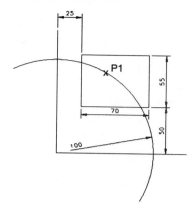

Figure 3.97

 Select **Dimension**
Add necessary dimensions as shown in Figure 3.97

**Step 4. Modify three dimensions. Use Figure 3.97 as reference.**

 Select **Modify Entity**
Change dimensions to desired values

**Divide the arc at a point. Use the pick point in Figure 3.97.**

 Select the **Divide At** icon
Pick the arc to divide
Pick at **P1** as the point for dividing
The arc is divided into two arcs. You do not
see this on screen. The drawing is redisplayed
in Figure 3.98.

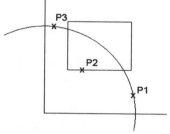

Figure 3.98

**Step 5. Create a section. Use the pick points in Figure 3.98.**

Select **Build Section**
Select **Section Options** to open its menu
Click the right mouse button,
   then set **Stop at intersections** parameter to **On**, then select **OK**
Sequentially pick **P1 - P3** to select four entities
Click the middle mouse button to terminate entity selection
The section is shown in thick purple lines as in Figure 3.99.

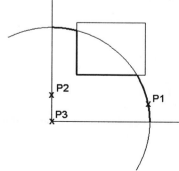

Figure 3.99

**Step 6. Mirror the section about a vertical line. Use the pick points in Figure 3.99.**

 Select the **Reflect** icon

Pick **P1** to select the selection, then click the middle mouse button

Click the right mouse button, then select **Point Normal** from the list

Pick **P2** to select the vector normal to plane

Pick **P3** to pick point plane passes through

Select **Keep Both** from the options list

The mirror result appears in Figure 3.100.

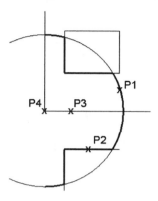

Figure 3.100

**Step 7. Mirror two sections about the horizontal line. Use the pick points in Figure 3.100.**

 Select the **Reflect** icon

Pick **P1** then press the **Shift** key and pick **P2**

Click the middle mouse button to terminate section selection

Click the right mouse button, then select the **Point Normal** option from the list

Pick **P3** as the vector normal to plane

Pick **P4** as the point plane passes through

Select **Keep Both** from the options list

The new drawing becomes Figure 3.101.

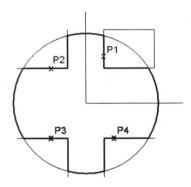

Figure 3.101

**Step 8. Build four sections into one single section.**

 Select the **Build Section** icon

Pick **P1 - P4** to select four sections, then click the middle mouse button

The four sections become a single section now.

Mastering I-DEAS,
Scholars International Publishing Corp., 1999

**Step 9. Offset the section by 15 mm.**

 Select the **Offset** icon
Pick the section to offset, then click the middle mouse button
A tentative result of offset should resemble Figure 3.102.

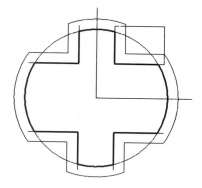

Figure 3.102

Set the Offset parameters as below.

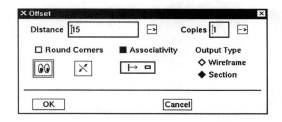

Select **OK** to complete the offsetting of the section

**Step 10. Make two sections becomes a single section.**

 Select the **Build Section** icon
Pick the outer section and inner section to make two sections into one section

**Step 11. Extrude the section by 30 mm.**

 Select the **Extrude** icon
Pick the section, then click the middle mouse button
Set the Extrude Section parameters as below.

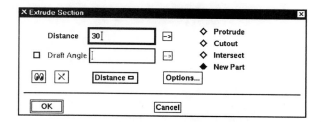

Select the **Isometric view** icon
The extrude feature should appear as Figure 3.103.

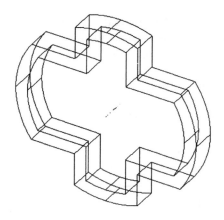

Figure 3.103

**Step 12.  Shade the feature.**

 Click **Shade Software** icon to shade the feature as in Figure 3.104.

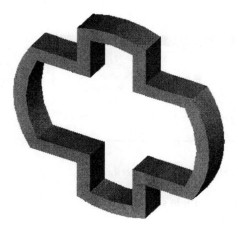

Figure 3.104

# Chapter 3. Review Questions

1.  What is a sketch?

2.  What is a section?

3.  What are the two section types?

4.  Describe how sections can be arranged in different configurations.

5.  Explain how the order of section looping affects the creation of solids and cavities of a feature.

Mastering I-DEAS,
Scholars International Publishing Corp., 1999

# Sketching and Constraints

6. Illustrate how to use Polylines command to create a series of line entities.

7. List the three methods of creating rectangles and explain when to use each method.

8. Illustrate the three methods of creating arcs and explain when to use each method.

9. Illustrate the four methods of creating circles and explain when to use each method.

10. Illustrate how a fillet can be added at a corner and between two intersecting entities.

11. What is the function of Make Corner?

12. What is a spline?

13. List the two ways of creating splines and explain their difference.

14. Describe the three methods of creating ellipses.

15. What are the two types of constraints?

16. Describe the purpose of constraints.

17. What are the three constraint conditions of a sketch? Briefly describe each condition.

18. List the three types of dimensional constraints. Use a drawing to show how they are used.

19. Describe the two methods to apply constraints in I-DEAS.

20. Explain how Dynamic Navigator help you in sketching.

21. Draw the symbols for the following pre-assigned constraints:
    Tangent
    End point
    Center
    Intersection
    Perpendicular
    Parallel
    Vertical
    Horizontal

22. What are variational constraints?

23. List the five showing constraints functions and describe what they are.

24. What are the three forms of linear dimensions? Use drawings to describe them.

25. What are the two methods of modifying dimensions? Explain their difference.

26. List the three functions to edit entities.

27. Explain why entities are built as a section before the offset function is used to offset them by a distance.

# Sketching and Constraints

28. What are the two ways to build sections?

29. Explain the purpose of haystacking in creating sections.

30. List and describe the four transform functions in I-DEAS.

31. Use a drawing to explain how the "Copy sw" parameter affects the use of transform functions.

32. List and describe the four move options.

33. What are the six options for rotating entities?

34. What does the drag function do?

35. Use drawings to describe the seven options for defining a plane using the Reflect function.

36. What are the two types of scale? Describe their differences.

37. Create a sketch as shown in Figure 3.105. Create two circles and a rectangle for the outside contour. Add dimensions as shown to fully constrain the outside contour. Create two circles and two lines to form the profile of the inside contour. Two lines are tangent to two circles. Use the Build function to define a section as shown in Figure 3.105b.

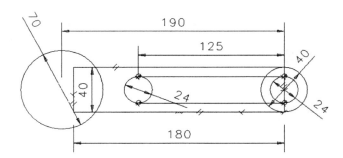

Figure 3.105a

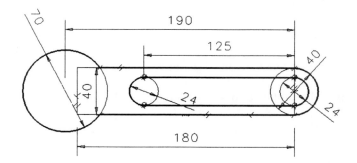

Figure 3.105b

Mastering I-DEAS,
Scholars International Publishing Corp., 1999

38. Create a sketch as shown in Figure 3.106. The section consists of a rectangle, two circles, four lines, and a conic defined by using three points. The two ends of the conic must be tangent to their adjacent line. Use the Reflect function to copy the conic and a tangent line at its upper end to the other side. Use the Build Section functon to define a section as shown in Figure 3.106b.

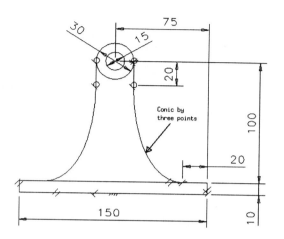

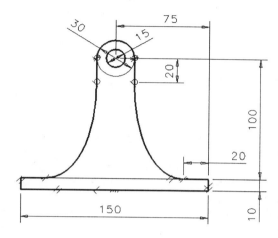

Figure 3.106a

Figure 3.106b

39. Create a sketch as shown in Figure 3.107. Create a larger circle and eight smaller circles and constrain them to their correct sizes and locations. Use the fillet function to add four fillets, each tangent to two circles. Toggle the "Trim/Extend" parameter OFF. Use the Build Section function to define a section as shown in Figure 3.107b.

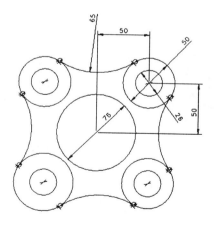

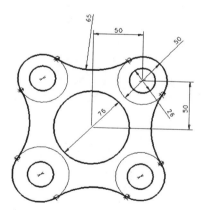

Figure 3.107a

Figure 3.107b

40. Create a sketch as shown in Figure 3.108. Create four circles, two fillets, and three construction lines.Constrain entities to.their correct sizes and locations. Use the Build Section function to define a section as shown in Figure 3.108a. Use the Rotate function with the "Copy sw" option to copy the initial section to two locations. The rotation angle is 120 degrees about the Z axis. Figure 3.108b shows the final section.

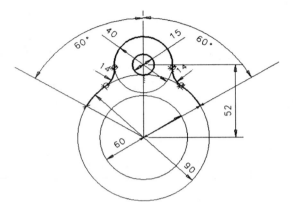

Figure 3.108a

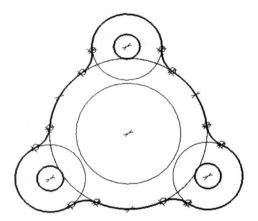

Figure 3.108b

Mastering I-DEAS,
Scholars International Publishing Corp., 1999

# Chapter

# Extrude and Revolve Features

## Highlights of the Chapter

- Feature-based modeling
- Base features and added features
- Creating base features using extrude and revolve functions
- Creating added features
- Draft features
- Sketch planes
- Adding material features
- Removing material features

## Overview

A part normally consists of a number of distinctive features. The first part feature created is referred to as the **base feature.** The remaining added features defining the part details are called **added features**. Added features mainly fit one of two categories: **adding material features** and **removing material features**. Those features that increase the material volume to the part, such as extruding a section or adding a flange, are "adding material features". The features that reduce material volume from the part, such as cutting a hole or chamfering an edge, are "removing material features".

I-DEAS provides two basic feature functions to model the parts from simple to complicated. They are extrude and revolve. The adding or removing of a part's material is controlled by the selection of the feature relation parameter. The feature relation parameter has four options; **protrude, cutout, intersect**, and **new part**. The use of the protrude option adds material to the part. The use of cutout and intersect options removes material from the part. The new part option creates a new separate part that bears no relationship between the new feature and existing part. This chapter presents basic concepts of feature-based modeling.

# 4.1   Feature Types

I-DEAS uses a feature-based construction approach to create parts. Features are the building blocks of a part. There are two types of features: **base features** and **added features**. An object or a part normally consists of a combination of a base feature and several added features. The base feature is the initial workblock that defines the basic shape of the part. In other words, the base feature is the basic form of the part. Figure 4.1 shows some typical examples of base features. The base feature can be analogous to raw stock.

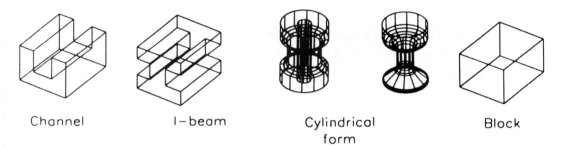

| Channel | I−beam | Cylindrical form | Block |

Figure 4.1

The base feature is the most basic element in the part design and should be represented in its simplest shape and form. I-DEAS does not require that every detail of the part be shown, only the most primitive shape. The added features are added to the base feature to define the details of a part. Added featues are also referred to as construction featues. Figure 4.2 shows an example of two parts that are created by adding different construction features to the same base feature.

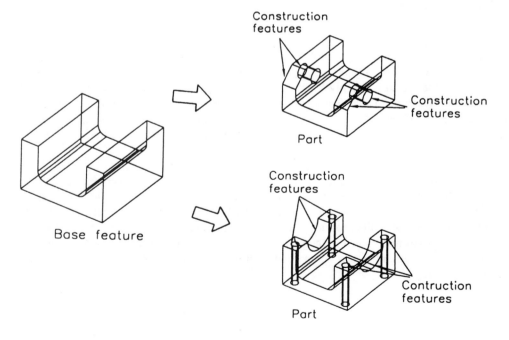

Figure 4.2

Mastering  I-DEAS
Scholars International Publishing Corp., 1999

# 4.2   Creating Base Features

I-DEAS provides two functions to create various forms of base features; **extrude** and **revolve**. Table 4.1 summarizes these two base feature functions.

## Table 4.1   Two base feature functions

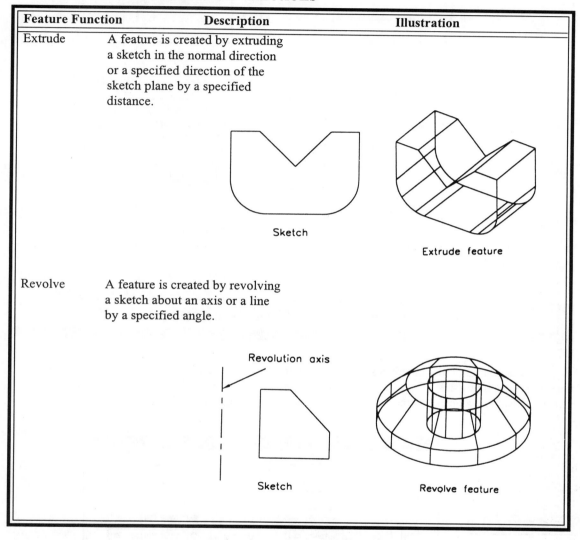

| Feature Function | Description | Illustration |
|---|---|---|
| Extrude | A feature is created by extruding a sketch in the normal direction or a specified direction of the sketch plane by a specified distance. | |
| Revolve | A feature is created by revolving a sketch about an axis or a line by a specified angle. | |

**The procedure for creating a base feature is listed below (Figure 4.3):**

1. Create a sketch.
2. Constrain the sketch by adding geometric and/or dimension constraints.
3. Use a feature function to create the feature.
4. Modify the feature if necessary.

## Extrude and Revolve Features

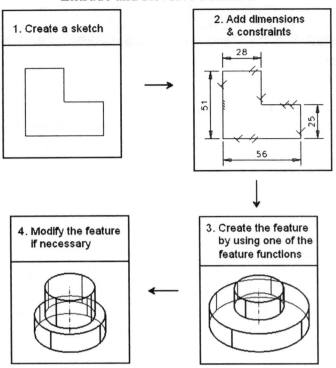

Figure 4.3

## 4.3   Creating Extrude Base Features

The Extrude function creates a feature by extruding a section by a given distance in the specified direction (Figure 4.4). The extrusion parameters are grouped under the Extrude Section menu as shown below. The icon command for creating extrude features appears as below.

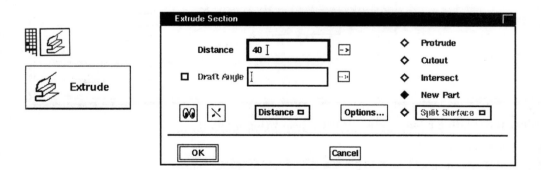

# Extrude and Revolve Features

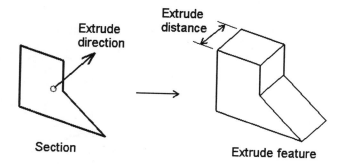

Figure 4.4

The seven defining parameters for creating an extrude feature are briefly described below:

| | |
|---|---|
| **Feature relation:** | specifies the feature relation between the new feature and existing model. |
| **Termination method:** | selects the option for terminating the feature. |
| **Draft angle:** | specifies the draft angle in the extrusion direction. |
| **Flip direction button:** | reverses the extrusion direction of the feature. |
| **Options:** | opens the option menu for defining the extrusion vector, twist angle, and draft parameters. |
| **Distance:** | specifies the extrusion distance. |
| **Preview button:** | shows the preview of the feature before it is actually created. |

## Feature relation

This parameter selects the extrusion relation between the new feature and existing part. It has the following four options:

| | |
|---|---|
| **Protrude:** | adds and integrates the resulting extrude feature to the existing part. |
| **Cutout:** | removes the volume of the extruded feature from the existing part. |
| **Intersect:** | produces a solid feature by retaining the common volume of the existing part and the new extruded feature. |
| **New part:** | creates a new separate extruded part. |

The "New part" option automatically will be selected when no existing feature is found. The remaining three options can be used only when there is at least one existing feature. They add or remove material to/from the part and do not produce a separate part. Protrude is the adding material function. It adds material volume to the existing part. Cutout and intersect remove material from the part.

## Termination method

I-DEAS provides a variety of methods to indicate where to terminate the feature. In other words, it controls the extrusion length. There are only two termination methods in the New Part options:

| | |
|---|---|
| **Distance:** | extrudes a section in a specified direction by a given distance (Figure 4.5). |
| **Thicken:** | extrudes the section equally in both directions with one-half of a specified distance (Figure 4.6). |

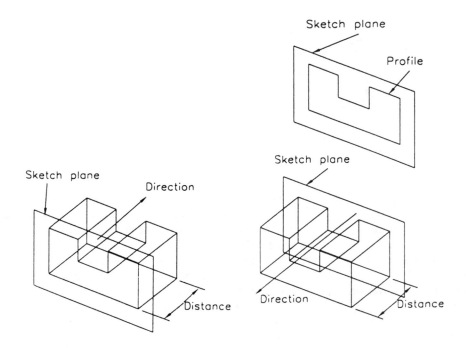

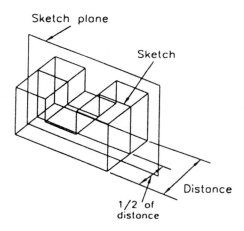

Figure 4.5

Figure 4.6 Thicken

## Draft angle

The Draft Angle parameter specifies the slope angle to be extruded. It can be a positive value or a negative value. A positive draft angle proportionally enlarges the feature in the extruded direction from the sketch plane (Figure 4.7). A negative draft angle proportionally shrinks the feature from the sketch plane (Figure 4.8). When the Thicken method is used, the draft is symmetrically extruded in both directions from the sketch plane (Figure 4.9).

Mastering I-DEAS
Scholars International Publishing Corp., 1999

# Extrude and Revolve Features

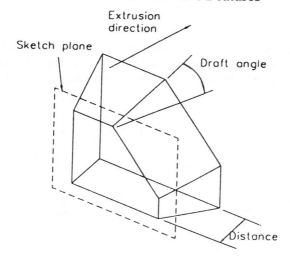

Figure 4.7

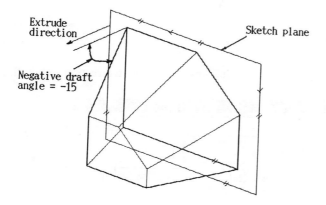

Figure 4.8

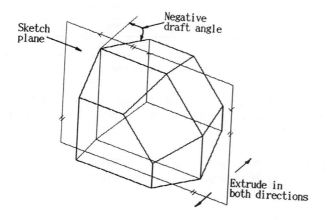

Figure 4.9

## Flip direction

This parameter is toggled to change the extrusion direction. The extrusion direction is indicated by an arrow. The system automatically assigns an extrusion direction that is perpendicular to the sketch plane (Figure 4.10a). Click the Flip Direction button to reverse the extrusion direction (Figure 4.10b).

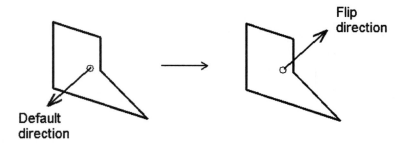

Figure 4.10a Default            Figure 4.10b Flip

## Option parameters

I-DEAS provides a group of option parameters for defining the extrusion direction and draft. Its menu appears as below.

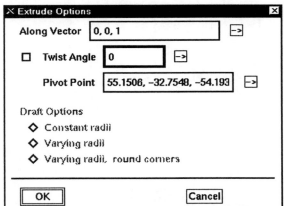

| | |
|---|---|
| **Along vector:** | defines the extrusion direction in the vector form. |
| **Twist angle:** | specifies the twist angle of the section along the extrusion direction. |
| **Pivot point:** | specifies the pivot point for twisting of the extrude feature. |
| **Draft options:** | controls how corners and fillets will be handled. This has three additional options: |

        **Constant radii:** draft the feature with a constant radius.
        **Varying radii:** draft the feature with a varying radius.
        **Varying radii,**
          **round corners:** draft the feature with a varying radius and round corners.

Mastering I-DEAS
Scholars International Publishing Corp., 1999

# Along vector

This parameter allows the extrude direction to be changed. The default extrusion direction is perpendicular to the sketch plane. You can specify three vector values for the direction vector of the three principal axes to define the extrusion direction. Figure 4.11 shows an extrusion that has an along vector of (-1,-1,1), while Figure 4.12 is the example showing an along vector of (2,0,1).

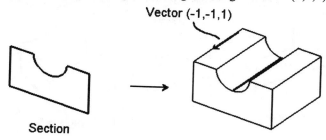

Figure 4.11

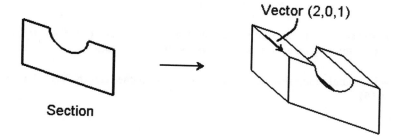

Figure 4.12

# Twist angle

This parameter specifies the angle value for the feature to be twisted. When this parameter is toggled to ON, you can specify the angle value and pivot point. The system automatically determines the pivot point based on the center of the sketch. You can specify any point as the pivot point. Figure 4.13 shows an extruded feature that has 30 degrees of twist angle.

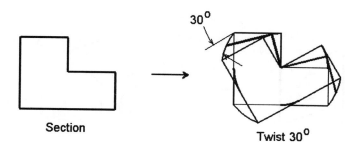

Figure 4.13

## Draft options

This parameter has three options; **constant radii, varying radii, varying radii with round corners**. Figure 4.14 shows the effect of varying radii with round corners on the extrude feature with a draft angle of 5 degrees.

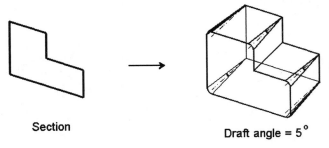

Figure 4.14

## Sections

I-DEAS allows multiple sections to be used in creating features. Section configuration has been presented in chapter 3. Two things you need to know about sections in extrusion are:

    1. Sections in a single loop produce separate features. Those features have the same distance (Figure 4.15).

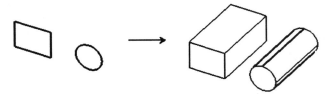

Figure 4.15

    2. Multiple-loop sections produce a single feature (Figure 4.16). The even numbered loops form a cavity and odd numbered loops create a solid.

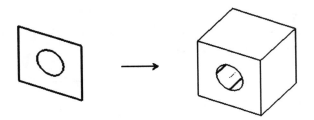

Figure 4.16

Mastering I-DEAS
Scholars International Publishing Corp., 1999

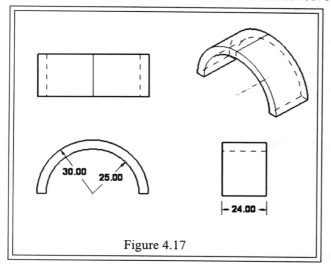

Figure 4.17

# Project 1.
# Creating a bushing part

The bushing part has only one extrude feature (Figure 4.17). We use a horizontal line and two half-circles to form the section for extrusion. The horizontal line should be long enough to cover the diameter of the larger arc. The two half-circles are concentric. The start points and end points of the arcs are on the horizontal line. A hatching technique is used to define the section for extrusion. The part is checked into the library using the following file management data:

| | |
|---|---|
| **Project:** | **engine** |
| **Library:** | **engine-assembly** |
| **Part name:** | **bushing** |

**Step 1. Create a horizontal line and two half-circles. Use Figure 4.18 as reference.**

Select the **Lines** icon, then pick two points to create a horizontal line
Select the **Arc – Start End 180** icon
Create two arcs as shown in Figure 4.18.

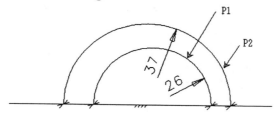

Figure 4.18

**Step 2. Constrain the two arcs. Use Figure 4.18 as a reference.**

Select **Constrain & Dimension** to open the Constrain panel

Select the **Coincident & Collinear** icon
Pick the outer arc (**P1**) as the first entity to constrain
Pick the inside arc (**P2**) as the second entity to constrain

Select the **Modify Entity** icon, then change the two diameter values as shown in Figure 4.19.

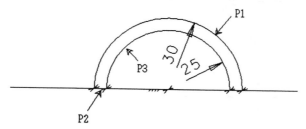

Figure 4.19

### Step 3. Extrude the section. Use Figure 4.19 as a reference.

Select the **Extrude** icon

Click the right mouse button, then select **Section Options**

Make sure that all three parameters are **On**

Sequentially pick entities (**P1 – P3**), then press **Enter** key

The section should appear as in Figure 4.20.

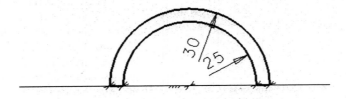

Figure 4.20

Set the Extrude Section parameters as below.

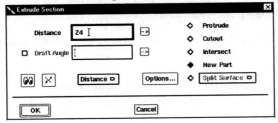

Select **OK** to complete the feature

Select the **Isometric View** icon to display the feature as in Figure 4.21.

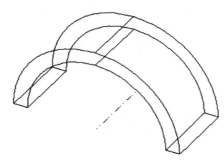

Figure 4.21

### Step 4. Check the part into the library.

Select the **Check In** icon, then pick the part to check in

Enter "**bushing**" into the Name field in the Name menu

Set the Check-In parameters as below.

Select **OK** to check the part into the library

# Project 2.
# Creating a pin part using extrude function

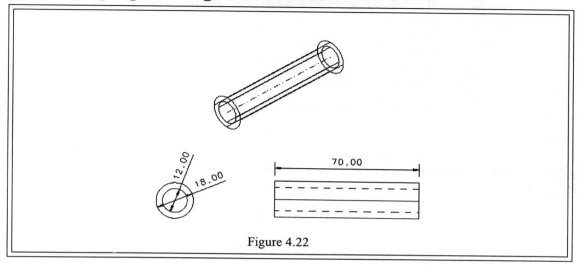

Figure 4.22

This project creates a single extrusion feature part (Figure 4.22). The section has two concentric circles with two loops. The outside circle produces the solid and the inside circle forms the cavity. This part is used in the engine assembly. Check the part into library using the following data:

| | |
|---|---|
| **Project:** | **engine** |
| **Library:** | **engine-assembly** |
| **Part:** | **pin** |

### Step 1. Create two concentric circles.

Select the **Circle – Center Edge** icon
Create two concentric circles as shown in Figure 4.23
Modify two diameters to their correct value as shown.

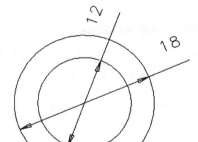

Figure 4.23

### Step 2. Extrude two circles.

Select the **Extrude** icon, the pick both circles to extrude

Set the extrusion parameters as below.

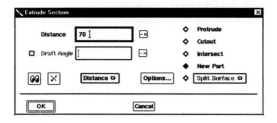

Select **OK** to complete the feature

 Select the **Isometric View** icon to shown the part as in Figure 4.24

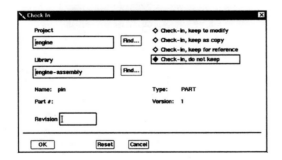

Figure 4.24

### Step 3.  Check the part into library.

Select the **Check In** icon, then pick the part to check in
Enter "**pin**" into the Name field in Name menu
Set the check-in parameters as below.

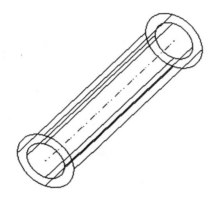

Select **OK** to check the part into library

Mastering  I-DEAS
Scholars International Publishing Corp., 1999

# 4.4 Creating Revolve Base Feature

The creation of a revolve feature requires a section and an axis of rotation. The system revolves the section along the axis of rotation by a given angle to produce the feature (Figure 4.25).

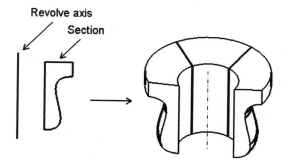

Figure 4.25

The section must be completely located on one side of the revolving axis. If the revolving axis intersects with the section (Figure 4.26), the system will fail to create the revolve feature and issue a "Revolve axis intersects the section" message.

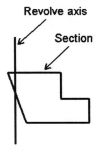

Figure 4.26

The revolve feature can be a solid type or center hole type. The center hole can have multiple steps. Table 4.2 illustrates various types of revolve features and their required section.

The size of the feature is decided by the distance between the revolving axis and the inner edge of the section when the hole center type is used. Figure 4.27 shows the effect of distance on the feature size. The longer distance produces the larger feature (Figure 4.27a). The shorter distance has the smaller feature (Figure 4.27b).

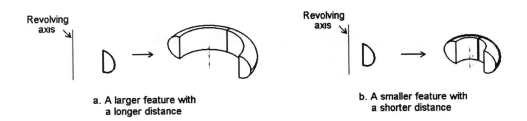

Figure 4.27

## Table 4.2   Various types of revolve features

| Feature Type | Description | Illustration |
|---|---|---|
| Solid center | No hole in the center. One of the lines on the section is used as the revolving axis. | |
| Straight center hole | A hole in the center. A separate line should be used as the revolving axis. The center hole size is determined by the distance between the revolving axis and the inner edge of the section. | |
| Slope center hole | A slope center hole is created by having a slope angle between the revolving axis and the inner edge of the section. | |
| Center hole with steps in the center | The center hole with steps is possible by making the inner edge with steps. | |

The Revolve feature icon appears as:

The revolving parameters are grouped under the Revolve Section dialog box as shown below.

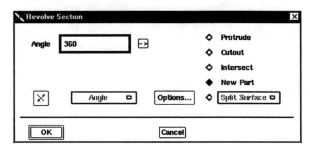

Five parameters in the Revolve Section menu include:

| | |
|---|---|
| **Revolution Angle:** | specifies the angle value of section revolution. |
| **Flip direction:** | changes the revolving direction of the feature. |
| **Termination:** | determines how to terminate the feature. |
| **Options:** | defines the additional revolving parameters. |
| **Feature relation:** | determines the relation between a new feature with an existing part. |

## Revolution angle

The angle determines the shape and size of a revolve feature. This angle can be set to any value between 0 and 360 degrees (Figure 4.28). The system determines the angle value in degrees using the right-hand rule. With the thumb pointing to the revolving axis direction, the four fingers curve in the rotation direction. The system automatically assigns a revolving direction. You can use the **Flip Direction** command to change the revolving direction (Figure 4.29).

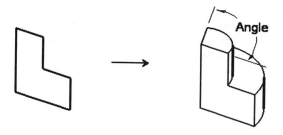

Figure 4.28

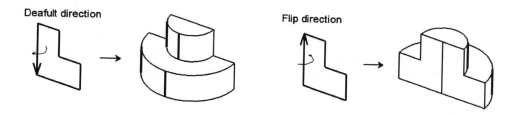

Figure 4.29

## Termination method

There are four feature termination methods available in creating revolve features including **angle**, **until next**, **until selected**, and **from/to**. Only the Angle option is available for creating the base revolve features.

## Option parameters:

The option parameters dialog box appears as below.

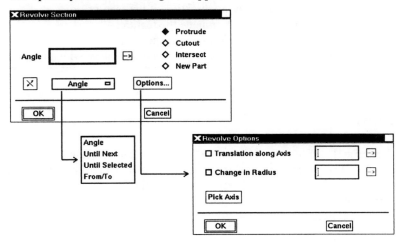

The two main parameters are **translation along axis** and **change in radius**. The "Translation along axis" parameter is used to shift the section along the axis of revolution by a given distance (Figure 4.30). It can be a positive value or a negative value. A positive value shifts the section in the direction of axis of revolution. A negative value shifts the section in the opposite direction of axis of revolution.

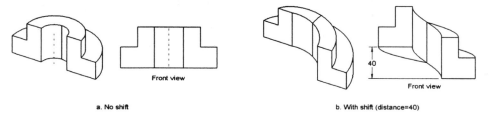

a. No shift        b. With shift (distance=40)

Figure 4.30

The "Change in radius" parameter is used to grow the radius of revolution by a given value during a revolution. Figure 4.31 shows the result of before and after using this parameter.

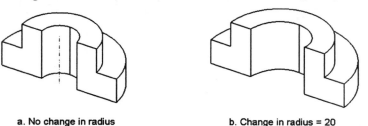

a. No change in radius        b. Change in radius = 20

Figure 4.31

### Feature relation

This parameter defines the relationship between the new feature and the existing part. It has four options; **Protrude, Cutout, Intersect,** and **New Part**. They are the same as in creating extrude features. Only the New Part option is available for creating base features.

## Selecting revolution axis

Any line entity can be used as the revolution axis. It can be a line segment of the section or any line outside the section. Figure 4.32 shows four revolved features that are produced from the same section, but using four different lines as the revolution axis.

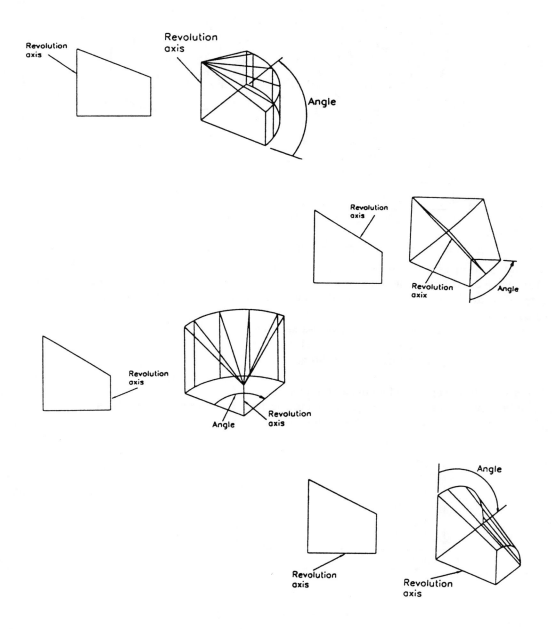

Figure 4.32

# Project 3.
# Creating a bushing part using revolve function

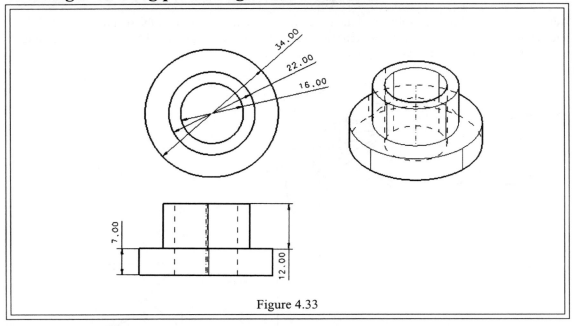

Figure 4.33

This part revolves a 6-line section about a line to form a bushing part for the wheel assembly. The distance between the revolution line and the closest section line is 8-mm. This makes a center hole with the diameter of 16-mm. Figure 4.33 shows the drawing views of the part.  Save the part using the following check-in data:

| | |
|---|---|
| **Project:** | **wheel-assembly** |
| **Library:** | **library1** |
| **Part name:** | **bushing** |

**Step 1.  Create a 6-line section and a horizontal line.**

  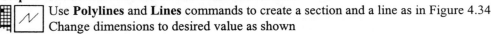

Use **Polylines** and **Lines** commands to create a section and a line as in Figure 4.34
Change dimensions to desired value as shown

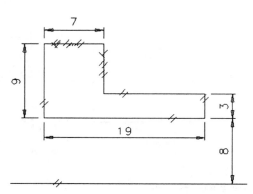

Figure 4.34

**Step 2. Revolve the section to complete the part.**

Select the **Revolve** icon

Pick the 6-line section as the revolving curves

Pick the horizontal line as the axis of revolution

Set the revolving parameters as below

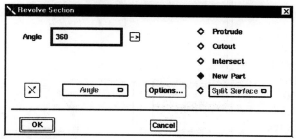

Select **OK**

 Select the **Isometric View** icon to display the part as in Figure 4.35.

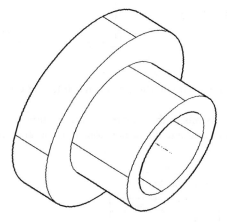

Figure 4.35

**Step 3. Check the part into the library.**

Select the **Check In** icon

Pick the part to check in

Enter "**bushing**" into the Name field, then select **OK**

Set the check in parameters as below.

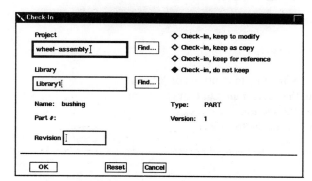

Select **OK** to check the part into the library

# Project 4.
# Creating a wheel part
# using revolve function

This project creates a revolve feature for a wheel. An initial profile which is the half section is created first. This half section is then reflected about the vertical plane to form the complete section. The section is then revolved by 360 degrees to produce the wheel part. Figure 4.36 shows the drawing views of the part. Check the part into library using the following data:

>**Project:**   **wheel-assembly**
>**Library: library1**
>**Part:**    **wheel-assembly**

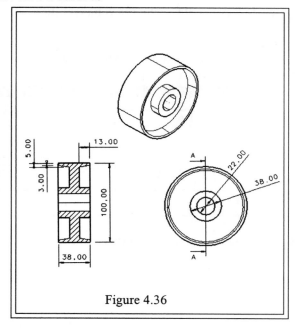

Figure 4.36

### Step 1. Create a section and a line.

  Use **Polylines** and **Line** commands to create an 8-line section and a horizontal line
   as in Figure 4.37
  Add and modify dimensions to their correct value as shown
  Use the right mouse button to make dimensions horizontal or vertical as needed.

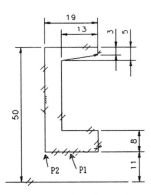

Figure 4.37

### Step 2. Reflect the 8-line section to the other side.

  Select the **Reflect** icon
  Pick the eight lines (Press the **Shift key** to continue pick lines)
  Click the right mouse button, then select the **On Curve** option
 Pick the bottom horizontal line on the section
 Pick the left end point as the point on curve to reflect
 Select **Keep Both** from the options list

Mastering I-DEAS
Scholars International Publishing Corp., 1999

The new sketch becomes Figure 4.38.

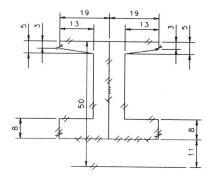

Figure 4.38

## Step 3. Revolve the section about the horizontal line.

 Select the **Revolve** icon

Click the right mouse button, then select **Section Options**

Set Section Options parameters as below.

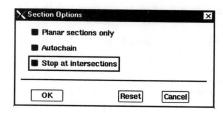

Select **OK**

Pick two sides of entities to form a section as shown in Figure 4.39.

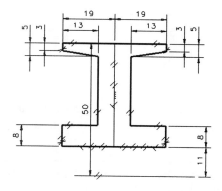

Figure 4.39

Pick the horizontal line as the axis of revolution

Set the Angle value to "**360**", then select **OK**

 Select the **Isometric View** icon to display the wheel model as in Figure 4.40.

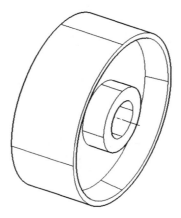

Figure 4.40

**Step 4. Check the part into the library.**

 Select the **Check In** icon
Pick the wheel part to check in
Enter "**wheel-assembly**" into the Name field in Name menu, then select **OK**
Set the check in parameters as below.

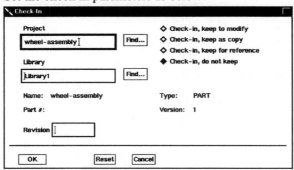

Select **OK** to check the part into the library

# Revolve function

There are two option parameters in Revolve function that can be used to create various types of common mechanical parts such as springs and threads. These two parameters are **translation along axis** and **change in radius**.

> **Translation along axis:**   specify the revolving distance in the direction perpendicular to the sketching plane of the section (Figure 4.41). It is the total distance the feature will move in the translation direction while revolving the section.
>
> **Change in radius:**   specify the change of radius between the beginning section and end section (Figure 4.42).

The above two parameters can be easily used to create various forms of springs and threads.

Mastering I-DEAS
Scholars International Publishing Corp., 1999

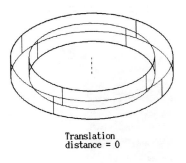

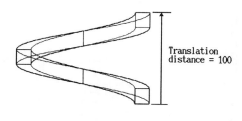

Translation
distance = 0

Translation
distance = 100

Figure 4.41

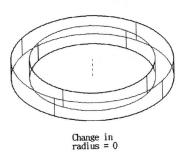

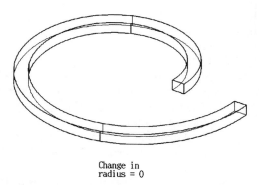

Change in
radius = 0

Change in
radius = 0

Figure 4.42

## Creating Springs

We can use revolve function to create springs. The angle and translation along axis parameters are used to determine the number of coils and pitch for straight springs. The formulas for spring calculation are:

**Angle value = Number of spring coils x 360**
**Translation along axis distance = Pitch x Number of spring coils**

Taper springs can be modeled by adding the "change in radius" parameter. Also, spiral springs can be created by using the **angle** and **change in radius** parameters.

# Project 5.
# Creating a helical spring

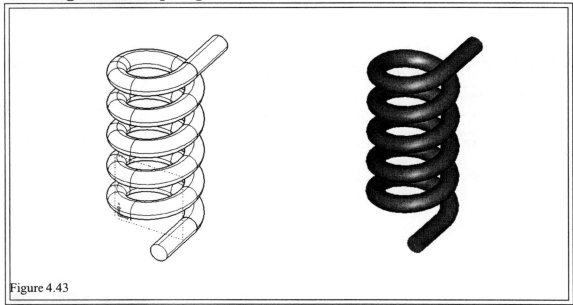

Figure 4.43

This project creates a spring having the following specifications:
      The number of coils = 5
      Pitch = 50 mm
      Coil diameter = 25 mm
      Radius to coil center = 50 mm

The angle value and translation along axis distance for this spring are calculated below:
      Angle value = Number of spring coils x 360 = 5 x 360 = 1800
      Translation along axis distance = pitch x Number of spring coils = 50 x 5 = 250

Figure 4.43 shows the isometric view of the spring.

**Step 1. Set the unit to mm-newton.**
      Select **Options → Units → mm** (milli newton)

**Step 2. Create a circle and a line.**

Create a circle and a line,
    then modify two dimensions
    as shown in Figure 4.44

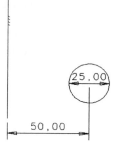

Figure 4.44

Mastering I-DEAS
Scholars International Publishing Corp., 1999

# Extrude and Revolve Features

**Step 3. Initiate the revolve function.**

 Select **Revolve**

Pick the circle as the section to revolve

Pick the line as the axis of revolution

Make sure that the arrow direction of axis is pointing upward

Set the angle value to **1800** in the Revolve Section menu as below.

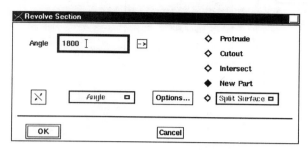

Click the "**Options**" button to open the "Revolve Options" menu

Click the "**Translation along axis**" button to **On**,

and enter "**250**" to this parameter as shown below.

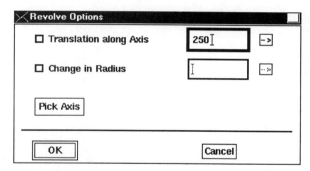

 Select **OK** → **OK** to generate the spring

Select the **Isometric View** icon to show the spring as in Figure 4.45

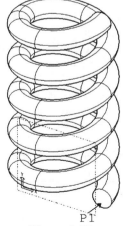

Figure 4.45

**Step 4. Extract a section. Use the pick point in Figure 4.45.**

 Select **Extract**

Pick the circle on th lower end face of the spring (**P1**) as the entity to extract

Press **Enter** to build a section

**Step 5. Extrude the circular section by 75 mm.**

Select the **Extrude** icon

Set the extrusion parameters as below.

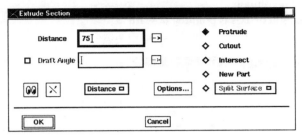

Select **OK**

Pick the spring as the part to be protruded to

The extrude feature is added as in Figure 4.46.

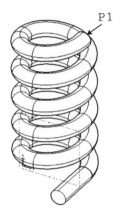

Figure 4.46

**Step 6. Build another circular section at the top end of spring. Use the pick point in Figure 4.46.**

Select **Extract**

Pick **P1** on the circle of the top end face

The circular section is created as shown in the model.

**Step 7. Create an extrude feature from the extracted section.**

Select the **Extrude** icon

Set the extrusion parameters as below.

| Note: | You may need to pick the extrusion direction icon to change the extrude direction away from the part. |
|---|---|

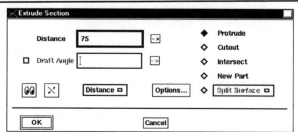

Select **OK**

Mastering I-DEAS
Scholars International Publishing Corp., 1999

Pick the spring as the part to be protruded to
The complete spring appears as in Figure 4.47.

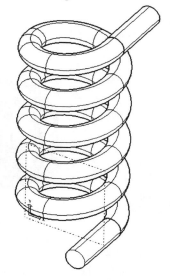

Figure 4.47

**Step 8.  Shade the model.**

 Select the **Shaded Software** icon to shade
the model as shown in Figure 4.48.

Figure 4.48

**Step 9.  Check the part into library.**

 Select the **Check In** icon
Pick the spring to check in
Enter "**spring**" into the Name field of the Name menu
Set the check-in parameters as below:

| | |
|---|---|
| **Project:** | **exercise** |
| **Library:** | **exercise** |
| **Part:** | **spring** |

Click the "**Check-in, do not keep**" option, then select **OK**

# Project 6.
# Creating a taper spring

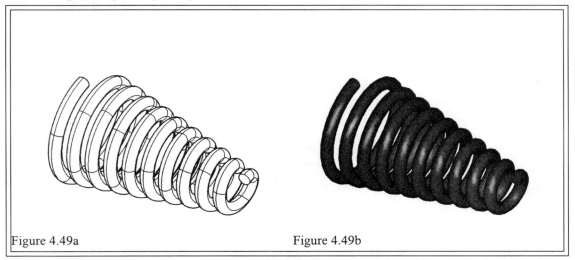

Figure 4.49a                          Figure 4.49b

The taper spring can be created by adding a value to the "Change in Radius" parameter. This project creates a taper spring having the following specifications:

Number of coils = 10
Pitch = 0.5-in
Coil diameter = 0.35-in
Distance from center line to coil center = 0.5-in
Change in Radius = 1-in

The angle value and translation along axis distance for this taper spring are calculated below:

Angle value = Number of spring coils x 360 = 10 x 360 = 3600
Translation along axis distance = Pitch x Number of spring coils = 0.5 x 10 = 5.0-in

Figure 4.49 shows the isometric view and shaded model of the taper spring.

**Step 1. Set the units system to Inch (pound f)**
Select **Options → Units → Inch** (pound f)

**Step 2. Create a circle and a horizontal line. Use Figure 4.50 as reference.**
Create a circle and a horizontal line, then modify two dimensions as shown in Figure 4.50

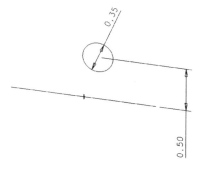

Figure 4.50

Mastering I-DEAS
Scholars International Publishing Corp., 1999

Extrude and Revolve Features

## Step 3.  Create a revolve feature.

Select the **Revolve** icon
Select the circle as the section to revolve
Select the line as the axis of revolution
Select the **"Direction arrow"** button to make the arrow pointing to left
Set the angle value to **3600** as below.

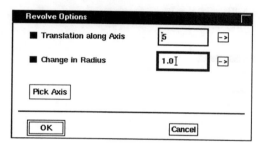

Select the **"Options"** button to open the Revolve Options menu
Set the option parameters as below.

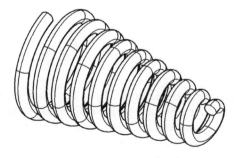

Select **OK → OK** to create the taper spring
Figure 4.51 shows the taper spring in isometric view.

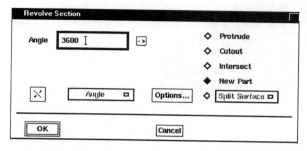

Figure 4.51

## Step 4.  Shade the model.

Select **Shaded Software** (or Shaded Hardware) to render the model as in Figure 4.52

Figure 4.52

**Step 5. Check the taper spring into library.**

 Select the **Check In** icon
Pick the taper spring as the part to check in
Enter "**taper-spring**" to the Name field in Name menu
Set the check-in parameters as below.

| Check In | | | |
|---|---|---|---|
| Project | | ◇ Check-in, keep to modify | |
| exercise | Find... | ◇ Check-in, keep as copy | |
| | | ◇ Check-in, keep for reference | |
| Library | | ◆ Check-in, do not keep | |
| exercise | Find... | | |
| Name: taper-spring | | Type: PART | |
| Part #: | | Version: 1 | |
| Revision I | | | |
| OK | Reset | Cancel | |

Select **OK** to check the part into library

## Creating Threads

Threads are commonly used when joining mechanical parts. Most of popular threads are Unified National threads and metric threads. Both have a 60-degree thread form as shown in Figure 4.53.The following equations are used to determine the necessary dimensions of the threads:

> Pitch (P) = 1 / number of threads per inch
>
> Thread height (h) = 0.6403 * Pitch      (unified)
>
> Thread height (h) = 0.6495 * Pitch      (metric)
>
> Thread root radius = Major radius – Thread height

Mastering I-DEAS
Scholars International Publishing Corp., 1999

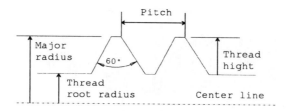

Figure 4.53

Any section of thread must be exactly the same as the thread form. The section is revolved about a center line to form the threads. **Translation along axis** and **angle parameters** in the revolve function are used to define straight threads. They are calculated as below:

**Translation = Pitch (P) x Number of threads**
**Angle = 360 x Number of threads**

It is possible to create taper threads using the revolve function. The change in radius parameter in the revolve function is added to specify the taper angle in taper threads. Figure 4.54 shows the parameters of a taper thread. Use the formula below to calculate the change in radius:

**Change in radius = Thread length x tan(taper angle)**

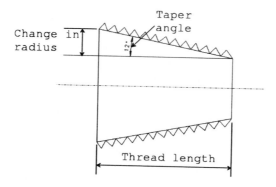

Figure 4.54

# Project 7.
# Creating a straight thread

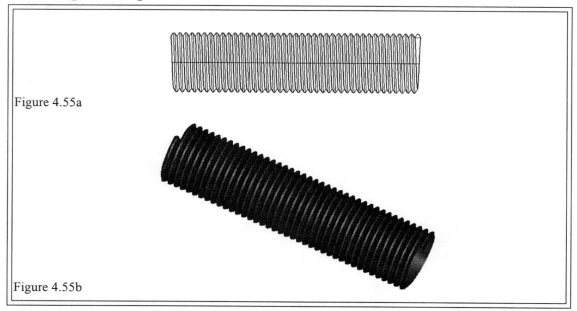

Figure 4.55a

Figure 4.55b

This project creates a UNC 1-10-2A thread which has a length of 4 inches. Figure 4.55 shows the thread in various views. The threading parameters for this thread are given below:

**Pitch (P) = 1/10 = 0.1"**
**Thread height (h) = 0.6403 P = 0.064"**
**Root radius (R) = (Major diameter – 2h)/2 = [1 – 2 (0.064)]/2 = 0.436"**
**Translation along axis = 0.1 x 10 x 4 = 4"**
**Angle = 360 x 10 x 4 = 14400 degrees**

**Step 1. Change the units to inch.**
Select **Options** → **Units** → **Inch**

**Step 2. Create a line and a section.**
 Select the **Polylines** icon
Create a section as the thread profile and a horizontal line as in Figure 4.56

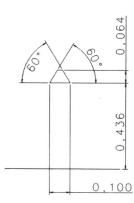

Figure 4.56

Modify the five dimensions for the section as in Figure 4.56

Mastering I-DEAS
Scholars International Publishing Corp., 1999

**Step 3. Save the section as "thread-profile".**

Select **File → Save As**

New model file name:   D:\ideas\ms6\thread-profile

**Step 4. Initiate the revolve function.**

Select the **Revolve** icon

Pick the section as the section to revolve

Pick the horizontal line as the axis of revolution

Select the **Options** button to open the Revolve Options menu

Set the Revolve Options parameters as below.

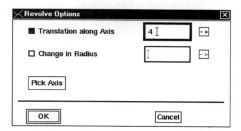

Select **OK** to return back to the Revolve Section menu

Set the angle value to "**14400**", then select **OK** to generate threads

| **Note** | Enter a value of 14399 if you experience a difficulty in creating the thread successfully. |
|---|---|

The thread is created as in Figure 4.57.

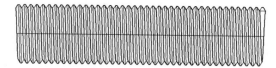

Figure 5.57

Use **F3** with the mouse to show the model in an orientation as in Figure 4.58

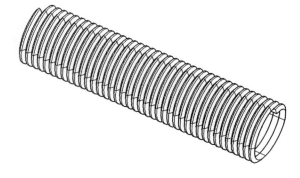

Figure 4.58

 Select the **Shaded Software** icon to shade the model as shown in Figure 4.59

Figure 4.59

**Step 5. Check the part into the library.**

 Select the **Check In** icon

Pick the thread part to check in

Enter "**straight-thread**" into the Name field in the Name menu, then select **OK**

Set the Check-In parameters as below.

Select **OK**

# Project 8.
# Creating a helical thread

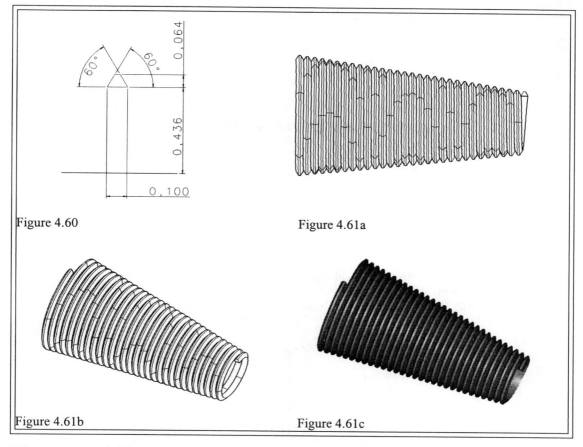

Figure 4.60

Figure 4.61a

Figure 4.61b

Figure 4.61c

This project uses the thread profile (Figure 4.60) created in the previous project to create helical threads that have a taper angle of 7.5 degrees. The thread length is 3 inches. Figure 4.61 shows the taper thread in various display modes. The calculations for this taper thread are:

**Translation along axis = 0.1 x 10 x 3 = 3-in**
**Angle value = 360 x 10 x 3 = 10800 degrees**
**Change in radius = Thread length x tan (taper angle) = 3 x tan (7.5) = 0.395-in**

**Step 1. Open the wireframe file "thread-profile".**
Select **File → Open**
Enter model file name:
D:\Ideas\Ms7\thread-profile.mf1
The thread profile is shown in Figure 4.62.

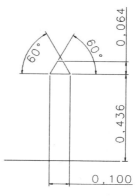

Figure 4.62

**Step 2.  Initiate the revolve function.**

 Select the **Revolve** icon
Pick the profile as the section to revolve
Pick the horizontal line as the axis to revolve about

| | |
|---|---|
| *Note:* | You may need to click the direction button to reverse the rotation to  have the arrow pointing in the  −X direction |

Click the **Options** button
Set the Revolve Options parameters as below.

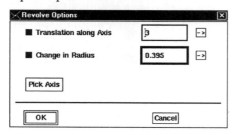

Select **OK**
Enter "**10800**" into the Angle field in Revolve Section menu
Select **OK** to create taper threads
Figures 4.63 – 4.65 show the taper thread in different display modes.

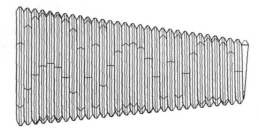

Figure 4.63

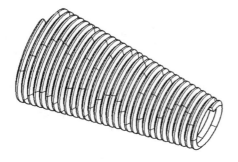

Figure 4.64

Figure 4.65

**Step 3.  Check the part into the library.**

 Select the **Check In** icon
Pick the taper threads as the part to check in
Enter "**taper-thread**" into the Name field, then select **OK**

Mastering  I-DEAS
Scholars International Publishing Corp., 1999

Set the check-in parameters as below.

| Check-In | |
|---|---|
| **Project** | ◇ Check-in, keep to modify |
| exercise [Find...] | ◇ Check-in, keep as copy |
| | ◇ Check-in, keep for reference |
| **Library** | ◆ Check-in, do not keep |
| exercise [Find...] | |
| Name: taper-thread | Type: PART |
| Part #: | Version: 1 |
| Revision I | |

[ OK ]    [Reset]    [Cancel]

# 4.5   Added Feature Functions

Most parts consist of more than one feature. The first feature created is referred to as the base feature. The second feature and all additional features are called added features. I-DEAS provides a wide variety of added feature functions for defining the details of the part. These added features can be grouped into the following two categories according to their functionality:

| | |
|---|---|
| **Adding material features:** | Those feature functions add material to the part. They include protrude, new part, etc. |
| **Removing material features:** | Those feature functions remove material from the part. They include cutout, intersect, chamfer, fillet, shell, etc. |

Table 4.3 summarizes features for adding material and removing material to/from the part.

# 4.6   Sketch Plane

Every feature requires a sketch plane to place its sketch section. A sketch plane is an infinite plane which is not a part of the model. It is a temporary object and only one can exist at a time. Creating a base feature does not require specifying a sketch plane because the system automatically uses the current system default as the sketch plane (Figure 4.66). This system default plane is also called the **global workplane**.

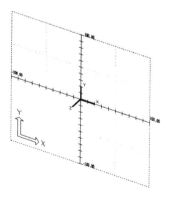

Figure 4.66

## Table 4.3  Added feature functions

| Feature Function | Description | Illustration |
|---|---|---|
| **Adding material feature functions** | | |
| Protrude | Produce the part features that add material. | |
| New Part | Create a new part that separates from the existing part. | |
| **Removing material feature functions** | | |
| Cutout | Produce the part features that remove material from the part. | |
| Intersect | Produce the part feature that is formed by retaining the material shared by two features. | |
| Chamfer | Create chamfers at selected edges or corners. | |
| Fillet | Create fillets between two adjacent surfaces or edges. | |
| Shell | Hollow out the inside of the solid to leave a shell of a given wall thickness. | |

Mastering I-DEAS
Scholars International Publishing Corp., 1999

# Extrude and Revolve Features

Adding any additional features to the base feature requires a sketch plane (Figure 4.67). The sketch plane should be identified by its placement and orientation.

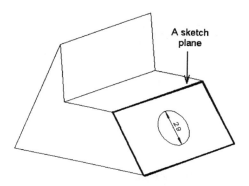

Figure 4.67

There are three ways for defining a sketch plane. They are:

> Using an existing part surface
> Using a reference plane
> Using a workplane

## Using an existing part surface

Any planar surface on the part can be used as the sketch plane for adding more features to the part. Figure 4.68 shows an example in which the right side face of the part as the sketch plane for the feature to be added. Click the "Sketch in place" icon, then select the desired surface as the sketch plane.

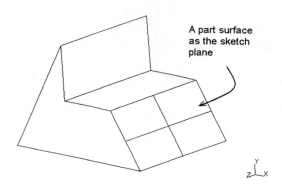

Figure 4.68

## Using a reference plane

A reference plane is a plane defined by the user which in general is not available as an existing planar surface. Figure 4.69 shows a reference plane defined by three points. The **sketch in place** icon command should be used to select a reference plane as the sketch plane.

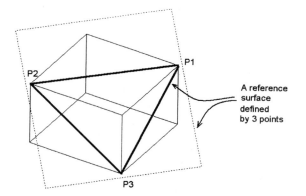

Figure 4.69

I-DEAS provides a variety of methods for defining reference planes.

**The procedure for creating a reference plane is:**

1. Select "Reference planes" icon

2. Click the right mouse button to open the option menu as shown here.

| Key In |
| --- |
| Three Point |
| Point Normal |
| Offset Surface |
| Axis Planes |
| On Curve |
| Surface Tangent |
| Angled Surface |

Table 4.4 summarizes the eight reference plane creating methods.

## Table 4.4   Reference plane creating methods

| Method | Description | Illustration |
| --- | --- | --- |
| Key In | Enter four plane coefficients to define a reference plane. The plane equation is: $Ax + By + Cz + D = 0$ | X=0 (A=1, B=C=D=0) |
| Three Points | Select three points to define a reference plane. | Plane |

Mastering I-DEAS
Scholars International Publishing Corp., 1999

Table 4.4 continued

| | | |
|---|---|---|
| Point Normal | Select a line element as the vector and a point for the plane to pass through. The reference plane is created to be perpendicular to the selected vector and pass through the point. | |
| Offset Surface | Define a reference plane by being parallel to a selected surface and offset by a given distance. | |
| Axis Planes | Select one of three principal planes (XY-plane, YZ-plane, and ZX-plane), an offset distance, and a part to associate with the plane to define a reference plane. | |
| On Curve | Select a curve and a point on the curve to define a reference plane that being normal to the curve at the given point. | |
| Surface Tangent | Select a surface, planar or curve, and a point on the surface to define a reference plane that being tangent to the selected surface at the given point. | |
| Angled Surface | Select a planar surface and a rotation axis, and enter the angle value between surfaces to define a reference plane that is formed by a given angle from the selected surface. | |

## Using a workplane

The workplane is a special reference plane. By default, the workplane's origin is coincident with the global origin of model space, and this workplane is referred to as the **Global Workplane.** When you move or rotate the workplane from the global origin, a global triad will be displayed to indicate the global origin of the modeling space, and the oriented workplane is called the **Local Workplane**. I-DEAS allows only a global workplane and a local workplane.

**The procedure for creating a local workplane is (Figure 4.70):**

1. Select Workplane

2. Select Move (or Rotate, Align, Drag) command, then select one move option
3. Move the workplane to a new location

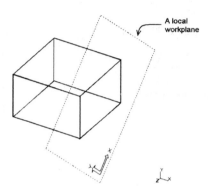

A local workplane

Figure 4.70

# 4.7   Adding Extrude Features

After the base feature is created, we can add additional features to define the details of the part. Extrude features and revolve features are often added to the part. This section presents how to add extrude features to the part. Adding revolve features steps are covered in next section.

The **feature relation** parameter defines the Boolean operation between the existing part and the new feature. It has four options; **protrude**, **cutout**, **intersect**, and **new part**. Table 4.5 summarizes these four Boolean operations.

## Feature direction

After defining the sketch plane and adding a wireframe profile on the plane, a feature direction arrow will appear to indicate in which direction the feature should extend. Select the Flip Direction option in the Extrude menu to toggle the arrow pointing to the opposite direction if necessary. The default feature direction is determined by the selection of the feature relation.

| | |
|---|---|
| Protrude: | arrow points in the opposite direction of the part (Figure 4.71). |
| Cutoff: | arrow points toward the direction of the part (Figure 4.72). |
| Intersect: | arrow points toward the direction of the part (Figure 4.72). |
| New Part: | arrow points toward the opposite direction of the part (Figure 4.71). |

Mastering I-DEAS
Scholars International Publishing Corp., 1999

## Table 4.5 Feature relation options

| Feature Relation | Description | Illustration |
|---|---|---|
| Protrude | Add and integrate the resulting feature to the existing part. | Protrude → One Integrated Part |
| Cutout | Remove the volume of the resulting feature from the existing part. | Cutout → |
| Intersect | Produce a solid feature by retaining the common volume of the existing part and new feature. | Intersect → |
| New Part | Create a new separate part. | New Part → Two Separate Parts |

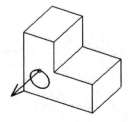

Figure 4.71

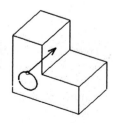

Figure 4.72

## Feature distance

The distance of the added feature is specified by using one of the seven distance options; **distance**, **depth**, **thicken**, **until next**, **until selected**, **from to**, and **thru all**. Table 4.6 illustrates distance options for three types of feature relation.

## Table 4.6   Feature distance options for adding extrude features

| Distance Option | Feature Relation | Description | Illustration |
|---|---|---|---|
| **Distance** | Protrude | To extrude a section from a surface by a given distance. | |
| **Depth** | Cutout | To cut a section from the part by a given depth. | |
| | Intersect | To retain the common material formed between the existing part and the feature created by extruding a section by a given depth. | |
| **Thicken** | Protrude | To produce a section equally in both directions from the sketch plane by a given total distance. | |
| | Cutout | To cut a section from the part equally in both directions from the sketch plane by a given total distance. | |
| | Intersect | To retain the common material formed between the existing part and the feature created by extruding a section equally in both directions from the sketch plane by a given total distance. | |

Mastering I-DEAS
Scholars International Publishing Corp., 1999

Table 4.6 continued

| | | | |
|---|---|---|---|
| **Until Next** | Protrude | To protrude a section until reaching the next surface. | |
| | Cutout | To cut a section from the part until reaching the next surface. | |
| | Intersect | To retain the common material formed between the existing part and the feature created by extruding a section until reaching the next surface. | |
| **Until Selected** | Protrude | To protrude a section until reaching the selected surface. | |
| | Cutout | To cut a section from the part until reaching the selected surface. | |
| | Intersect | To retain the common material formed between the existing part and the feature created by extruding a section until reaching the selected surface. | |

Table 4.6 continued

| From/To | Protrude | To protrude a section from a surface to another surface. | |
|---------|----------|----------|---|
| | Cutout | To cut a section from the part starting from a surface to another surface. | |
| | Intersect | To retain the common material formed between the existing part and the feature created by extruding a section starting from a surface to another surface. | |
| **Thru All** | Cutout | To cut a section from the sketch plane throughout the part in the specified direction. | |
| | Intersect | To retain the common material formed between the existing part and the feature created by extruding a section throughout the part. | |

Mastering I-DEAS
Scholars International Publishing Corp., 1999

# Project 9.
# Creating the cap part for engine project

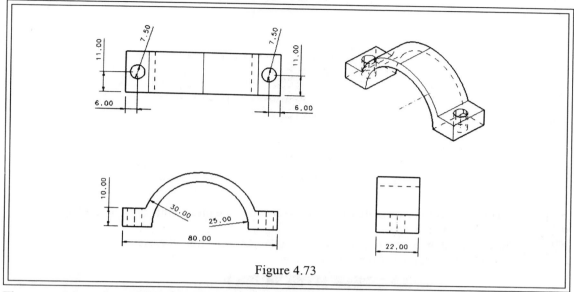

Figure 4.73

The cap consists of an extruded base feature with two hole features (Figure 4.73). The section for the base feature can be obtained by using the hatching technique from a rectangle and two concentric circles. This process simplifies the creating of a section. Check the part into the library using the data below.

| | |
|---|---|
| **Project:** | engine |
| **Library:** | engine-assembly |
| **part Name:** | cap |

### Step 1.  Create a rectangle.

Select the **Rectangle by 2 Corners** icon
Pick two points to create the rectangle
Modify its two dimensions as shown in Figure 4.74.

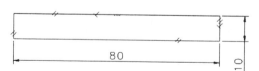

Figure 4.74

### Step 2.  Add two concentric circles.

Select the **Circle – Center Edge** icon

# Extrude and Revolve Features

Create two circles as shown (place the center at the midpoint of the bottom line of the rectangle)
Modify their diameter to correct value as shown in Figure 4.75

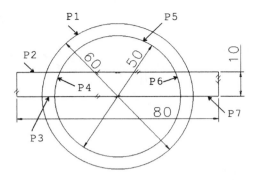

Figure 4.75

**Step 3. Extrude the section to create the base feature. Use the pick points in Figure 4.75.**

 Select the **Extrude** icon

Click the right mouse button, then select **Section Options** from the list

Set the Section Options parameters as below.

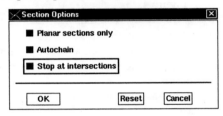

Select **OK**

Sequentially pick the entities (**P1 – P7**) as shown in Figure 4.75

The complete section should appear as in Figure 4.76.

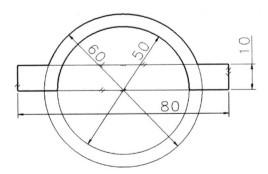

Figure 4.76

Press **Enter** to complete the section

Mastering I-DEAS
Scholars International Publishing Corp., 1999

# Extrude and Revolve Features

Set the Extrude Section parameters as below.

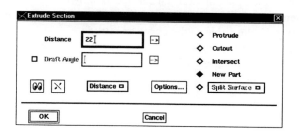

Select **OK** to complete the extrude feature

Select the **Isometric View** icon to show the feature as in Figure 4.77

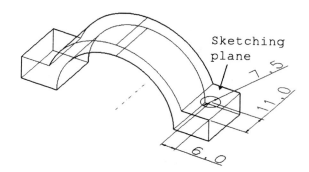

Figure 4.77

## Step 4.  Create a hole feature at the right flat surface. Use Figure 4.77 as reference.

Select the **Sketch in place** icon, then pick the surface at the right side as shown
Create a circle and add dimensions, then modify them to correct value as shown
Select the **Extrude** icon, then pick the circle as the curve to extrude

Set the Extrude Section parameters as below.

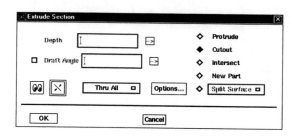

Select **OK** to add the hole feature as in Figure 4.78.

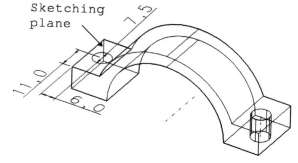

Figure 4.78

**Step 5.  Create a hole feature at the left flat surface. Use Figure 4.78 as reference.**

  Select the **Sketch in place** icon, then pick the left flat surface as shown

Create a circle and add dimensions, then modify them to their correct value as shown

Select the **Extrude** icon, then pick the circle as the curve to extrude

 Set the Extrude Section parameters as in step 4

Select **OK** to add the hole feature as in Figure 4.79

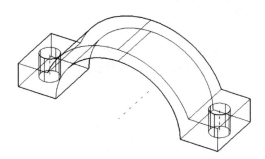

Figure 4.79

**Step 6.  Check the part into the library.**

Select the **Check In icon**, then pick the part to check in

Enter "**cap**" into the Name field in Name menu

Set Check-In parameters as below.

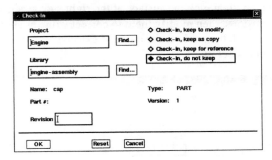

Select **OK** to check the part in

# Project 10.
# Creating the coupler part

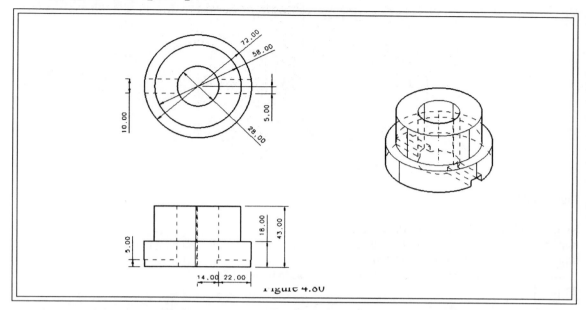

Figure 4.80

The coupler part consists of two features; revolve feature and extrude-cutout feature (Figure 4.80). A rectangle is created on the bottom face of the revolve feature. This rectangle is created somewhat longer than the size of the bottom face while the width is dimensioned to its exact size. The cutout function is used to cut the slot.

**Step 1.  Create a six-line section and a vertical line.**

Create a section and a line as in Figure 4.81

Modify dimensions to their desired value as shown

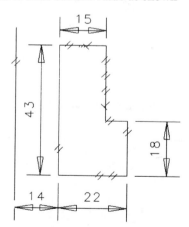

Figure 4.81

**Step 2.  Revolve the section about the left vertical line.**

Select the **Revolve** icon

Select the section as the curve to revolve

Select the left vertical line as the axis of revolution

Enter "**360**" to the Angle parameter in the Revolve Section menu

Select **OK** to complete the feature

# Extrude and Revolve Features

Select the **Isometric View** icon to display the feature as in Figure 4.82.

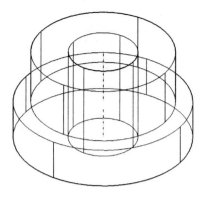

Figure 4.82

**Step 3.  Create a rectangle on the bottom face.**

Select **Sketch in place**, then pick the bottom face as the sketching plane
Select the **Top (ZX) View** icon

Create a rectangle with its dimensions as in Figure 4.83.

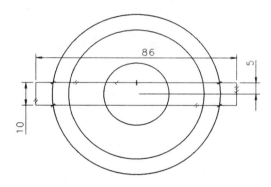

Figure 4.83

**Step 4.  Extrude cut the slot.**

Select the **Extrude** icon
Carefully pick entities to form a section as shown in Figure 4.84.

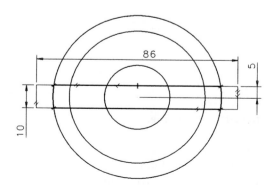

Figure 4.84

Mastering  I-DEAS
Scholars International Publishing Corp., 1999

# Extrude and Revolve Features

Set the Extrude Section parameters as below.

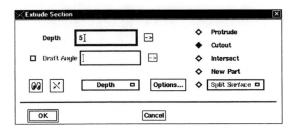

Select **OK** to extrude cut the feature
The slot feature is added as in Figure 4.85.

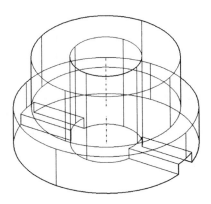

Figure 4.85

**Step 5. Check the part into the library.**

 Select the **Check In** icon, then pick the part to check in
Enter **"coupler"** into the Name field in Name menu, then select **OK**
Set the check-in parameters as below.

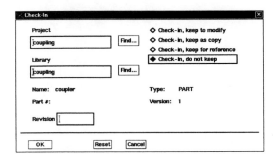

Select **OK** to complete the check in

# Project 11.
# Creating the connector part

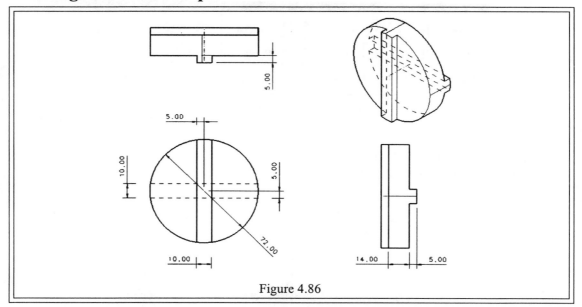

Figure 4.86

The connector part has three features; extrude base feature and two protrude flanges in each side (Figure 4.86). The protrude flanges are created by extruding a section from two lines and two arcs. The two lines are part of a rectangle and two arcs are from the profile edge of the base feature. Use the "Stop at intersection" option to define the section.

**Step 1. Create a circle with a diameter of 72.**

Use the **Circle-Center Edge** icon to create a circle and modify its value to **72** as Figure 4.87

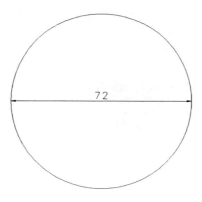

Figure 4.87

**Step 2. Extrude the circle by a distance of 14.**

Select the **Extrude** icon
Pick the circle as the curve to extrude
Enter "**14**" to the Distance parameter in the Extrude Section menu
Select **OK** to create the feature
Select **Isometric View** to display the model as in Figure 4.88

Mastering I-DEAS
Scholars International Publishing Corp., 1999

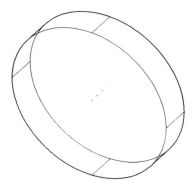

Figure 4.88

### Step 3. Create a rectangle using the front face as the sketching plane.

 Select the **Sketch in place** icon, then pick the front face
Click the **Front (XY) view** icon

 Select **Rectangle by 2 Corners** icon, then create a rectangle as shown in Figure 4.89
Add a dimension and modify three dimensions to their correct value as in Figure 4.89

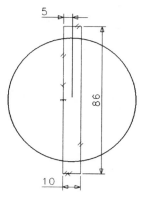

Figure 4.89

### Step 4. Create an extrude-protrude feature.

 Select the **Extrude** icon
Click the right mouse button, then select **Section Options** from the list
Set the parameters as below.

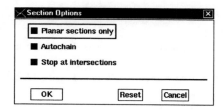

Select **OK**

# Extrude and Revolve Features

Carefully pick four elements to form a section as in Figure 4.90.

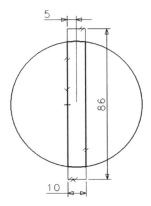

Figure 4.90

Define the Extrude Section parameters as below.

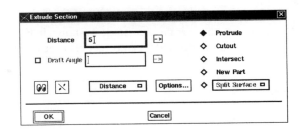

Select **OK** to add the extrude feature

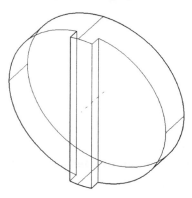

Select the **Isometric View** icon to display the model as in Figure 4.91.

Figure 4.91

**Step 5.  Create another rectangle on the back face.**

Select the **Sketch in place** icon, then pick the back face as the sketching plane

Select the **Front (XY) View** icon

Select **Rectangle by 2 Corners**, then create a rectangle as in Figure 4.92.

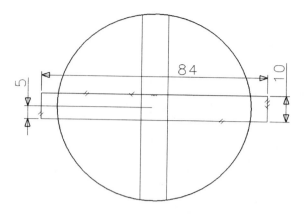

Figure 4.92

## Step 6. Extrude a section.

 Select the **Isometric View** icon
Select the **Extrude** icon
Carefully pick the four entities to form a section as shown in Figure 4.93.

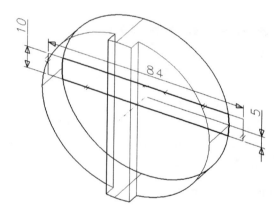

Figure 4.93

Set the Extrude Section parameters as below.

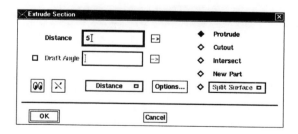

Select **OK** to add another extrude feature as in Figure 4.94.

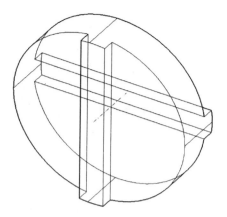

Figure 4.94

**Step 7.  Check the part into the library.**

 Select the **Check In** icon, then pick the part to check in
Enter "**connector**" into the Name field in Name menu, then select **OK**
Set the check in parameters as below.

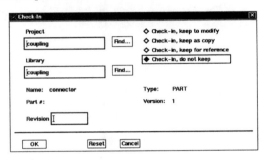

Select **OK** to check the part into the library

# Project 12.
# Creating the connecting rod part

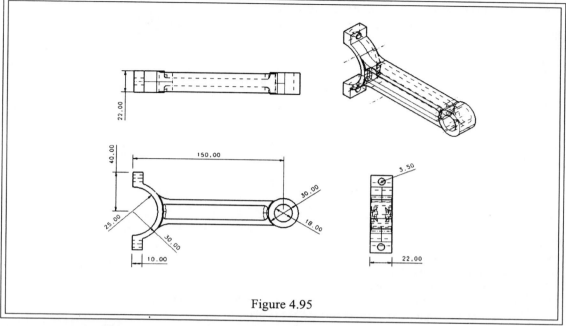

Figure 4.95

The connecting rod consists of eight features including (Figure 4.95):

    Base extrude I-section body
    Eye feature with the hole
    Flange feature
    Two hole features on the flange

**The sequence for creating features is listed below:**

    1. Extrude the I-section for the beam rod as the base feature.
    2. Create the eye of the connecting rod, then add a hole feature.
    3. Add an extrude feature to the other side of the rod as flange.
    4. Extrude – cut a semi-circle from the flange.
    5. Add two hole features to the flange.

**Step 1.  Create a I-section.**

 Use the **Polylines** command to create
    a 12-line sections as shown in Figure 4.96
    Add dimensions and modify them to
      their correct values as shown

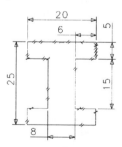

Figure 4.96

# Extrude and Revolve Features

**Step 2. Extrude the section by a distance of 150.**

Select the **Extrude** icon, then pick the section to be extruded
Enter "**150**" to the Distance field in Extrude Section menu
Select **OK** to create the extrude feature
Select the **Isometric View** icon to display the feature as in Figure 4.97.

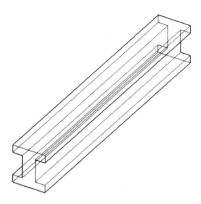

Figure 4.97

**Step 3. Create a reference plane.**

Select the **Reference Planes** icon
Click the right mouse button and select **Offset Surface** from the list
Pick the right most vertical surface as the plane to offset
Enter offset distance: **1**
The reference plane is added
as in Figure 4.98.

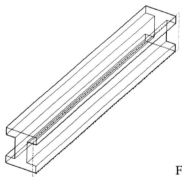

Figure 4.98

**Step 4. Create an extrude feature at the left end of the base feature.**

Select **Sketch in place**, then select the reference plane just created

Select the **Side View (YZ)** icon to display the part as in Figure 4.99.

Figure 4.99

4-62

Select the **Circle – Center Edge** icon
Click the right mouse button, then select **Focus** from the list
Pick the left vertical line to focus
Use the midpoint of the left vertical line as the circle center to create a circle as shown
Modify its diameter to **30** as shown

Select the **Extrude** icon, then pick the circle to extrude
Set Extrude Section parameters as below.

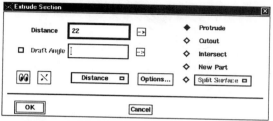

Select **OK** to complete the extrude feature

Select the **Isometric View** icon to display the model as in Figure 4.100.

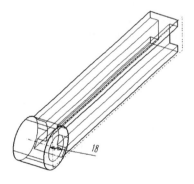

Figure 4.100

## Step 5. Add a hole feature. Use Figure 4.100 as a reference.

Select the **Sketch in place** icon, then pick the right face of the feature just extruded
Add a circle and modify its diameter to **18** as shown in Figure 4.100
Select the **Extrude** icon, then pick the circle to extrude

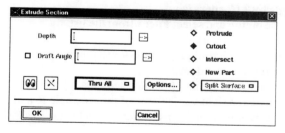

Select **OK** to produce the hole feature as in Figure 4.101.

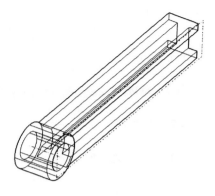

Figure 4.101

### Step 6. Create a rectangle and a semi-circle.

Select the **Sketch in place** icon, then pick the reference plane as the sketching plane
Select the **Side View (YZ)** icon to display the part as in Figure 4.102

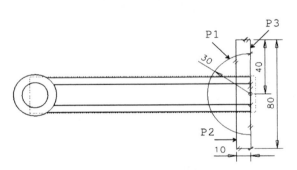

Figure 4.102

Select the **Rectangle by 2 Corners** icon
Click the right mouse button and select **Focus** from the list
Pick the right vertical line to focus
Create a rectangle as shown (left line align with the focus point)

Select the **Arc – Center Start End** icon
Pick the center point at the midpoint of the focused line
Then pick two points on the right vertical line of the rectangle to add an arc
Add a dimension and modify four dimensions to their correct value as shown in Figure 4.102

### Step 7. Extrude the flange. Use **Figure 4.102 as reference.**

Select the **Extrude** icon
Sequentially pick entities (**P1 – P3**) as in Figure 4.102 to define
the section as shown in Figure 4.103

Mastering I-DEAS
Scholars International Publishing Corp., 1999

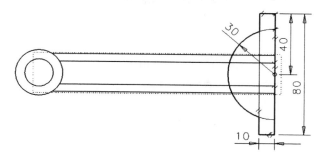

Figure 4.103

Set Extrude Section parameters as below.

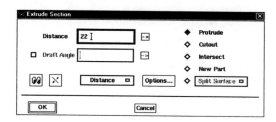

Select **OK** to add the extrude feature

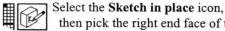 Select the **Isometric View** icon to show the model as in Figure 4.104

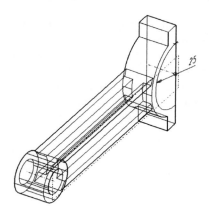

Figure 4.104

**Step 8. Create a half-circle to the right end face of the flange. Use Figure 4.104 as reference.**

Select the **Sketch in place** icon,
  then pick the right end face of the flange feature as the sketching plane

Select the **Arc – Center Start End** icon
  Pick the right end point of the center line of the flange as the center point
  Pick two points along the right vertical line to add the arc as in Figure 4.104
  Modify its radius value to **25**

**Step 9. Extrude – cut the arc.**
  Select the **Extrude** icon, then pick the arc and right vertical line to define a section

# Extrude and Revolve Features

Set Extrude Section parameters as below.

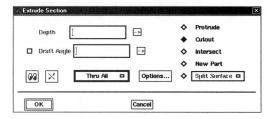

Select **OK** to extrude – cut the section as shown in Figure 4.105

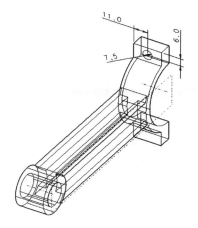

Figure 4.105

**Step 10. Create a hole feature on the top end of flange. Use Figure 4.105 as reference.**

 Select **Sketch in place**, then pick the front-top vertical face of the flange
Create a circle and modify three dimensions to their correct value as shown in Figure 4.105

 Select the **Extrude** icon, then pick the circle just created
Select "**Cutout**" from relation parameter and "**Thru All**" from distance parameter
Select **OK** to create the hole feature as in Figure 4.106.

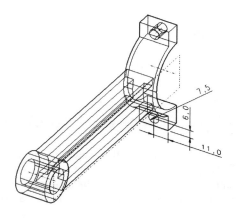

Figure 4.106

**Step 11. Create a hole feature on the bottom end of flange. Use Figure 4.106 as reference.**

 Select **Sketch in place**, then pick the front-bottom vertical face of the flange
Create a circle and modify three dimensions to their correct value as shown in Figure 4.106

Mastering I-DEAS
Scholars International Publishing Corp., 1999

# Extrude and Revolve Features

 Select the **Extrude** icon, then pick the circle just created
Select "**Cutout**" from relation parameter and "**Thru All**" from distance parameter
Select **OK** to create the hole feature as in Figure 4.107.

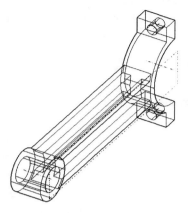

Figure 4.107

Figures 4.108 and 4.109 show two different display modes of the model.

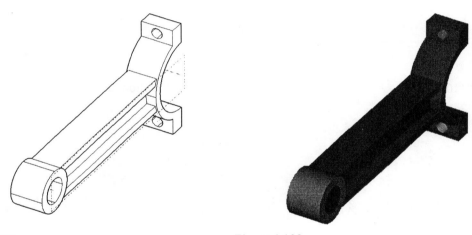

Figure 4.108                               Figure 4.109

## Step 12. Check the part into library.

 Select the **Check In** icon, then pick the part to check in
Enter "**connecting-rod**" to the Name field in Name menu
Set the Check-In parameters as below.

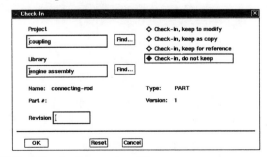

Select **OK** to check the part into library

# Adding Revolve Features

The procedure of adding a revolve feature to the part is similar to that for creating a revolve base feature. There are only two differences between creating a revolve base feature and a revolve added feature. One is the selection of feature relation and the other is the selection option of revolve angle.

## Feature relation

There are three feature relation options available in creating revolve added features; **protrude**, **cutoff**, and **intersect** (Figure 4.110a-d).

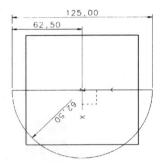

Figure 4.110a Sketch

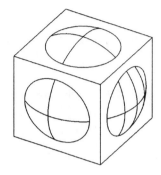

Figure 4.110b Protrude

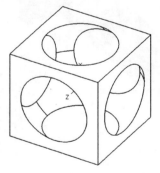

Figure 4.110cCutoff

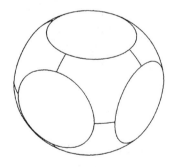

Figure 4.110d Intersect

## Feature angle

The revolve angle of the added feature is specified by using one of four angle options; **angle**, **until next**, **until selected**, and **from/to**, Table 4.7 illustrates angle options for the three types of feature relation.

Mastering I-DEAS
Scholars International Publishing Corp., 1999

# Table 4.7  Angle options for adding revolve features

| Angle Option | Feature Relation | Description | Illustration |
|---|---|---|---|
| Angle | Protrude | To add a feature by revolving a section by a given angle in the specified direction. | |
| | Cutout | To cut a feature by revolving a section by a given angle in the specified direction. | |
| | Intersect | To retain the common material formed between the existing part and the feature created by revolving a section by a given angle. | |
| Until Next | Protrude | To add a feature by revolving a section until reaching the next surface. | |
| | Cutout | To cut a feature by revolving a section until reaching the next surface. | |
| | Intersect | To retain the common material formed between the existing part and the feature created by revolving a section until reaching the next surface. | |

Table 4.7 continued

| **Until Selected** | Protrude | To add a feature by revolving a section until reaching a selected surface. | |
| | Cutout | To cut a feature by revolving a section until reaching a selected surface. | |
| | Intersect | To retain the common material formed between the existing part and the feature created by revolving a section until reaching a selected surface. | |
| **From /To** | Protrude | To add a feature by revolving a section starting from a surface to another surface. | |
| | Cutout | To cut a feature by revolving a section starting from a surface to another surface. | |
| | Intersect | To retain the common material formed between the existing part and the feature created by revolving a section starting from one surface to another surface. | |

Mastering I-DEAS
Scholars International Publishing Corp., 1999

# Project 13.
# Creating added revolve feature using three feature relation options

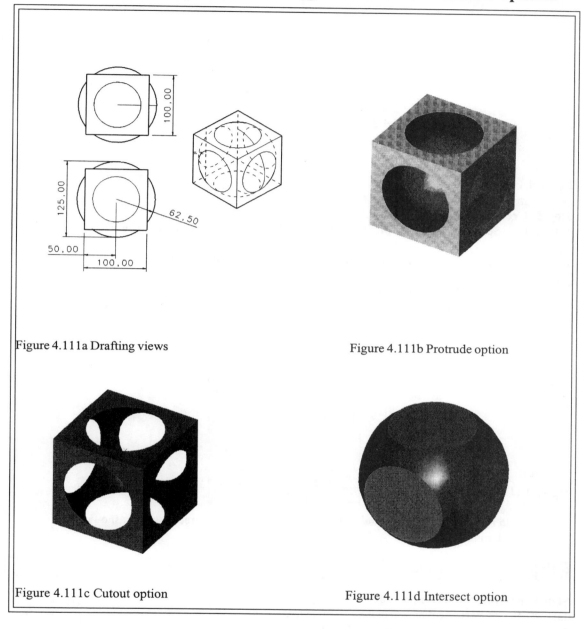

Figure 4.111a Drafting views

Figure 4.111b Protrude option

Figure 4.111c Cutout option

Figure 4.111d Intersect option

This project shows how to create a base feature then add a revolve feature to it to complete the part. The added revolve feature can be defined by three feature relation options; protrude, cutout, and intersect. Figure 4.111 shows the models using three feature relation options.

### Step 1. Create a coordinate system.

   Select the **Coordinate Systems** icon,
  then pick the reference coordinate as the entity to reference
  Select **Done** to make the coordinate system as in Figure 4.112

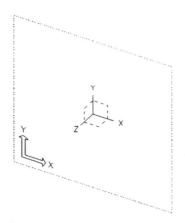

Figure 4.112

## Step 2. Create a rectangle.

 Select the **Sketch in place** icon then pick **XY-plane** from the coordinate system

Select **Front (XY) View** to show the coordinate system in the front view

 Select **Rectangle by 2 Corners**
Pick two points to create a rectangle as in Figure 4.113

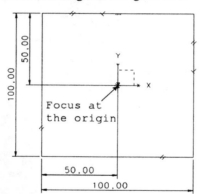

Focus at
the origin

Figure 4.113

Add two dimensions and modify four dimensions to their correct values as shown
in Figure 4.113

**Note:** You need to use the "Focus" function to pick the origin for adding two dimensions.

## Step 3. Extrude the section by 100-mm using Thicken option.

 Select **Extrude** then select the rectangle to extrude
Set the extrusion parameters as below.

Mastering  I-DEAS
Scholars International Publishing Corp., 1999

# Extrude and Revolve Features

Select **OK** to create the extrude feature

 Select the **Isometric View** icon to show the feature as in Figure 4.114

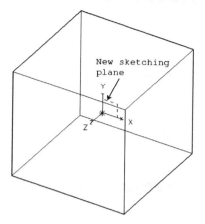

New sketching
plane

Figure 4.114

## Step 4. Create an arc and a vertical line.

 Select the **Sketch in place** icon,
then pick **XY-plane** of the coordinate system (Figure 4.114) as sketching plane

Select **Front (XY) View**
Create a vertical line aligned with the Y axis

Use the **Arc – Start End 180** command to create an arc with two end points located at
the two end points of the line (Figure 4.115)

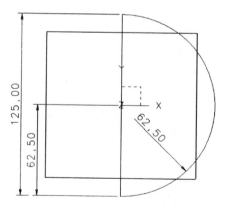

Figure 4.115

Add dimensions and modify them to their correct value as in Figure 4.115

## Step 5. Revolve the section.

Select the **Revolve** icon
Click the right mouse button and select the **"Section Options"** from the list

# Extrude and Revolve Features

Set the section options as below.

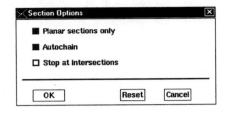

Select **OK**

Pick the arc as the curve to revolve

Pick the vertical line as the axis of revolution

Set the revolving parameters as below.

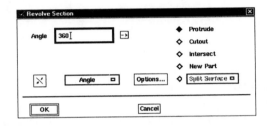

Select **OK**

Pick the extrude feature as the part to be protruded to

 Select the **Isometric View** icon to show the new model as in Figure 4.116

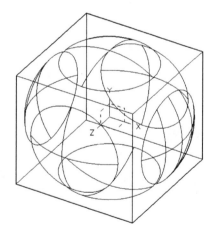

Figure 4.116

Figures 4.117 and 4.118 show two different display modes of the model.

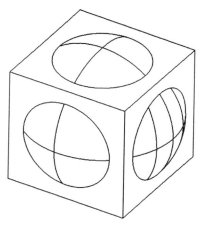

Figure 4.117

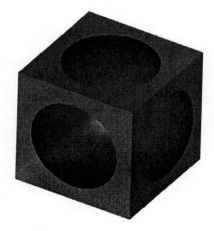

Figure 4.118

**Step 6.  Modify the feature relation option to "Cutout".**

Select the **Modify Entity** icon
Double click the revolve feature
  to open the options list as shown here.

Show Dimensions
Feature Parameters
Dimension Values
Quick Wireframe
Suppress Feature
Replace Feature
Delete History
Add Relations
Wireframe
Rename Feature
Backup
Cancel

Select **Feature Parameters** from the list
The revolving parameter menu should appear as below for change.

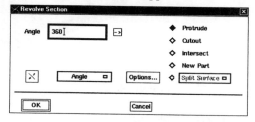

Change the feature relation option to "**Cutout**" as below.

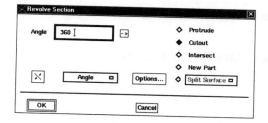

Select **OK** to make the change
Select the **Update** icon to update the change from protrude to cutout

# Extrude and Revolve Features

The update model appears as in Figure 4.119.

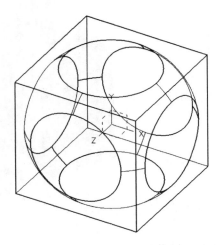

Figure 4.119

Figures 4.120 and 4.121 shows the two different display modes of the model.

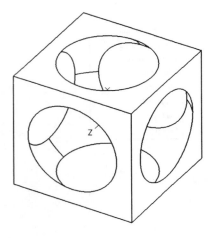

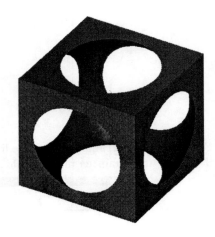

Figure 4.120                                    Figure 4.121

**Step 7. Modify the feature relation parameter to intersect.**

 Select the **Modify Entity** icon
Double click on the revolve feature to select it
Select "**Feature Parameters**" from the options list
Set the new revolving parameters as below.

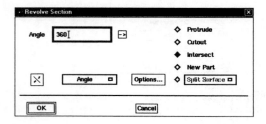

Mastering  I-DEAS
Scholars International Publishing Corp., 1999

Select **OK** to make the change
Select the **Update** icon to update the change to the model
The new model becomes Figure 4.122.

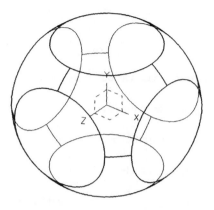

Figure 4.122

Figures 4.123 and 4.124 shows two different display modes of the model.

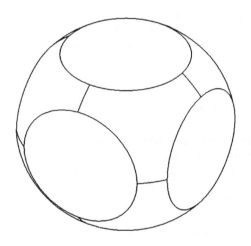

Figure 4.123

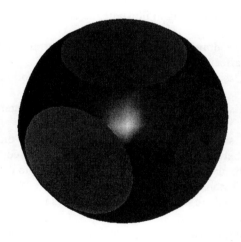

Figure 4.124

# Chapter 4. Review Questions

1.  What are the two types of features?

2.  What is a base feature?

3.  What are added features?

4.  What are the two feature functions used to create various forms of base features?

5.  List the four-step procedure of creating a base feature.

6.  Describe the purpose of the feature relation parameter.

7.  List the four options of the feature relation parameter and briefly describe what they are.

8.  What are the two options of the termination parameter when creating an extrude base feature?

9.  Use a drawing to illustrate the effect of the draft angle when extruding a feature.

10. Describe the purpose of the "Flip direction" parameter when extruding a feature.

11. Use a drawing to illustrate the effect of the along vector when extruding a feature.

12. Use a drawing to illustrate the effect of twist angle when extruding a feature.

13. Use drawings to explain how to determine the loops of sections and how the order of loops affects the features.

14. Use a drawing to show how to create a solid center of a revolve feature.

15. Use a drawing to show how to create a center hole of a revolve feature.

16. Use a drawing to illustrate how the size of the revolve feature is determined by the distance between the revolving axis and the inner edge of the revolving section.

17. Explain how the right-hand rule is used to determine the rotation direction in creating revolve features.

18. What are the two option parameters in the revolve function?

19. Explain how the angle and translation along axis parameters in the revolve function are used in creating a spring.

20. Explain how the angle, translation along axis, and change in radius parameters in the revolve function are used in creating a taper spring.

21. How do you determine the value for the following two parameters in creating a straight thread:
    > Translation along axis
    > Angle

22. What are the two groups of added feature functions?

23. What is the sketch plane?

24. What are the three ways of defining a sketch plane?

Mastering I-DEAS
Scholars International Publishing Corp., 1999

25. Illustrate how to select an existing part surface as the sketch plane.

26. List the eight reference plane creation methods.

27. What are the four Boolean operation functions to determine the relation between the existing part and the new feature?

28. List the four options for specifying the revolving angle in adding revolve features.

# Chapter

5

# Modifying Features

## Highlights of the Chapter
- Copying features with transform functions
- Boolean operations for features
- Deleting with the delete command
- History tree
- Modifying dimensions, feature parameters and wireframe
- Replacing features and updating the part

## Overview

After the features are created, you may want to change their shapes and sizes. I-DEAS provides various methods for modifying features. There are three transform functions that can be easily used to move or copy the selected features to new locations. These three transform functions are move, rotate, and reflect. The "Copy sw" option is used to determine whether the selected features are merely changing their locations or making copies to new locations while retaining the original feature. Boolean operations perform logic operations between separate, unrelated features. Boolean operations include cut, join, intersect, and partition. The cut operation subtracts a feature from the part. The join feature adds a feature to a part. The intersect operation retains the common volume of two features. The partition operation distinguishes separate objects that are not physically connected, but considered one part.

There are two ways to delete wireframe elements or features; using the delete command and history tree access. Single elements or features, even the entire part can be deleted using these two deleting methods. Two commonly used methods for modifying features are modifying dimensions and modifying entity. The modifying dimensions method allows you to modify the dimensions of the feature, which in turns changes the shape and size of the features. The modifying entity method is a more versatile approach that can be used to perform more modifying functions on dimensions, feature parameters, replace features, wireframe, etc. The update command must be used to update changes to modified dimensions and parameters. Delete and modify functions can be accessed from the history tree.

# 5.1  Using Transform Functions to Copy Features

Features can be copied to any locations as many times as possible. The "Copy sw" option is used in conjunction with transform functions to copy features. There are four transform functions including **move**, **rotate**, **reflect**, and **scale**. The move and rotate functions can be used to make as many copies of the selected features as desired. The reflect function can make one copy of the selected features at a time. The scale function only allows changing the size of the selected features and does not produce an extra copy of features. Table 5.1 summarizes the three transform functions that can copy features.

## Table 5.1  Transform functions

| Function | Description | Illustration |
|----------|-------------|--------------|
| Move | Move or copy the selected feature a given number of times offset by a specified distances in X, Y, and Z axes. | |
| Rotate | Move or copy the selected feature a given number of times at the specified angles about the X, Y, and Z axes. | |
| Reflect | Move or copy the selected feature by mirroring it about a given plane. It produces only one copy at a time. The "Copy sw" option is not available in this function. | |

The three transform functions in Table 5.1 can also be used to move or copy wireframe entities that are presented in Chapter 3. When using a **move** or **rotate function**, the system will prompt with an option menu as shown here to select the "Copy sw" option. When "Copy sw" is toggled to **On**, the system will prompt to "Enter number of copies". Enter the desired number of copies to produce. The copied features are treated as separate features. Boolean functions should be used to associate features, and are presented in the next section. **Pattern functions** are also used to copy features in rectangular and circular manners. Patterned features are treated as a single entity, while copied features using transform functions are individual features. Transformed features provide flexibility for manipulating individual features.

```
Move To
Move Along
Slide On Screen
Copy sw
Measure
Backup
Cancel
```

Mastering  I-DEAS
Scholars International Publishing Corp., 1999

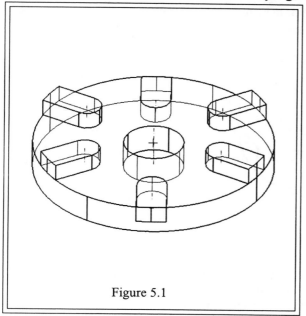

Figure 5.1

# Project 1.
# Copying features using the move and rotate functions

This project uses move and rotate functions to copy a feature to a new location (Figure 5.1). The base feature is a revolve feature. An extrude feature is created on the top of the face of the base feature. This extrude feature is created as a new part. The Rotate function is then used to copy this feature to five locations. The Move function is then used to move two features a distance of 15 in the –Z direction. Save the model file as "transform". This model will be used in project 2 of this chapter to perform Boolean operations for joining and cutting features from/to the base feature.

**Step 1. Create a revolve feature.**

Create a rectangle and a line, then modify their dimensions as shown in Figure 5.2

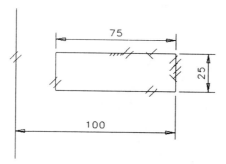

Figure 5.2

 Select **Revolve** and pick the rectangle as the section to revolve
Pick the vertical line as the axis of revolution
Set the revolving parameters as below.

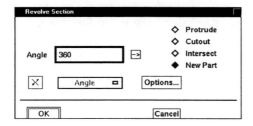

Select **OK** to complete the feature

# Modifying Features

Select **Isometric View** to show the feature as in Figure 5.3

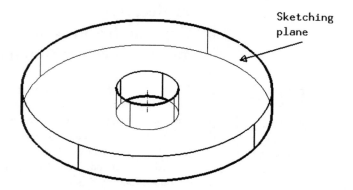

Figure 5.3

**Step 2. Create a rectangle and an arc of 180 degrees. Use Figure 5.4 as reference.**

 Select the **Sketch in place** icon and select the top surface as the sketching plane
Select **Top (XZ) View** to display the model in the top view
Select the **Rectangle by 2 Corners** icon, then add a rectangle as shown
Select the **Arc – Start End 180** icon,
    then pick the upper left corner of rectangle as the start point
Pick the lower left corner of rectangle as the end point to add an arc
Add and modify necessary dimensions as shown

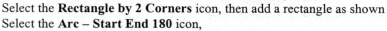

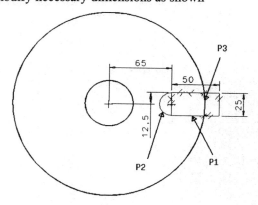

Figure 5.4

**Step 3. Extrude the section. Use Figure 5.4 as reference.**

 Select **Isometric View**
Select **Extrude** and click the right mouse button, then select **Section Options** from the list
Set the section options parameters as below.

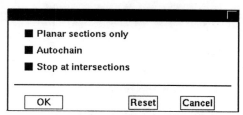

5-4

Sequentially pick at **P1 – P3** to define the section
Set the extrusion parameters as below.

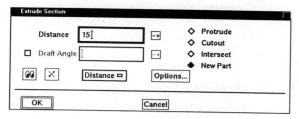

Select **OK** to add the feature as in Figure 5.5.

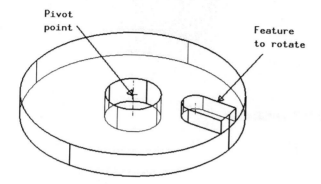

Figure 5.5

**Step 4. Copy the extrude feature 5 times using Rotate function. Use Figure 5.5 as reference.**

 Select the **Rotate** icon and pick the extrude feature as the entity to rotate
Pick the top end point of the center line as a pivot point
Select "**Copy sw**" from the options list, then select **On**
Select **About Y**
Enter angle about Y: **60**
Enter number of copies: **5**
The feature is copied to five locations as in Figure 5.6.

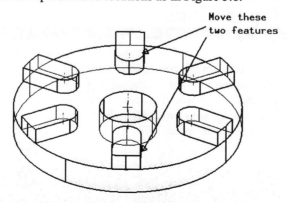

Figure 5.6

**Step 5. Move two features to new locations. Use Figure 5.6 as reference.**

 Select the **Move** icon
Pick two features (press Shift key to select) to move
Enter translation X, Y, Z: enter **0,-15,0**

The two features are moved to new locations as in Figure 5.7.

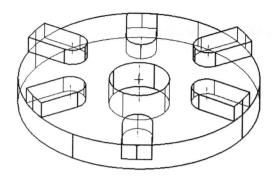

Figure 5.7

**Step 6. Save the model file as "transform".**
Select **File → Save As**
Enter the file name as below.

| File Name Input | ✕ |
| --- | --- |
| **New model file name** | |
| D:\Ideas\Ms7\transform | 🗁  Find... |
| Item name: | |
| OK | Cancel |

Select **OK** to save the model


# 5.2   Boolean Operations


Features in I-DEAS can be created as independent, separate parts. In this case, they do not bear any relationship among themselves. They can be moved or modified independently. Boolean functions are logic operations that can be used to add a relation to two independent features. The four Boolean functions are summarized in Table 5.2.

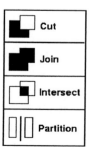

# Table 5.2  Boolean logic operations

| Logic Function | Description | Illustration |
|---|---|---|
| Cut | Subtract a feature from the part. It is used in where you want to remove a feature from the part. | |
| Join | Add a feature to the part. It is used in where you want to retain volumes in both parts including volumes shared by them. | |
| Intersect | Retain the common volume of two features. It is commonly used to trim a part. The larger part has the rough shape of the desired Part. The smaller part serves as the trimming boundary to remove volume outside the boundary. | |
| Partition | Distinguish separate objects that are not physically connected, but considered one part. | |

Two features must be aligned before performing a Boolean operation. The two features used in a Boolean operation can be created in any location. We need to bring them to a desired location and orientation while performing a Boolean operation. The Relation function can be toggled to On or Off by using "Turn Relation" option. When "Relation" is toggled to Off, both features stay in the same locations after the Boolean operation (Figure 5.9). When "Relation" is toggled to On, the movable part or cutter part changes its location in the way defined by aligning planar surfaces from two features (Figure 5.10).

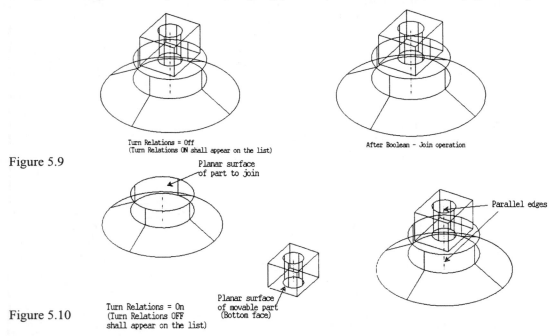

Figure 5.9

Figure 5.10

The relation statement appearing in the options list is somewhat confusing. It appears in one of two forms: "Turn Relation On" and "Turn Relation Off". When "Turn Relation On" appears on the option list, it indicates that the current relation status is "Off". Therefore, click "Turn Relation On" to toggle the "Relation" function to "ON". Similarly, when "Turn Relation Off" appears on the option list, it means that the current relation status is "On". Therefore, click "Turn Relation Off" to toggle the "Relation" function to "Off". Table 5.3 summarizes the two options of the Relation function and their applications.

## Table 5.3 Relation status and applications

| Relation Status | Statement in Options List | System Prompts | When to Use |
|---|---|---|---|
| Relation On | Turn Relation Off | 1. Pick planar surface from the movable part. <br> 2. Pick planar surface from the part to cut/joint. | The two parts are not located at their proper location. |
| Relation Off | Turn Relation On | 1. Select cutter part (for Cut Operation) or pick 1st part to join (for Join operation). <br> 2. Select the part to cut (for Cut operation) or pick 2nd part (for Join operation). | The two parts have been positioned in their correct location. |

Mastering I-DEAS
Scholars International Publishing Corp., 1999

# Modifying Features

When the "Relation" function is toggled to On and two planar surfaces have been selected from the two parts, the system will open a positioning menu for you to constrain the two parts to their desired location. The positioning menu is shown here.

| Surface Operations |
| --- |
| Parallel at distance |
| Parallel Edges |
| Angle Between Edges |
| Coincident Points |
| From Edges |
| Along Edges |
| From & Along Edge |
| Done |
| View |
| Backup |
| Cancel |

Three constraints must be applied to fully define the positioning locations of the two parts. Figure 5.11 shows an example of two parts being constrained by three constraints.

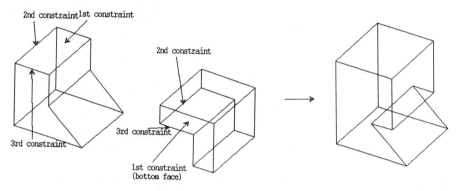

Figure 5.11

There are two ways to locate the moving part at its correct location for performing Boolean operations when the two involved parts are not initially at their correct locations. One way is to use transform functions, move and/or rotate, to move the movable part to the exact location before performing any Boolean operation. When using this method, the "Relation" function must be toggled to Off. No positioning on a movable part is required in this case. The other way to locate the moving part that is not yet at the desired location is to use the "Relation On" function and positioning commands to constrain the part while performing the Boolean operation. The first method is probably the better way to locate the proper location for the movable part.

# Project 2.
# Using Boolean Cut and Join functions

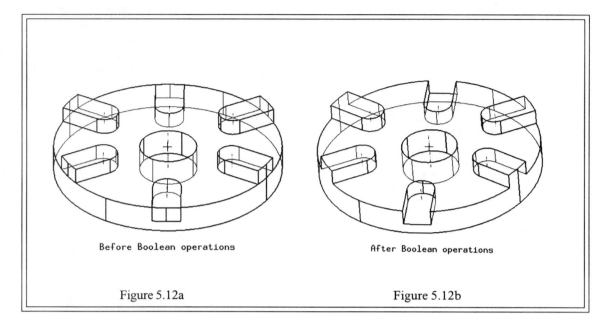

Before Boolean operations

After Boolean operations

Figure 5.12a

Figure 5.12b

The parts created in project 1 of this chapter are used to show how to use Boolean Cut and Join functions. The two parts which are lower than the other four parts are used as the cutter parts to cut the cylindrical feature. The other four parts are joined to the existing part. Figure 5.12 shows the part before and after two Boolean operations.

**Step 1. Open the model file "transform" if necessary.**

Start at step 2 if your model "transform" is still in the workbench.

Select **File → Open** ·

Set the open model file parameters as below.

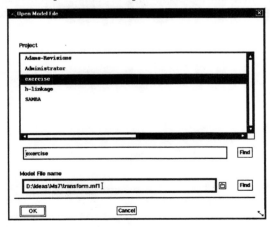

Select **OK** to open the model and it will appear as in Figure 5.13

Mastering I-DEAS
Scholars International Publishing Corp., 1999

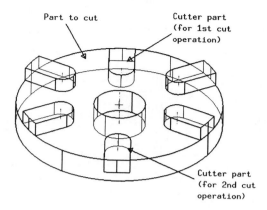

Figure 5.13

**Step 2. Cut two parts from the cylindrical part. Use Figure 5.13 as reference.**

 Select the **Cut** icon

Click the right mouse button, then make sure "Turn Relation On" statement appears

Pick the cutter part as shown for the first cut operation

Pick the cylindrical part as the part to cut

Select the **Cut** icon again

Pick the cutter part for the second cut operation as shown

Pick the cylindrical part as the part to cut

The new drawing should resemble Figure 5.14.

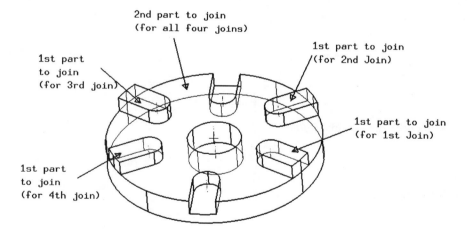

Figure 5.14

**Step 3. Join the remaining four parts to the cylindrical part. Use Figure 5.14 as reference.**

 Select the **Join** icon

Pick the first part to join as shown, then pick the second part to join

Repeat this procedure for the three remaining parts to join

## Modifying Features

The final part model should resemble Figure 5.15.

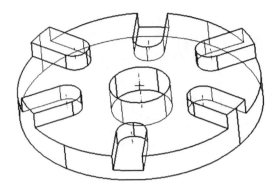

Figure 5.15

### Step 4. Check the model into library.

 Select the **Check in** icon, then pick the model as the part to check in
Enter **"transform"** in the Name field of the Name menu
Set the check-in parameters as below.

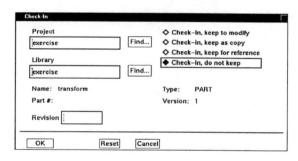

Select **OK** to check the part into library

# Project 3.
# Creating the crankshaft part using Transform and Boolean functions

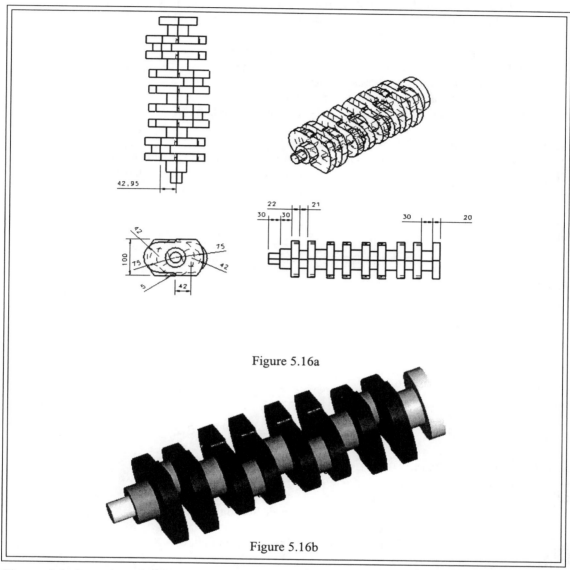

Figure 5.16a

Figure 5.16b

The crankshaft consists of eight pieces of counterweights connected by short circular bars (Figure 5.16). Those counterweights are identical, so that we need only to create one and copy it to produce others. The orientation of the four inside counterweights is 180 degrees apart from the four outside ones. The gaps between counterweights are also different. This complicates the copying of the counterweights. A counterweight is created first as the base feature by extruding a section. This base feature is copied to produce another feature by using the Move-copy command. Two cylindrical features are added to the new feature. The two counterweights are joined as one feature by using the Join command. The joined feature is then copied to three locations by using Move-copy commands. The two inside features are rotated by 180 degrees about the Y axis to obtain their correct orientation. The Join command is used again to join all four features into one. Extra cylindrical features are finally added to both ends of the part to complete the model. Figure 5.16a shows the drawing views of the model and Figure 5.16b is the shaded isometric view.

# Modifying Features

**The Procedure for project 3:**

1. Create an extrude feature as the basic counterweight part.

2. Copy this feature by using Move function by a distance of 43 in X direction.
3. Add two circular features to each side of the right counterweight part.
4. Use Join function to join two counterweights.
5. Copy the part to three locations using Move function.
6. Rotate the two middle parts 180 degrees about X axis.
7. Join the four parts together as one part.
8. Add cylindrical features to both sides of the part.
9. Check the part into library using the part name "crankshaft".

**Step 1. Create a section for the base feature.**

Use **Lines, Arc-Three Points On**, and **Fillet** to create a section as shown in Figure 5.17. You may need to apply Tangent constraint to the two end points of the left arc.

Add dimensions and change them to the correct values as shown.

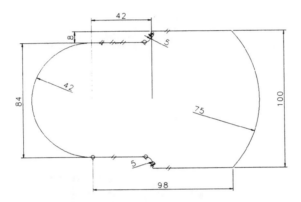

Figure 5.17

**Step 2. Extrude the section.**

Select the **Extrude** icon
Pick the section to be extruded
Enter "**21**" to the Distance parameter in Extrude Section menu
Select **OK** to create the extrude feature
Select the **Isometric View** icon to show the feature as in Figure 5.18.

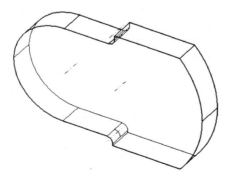

Figure 5.18

Mastering I-DEAS
Scholars International Publishing Corp., 1999

**Step 3. Rotate the feature by 90 degrees about the Y axis.**

 Select the **Rotate** icon, then pick the feature to rotate
Pick any point on the feature as the pivot point
Select **About Y** axis
Enter angle about Y (90.0): **90**
The new drawing becomes Figure 5.19.

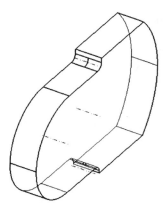

Figure 5.19

**Step 4. Copy the feature using the Move command.**

 Select the **Move** icon, then pick the feature to move
Select **"Copy sw"** from the list
Set "Copy Switch" to **On**
Enter translation X, Y, Z: **43,0,0**
Enter the number of copies: **1**
The copied feature is added as in Figure 5.20.

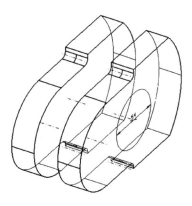

Figure 5.20

**Step 5. Add a circular feature to the right face of the feature at the right side. Refer to Figure 5.20.**

 Select the **Sketch in place** icon, then pick the right face at the feature on the right side
Select the **Circle-Center Edge** icon
 Add a circle and change its diameter to **54** as shown in Figure 5.20
Select the **Extrude** icon, then pick the circle to extrude

Set the Extrude Section parameters as below.

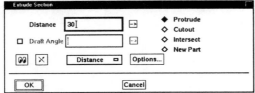

Select **OK** to add the circular feature as in Figure 5.21.

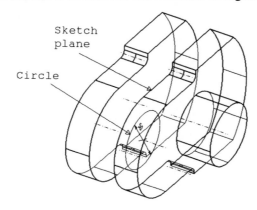

Figure 5.21

**Step 6. Add another circular feature to the left face. Use Figure 5.21 as reference.**

Select the **Sketch in place** icon, then pick the left face of the right feature as shown
Select the **Circle-Center Edge** icon, then add a circle being concentric with the arc

Modify its diameter value to **50**
Select the **Extrude** icon, then pick the circle as the curve to extrude

Set the Extrude Section parameters as below.

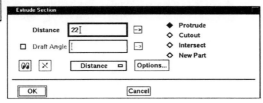

Select **OK** to add the second circular feature as in Figure 5.22.

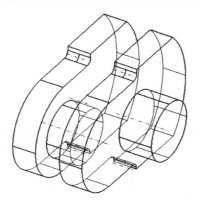

Figure 5.22

Mastering I-DEAS
Scholars International Publishing Corp., 1999

### Step 7. Join the two counterweights.

Select the **Join** icon

Pick the right counterweight as the first part to join

Pick the left counterweight as the second part to join

The two features are now joined as one.

### Step 8. Copy the part to three locations.

Select the **Move** icon, then pick anywhere on the part to select it

Select "**Copy sw**" from the list

Set the copy switch to **On**

Enter translation X, Y, Z:  **-94,0,0**

Enter number of copies:  **3**

The new drawing becomes Figure 5.23.

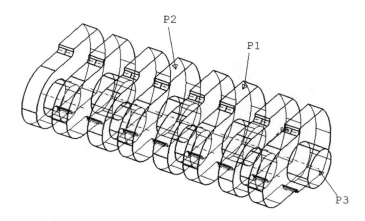

Figure 5.23

### Step 9. Rotate the two middle features. Use Figure 5.23 as reference.

Select the **Rotate** icon,

Pick the two middle features (**P1** and **P2**) with the **Shift key** to select them

Pick the center of the right end face (**P3**) of the circular feature as the pivot point

Select **About X** from the list

Enter angle about X:  **180**

The new drawing appears as in Figure 5.24.

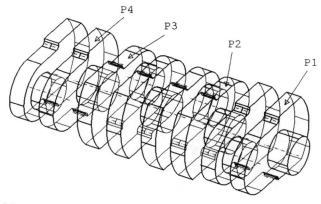

Figure 5.24

**Step 10. Join the four features together. Use Figure 5.24 as reference.**

Select the **Join** icon
Pick the right most feature (**P1**) as the 1st part to join
Pick the 2nd feature from right (**P2**) as the 2nd part to join
Pick the **Join** icon again
Pick the right most feature (**P1**) as the 1st part to join
Pick the 2nd feature from the left (**P3**) as the 2nd part to join
Select the **Join** icon again
Pick the right most feature (**P1**) as the 1st part to join
Pick the left most feature (**P4**) as the 2nd part to join
All features now are joined as one.
The part is redisplayed as Figure 5.25.

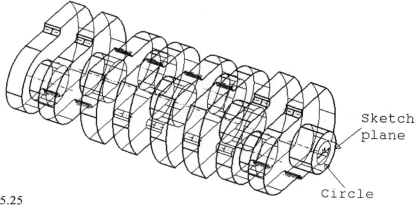

Figure 5.25

**Step 11. Add a cylindrical feature to the right end face. Use Figure 5.25 as reference.**

Select the **Sketch in place** icon, then pick the right end face
Create a concentric circle and modify its diameter to **30**
Select the **Extrude** icon, then select the circle just created as the curve to extrude
Set the Extrude Section parameters as below.

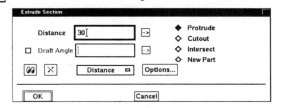

Select **OK** to add the feature as in figure 5.26.

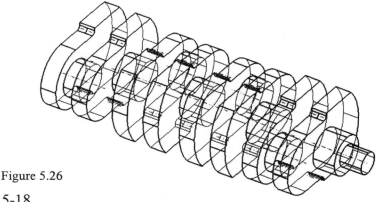

Figure 5.26

Mastering I-DEAS
Scholars International Publishing Corp., 1999

**Step 12. Rotate the part 90 degrees about the Y axis.**

 Select the **Rotate** icon, then pick the part

Pick the center point of the right most face as the pivot point

Select **About Y** from the list

Enter angle about Y: **90**

The new drawing becomes Figure 5.27.

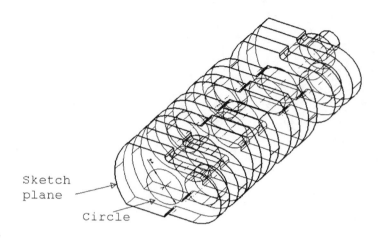

Figure 5.27

**Step 13. Add an extrude feature to the front face of the part. Use Figure 5.27 as reference.**

 Select the **Sketch in place** icon, then pick the front end face as sketching plane

Create a concentric circle with a diameter of **54**

 Select the **Extrude** icon, then pick the circle as the curve to extrude

Set the Distance to "**30**" and feature relation to "**Protrude**"

Select **OK** to add the cylindrical feature as in Figure 5.28.

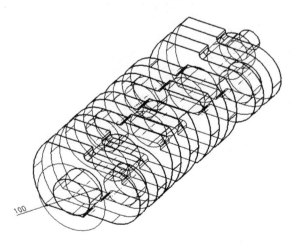

Figure 5.28

**Step 14. Add another cylindrical feature. Use Figure 5.28 as reference.**

Create a circle with a diameter of **100** on the front end face as shown in Figure 5.28

Extrude this circle by a distance of **20** applying the Protrude relation to the part

The final part should resemble Figure 5.29.

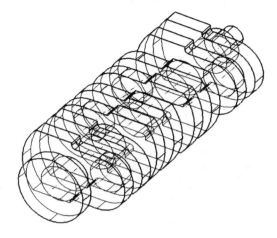

Figure 5.29

**Step 15. Rotate the part 180 degrees about the Y axis.**

 Select the **Rotate** icon, then pick the part to rotate
Pick the center point on the front end face as the pivot point
Select **About Y** from the list
Enter angle about Y: **180**
The orientation of the part becomes Figure 5.30.

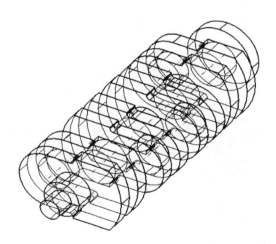

Figure 5.30

Figures 5.31 and 5.32 show the part shown in two different modes.

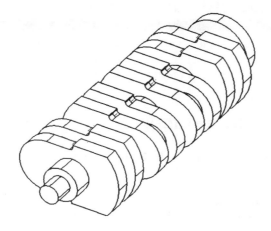

Figure 5.31

Figure 5.32

## Step 16. Check the part into the library.

 Select the **Check In** icon, then pick the part to check in
Enter "**crankshaft**" in the Name field in Name menu, then select **OK**
Set the Check-In parameters as below.

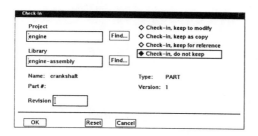

Select **OK** to check the part into library

# 5.3  Using the Delete Command

The Delete command can be used to delete a geometry entity, a feature, or the entire model. There are many possibilities you may face when using this Delete command. This section presents various ways for you to delete wireframe entities and features in modeling parts.

## Deleting a single wireframe entity

**The procedure for deleting a single wireframe entity is (Figure 5.33):**

1. Select the **Delete** command

2. Click the wireframe entity to delete
3. Click the middle mouse button to confirm the selection
4. Select **Yes** from the Options menu

*Note:* Repeat the above procedure to delete entities one by one.

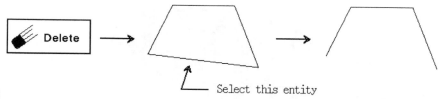

Figure 5.33

## Deleting multiple wireframe entities

The key to delete multiple wireframe entities are to pick two points to form a window for including all entities to delete.

**The procedure for deleting multiple entities is (Figure 5.34):**

1. Select the **Delete** command

2. Pick two corner points to form a window to include the entities to be deleted
3. Click the middle mouse button to confirm the selection
4. Select **Yes** from the Options menu

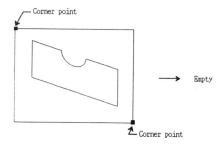

Figure 5.34

# Deleting a face of a feature

A feature consists of several faces or surfaces. Each face can be regarded as a separate entity in I-DEAS.

**The procedure to delete a face from a feature (Figure 5.35):**

    1. Select the **Delete** command

    2. Pick the surface at the grid line (not the surface edge) to select the surface
    3. Click the middle mouse button to confirm the selection
    4. Select **Yes** from the Options menu

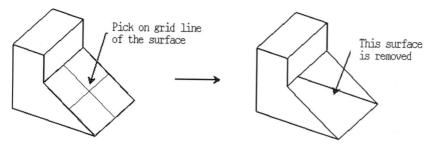

Figure 5.35

# Deleting a single feature

**The procedure for deleting a single feature is (Figure 5.36):**

    1. Select the **Delete** command

    2. Pick any edge line of the feature
    3. Click the middle mouse button to confirm the selection
    4. Select **Yes** from the Options menu

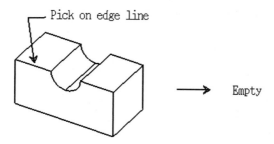

Figure 5.36

# Deleting a feature from the workbench which has more than one independent feature

When more than one unrelated feature is present in the workbench, each feature is regarded as an independent feature. We can delete a single feature or all of the features.

**The procedure below to delete a single feature (Figure 5.37):**

1. Select the **Delete** command

2. Pick on any edge of the feature to delete
3. Click the middle mouse button to confirm the selection
4. Select **Yes** from the Options menu

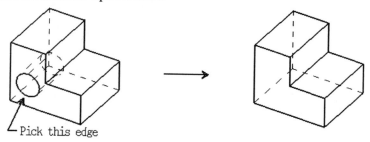

Figure 5.37

# Deleting more unrelated features from the workbench

Pick two points to define a window which includes the features to be deleted is the best way to delete unrelated features from the workbench.

**The procedure for deleting unrelated features from the workbench is (Figure 5.38):**

1. Select the **Delete** command

2. Pick two corner points to form a window which includes all features to be deleted
3. Click the middle mouse button to confirm the selection
4. Select **Yes** from the Options menu

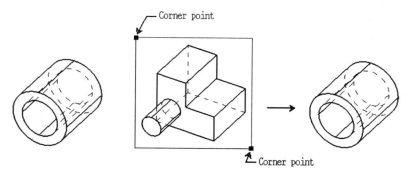

Figure 5.38

Mastering I-DEAS
Scholars International Publishing Corp., 1999

# Deleting the entire part

A part model normally consists of a base (or root) feature and several added features. The Delete command can be used to delete the entire part, a single added feature, or the base (root) feature.

**The procedure for deleting the entire part is (Figure 5.39):**

1. Select the **Delete** command
2. Pick a surface edge of any feature of the part
3. Click the middle mouse button to confirm the selection
4. Select **Yes** from the Options menu

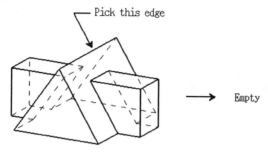

Figure 5.39

# Deleting an added feature

**The procedure below deletes an added feature (Figure 5.40):**

1. Select the **Delete** command
2. Double-click on a surface edge of the feature to be deleted
3. Click the middle mouse button to confirm the selection
4. Select **Yes** from the Options menu

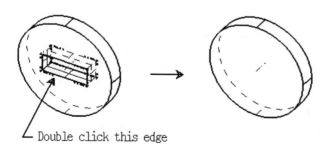

Figure 5.40

## Deleting the base (root) feature

The base feature is the first feature to be created. It is the parent to all added features. Deleting the base feature subsequently deletes all child (added) features from the model.

**The procedure for deleting the base feature is (Figure 5.41):**

1. Select the **Delete** command
2. Double Click on a surface edge of the root feature twice
3. Click the middle mouse button to confirm the selection
4. Select **Yes** from the Options menu

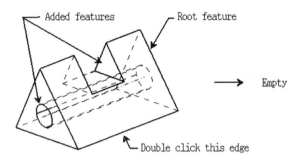

Figure 5.41

# 5.4 History Tree

Every solid model created in I-DEAS has a history. I-DEAS records each modeling event used to create a part and provides several tools you can use to access these events. A history tree is a sequential record of the modeling events used to create a part. It is organized by three elements; **nodes**, **leafs**, and **root** (Figure 5.42).

| | |
|---|---|
| **Node:** | A node is a data structure that represents the result of a construction operation such as cut, join, and intersection. A node typically has a parent and two children. |
| **Leaf:** | A leaf is a terminal node in a tree. It is an end of the line. A leaf represents an initial creation event such as extrude, revolve, sweep, get, etc. It is a primitive block with no children. |
| **Root:** | A root is the last operation performed on the part. In other words, it represents the current part as fully defined by its history. |

Figure 5.42 shows a part and its history tree. This part has four features including the base feature, one protrude feature and two cut features. The protrude feature is added first, followed by the hole and slot.

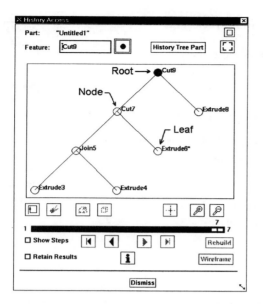

Figure 5.42

# Accessing the History Tree

There are two ways for you to access the history tree of a part model; **icon command** and the **options menu**.

## Icon command

**The procedure for using the icon command to access the history tree is (Figure 5.43):**

1. Select the **History Tree** icon
2. Pick the part, feature or reference geometry from the model.
3. Click the middle mouse button to accept the selection.
4. The History Access menu should appear as shown here.

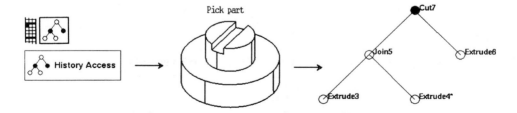

Figure 5.43

## Options menu

The other way to access the history tree of a part is to select the **History Access** command from the Options menu. Click the **right mouse button** to open the Options menu as shown here.

| |
|---|
| Visible |
| Label |
| Filter... |
| Area Options... |
| Reconsider |
| Deselect All |
| Related To |
| History Access... |
| Use Design Groups... |
| All |
| Show |
| Highlight Selection |
| Backup Selection |

The procedure for using the options menu to access the history tree:

1. Click the right mouse button to select the **History Access** option.
2. The system will prompt "Pick part, feature or reference geometry".
3. Pick an edge of the feature, then click the middle button to accept the selection.
4. The History Access menu should appear.

# 5.5 Deleting Using History Tree Access

I-DEAS allows you to delete a feature (leaf) or an operation (node) from the History Tree. The examples given below illustrate the procedure for deleting a feature from the History Tree.

**The procedure for deleting a feature from the History Tree (Figures 5.44 and 5.45).**

1. Click on the **History Tree** icon

2. Pick any part entity to open the History Tree as shown below.

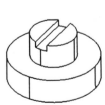
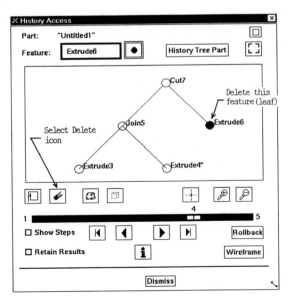

Figure 5.44

Mastering I-DEAS
Scholars International Publishing Corp., 1999

3. Click the node or leaf you want to delete
4. Select the **Delete** icon in the History Access menu
5. Select **Yes** from the options menu to accept the delete operation.
6. The model and history tree after deleting a feature appear as in Figure 5.45.

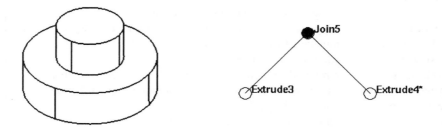

Figure 5.45

# 5.6 Modifying Features

A part or a feature can be modified after it is created. I-DEAS has two ways to access the feature modifying function, history tree access and modify icon. Both methods access the same modifying functions.

## History Tree Modifying

Click the Modify icon in the History Tree menu (Figure 5.46) to open the Options menu that includes the following options:

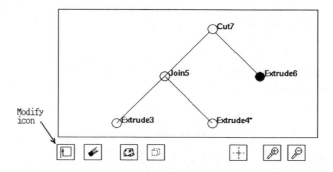

Figure 5.46

## Modifying Features

| | |
|---|---|
| **Show Dimensions:** | shows all dimensions of part features. |
| **Dimension Values:** | open the Dimensions dialog box for changing dimension values of the dimensions. |
| **Feature Parameters:** | open the feature section dialog box for defining feature parameters. |
| **Quick Wireframe:** | extract the wireframe section of the selected feature to be used for creating another feature. |
| **Suppress Feature:** | suppress a selected feature from being modified. |
| **Replace Feature:** | replace a feature by a new one. |
| **Adding Relations:** | add relations between frames |
| **Delete Relations:** | remove the parent-child relationship between features. |
| **Wireframe:** | extract wireframe section from a feature for further use. |
| **Rename Feature:** | rename a feature. |
| **Backup:** | return to one previous operation. |
| **Cancel:** | terminate the modify operation. |

### Show dimensions

This parameter sets the system to display all dimensions of features in the part model. Click "Show Dimensions" from the menu list to show dimensions of the part as shown in Figure 5.47.

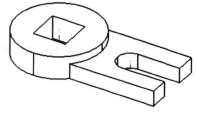 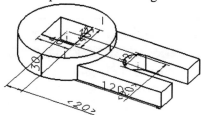

Original geometry

After show dimensions

Figure 5.47

### Dimension values

This parameter opens the Dimensions dialog box that lists all dimensions of the part model for you to modify. Figure 5.48 shows an example of the Dimensions dialog box for the part having four features. Click the dimension you want to modify from the Dimensions dialog box. The selected dimension will be highlighted in white in the part model. Enter the new value for the selected dimension. Repeat this process until all dimensions has been modified. Select OK to accept the dimension changes and close the Dimensions dialog box. Click the Update icon to update changes to the modified geometry. Figure 5.48 shows the change made to the model according to the new dimensions.

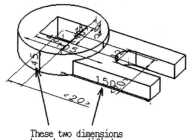 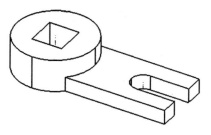

These two dimensions have been modified (before Update command)

New geometry after Update

Figure 5.48

### Feature parameters

This parameter opens the selected feature parameters menu for you to modify. It only opens the feature parameters menu for the selected feature. The selected feature will be highlighted in pink. Figure 5.49shows a feature parameters menu for a selected extrude feature with its part model. Make all necessary change to the parameters, then select OK to close the parameters menu. Select the Update icon to update the parameter changes to the part model as shown in Figure 5.50.

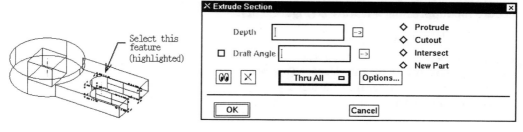

Figure 5.49

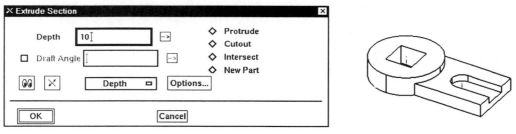

Update to new feature parameters                    New part after Update

Figure 5.50

### Quick wireframe

This function is used to define a wireframe section that can be used to create another feature. The system will prompt you to select a feature on the part. The wireframe section of the selected feature will be highlighted as the section for creating a new feature. Figure 5.51 shows an example of using the wireframe of the base feature to create a new feature that extrudes in the vector direction (2,1,-1) with a distance of 30.

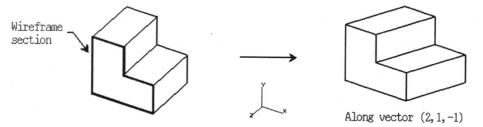

Figure 5.51

The feature created from the quick wireframe section must be the same type as the original feature. In other words, the wireframe section derived from the extrude feature must only be used to create an extrude feature.

### Suppress and unsuppress features

The Suppress Feature function temporarily disables a node or leaf in the part's history. The suppressed feature still exists but it is ignored until you **un**suppress it. This function is especially usefull when you troubleshoot a part with modeling errors. Just suppress the suspected feature. It can also be used for finishing the design of a feature especailly if you want to increase your computer's performance by reducing the calculations required for each update.

**The procedure for suppressing a feature is (Figure 5.52):**

     1. Select the **History Tree** icon

2. Pick the feature you want to suppress
3. Pick the **Modify** icon from the History Tree menu
4. Select **Suppress Feature** from the menu
5. Pick the **Update** icon

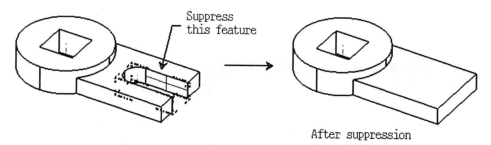

Figure 5.52

**The procedure for unsupressing a feature is (Figure 5.53):**

     1. Select the **Modify** icon

2. Pick the entire part to modify
3. Select **Unsuppress Features** from the menu
4. Select "**All of Above**" from the list
5. Select the **Update** icon to update the part

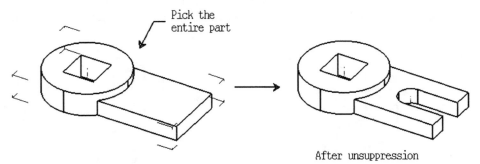

Figure 5.53

### Replace feature

This function is used to substitute one node or leaf for another in a part's history. The old (replaced) feature and its construction relationships will be deleted. The new feature will be constructed to the part in its current orientation. You may need to use Move or Rotate functions to reposition the new feature.

**The procedure for replacing a feature is (Figure 5.54):**

 1. Create the replacing feature as a new part on the workbench

 2. Select the **Modify** icon
3. Pick the feature to be replaced
4. Select **Replace Feature** from the option list
5. Pick the part to replace the feature with (new feature)

 6. Select the **Update** icon to update the change

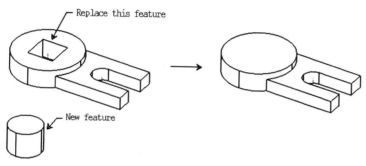

Figure 5.54

### Adding relations

This function is often used after the "Replace Feature" function to replace one feature with another. The new feature will not inherit the construction relationships of the old (replaced) feature.

**The procedure for adding relations is (Figure 5.55):**

1. Select the **Modify** icon

2. Pick the new feature added from using Replace Feature function
3. Select **Add Relations** from the option list
   The system will prompt you to select the planar faces to be related, then prompt you to select the kind of relationship: face-to-face, line-to-line, point-to-point, from edges, etc.

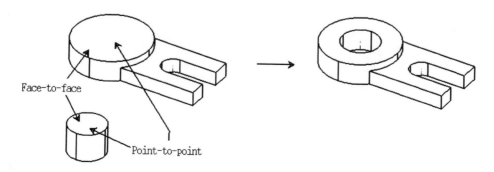

Figure 5.55

### Deleting relations

This function is used to delete positional relations of a selected feature with the part. It is used to remove a feature from a part. The released feature can be moved to any location by using Move or Rotate commands. The slot feature has a cut relation with the part in Figure 5.56. Deleting this cut relation from this feature frees it from the feature and frees it from the part. The feature is still removed, but as a separate part. It can be freely moved to a new location.

**The procedure for deleting relations of a feature is (Figure 5.56):**

1. Select the **Modify** icon
2. Pick the feature to delete relations
3. Select **Delete Relations**

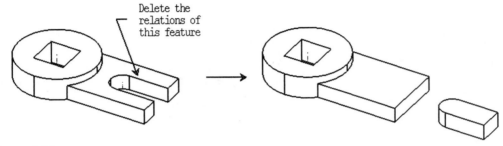

Delete the relations of this feature

Figure 5.56

Mastering I-DEAS
Scholars International Publishing Corp., 1999

# Project 4.
# Modifying part features using modify entity function

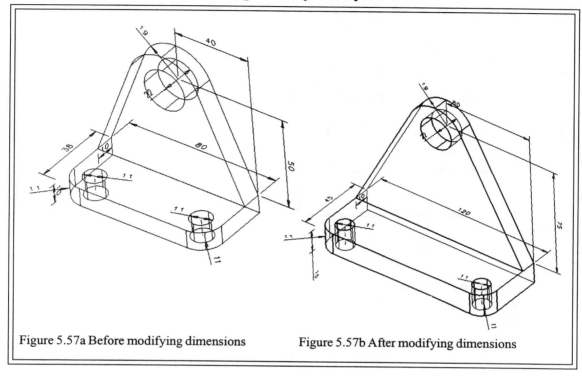

Figure 5.57a Before modifying dimensions          Figure 5.57b After modifying dimensions

The "support" part will be created in project 2 of chapter 6. After creating the project, the part can be retrieved from the library. We use the "Modify Entity" function to modify five dimensions in the part. Figure 5.57 shows the part before and after the modification.

### Step 1. Check the "support" part out from the library.

 Select **Get From Library** to open "Get from Project Library" menu as below.

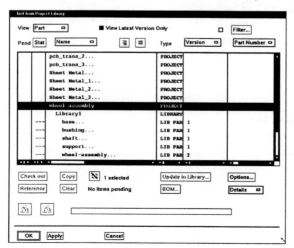

# Modifying Features

Scroll the menu list to find the **"wheel-assembly"** project and double click it
Double click **"Library1"** to open the library part list
Click the **"support"** part from the list
Select the **"Copy"** button near the bottom of the library menu
Select **OK** to make a copy of the support part

### Step 2. Get the part from the bin.

Select the **Get** icon to open the "Get" menu as below.

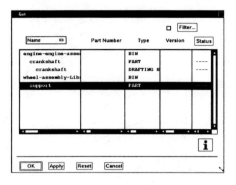

Click the **"support"** part from the Get menu
Select **OK** to return to graphic window
The "support" part should appear as in Figure 5.58.

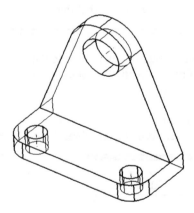

Figure 5.58

### Step 3. Initiate the Modify Entity function.

Select the **Modify Entity** icon
Click on any edge of the part
Select **"Show Dimensions"** from the options list

All dimensions associated with this part should appear as in Figure 5.59.

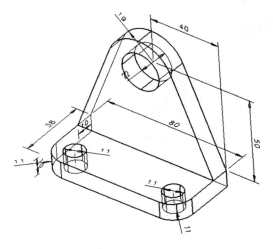

Figure 5.59

**Step 4. Modify five dimensions. Use Figure 5.60 as reference.**

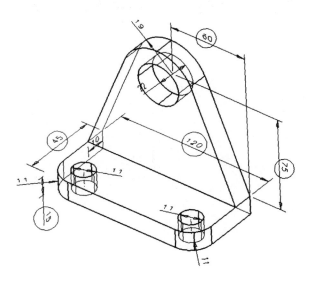

Figure 5.60

 Click on the **Modify Entity** icon
Pick the height dimension "**50**", then enter "**75**" for the new value
Continue the above procedure to change the four remaining dimensions

## Step 5. Update the model to reflect the changes.

 Select the "**Update**" icon to update the changes
The new part becomes Figure 5.61.

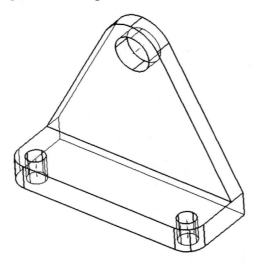

Figure 5.61

# Project 5.
# Using history tree to modify a feature

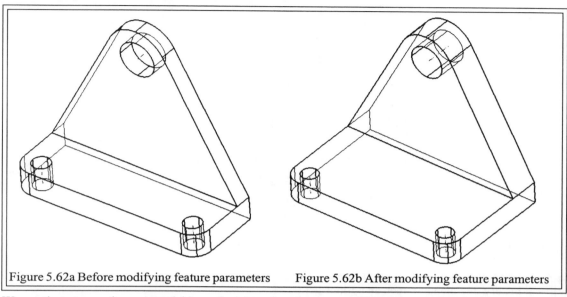

Figure 5.62a Before modifying feature parameters    Figure 5.62b After modifying feature parameters

We continue to use the part model in project 4 to show how to modify a feature using the history tree approach. Two features are modified in this project. The thickness of the vertical extrude feature is changed from 10 to 20. The width dimension of the wireframe for the base extrude feature is changed from 45 to 80. Figure 5.62 shows the part model before and after modifications.

### Step 1. Initiate history tree function.

 Select the "**History Access**" icon
Pick any edge on the part to select it
The history tree menu should appear.
Click the "**Magnifies**" button to make the graphic larger as shown next.

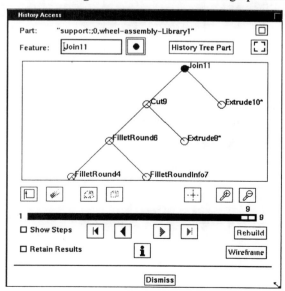

# Modifying Features

**Step 2. Select the vertical extrude feature (Extrude10).**

Click "**Extrude10**" from the history tree to select it

The selected feature is highlighted in the graphic window as in Figure 5.63.

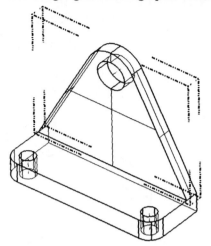

Figure 5.63

 Select the "**Modify**" button from the history tree menu to open an options list as shown at the side here.

Show Dimensions
Feature Parameters
Dimension Values
Quick Wireframe
Multiple Draft
Suppress Feature
Replace Feature
Delete Relations
Wireframe
Rename Feature
Backup
Cancel

Select **Feature Parameters** from the list

The existing extrusion parameters menu should appear as below.

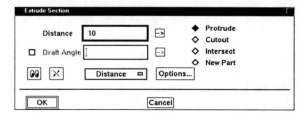

# Modifying Features

Change the distance value to "**20**" as below.

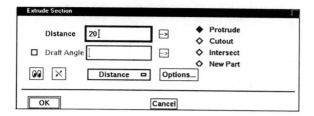

Select **OK** to return to graphic window mode
Select the "**Update**" icon to update the change as shown in Figure 5.64

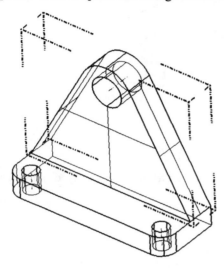

Figure 5.64

## Step 3. Modify the wireframe geometry.

Select the "**History Access**" icon again to reopen the history access menu
Move the graphic display in history access to show the first feature (Extrude3) as below.

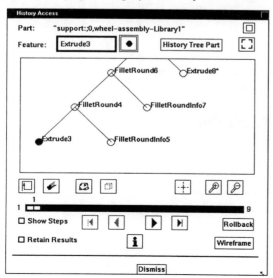

# Modifying Features

The selected feature is highlighted as in Figure 5.65.

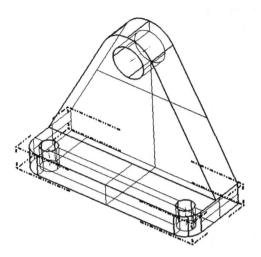

Figure 5.65

 Click the "**Modify**" button to open the options list
Select **Wireframe** from the list
The wireframe geometries of the extruded feature are displayed as in Figure 5.66.

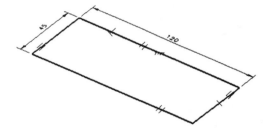

Figure 5.66

**Step 4. Change the width dimension to 80.**

Select the "**Modify Entity**" icon, then select the width dimension
Enter **80** to the modify dimension menu as below.

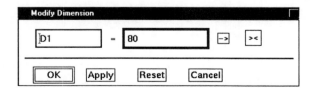

Mastering I-DEAS
Scholars International Publishing Corp., 1999

### Step 5. Update the model for two changes.

Select the "**Complete Update**" icon, then pick any entity on the wireframe
The model is updated for two changes as shown in Figure 5.67.

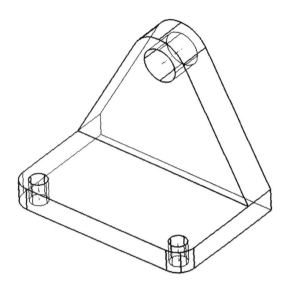

Figure 5.67

### Step 6. Delete the part from the graphic window.

Select the **Delete** icon
Pick on any edge of the part to select the entire part model
Select **OK** to "Parts have been selected for deletion. OK to delete these parts?"

# Chapter 5. Review Questions

1. What are the three transform functions that can be used in copying features to other locations?

2. Explain how to use "Copy sw" parameter in using move and rotate functions.

3. List the four Boolean functions.

4. Explain the reasons of using Boolean functions in part modeling.

5. Use a drawing to describe the cut function.

6. Use a drawing to describe the join function.

7. Use a drawing to describe the intersect function.

8. Explain how to correctly use "Relation" function in performing Boolean operations.

9. Explain how "Relation On" means and when to use it.

10. Explain how "Relation Off" means and when to use it.

11. What are the two ways to locate the movable parts to their desired location while performing Boolean operations?

12. Explain how to use the delete command to delete a single wireframe entity, multiple wireframe entities, a face of a feature, a single feature, and the entire part.

13. What is the history tree?

14. What are the three elements of history tree? Describe what they are.

15. List the two ways to access the history tree.

Mastering I-DEAS
Scholars International Publishing Corp., 1999

# Chapter 6

# Adding Construction Features

## Highlights of the Chapter

- Construction features
- Fillets and their controlling parameters
- Chamfers and their defining parameters
- Shell features
- Draft features

## Overview

I-DEAS provides extrude and revolve functions to create solid features and various modeling functions to create surface features. These modeling functions are extensively used to create most part models, simple or complex. I-DEAS also provides additional feature creating functions to make some features easily. Those feature functions include fillet, chamfer, shell, and draft. This group of functions are referred to as *construction features* in this text. This chapter presents the modeling principle and defining parameters of these four construction functions. Seven tutorial projects are included to show effectively how to use construction features.

## 6.1 Construction Features

The main characteristics of construction features are used to modify existing features by changing part shape and volume. I-DEAS provides four construction feature functions to facilitate defining details of the part. Table 6.1 summarizes these four construction feature functions. These four construction features are presented in the next four sections, respectively.

## Table 6.1  Construction features

| Feature Type | Description | Illustration |
|---|---|---|
| Fillet | Creates fillets or rounds at selected edges or surfaces. | |
| Chamfer | Creates chamfers at selected edges or surfaces. | |
| Shell | Removes the inside material of a solid feature to make it a shell.  It also can be used to add a specified thickness of material to a surface. | |
| Draft | Creates a draft at selected faces. | |

Mastering I-DEAS,
Scholars International Publishing Corp., 1999

# 6.2 Fillets

Fillets are concave or convex transitions at intersecting surfaces and vertices. Fillets are also referred to as *rounds*. There are two fillet types, **constant radius fillets** and **variable radius fillets** (Figure 6.1). The shape of a fillet can be manipulated by these three parameters:

- Radius for selected edges:  specifies the radius for constant radius fillets.
- Variable radius:  allows the radius of the fillet to vary linearly along the filleting edges.
- Conic parameter:   controls the shape of the fillet to range from flat, circular, to sharp.

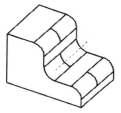

Figure 6.1 Constant radius

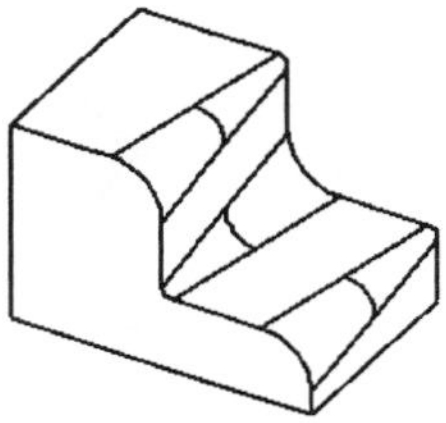

Variable radius

## Variable Radius

The variable radius parameter allows you to specify different radius values to control points (corners). The system automatically will have a circle on the current control point and prompt "Enter radius for highlighted point of edge (5.0)". Enter the radius for the selected point. The system will move to the next control point and wait for you to enter the radius. Repeat this process until radius values are assigned to all points. Each edge has two control points. Two edges may share the same point for different edges. However, it is possible to assign different radius values to the same point that is intersected by two or three edges. Figure 6.2 is an example of using variable radius at an edge, while Figure 6.3 is an example of using variable radius at three edges that intersect at one vertice.

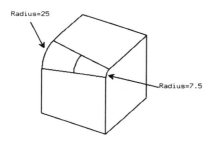

Figure 6.2

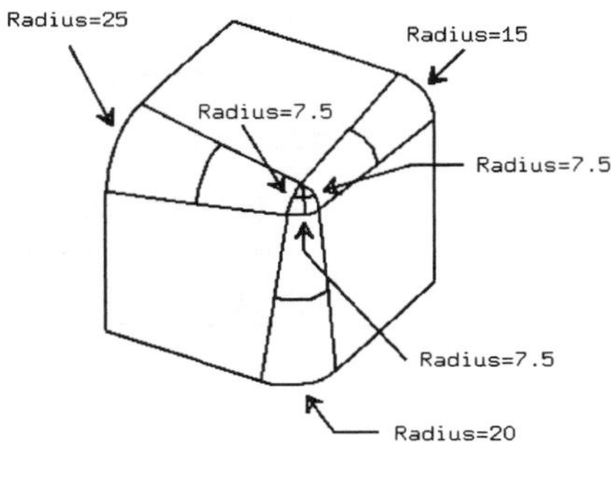

Figure 6.3

## Conic Parameter

The conic parameter controls the shape and type of conical cross section used in fillets. When you click the Conic parameter from the options menu, the system will prompt "Enter conic parameter for cross section (0.5)". The value you can enter ranges from 0.01 to 0.99. Smaller values produce a flat cross section and larger values create a sharp cross section. The default value is 0.5 which produces a circular cross section. Figure 6.4 shows examples of using four different values; 0.01, 0.25, 0.5, 0.99.

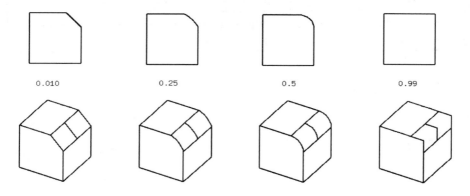

Figure 6.4

## Options Menu

The fillet options menu contains parameters to manipulate color, line style, radius curves display, corner patch, and miter bevels. Its menu appears as below.

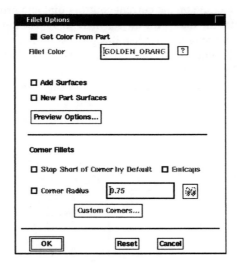

| | |
|---|---|
| **Get color from part:** | changes the color of the filleted edges or surface intersections. |
| **Fillet color:** | assigns the fillet color when Get color from part is Off. |
| **Radius curves display:** | |
| Color: | assigns the color of the preview lines of fillets. |
| Style: | specifies the preview line style of fillets as unbroken, dashed, etc. |
| Number: | specifies the preview line number of fillets. |
| **For 5 or 6 sided corners:** | |
| Corner patch: | creates a surface patch at the corner. |
| Miter: | bevels all the intersecting filleted edges. |

## Selecting Elements to Add Fillets

The valid fillet edge selection elements used for adding fillets are edges, vertices, and surfaces.

### Edges option

Selecting the Edges option is to pick those edges to add fillets one-by-one, then click the middle button to terminate the edge selection (Figure 6.5). The system will prompt "Enter radius for selected edges (5.0)" and open the options menu as below.

```
Variable Radius

Options...

Conic Parameter

Measure

Backup

Cancel
```

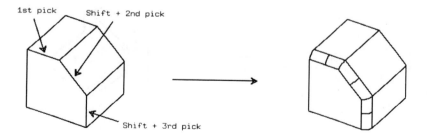

Figure 6.5

### Vertices option

Use the vertices option to pick a vertex to automatically trap three edges that intersect at that vertex for adding fillets (Figure 6.6). Each vertex in the model is identified by a letter V followed by a number. For example, V6 indicates the vertex #6 in the model. Click the vertices one-by-one, then click the middle mouse button to terminate the vertex selection. Press the Shift key to continuously select multiple vertices.

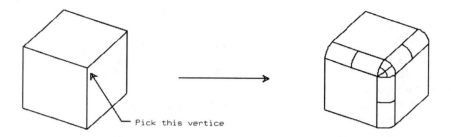

Figure 6.6

### Surfaces option

Use the surfaces option to pick a surface to automatically trap its edges for adding fillets (Figure 6.7). Each surface in the model is identified by a letter F followed by a number. For example, F3 indicates the surface #3 in the model. Click the surfaces one-by-one, then click the middle mouse button to terminate the surface selection. Press the Shift key to continuously select multiple surfaces. Figure 6.8 shows that three surfaces are selected to added fillets.

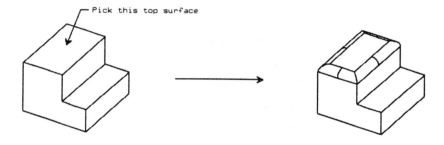

Figure 6.7

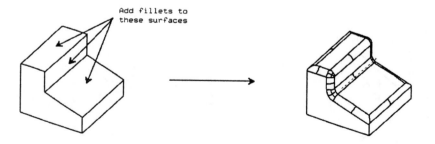

Figure 6.8

Mastering I-DEAS,
Scholars International Publishing Corp., 1999

# Project 1.
# Creating the base part for the wheel assembly

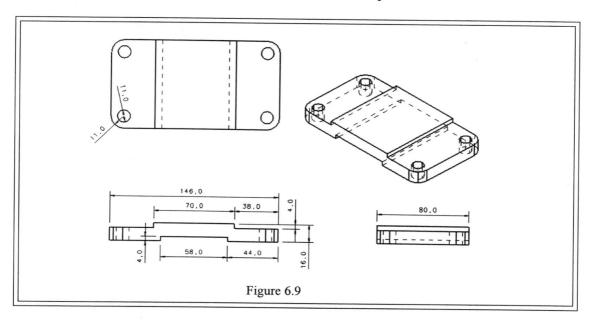

Figure 6.9

The base part consists of three features; extrude base feature, fillet features, and hole features. After the extrude base feature is created, add fillets to its four corners. The four holes are added last. Figure 6.9 shows the drawing views of the project. Check the part into the library using the following data:

| | |
|---|---|
| **Project:** | **wheel-assembly** |
| **Library:** | **Library1** |
| **Name:** | **base** |

**Step 1. Set the unit to mm.**

Select **Options → Units → mm (milli newton)**

**Step 2. Create a section.**

Use the **Polylines** function to create a section and add dimensions as in Figure 6.10.

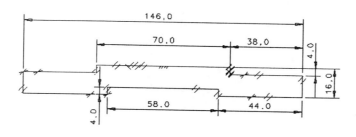

Figure 6.10

### Step 3. Extrude the section.

Use the **Extrude** function to extrude the section by **80**
The extrude feature should look like Figure 6.11.

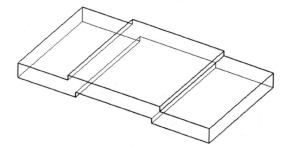

Figure 6.11

### Step 4. Add fillets at four corners.

Select the **Fillet** icon
Pick the vertical edges at the four corners
    (press the Shift key to continue selecting corner lines)
Enter radius for selected edges (0.8):  **11**
Select **Done**
Four fillets are added as in Figure 6.12.

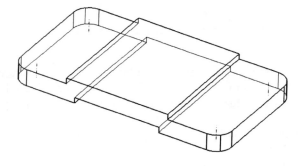

Figure 6.12

### Step 5. Create two circles.

Select the **Sketch in place** icon,
    then pick the second horizontal surface from the top at the right end
Create two circles and change the diameters to the desired value as in Figure 6.13
      (concentric with the fillets)

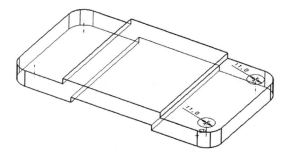

Figure 6.13

### Step 6. Extrude cut the two holes.
Select the **Extrude** icon

Mastering I-DEAS,
Scholars International Publishing Corp., 1999

Pick two circles to extrude
Set the Extrude Section parameters as below.

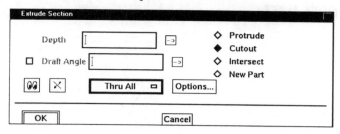

The two hole features are added as in Figure 6.14.

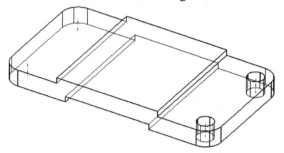

Figure 6.14

### Step 7.  Add two hole features at the left side.

 Select the **Sketch in place** icon
Pick the left top flat surface as the sketch plane
Follow the instructions in step 6 to add two hole features as in Figure 6.15

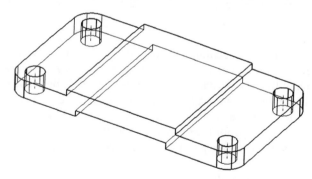

Figure 6.15

### Step 8.  Check the part into library.

Use the check in parameters as below to check the part into the library

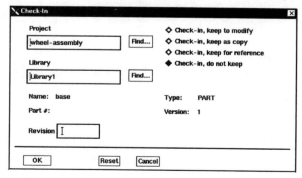

# Project 2.
# Creating the wheel support part

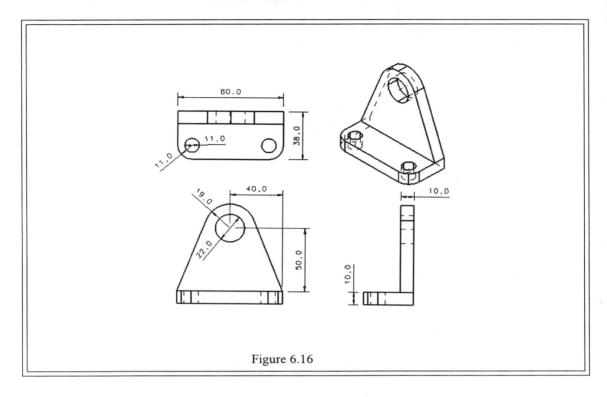

Figure 6.16

The wheel support part consists of four features including the base extrude feature, two fillet features, two hole features, and another extrude feature joined to the base feature. The two fillets are added to the two corner vertical lines. The sketch of the last extrude feature consists of two loops. The outer loop consists of two lines and one arc. These two lines must be tangent to the arc. The back top edge of the base feature is used in conjunction with the three entities to form the outer closed loop. The inner loop is a circle. Extrude these two loops to form a solid for the outer loop and cavity for the inner loop. Figure 6.16 shows the drawing views of the part. Check the part into the library using the following data:

| | |
|---|---|
| **Project:** | **wheel assembly** |
| **Library:** | **Library1** |
| **Part:** | **support** |

## Step 1.  Create a rectangle.
Select the **Rectangle by 2 Corners** icon
Create a rectangle and change two dimensions to their desired values as in Figure 6.17

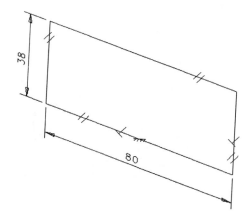

Figure 6.17

## Step 2.  Extrude the rectangle.

 Select the **Extrude** icon

Extrude the section by **10 mm**

The extruded base feature appears as in Figure 6.18.

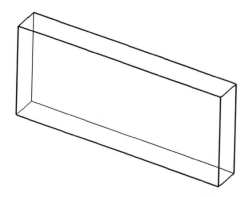

Figure 6.18

## Step 3.  Rotate the feature about X-axis by 90 degrees.

 Select the **Rotate** icon

Pick the base feature to rotate

Pick the lower right front corner as the pivot point

Select **About X axis**, enter **90** degrees

The new drawing becomes Figure 6.19.

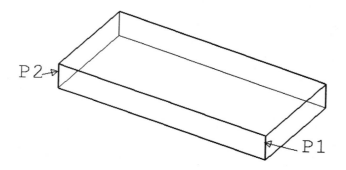

Figure 6.19

**Step 4. Add two fillets to two corners. Use Figure 6.19 as reference.**

 Select the **Fillet** icon
Select the two vertical edges (**P1** and **P2**) of the front face
Enter the fillet radius: **11**
The two fillets are added as in Figure 6.20.

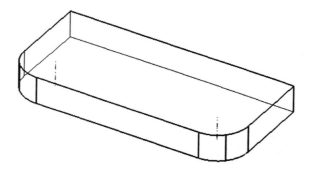

Figure 6.20

**Step 5. Add two circles concentric to two fillets.**

 Select the **Sketch in place** icon, then pick the top face
Create two circles that are concentric to two fillets
Change circle diameter to **11**
The two circles are shown in Figure 6.21.

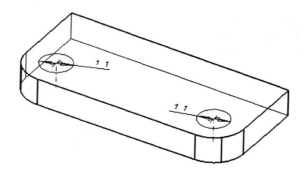

Figure 6.21

6-12

### Step 6. Extrude-cut two circles.

Select the **Extrude** icon

Pick two circles as the section to extrude

Set the Extrude Section parameters as below.

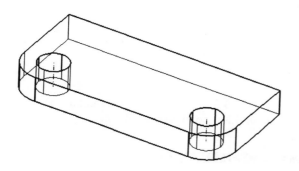

Select **OK** to cut two holes as in Figure 6.22.

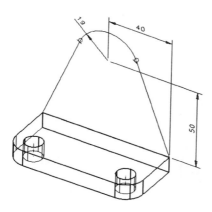

Figure 6.22

### Step 7. Create a section.

Select the **Sketch in place** icon, then pick the back vertical surface as the sketch plane

Create a sketch and constrain and add dimensions as shown in Figure 6.23

Figure 6.23

**Step 8. Add a concentric circle.**

Add a circle that is concentric to the arc
and modify its diameter to a proper value as in Figure 6.24

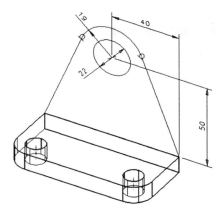

Figure 6.24

**Step 9. Extrude the section and the circle.**

 Select the **Extrude** icon
Pick the section (must include the base line to form a closed section) and the circle
Click on the **Extrusion direction** icon until it is pointing toward you
Set Extrude Section parameters as below.

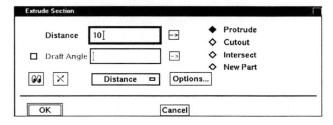

Select **OK** to complete the model as in Figure 6.25.

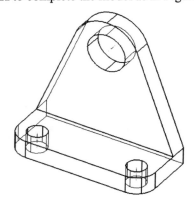

Figure 6.25

Mastering I-DEAS,
Scholars International Publishing Corp., 1999

### Step 10. Check the part into the library.

 Select the **Check In** icon
Pick the part to check in
Enter "**support**" into the Name field to name it
Set the Check In parameters as below.

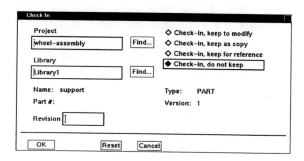

Select **OK** to check the part into the library

# Project 3.
# Adding fillets to the connecting rod part

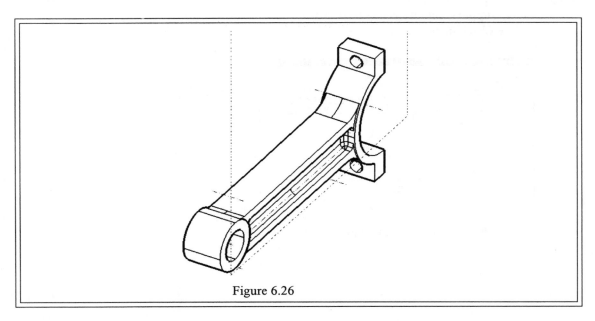

Figure 6.26

This project adds fillets to the connecting rod created in project 12 of chapter 4. There are three sizes of fillets. A fillet of 15-mm is added to two edges at the larger end of the rod. A fillet of 10-mm is added to two edges at the smaller end of the rod. A fillet of 3-mm is added to 16 edges at the recesses of both sides of the rod. Figure 6.26 shows the complete connecting rod.

## Step 1.  Get the connecting rod from the library.

Select the **Get From Library** icon to open Get from the Project Library menu
Set project, library, and part parameters as below.

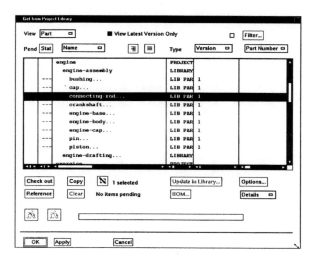

Click on the "**Check Out**" button, then select **OK** to exit the Get From Library menu

Mastering I-DEAS,
Scholars International Publishing Corp., 1999

# Adding Construction Features

**Step 2. Get the part from the bin.**

Select the **Get** icon to open the Get menu as below
(Your list in the Get menu may differ from what is shown below.)

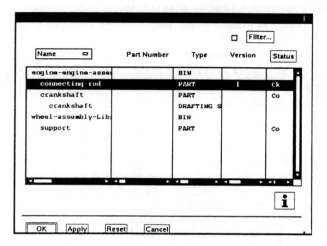

Click the "**connecting-rod**" from the list to highlight it
Select **OK** to make the part appear on the graphic window as in Figure 6.27.

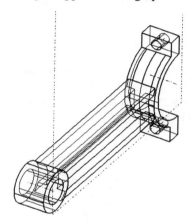

Figure 6.27

**Step 3. Add two fillets to two edges at the top side of the part. Use Figure 6.28 as reference.**

Press **F3** and manipulate the mouse to change the view orientation as shown in Figure 6.28

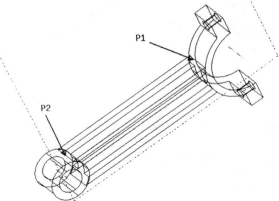

Figure 6.28

# Adding Construction Features

Select the **Fillet** icon
Press the right mouse button then select **Filter** from the list
Click **Edge** from the Filter list, then select the **Pick Only** button
Pick the edge (**P1**) shown in Figure 6.28 as the edge to fillet
Click the middle mouse button to finish the selection
Enter radius for selected edges(1.1):  **15**
Click the middle mouse button to complete the first fillet
Select the **Fillet** icon, pick the edge (**P2**) as shown as the entity to fillet
Enter radius for selected edges (1.1):  **10**
The two fillets are added as in Figure 6.29.

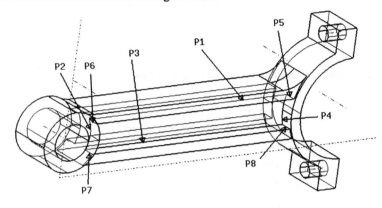

Figure 6.29

**Step 4.  Add a fillet of 3-mm to eight edges. Use Figure 6.29 as reference.**

Select the **Fillet** icon, and use the filter to select edges only
Pick eight edges as shown in Figure 6.29 (press the Shift key to continue picking edges)
Enter radius for selected edges (1.1):  **3**
The fillets are added as in Figure 6.30.

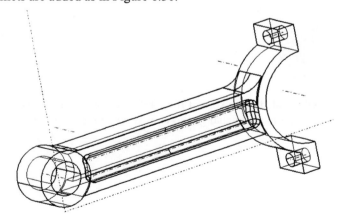

Figure 6.30

**Step 5.  Rotate the part 180 degrees about the Y axis.**

Select the **Rotate** icon, then pick the part as the entities to rotate
Pick a point at the right end as the pivot point
Select **About Y** from the list
Enter angle about Y (90.0):  **180**

Mastering I-DEAS,
Scholars International Publishing Corp., 1999

The new part orientation appears as in Figure 6.31.

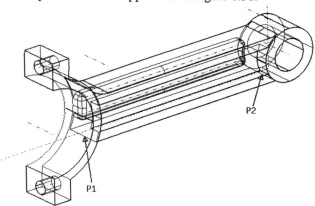

Figure 6.31

**Step 6. Add two fillets to two edges at the bottom face. Use Figure 6.31 as reference.**

 Select **Fillet**, then use the filter option to select **Edges only**
Pick the edge (**P1**) as the edge to fillet
Enter radius for selected edges (1.1): **15**
Select **Fillet** again, then pick the edge (**P2**) as the edge to fillet
Enter radius for selected edges (1.1): **10**
The two fillets are added as in Figure 6.32.

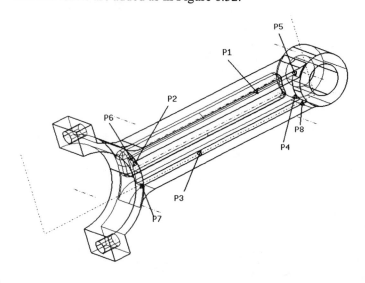

Figure 6.32

**Step 7. Add a fillet of 3-mm to eight edges. Use Figure 6.32 as reference.**

Select **Fillet**, and set the filter to pick **Edges only**
Pick eight edges as shown in Figure 6.32 (press the Shift key to continue picking edges)
Enter radius for selected edges: **3**
The fillets are added as in Figure 6.33.

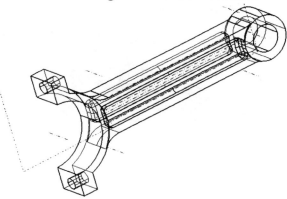

Figure 6.33

### Step 8. Rotate the part 180 degrees about the Y axis.

 Select **Rotate**, then pick the part to rotate
Pick a point at the right end as the pivot point
Select **About Y** from the list
Enter angle about Y (90.0): **180**

 Select **Isometric (XYZ) View** to show the part model as in Figure 6.34

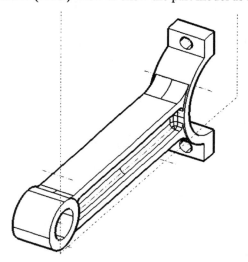

Figure 6.34

### Step 9. Check the part into library.

 Select the **Check In** icon
Pick the part for checking in
Set check-in parameters as below.

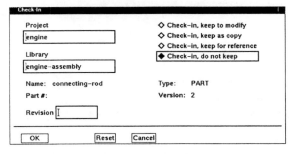

Select **OK** to check the part into library

Mastering I-DEAS,
Scholars International Publishing Corp., 1999

# 6.3 Chamfers

Chamfers are beveled edges of a part. There are three types of chamfers; **equal offset, unequal offset**, and **angle and offset**. They are summarized here.

· Equal offset:     creates chamfers of equal distance in each surface (Figure 6.35). This is the default selection.

· Unequal offset:  allows to independently set the chamfer distance for each adjacent surface along a picked edge (Figure 6.36).

· Angle and offset: sets the distance and angle for the adjacent surfaces along a picked edge (Figure 6.37).

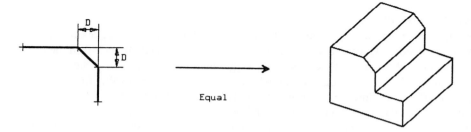

Figure 6.35

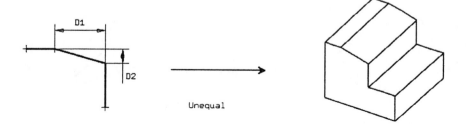

Figure 6.36

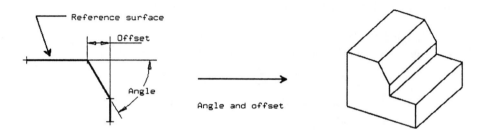

Figure 6.37

## Equal offset

The equal offset is the default selection which creates equal offset distance in all selected surfaces along the edges. The system will prompt "Enter offset for selected edges (5.0)". Enter your desired value to create chamfers. Figure 6.38 shows an equal offset chamfer is added to a selected edge.

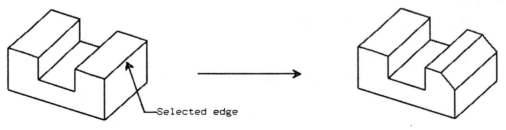

Figure 6.38

## Unequal offset

Unequal offset option is to create chamfer along selected edges that have different values in those involved surfaces. After selecting edges, select "Unequal Offset" from the options menu. The system will issue "Enter offset along highlighted surface (5.0)" and the along surface will be highlighted in white in the part model. Enter the desired offset value for that surface. The system will issue "Enter offset from highlighted surface (5.0)" with highlighted surface in the part model. Enter new offset value for the highlighted surface. Repeat the same procedure until all involved edges and surfaces are completed. Figure 6.39 shows adding an unequal offset chamfer on a selected edge.

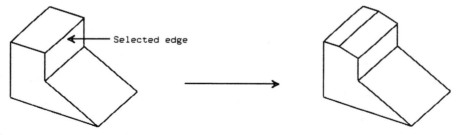

Figure 6.39

## Angle and offset

This option allows you to specify the shape and size of chamfers by its angle and offset distance (Figure 6.40).
The system will prompt the following two inputs to define the chamfer:

Enter angle from highlighted surface (45.0):  30
Enter offset along highlighted surface (5.0):  25

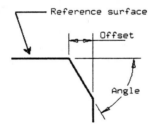

Figure 6.40

Mastering I-DEAS,
Scholars International Publishing Corp., 1999

# Selecting elements to add chamfers

The valid chamfer edge selection elements for adding chamfers are edges, vertices, and surfaces.

### Edges option

Selecting the Edges option allows picking the desired edges one-by-one, then click the middle button to terminate the edge selection (Figure 6.41). Press the Shift key to continuously selecting multiple edges. The system will prompt "Enter offset for selected edges (5.0)" and open the options menu as below.

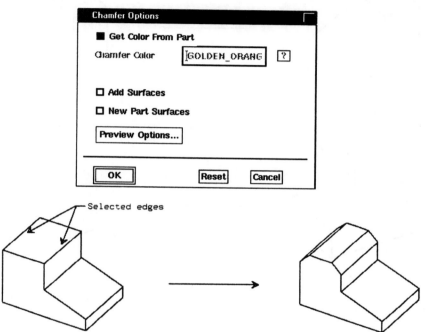

Figure 6.41

### Vertices option

Use the Vertices option to pick a vertex to automatically trap three edges that intersect at that vertice for adding chamfers (Figure 6.42). Click the vertices one-by-one, then click the middle mouse button to terminate the vertice selection. Press the Shift key to continuously select multiple vertices.

Figure 6.42

## Surfaces option

Use the Surfaces option to pick a surface to automatically trap its edges for adding chamfers (Figure 6.43). Click the surfaces one-by-one, then click the middle mouse button to terminate the surface selection. Press the Shift key to continuously select multiple surfaces. Figure 6.44 shows that three surfaces are selected to added chamfers

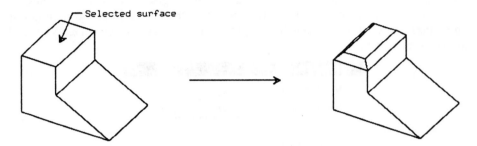

Figure 6.43

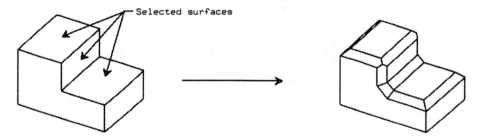

Figure 6.44

# Project 4.
# Creating a shaft part for the wheel assembly

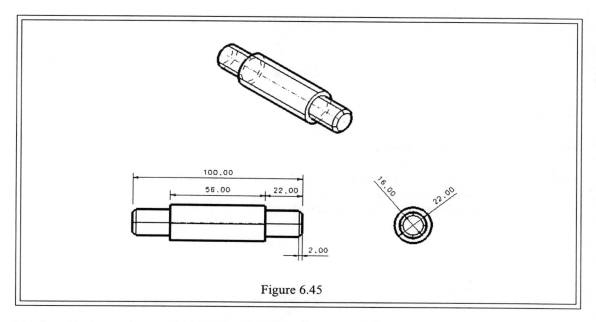

Figure 6.45

This is a simple part that consists of only two features; a revolve base feature and two chamfers at two end faces. Figure 6.45 shows the drawing views of the part. Check the part into the library using the following data:

| | |
|---|---|
| **Project:** | **wheel-assembly** |
| **Library:** | **Library1** |
| **Part:** | **shaft** |

### Step 1. Create a 8-line section.

Use the **Polylines** command to create a section as in Figure 6.46.
Change dimensions to their correct value as shown

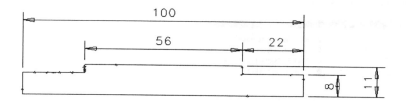

Figure 6.46

### Step 2. Revolve the section.

Select the **Revolve** icon
Pick any entity on the section to select the entire section
Pick the bottom line of the section as the axis of revolution
Set the Angle to "**360**", then select **OK**

# Adding Construction Features

Select the **Isometric View** icon to show the revolve feature as in Figure 6.47.

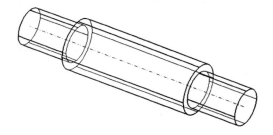

Figure 6.47

## Step 3. Add chamfers to two end faces.

Select the **Chamfer** icon

Pick the edges of the two end faces as the edges to add chamfer

Enter offset for selected edges (1.1): **2**

The two chamfers are added as in Figure 6.48.

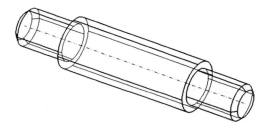

Figure 6.48

## Step 4. Check the part into the library.

Select the **Check In** icon

Pick the part to check in

Enter "**Shaft**" into the Name field in the Name menu, then select **OK**

Set the check in parameters as below.

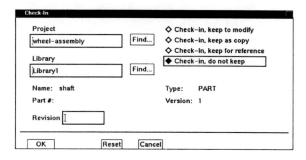

Select **OK** to check in the part

# 6.4  Shell

The shell function allows to create a thin-walled part from solids or surfaces. It hollows out the inside of the solid, leaving a shell of a specified wall thickness (Figure 6.49). I-DEAS also allows surface(s) to be removed in the shell features.

### The procedure for creating a shell is (Figure 6.49):

1. Select the **Shell** icon

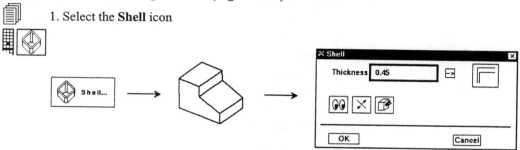

2. Pick a part or volume to shell
3. Define the Shell parameters (thickness and direction) in the Shell menu as below.

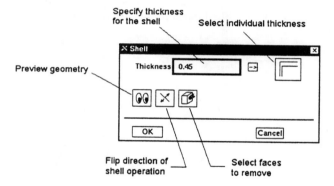

4. Click the "Select faces to remove" icon in Shell menu
5. Pick the face to be removed
6. Select OK from the Shell menu

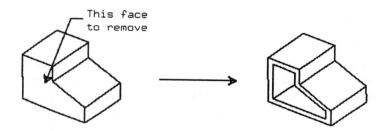

Figure 6.49

## Thickness and Individual Thicknesses

You are allowed to assign different thicknesses to selected surfaces. (Figure 6.50)

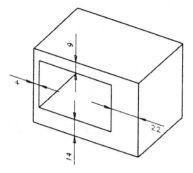

Figure 650

**Follow this procedure to assign different thicknesses (Figure 6.51):**

1. Click on the **Individual thicknesses** icon from the shell menu
2. Pick the face with different thickness:  pick a face
3. Enter wall thickness for face (20.0):  10
4. Repeat the above two steps for assigning different thickness to all desired faces
5. Set the Thickness value to 20 from the Shell menu for the rest of the faces
6. Pick the face to remove
7. Select OK

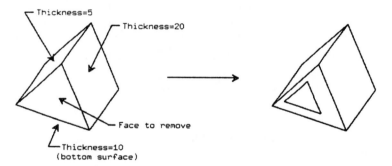

Figure 6.51

## Offset Direction

This parameter is to flip the direction of shell or offset direction. The default direction is pointing toward the part (Figure 6.52a). Click the Offset Direction icon to have the offset direction pointing away from the part (Figure 6.52b). The offset direction has an effect on the size of the feature. When the offset direction is pointing toward the part, the offset distance is measured from the existing surface edges toward inside (Figure 6.53). This results in no size change in existing feature. When the offset direction is pointing away from the part, the offset distance is measured from the existing surface edges toward outside (Figure 6.54). The resulting feature is larger than the existing feature by the thickness in all sides.

Mastering I-DEAS,
Scholars International Publishing Corp., 1999

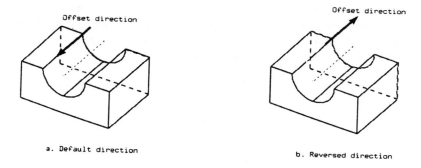

a. Default direction          b. Reversed direction

Figure 6.52

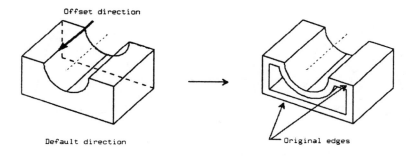

Default direction                Original edges

Figure 6.53

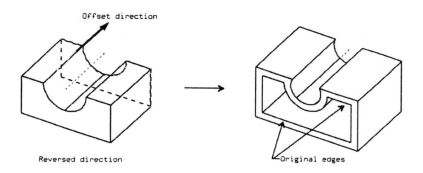

Reversed direction               Original edges

Figure 6.54

## Face(s) to Be Removed

This parameter selects faces on the part to be removed while creating shell feature. I-DEAS allows you to remove multiple faces in the shell features. To selecting multiple faces, select the first face to remove, then press the Shift key and continue to select next faces. Figure 6.55 shows no face is removed in the shell. Figure 6.56 illustrates a single face is removed from the shell. Figure 6.57 shows three faces are removed from the shell.

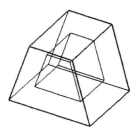

Figure 6.55

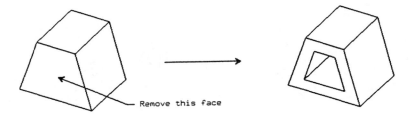

Figure 6.56

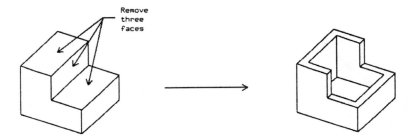

Figure 6.57

# Project 5.
# Creating the piston part for engine assembly

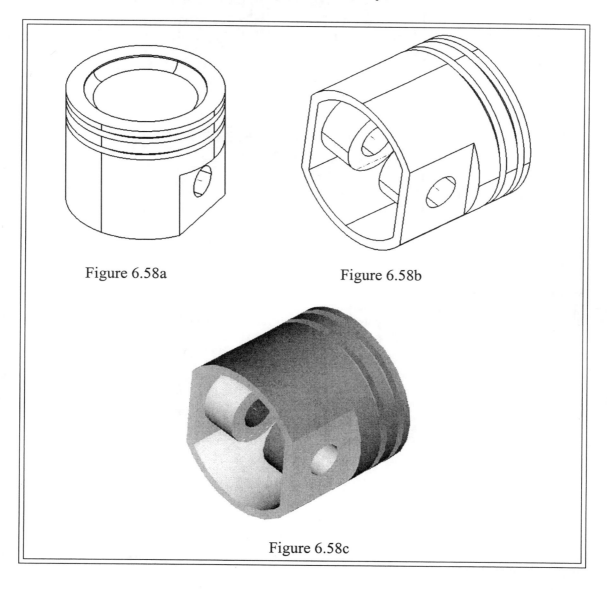

Figure 6.58a                      Figure 6.58b

Figure 6.58c

This project is a tutorial creating the piston part as shown in Figure 6.58. The part consists of a main body feature, two cutout slot features, a shell feature with variable thickness, two bushing features inside the shell, two hole features on bushings, cutout ring groove features, cutout recess feature on the piston head, and fillet features. This is a rather complicated part using a combination of feature creation functions. Fillet and shell functions are used to define the inner details of the part. Figure 6.59 shows the drawing views of this part. Check the part into the library using the following data:

|  |  |
|---|---|
| **Project:** | **engine** |
| **Library:** | **engine-assembly** |
| **Part:** | **piston** |

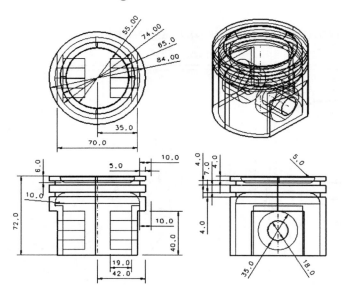

Figure 6.59

### Step 1.  Create a rectangle.

 Select the **Rectangle by 2 Corners** icon
Create a rectangle and modify its two dimension values as shown in Figure 6.60

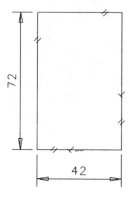

Figure 6.60

### Step 2.  Revolve the section.

Select the **Revolve** icon
Pick the rectangle as the section to revolve
Pick the left vertical line as the axis of revolution
Set the Angle to "**360**",
 then select **OK** to create the feature
Select the **Isometric View** icon
 to display the feature as in Figure 6.61

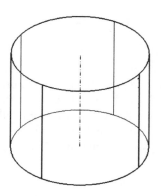

Figure 6.61

Mastering I-DEAS,
Scholars International Publishing Corp., 1999

**Step 3. Create two lines on the bottom face of the revolve feature.**

  Select the **Sketch in place** icon, then pick the bottom face of the feature as the sketching plane
Select the **Bottom View (ZX)** icon to show the model as in Figure 6.62

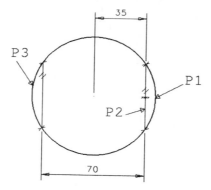

Figure 6.62

Select the **Polylines** icon, then create two vertical lines as shown in Figure 6.62
Add dimensions and modify their values as shown

**Step 4. Extrude-cut the feature. Use Figure 6.62 as reference.**

 Select the **Extrude** icon
Pick three entities (**P1 – P3**) to define sections to extrude
The sections should look like Figure 6.63.

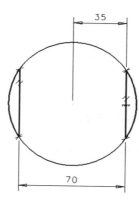

Figure 6.63

Set the Extrude Section parameters as below.

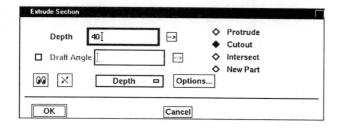

 Select **OK** to complete the extrude-cut feature
Select the **Isometric View** icon to display the model as in Figure 6.64.

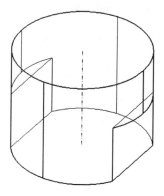

Figure 6.64

**Step 5. Create a hollow shell with variable thickness.**

Select the **Shell** icon
Click on any element of the feature
Set the Shell parameters as below.

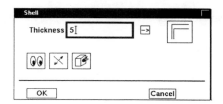

Select the **Individual thickness** icon ( ⌐ ) from the Shell menu

Pick the top surface of the feature
Enter wall thickness for face: **15**
Select the **Remove faces** icon ( ⬚ ) from the Shell menu

Click on the bottom most surface of the feature to remove face
Select **OK** to create the shell feature
Press **F3** and manipulate the mouse to rotate the orientation of the part as shown in Figure 6.65.

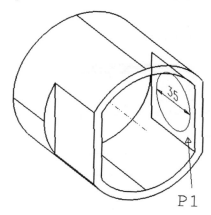

Figure 6.65

6-34

**Step 6. Create a circle on the right inner side of the part. Use Figure 6.65 as reference.**

 Select the **Sketch in place** icon
Pick the right inner flat plane (**P1**) as the sketching plane
Create a circle located at the center of the face as shown in Figure 6.65
Modify its diameter value to **35**

**Step 7. Extrude the circle.**

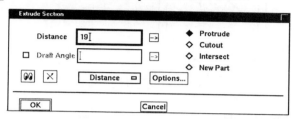 Select the **Extrude** icon, then pick the circle to extrude
Set the Extrude Section parameters as below.

Select **OK** to add the extruded circle as in Figure 6.66.

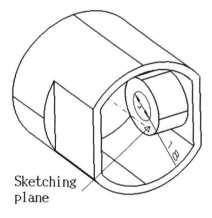

Sketching
plane

Figure 6.66

**Step 8. Create a circle on the left side of the extruded circle. Use Figure 6.66 as reference.**
Select the **Sketch in place** icon, then pick the left face of the extruded circle
Create a concentric circle and modify its diameter value to **18** as shown in Figure 6.66

**Step 9. Extrude-cut the circle.**
Select the **Extrude** icon
Pick the circle to extrude
Set the Extrude Section parameters as below.

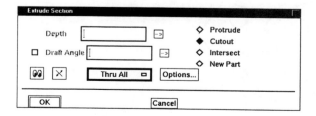

Select **OK** to complete the extrude-cut feature as in Figure 6.67

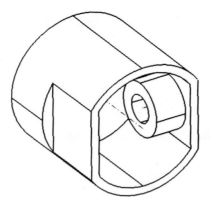

Figure 6.67

**Step 10.  Create two extruded features at the left side.**

Press **F3** and move the mouse to orient the part as shown in Figure 6.68

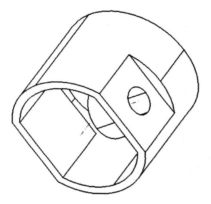

Figure 6.68

Repeat the steps 6 – 9 to create the same features on the left side
The new drawing should resemble Figure 6.69.

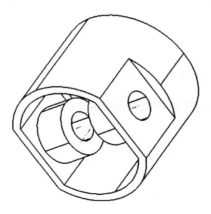

Figure 6.69

6-36

# Adding Construction Features

**Step 11.  Create a fillet at the top inside face.**

 Change the display to **Line** mode

Rotate the model to the orientation shown in Figure 6.70

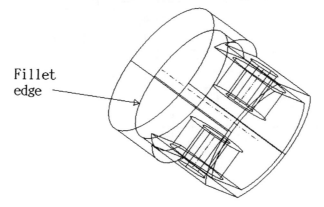

Fillet edge

Figure 6.70

 Select the **Fillet** icon, then pick the circle edge as shown in Figure 6.70 to fillet

Enter radius for selected edges:  **10**

Select the **Front View (XY)** icon to display the model as in Figure 6.71

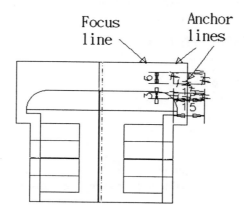

Focus line

Anchor lines

Figure 6.71

**Step 12.  Create two rectangles for piston ring grooves. Use Figure 6.71 as reference.**

Select the **Rectangle by 2 Corners** icon, then create two rectangles as shown in Figure 6.71

 Select the **Dimension** icon

Click the right mouse button, then select **Focus** from the list

Pick the top horizontal line (focus line) to focus

Pick the top line as the first entity to dimension

Pick the top horizontal line of the top rectangle as the second entity to dimension

Place the dimension at the proper location

 Select the **Constrain & Dimension** icon to open the Constrain panel

 Select the **Anchor** icon,

then pick the top horizontal line and right vertical edge of the part as the anchor edges

Add the remaining dimensions and modify them to correct value as shown in Figure 6.72

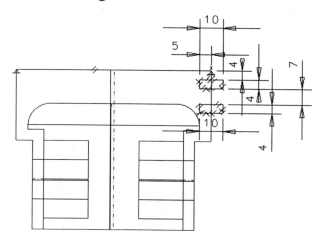

Figure 6.72

**Step 13.  Revolve the two rectangles about the part center line.**

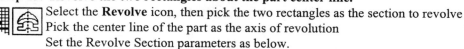
Select the **Revolve** icon, then pick the two rectangles as the section to revolve
Pick the center line of the part as the axis of revolution
Set the Revolve Section parameters as below.

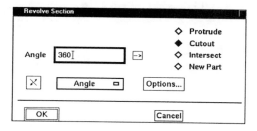

Select **OK**, then pick the part to be cutout
Select the **Isometric View** icon and **Hidden Software** icon to display the part as in Figure 6.73.

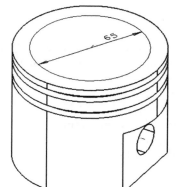

Figure 6.73

**Step 14.  Extrude-cut a circle on top of the head.  Use Figure 6.73 as reference.**

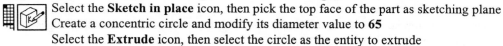
Select the **Sketch in place** icon, then pick the top face of the part as sketching plane
Create a concentric circle and modify its diameter value to **65**
Select the **Extrude** icon, then select the circle as the entity to extrude

Mastering I-DEAS,
Scholars International Publishing Corp., 1999

Set Extrude Section parameters as below.

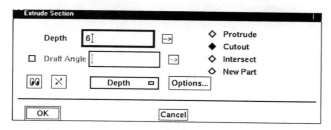

Select **OK** to add the cutout feature as in Figure 6.74.

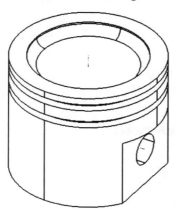

Filleting
curve

Figure 6.74

**Step 15.  Add a fillet to the top of recess. Use Figure 6.74 as reference.**

 Select the **Fillet** icon, then pick the curve as shown in Figure 6.74
Enter radius for selected edges:  **5**
The final part model should look like Figure 6.75.

Figure 6.75

# Adding Construction Features

Figures 6.76 and 6.77 show the model in a different orientation and its render model.

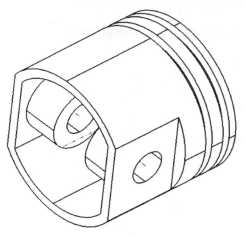

Figure 6.76

Figure 6.77

## Step 16.  Check the part into library.

 Select the **Check In** icon, then pick the part to check in
Enter "**piston**" into the Name field in the Name menu
Set Check-In parameters as below.

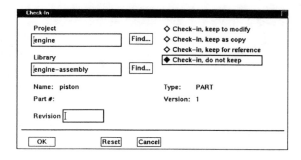

Select **OK** to check the part into the library

Mastering I-DEAS,
Scholars International Publishing Corp., 1999

# 6.5  Draft Features

The draft function adds a draft to selected surfaces. Many parts incorporate drafts in their design especially in casting, injection mold and die parts. The following elements are required to complete a simple draft feature (Figure 6.78):

> · Draft faces:      selected surfaces for drafting.
> · Stationary edge: selected surface edge from which the draft starts.
> · Pull direction:   specifies the direction a surface is pulled from a part.
> · Draft angle:      specifies the draft angle.

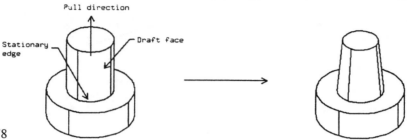

Figure 6.78

### Selecting Draft Faces
I-DEAS allows a single face or multiple faces to be drafted in one operation.

**The procedure for selecting draft faces is (Figure 6.79):**

1. Select the **Draft** command icon
2. Pick the direction of pull

3. Pick the front face for drafting
4. Select a surface edge as the stationary edge
5. Repeat the previous two steps to continu ously select left face to draft
6. Click the middle mouse button to terminate draft face selection
7. Define the draft parameters in the General Draft menu as below.

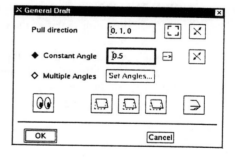

Select OK to complete drafting operation

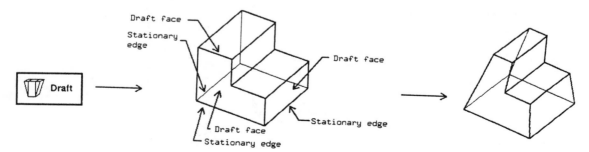

Figure 6.79

## Stationary Edges or Faces

Stationary edges are the selected face edges from which the draft starts. It can be a single edge or multiple edges or a face. The stationary edges cannot be parallel to the pull direction. Figure 6.80 shows an example of using one stationary edge with the pull direction pointing upward. Figure 6.81 uses three stationary edges having the pull direction pointing upward.

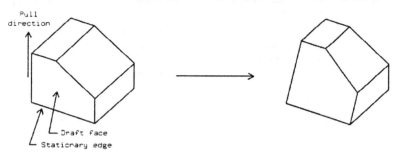

Figure 6.80

Figure 6.81

## Pull Direction

The pull direction specifies the reference plane (or direction) from which the surface is pulled. The draft angle is measured from this direction. When a face is selected for draft, the system automatically assigns a default pull direction (Figure 6.82). Select "no" from the options list to reverse the pull direction. The pull direction can be redefined by using the "Pull direction" parameter in the General Draft menu. This direction is defined by three direction vector values in three principal axes. You can define the direction vectors in the following two ways:

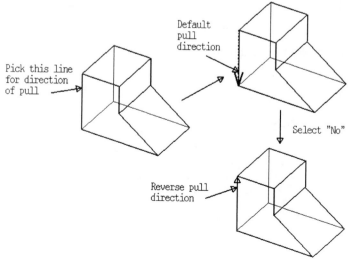

Figure 6.82

Mastering I-DEAS,
Scholars International Publishing Corp., 1999

**Vector values:**    specify three vector direction values (eg. 1,2,-1).
**Graphic element:**  select the vector direction of a line element in the part model as the pull direction.

Figure 6.83 shows a draft face that uses vector values of (1,2,-1) with the draft angle of 15 degrees.

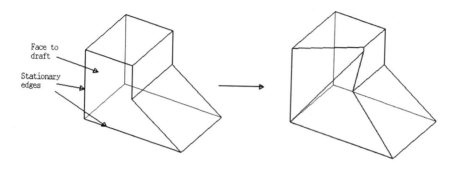

Figure 6.83

**The procedure for defining the pull direction vector values is given below (Figure 6.83):**

1. Select **Draft** icon
2. Press right mouse button to open the options list
3. Select **Key In** from the options list
4. The system prompt "Enter direction vector XYZ of Direction of Pull":  enter 1,2,-3
5. Select **Yes** to accept the direction
6. Pick the part to associate this vector to
7. Pick face to draft:  pick the front face as shown then click the middle mouse button
8. Pick stationary edge or face:  pick the front bottom edge
                and front left vertical edge as the stationary edge
9. Pick parting edge or face:  click the middle mouse button
   The general draft menu should appear as below.

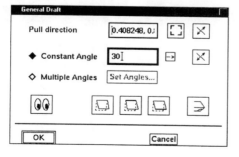

10. Set Constant Angle = **15**
11. Select **OK** to complete the draft

After entering the draft parameters menu, I-DEAS provides options for you to add draft faces, stationary edges or faces, etc. using existing graphic elements.

**The procedure for adding a draft face using graphic elements is listed below (Figure 6.84):**

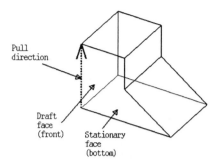

Figure 6.84

1. Select the **Draft** icon
2. Pick a direction of pull:  pick the front left vertical line as shown
3. Select **No**, then **Yes** to make the pull direction point upward
4. Pick the front face as the face to draft
5. Pick the bottom face as the stationary face
6. Click middle mouse button at the prompt "Pick parting edge or face"
7. Set Constant Angle = **15** to the drafting parameters menu as shown below

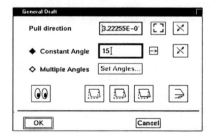

8. Click the **Preview** icon to show the preview drawing of the draft as in Figure 6.85

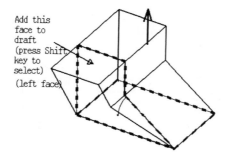

Add this
face to
draft
(press Shift
key to
select)
(left face)

Figure 6.85

9. Click the **Graphically select face to draft** icon
10. Press the Shift key, then pick the left face to draft as shown in Figure 6.85
11. Select **OK** to add the draft
    The draft is added to two faces as shown in Figure 6.86.

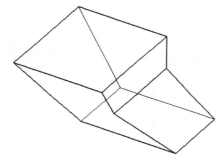

Figure 6.86

## Draft Angle

The draft angle parameter specifies the angle to draft measured from the pull direction in the indicated direction. You can use the "Reverse angle direction" icon to change the direction of the draft angle. The direction of draft angle has a significant effect on the material volume. The default draft direction reduces the volume, while the reversed draft direction adds the volume (Figure 6.87).

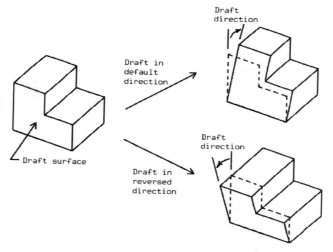

Draft
direction

Draft in
default
direction

Draft surface

Draft in
reversed
direction

Draft
direction

Figure 6.87

# Adding Construction Features

Figure 6.88 shows the results of drafting the four sides of a cube by 10 degrees and 20 degrees, respectively.

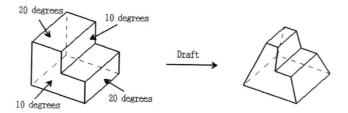

Figure 6.88

## Multiple Angles

When more than one face is used in drafting, I-DEAS allows you to independently specify the draft angle for each face (Figure 6.89). Click the "Multiple angles" icon to open the "Individual Draft Angles" menu. The menu for three selected faces is shown below.

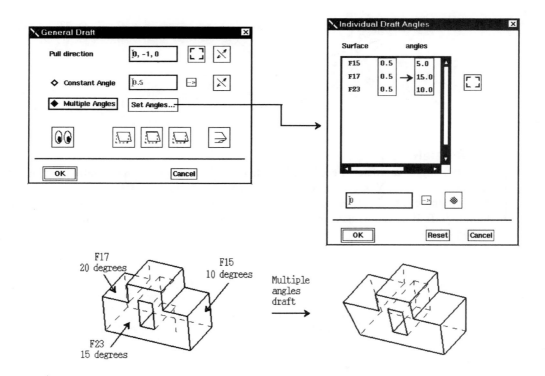

Figure 6.89

Change the angle parameters to their desired value, then select OK to return back to the General Draft menu. Click OK to complete the draft operation.

Mastering I-DEAS,
Scholars International Publishing Corp., 1999

# Project 6.
# Adding drafts to the part surfaces

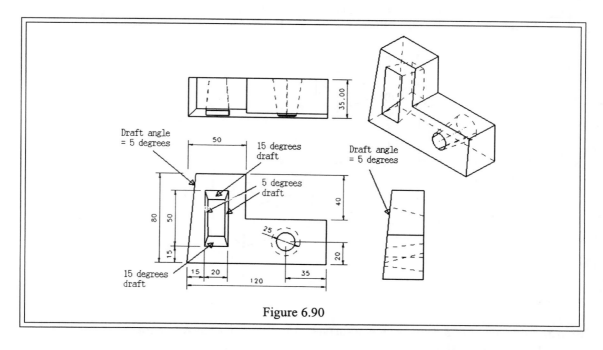

Figure 6.90

The base feature of the part consists of three elements; **step**, **slot**, and **hole**. Three sets of drafts are added to the base feature. The first set adds a 5-degree draft to the front face and left face. The second set adds drafts to four sides of the slot. The top face and bottom face of the slot have 15-degree drafts and the other two sides each have 5-degree draft. A multiple angle parameter is used to assign different draft angles to these four sides. The last set of draft is applied to the hole. Figure 6.90 shows the drawing views of the part.

### Step 1. Create three sections with two loops.
Create three sections with two loops
Constrain them with dimensions as shown in Figure 6.91

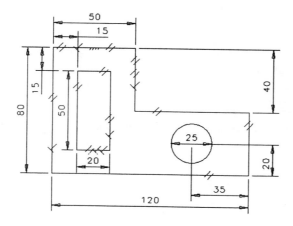

Figure 6.91

### Step 2. Extrude the three sections by 35-mm.

 Select **Extrude**, then pick three sections to extrude
Enter "35" into the Distance field in the Extrude Section menu
Select **OK** to produce the extrude feature as in Figure 6.92

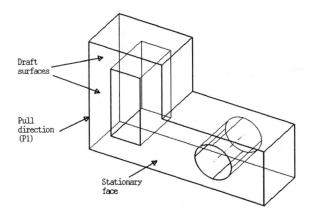

Figure 6.92

### Step 3. Add a taper of 5-degrees on two surfaces. Use Figure 6.92 as reference.

 Select the **Draft** icon
Pick the front vertical line **(P1)** as the direction of pull
Make sure the direction arrow is pointing upward, otherwise select No to change it
Select **Yes** to accept the pull direction
Pick the front vertical face and left vertical face as faces to draft
  (press the Shift key to continuously select the second face)
Pick the bottom face as the stationary face
Press the **Enter** key to the prompt "Pick parting edge or face"
Set the drafting parameters as below.

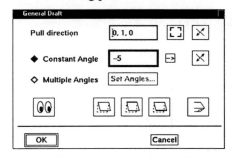

Select **OK** to make two draft surfaces as shown in Figure 6.93.

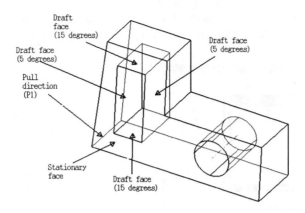

Figure 6.93

**Step 4. Add drafts with different angles to four surfaces. Use Figure 6.93 as reference.**

 Select the **Draft** icon

Pick the left bottom line (**P1**) as the pull direction

Make sure that the arrow is pointing toward the screen, then select **Yes** to accept it

Pick four faces around the slot features as shown in Figure 6.93 to draft

(press the Shift key to continuously pick the next faces)

Pick the front face as the stationary face

Press **Enter** to "Pick Parting Edge or Face" prompt

The initial draft menu should appear as below.

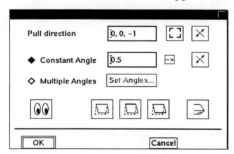

Click on the "**Multiple Angles**" button to toggle it to **On**

Select the "**Set Angles**" button to open the "Individual Draft Angles" menu as below

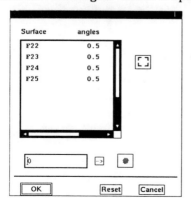

# Adding Construction Features

Change the angle values for the four surfaces as below.
(Click the surface row in the menu, enter the desired value at the prompt line located near the bottom of the menu, and click the **Change button** appearing as a green circle dot in the menu to change the draft angle value.)

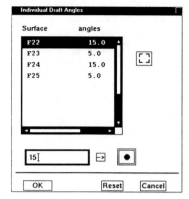

Select **OK** → **OK** to add four drafts as shown in Figure 6.94

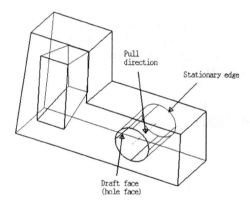

Figure 6.94

**Step 5. Add another draft to the hole feature. Use Figure 6.94 as reference.**

 Select the **Draft** icon
Pick the center line of the hole feature as the pull direction
(make sure the arrow points toward you)
Select **Yes** to accept the pull direction
Pick the hole surface as the face to draft
Pick the back circle of the hole as the stationary edge
Press "**Enter**" at the prompt "Pick Parting Edge or Face"
Set the drafting parameters as below.

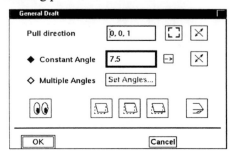

Mastering I-DEAS,
Scholars International Publishing Corp., 1999

# Adding Construction Features

Select **OK** to add the draft to the hole as shown in Figure 6.95

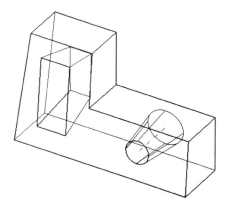

Figure 6.95

## Step 6. Name the part as "draft".

Select the **Name Parts** icon
Pick the part to name
Enter "**draft**" into the Name field in the name menu, then select **OK** to name it

## Step 7. Check the part into library.

Select the **Check In** icon
Pick the part to check in
Set the checking in parameters as below.

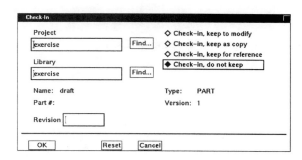

Select **OK** to check the part into library

# Chapter 6.  Review Questions

1. What are the main characteristics of construction features?

2. What are the four construction feature functions? Briefly describe each feature function.

3. List the two types of fillets.

4. Use drawings to illustrate the effect of the conic parameter on fillets.

5. List the valid fillet edge selection elements.

6. What are the three types of chamfers?

7. Describe the shell function.

8. Describe how to use the "Faces to remove" option to remove selected surfaces from the part.

9. Explain the purpose of using the individual thickness option.

10. Use drawings to illustrate the effect of the"offset direction" option on the shell.

11. Explain the function of the following drafting parameters:
    Pull direction
    Draft faces
    Stationary edges or faces
    Draft angle

12. Describe the purpose of using "Multiple Angles" option in creating drafts.

# Chapter

**7**

# Patterning Features

---

**Highlights of the Chapter**

- Patterns and pattern types
- Creating rectangular patterns
- Creating circular patterns

---

## Overview

Many part models consist of identical features that are arranged in an ordered fashion. The arrangement of identical features can be in the rectangular form or rotational form. I-DEAS uses the **Pattern function** to copy a feature to other locations in rectangular or circular fashion. The feature to be duplicated in the pattern is referred to as the **pattern leader** and the features produced by using the Pattern function are called **instances**. The pattern leader should be created as a separate part. The patterned instances are treated as a single element.

Selecting the patterning plane is a very important step in placing the patterned instances in the proper orientation. The planar surfaces on the lead feature can be chosen as the patterning plane. Cylindrical features have a limited number of planar surfaces to choose from. A reference plane needs to be created on the fly to help define the patterning orientation. This is especially true for creating circular patterns. This chapter presents essential concepts and techniques for creating various types and forms of feature patterns.

# 7.1  Pattern Types

The pattern concept is to duplicate a feature onto different locations appearing in a linear or circular array. The feature to be duplicated is referred to as the pattern leader and the duplicated features are called instances. Instances are not regarded as separate features (Figure 7.1). They are manipulated as a whole. For example, deleting an instance will result in removing all instances in the pattern.

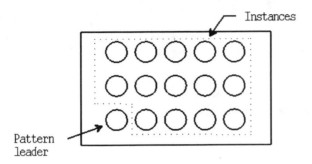

Figure 7.1

**The process of using patterns has these benefits:**

1. Creating a pattern is a quick and easy way to reproduce a feature.
2. It is easier and more effective to perform operations once on the patterned features, rather than on the individual features.
3. A pattern is parametrically controlled. It is rather easy to modify a pattern by changing pattern parameters, such as the number of instances, spacing between instances, and original feature dimensions.
4. Modifying patterns is more efficient than modifying individual features.

Two types of patterns in I-DEAS are rectangular patterns (Figure 7.2) and circular patterns (Figure 7.3). These two pattern types are presented in next two sections.

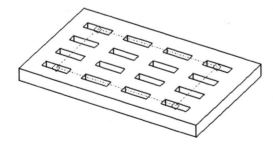

Figure 7.2 Rectangular patterns

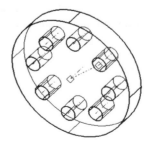

Figure 7.3 Circular patterns

Mastering I-DEAS,
Scholars International Publishing Corp., 1999

# 7.2 Rectangular Patterns

Instances can be placed in one or two directions in rectangular patterns. Patterns which are defined in only one direction are referred to as **unidirectional** patterns (Figure 7.4). A linear pattern is a typical example of a unidirectional pattern. Those patterns that have their instances defined in two directions are called **bidirectional** patterns (Figure 7.5).

The defining elements for creating a rectangular pattern include:

| | |
|---|---|
| · Pattern leader: | The part that makes a pattern. |
| · Patterning plane: | The plane on which the feature is duplicated to. |
| · Patterning parameters: | Specify the number of instances and their spacing in X and Y directions. |

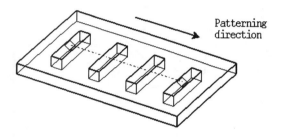

Figure 7.4 Unidirectional patterns

Figure 7.5 Bidirectional patterns

## Patterning Plane

The patterning plane controls the orientation and location of a patterned instance. The sketching plane of the lead feature is normally the plane used as the patterning plane for creating patterned features (Figure 7.6). Sometimes we need to use a different reference plane other than the existing plane of the pattern leader as the patterning plane (Figure 7.7). There are a variety of ways to define a reference plane in I-DEAS. Table 7.1 summarizes the **eight methods of defining a reference plane.**

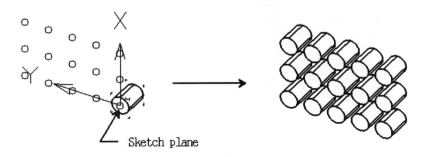

Figure 7.6

## Table 7.1   Methods of defining reference planes

| Method | Description | Illustration |
|--------|-------------|--------------|
| Key In | Defines a reference plane by entering the four plane coefficients for X, Y, Z, and offset. | (0, 0, 1, 40)   (1, 0, 0, 40) |
| Three Point | Defines a reference plane by using three existing points. | |
| Point Normal | Defines a reference plane by using a line element as the vector normal and a point to contain the plane. | Thru point   Line vector |
| Offset Surface | Defines a reference plane by being parallel to an existing plane and offset by a given distance. | Offset surface   Reference plane |

Mastering I-DEAS,
Scholars International Publishing Corp., 1999

Table 7.1 continued

| Method | Description | Illustration |
|--------|-------------|--------------|
| Axis Planes | Uses one of the existing principal planes as the reference plane. The three principal planes are XY-plane, YZ-plane, and ZX-plane. Their negative counterparts are also available. The new reference plane can be offset from the selected principal plane. | |
| Curve Normal | Defines a reference plane using a selected point on an existing curve and normal to the existing sketch plane. | |
| Surface Tangent | Defines a reference plane as tangent to a surface at a selected point. | |
| Angled Surface | Defines a reference plane using an existing planar surface a rotation axis, and an angle value. | |

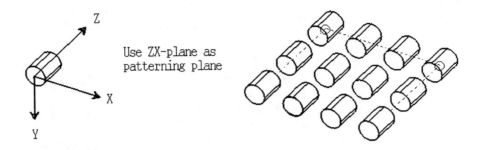

Figure 7.7

There are three basic pattern orientations: **front view, top-view,** and **right-side view** (Figure 7.8)

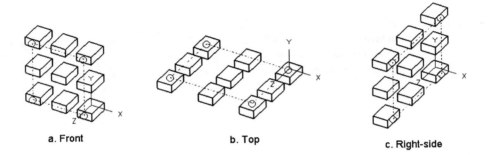

a. Front          b. Top          c. Right-side

Figure 7.8

After selecting the part as the lead feature, the system will prompt "Pick patterning plane". Pick a face on the lead feature. The system will show a reference coordinate system (Figure 7.9) with the Rectangular Pattern menu.

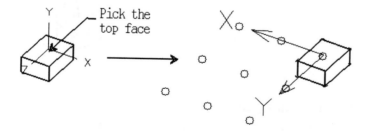

Figure 7.9

Mastering I-DEAS,
Scholars International Publishing Corp., 1999

# Patterning parameters

After selecting the patterning plane, the system will prompt with the Rectangular Pattern menu as shown here.

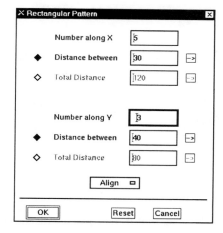

**The patterning parameters include (Figure 7.10):**

| | |
|---|---|
| **Number along X:** | Number of instances to create in the X direction. |
| **Distance between (X):** | Incremental (spacing) dimension in the X direction. |
| **Total Distance (X):** | Total distance between the pattern leader and last instance in the X direction. |
| **Number along Y:** | Number of instances to create in the Y direction. |
| **Distance between (Y):** | Incremental (spacing) dimension in the Y direction. |
| **Total Distance (Y):** | Total distance between the pattern leader and last instance in the Y direction. |

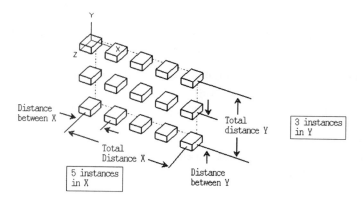

Figure 7.10

The number of instances to create in a direction must include the exiting feature (pattern leader). The total number of instances in the pattern is the product of the instance number along X and instance number along Y. A total of 15 instances will be created when the instance number along X = 5 and the instance number along Y = 3.

There are two ways to specify the spacing between instances; **incremental distance** and **total distance**. In incremental distance mode, the "Distance between" parameter assigns the spacing distance between two instances (Figure 7.11). In total distance mode, the "Total Distance" parameter specifies the distance between the lead feature and the last instance in the specified direction (Figure 7.12). The system automatically calculates the spacing distance based on the number of instances in the direction and the total distance value.

# Patterning Features

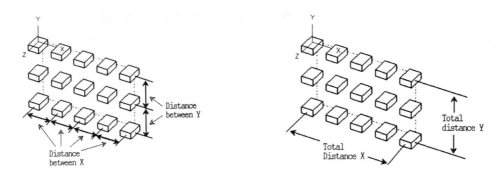

Figure 7.11                                    Figure 7.12

It is possible to specify a set of different spacing distances to the "Distance between" parameters. Figure 7.13 shows a rectangular pattern with a set of spacing distances given in the X direction. Its pattern parameters appear as shown here.

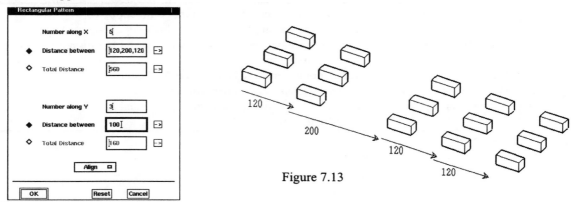

Figure 7.13

**The procedure for creating a rectangular pattern is (Figure 7.14):**

1. Create a pattern leader to be patterned
2. Select the Rectangular Pattern command icon
3. Pick the leader feature
4. Select the patterning plane
5. Defining the rectangular pattern parameters
6. Select OK to complete the patterning

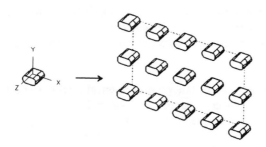

Figure 7.14

Mastering I-DEAS,
Scholars International Publishing Corp., 1999

# Deleting a Pattern

**Follow these steps to delete a pattern from the model (Figure 7.15):**

1. Click the "History Tree" icon
2. Pick an instance of the pattern
3. The History Access menu appears
4. Click the leaf "RectPatinfo9" to
   select the rectangular pattern
5. Click the Delete icon in the
   History Access menu
6. Select Yes → Yes from the options menu
7. Select Dismiss to exit the menu
8. The rectangular pattern is removed
   from the model.

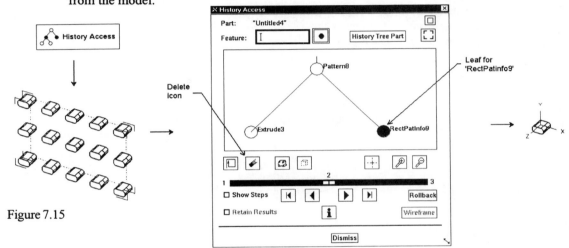

Figure 7.15

# Aligning a Pattern to the Part

Normally the pattern leader for creating a pattern is created as a new part. After a pattern is created, we need to use Boolean operation functions to join the pattern to the part. Aligning a pattern to the part is somewhat confusing because it requires you to use the Relations function, which is not easy to find in the menu. The example below (Figure 7.16) shows (1) how to join a pattern to the part and (2) how to align the pattern to the part. A rectangular block feature and a rectangular pattern are created as separate parts. Follow the procedure below to join two features at the desired locations:

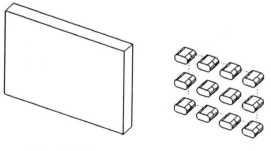

Figure 7.16          Rectangular block          Rectangular pattern

# Patterning Features

**Use this Procedure to join two features:**

1. Select the "Cut" command icon
2. Press the right mouse button to open the Options menu
3. Select "Turn Relations On" from the Options menu
4. Pick the front planar surface of any instance on the pattern
5. Pick the front planar surface of the rectangular block
6. Select "From Edges" from the Options menu
7. Pick the front left corner point in the front face of the rectangular block
8. Pick the left vertical line of the rectangular box in the pattern as the first edge of the movable part
9. Enter distance from first edge: 40
10. Pick the bottom horizontal line of the rectangular box in the pattern as the second edge of movable part
11. Enter distance from the second edge: 40
12. Select Done from the Options menu
13. The final part appears as Figure 7.17.

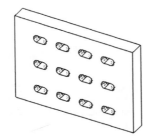

Figure 7.17

14. Select "Cut" command icon again
15. Press the right mouse button to open the Options menu
16. Select "Turn Relations Off" from the options list

Mastering I-DEAS,
Scholars International Publishing Corp., 1999

# Project 1.
# Creating the Engine Cap Part

The engine cap consists of five features including a rectangular base feature, five blind holes, ten through holes, ten counterbore holes, and fillets at four sides (Figure 7.18). We use the rectangular pattern function to create ten through holes. A single hole is created first. It is then copied to nine locations using the rectangular pattern function. The distances between patterning instances in the X direction are not evenly spaced, so we need to specify individual distance values for instances. The ten counterbore holes are created concentric to the ten through holes. Check the part into the library using the name "engine-cap".

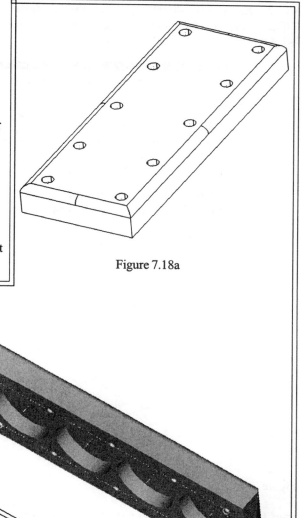

Figure 7.18a

Figure 7.18b

Figure 7.18c

## Step 1. Sketch a rectangle.

Select the **Rectangle by 2 Corners** icon, then create a rectangle
Modify its two dimensions to their correct value as shown in Figure 7.19

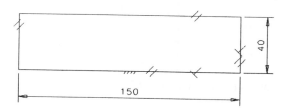

Figure 7.19

# Patterning Features

**Step 2. Extrude the sketch to produce the base feature.**

Select the **Extrude** icon, then pick the rectangle to extrude
Set extrude parameters as below.

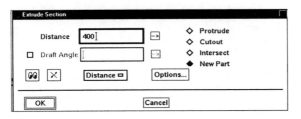

Select **OK** to complete the feature
Select the **Isometric View** icon to show the model as in Figure 7.20.

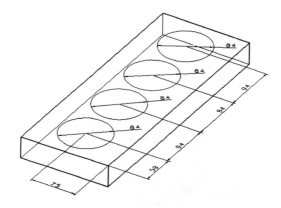

Figure 7.20

**Step 3. Create four circles on the top surface. Use Figure 7.20 as reference.**

Select the **Sketch in place** icon and pick the top surface as the sketching plane
Create four circles as shown in Figure 7.20
Add and modify dimensions to their correct values as shown

**Step 4. Extrude-cut four circles to produce four holes.**

Select the **Extrude** icon and select the four circles to extrude
Set the extrude parameters as below.

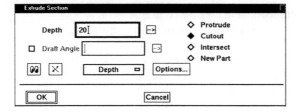

Select **OK** to add extrude-cut features as in Figure 7.21

Mastering I-DEAS,
Scholars International Publishing Corp., 1999

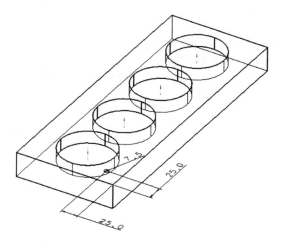

Figure 7.21

**Step 5. Create a cylinder. Use Figure 7.21 as reference.**

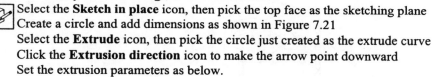 Select the **Sketch in place** icon, then pick the top face as the sketching plane
Create a circle and add dimensions as shown in Figure 7.21
Select the **Extrude** icon, then pick the circle just created as the extrude curve
Click the **Extrusion direction** icon to make the arrow point downward
Set the extrusion parameters as below.

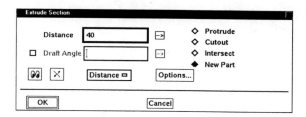

Select **OK** to create the cylindrical feature as in Figure 7.22.

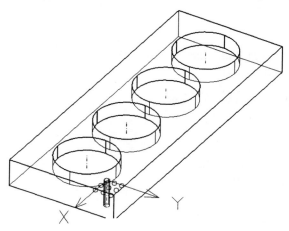

Figure 7.22

# Patterning Features

**Step 6.**  **Copy the cylindrical feature to nine locations using rectangular pattern.**

 Select the **Rectangular Pattern** icon
Pick the cylindrical feature as the part to make into a pattern
Pick the top face of the cylinder (**F1**) as the patterning plane
The initial patterning layout should resemble Figure 7.22.

Set rectangular patterning parameters as here.
(Distance between inputs should be –81,-94,-94,-81)

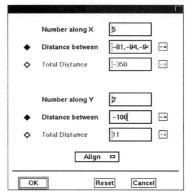

Select **OK** to add nine cylinders as in Figure 7.23.

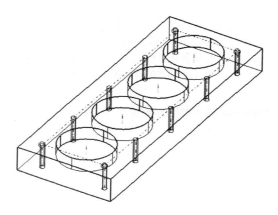

Figure 7.23

**Step 7.**  **Cut the cylinder pattern from the base.**

 Select the **Cut** icon
Click the right mouse button,
  make sure the relation option is toggled to **"Turn Relation OFF"**
Pick the **cylinder pattern** as the cutter part
Pick the **base part** as the part to cut
The two features are combined into one to make cylinders into holes
(The new drawing still looks like Figure 7.23.)

**Step 8.**  **Rotate the part 180 degrees about Z axis.**

Select the **Rotate** icon, then pick the part to rotate
Pick the left front corner as the pivot point to rotate
Select **About Z** from the list
Enter angle about Z:   **180**
The new drawing becomes Figure 7.24.

Mastering I-DEAS,
Scholars International Publishing Corp., 1999

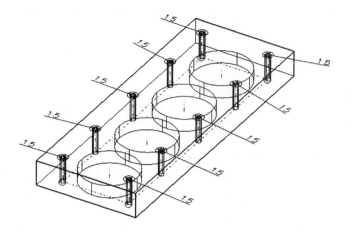

Figure 7.24

**Step 9.    Create ten circles being concentric to existing holes. Use Figure 7.24 as reference.**

 Select the **Sketch in place** icon, then pick the top face as the sketching plane
Create ten circles and modify their diameters to 15 as shown in Figure 7.24

**Step 10. Extrude-cut ten circles.**

Select the **Extrude** icon, then pick the ten circles just created
Set the extrusion parameters as below.

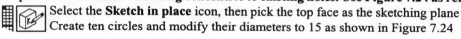

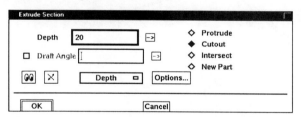

Select **OK** to produce ten counterbore holes as in Figure 7.25

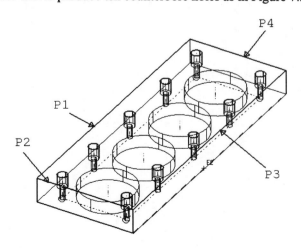

Figure 7.25

**Step 11. Add fillets to four edges of the top surface. Use Figure 7.25 as reference.**

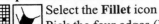 Select the **Fillet** icon

Pick the four edges (**P1 – P4**) of the top surface as edges to fillet (Press Shift key)

Enter radius for selected edges: **10**

The fillets are added as in Figure 7.26.

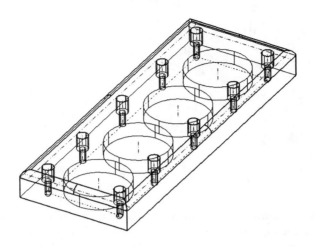

Figure 7.26

Figures 7.27, 7.28 and 7.29 show the model in different modes.

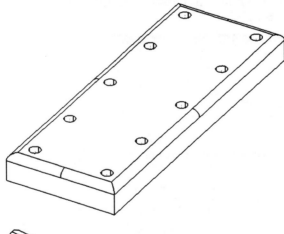

Figure 7.27

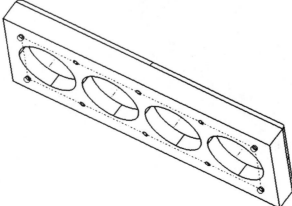

Figure 7.28

Mastering I-DEAS,
Scholars International Publishing Corp., 1999

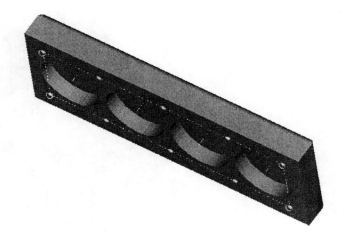

Figure 7.29

**Step 12. Check the part into the library.**
 Select the **Check In** icon, then pick the part to check in
Enter "**engine-cap**" into the Name field in the Name menu
Set the check-in parameters as below.

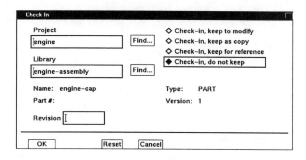

Select **OK** to check the part into library

# Project 2.
# Creating an Engine Base Part

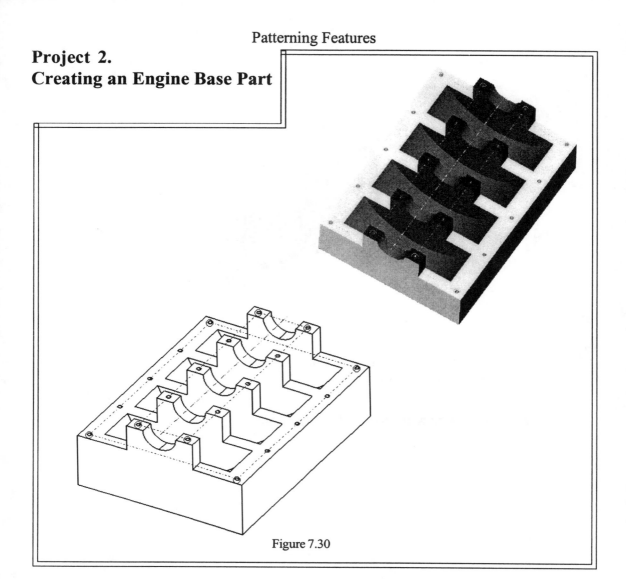

Figure 7.30

The engine base part consists of a base feature, a revolve-cut feature for forming the cavity of the crankshaft, and two sets of rectangular patterns for bolt holes.

**Step 1.   Create a section. Use Figure 7.31 as reference.**

Select **Polylines** to create an 8-line section as shown in Figure 7.31
Add necessary dimensions and modify them to their correct values as shown

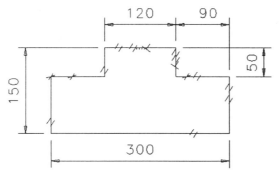

Figure 7.31

Mastering I-DEAS,
Scholars International Publishing Corp., 1999

**Step 2.   Extrude the section to form the base feature.**

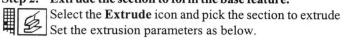 Select the **Extrude** icon and pick the section to extrude
Set the extrusion parameters as below.

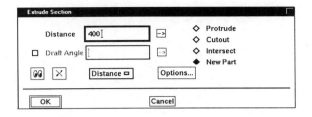

Select **OK** to complete the extruded feature
Select the **Isometric View** icon to show the feature as in Figure 7.32

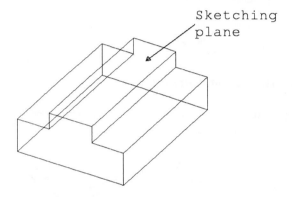

Figure 7.32

**Step 3.   Create a multiple-line section. Use Figure 7.33 as reference.**

Select the **Sketch in place** icon,
 then pick the top-most face as the sketching plane (Figure 7.32)
Select the **Top (XZ) View** icon to show the model (Figure 7.33)

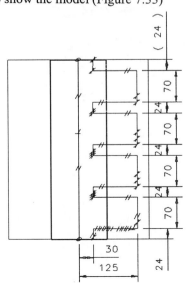

Figure 7.33a

# Patterning Features

Select the **Polylines** icon, then create a section as shown in Figure 7.33b
Add necessary dimensions and modify them to correct values as shown

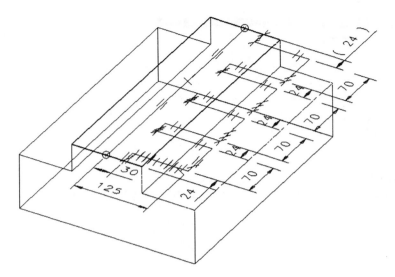

Figure 7.33b

**Step 4.  Revolve-cut the section for forming crankshaft cavity.**

 Select the **Revolve** icon
Sequentially and carefully pick the entities to form the section as shown in Figure 7.34

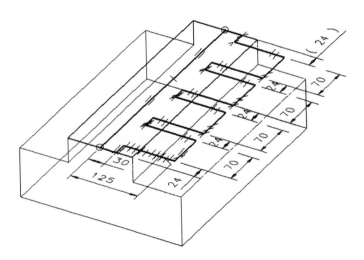

Figure 7.34a

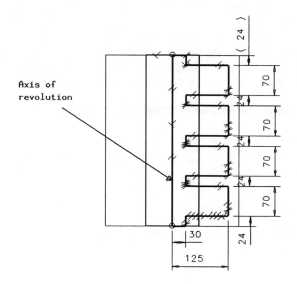

Figure 7.34b

Pick the **center line** as the axis of revolution
Set the revolving parameters as below.

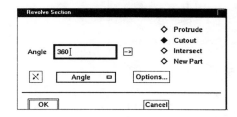

Select **OK** to cut the crankshaft cavity as in Figure 7.35

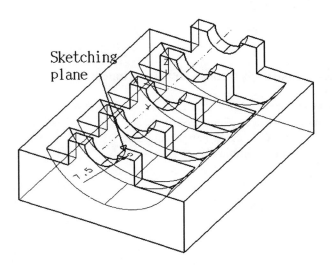

Figure 7.35

Mastering I-DEAS,
Scholars International Publishing Corp., 1999

# Patterning Features

**Step 5.** **Create a cylinder on the top surface. Use Figure 7.35 as reference.**

 Select the **Sketch in place** icon,
 then pick the top surface as sketching plane (Figure 7.35)

 Create a circle at the center of the surface and modify its diameter to **7.5**

Select the **Extrude** icon and select the circle just created as the entity to extrude
Set the extrusion parameters as below (direction arrow must point downward).

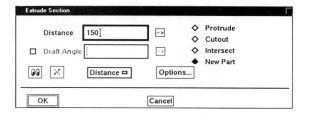

Select **OK** to complete the cylinder as shown in Figure 7.36

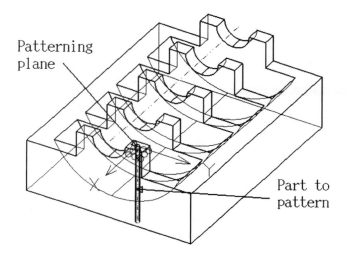

Patterning plane

Part to pattern

Figure 7.36

**Step 6.** **Copy the cylinder to nine locations using rectangular pattern function.**

 Use Figure 7.36 as reference.
Select the **Rectangular Pattern** icon
Select the cylinder as the entity to pattern (Figure 7.36)
Pick the top surface of the cylinder (**F1**) as the patterning plane
The initial patterning layout should resemble Figure 7.36

Mastering I-DEAS,
Scholars International Publishing Corp., 1999

# Patterning Features

Set patterning parameters as here.

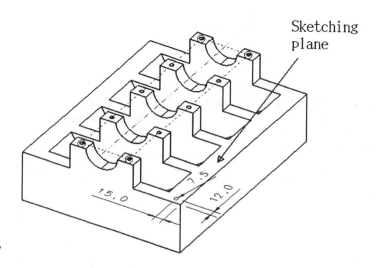

Select **OK** to copy the cylinder
The new drawing becomes Figure 7.37.

Sketching
plane

Figure 7.37

**Step 7. Cut the cylinder pattern from the part to form bolt holes.**

 Select the **Cut** icon
Pick the **cylinder pattern** as the cutter part
Pick the **main part** as the part to cut
The bolt holes are created as in Figure 7.37.

**Step 8. Create another cylinder feature on the step surface. Use Figure 7.37 as reference.**

 Select the **Sketch in place** icon,
   then pick the step surface as sketching plane (Figure 7.37)

Create a circle and add dimensions as shown
Select the **Extrude** icon and pick the circle just created as the entity to extrude
Set the extrusion parameters as below (direction arrow must point downward).

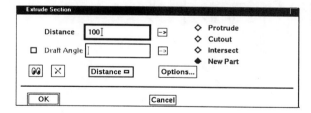

# Patterning Features

Select **OK** to add the cylinder feature as in Figure 7.38

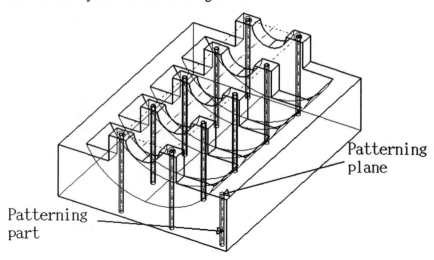

Figure 7.38

**Step 9.** **Copy the cylinder feature to nine locations using rectangular pattern function.**

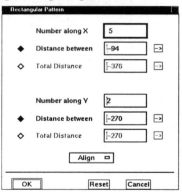

Use Figure 7.38 as reference.
Select the **Rectangular Pattern** function
Select the **cylinder feature** just created
  as the patterning part
Pick the **top surface** of the cylinder
  as the patterning plane
Set the patterning parameters as below.

| Rectangular Pattern | | |
|---|---|---|
| Number along X | 5 | |
| ◆ Distance between | -94 | ⇨ |
| ◇ Total Distance | -376 | ⇨ |
| Number along Y | 2 | |
| ◆ Distance between | -270 | ⇨ |
| ◇ Total Distance | -270 | ⇨ |
| Align ▫ | | |
| OK | Reset | Cancel |

Select **OK** to copy the cylinder to nine locations as in Figure 7.39

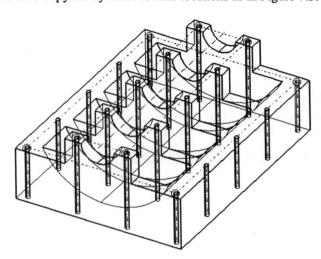

Figure 7.39

7-24

**Step 10. Cut the cylinder pattern from the part to form bolt holes.**

 Select the **Cut** icon

Pick the **cylinder pattern** just created as the cutter part

Pick the **main part** as the part to cut

Figures 7.40 and 7.41 show various modes and configurations of the complete model

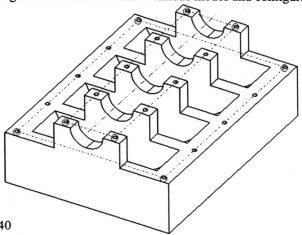

Figure 7.40

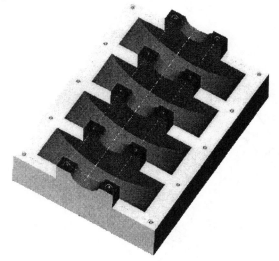

Figure 7.41

**Step 11. Check the part into library**

 Select the **Check In** icon

Pick the part to check in

Enter **"engine-base"** into the Name field in the Name menu

Set the check-in parameters as below.

| Check-In | | |
|---|---|---|
| **Project** | | ◇ Check-in, keep to modify |
| engine | Find... | ◇ Check-in, keep as copy |
| | | ◇ Check-in, keep for reference |
| **Library** | | ◆ Check-in, do not keep |
| engine-assembly | Find... | |
| Name: engine-base | | Type: PART |
| Part #: | | Version: 1 |
| Revision [ | | |
| OK | Reset | Cancel |

Select **OK** to check the part into the library

# Project 3.
# Creating the engine body part

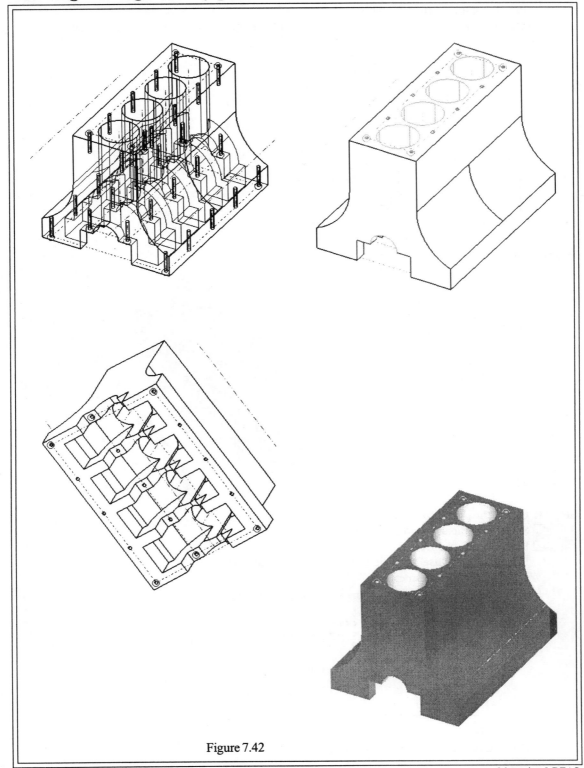

Figure 7.42

Mastering I-DEAS,
Scholars International Publishing Corp., 1999

# Patterning Features

The engine body part is used to house pistons, connecting rods, bushes, and a crankshaft. It consists of an extrude base feature as the main body, an extrude-cut feature and a revolve-cut feature for forming the cavity, four cylinder holes, and three sets of hole patterns (Figure 7.42). The cavity features are produced first from extruding a multiple-line section. The half section is created first and reflected to form the complete section for extrusion. The step-plane is used as the sketching plane for creating the section for a revolve-cut feature. This section also consists of multiple lines with the left edge located at the center line of the part. Two rectangular patterns are used to copy two cylinders to nine locations. The two cylinders used as the patterning part must be created as a new part. After patterning, the pattern features use the cutter part to cut from the part to form the holes. The big cylinder holes are added on the top of the part. Finally, the ten bolt holes are created on the top surface of the part by copying a small cylinder to nine locations using the rectangular pattern function.

    **The Procedure steps are:**

1. Extrude a section to form the base feature of the part.
2. Rotate the part 180 degrees about the Z axis to make the orientation of the part downward.
3. Extrude-cut a section to form the cavity of the crankshaft housing.
4. Revolve-cut a section to further define the cavity of the crankshaft housing.
5. Create an extruded cylinder and copy it to nine locations using the rectangular pattern function.
6. Use the Cut function to produce ten bolt holes from the first rectangular pattern features.
7. Create another extruded cylinder and copy it to other nine locations using the rectangular pattern function.
8. Use the Cut function to produce ten bolt holes from the second rectangular pattern features.
9. Rotate the part 180 degrees about the Z axis to make the orientation of the part upward.
10. Create four extrude-cut holes for the cylinder housing.
11. Create an extruded cylinder and copy it to nine locations using the rectangular pattern function.
12. Use the Cut function to produce ten bolt holes from the third rectangular pattern features.
13. Check the part into the library using the name "engine-body".

**Step 1.  Create a section for the base feature. Use Figure 7.43 as reference.**

  Use **Polylines** and **Three Points On** commands to create a section as shown in Figure 7.43
Use **Constraint-Tangent** to make two arcs tangent with their upper join line
Add dimensions and modify them to their correct values as shown

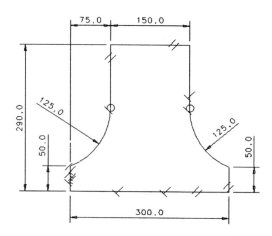

Figure 7.43

# Patterning Features

## Step 2. Extrude the section to produce the base feature.

 Select the **Extrude** icon, then pick the section to extrude
Set the extrusion parameters as below.

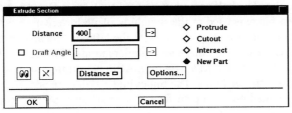

**Extrude Section**

| Distance | 400 | ⊡ | ◇ Protrude |
| Draft Angle | | ⊡ | ◇ Cutout |
| | | | ◇ Intersect |
| | | | ◆ New Part |

[ OK ]   [ Cancel ]

Select **OK** to create the feature
Select the **Isometric View** icon to show the feature as in Figure 7.44

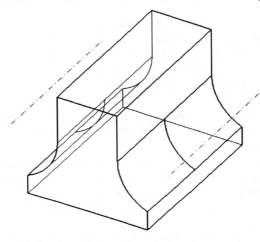

Figure 7.44

## Step 3. Rotate the part about Z axis by 180 degrees.

Select the **Rotate** icon, then pick the part to rotate
Pick the **lower left-front corner** as the pivot point
Select **About Z** from the list
Enter angle about Z: **180**
The new drawing becomes Figure 7.45.

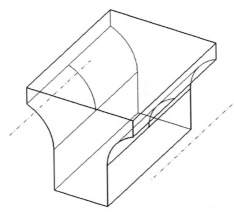

Figure 7.45

## Step 4. Create a section for extrusion. Use Figure 7.46 as reference.

Select the **Sketch in place** icon, then pick the top surface as the sketching plane

# Patterning Features

Select the **Top View** icon to display the part as in Figure 7.46

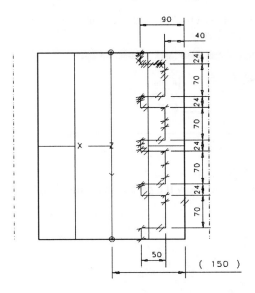

Figure 7.46

Use the **Polylines** command to create a section and a line as shown in Figure 7.46
Add and modify dimensions to their correct values as shown

**Step 5. Mirror the section about the center line.**

Select the **Reflect** icon,
then pick the section (press the Shift key to continue picking the entities) to reflect
Click the right mouse button, then select **On Curve** from the list
Pick the **bottom horizontal line** as the curve
Click the right mouse button, then select **Key In** from the list
Enter percent along curve: **50**
Select **Keep Both** from the list
The section is mirrored to the other side as shown in Figure 7.47.

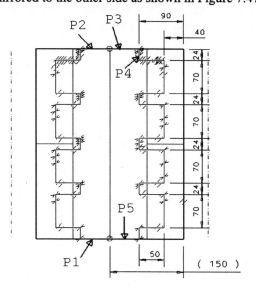

Figure 7.47

### Step 6. Extrude-cut the section. Use Figure 7.47 as reference.

 Select the **Extrude** icon

Pick the entities (**P1 – P5**) as shown to define the section to extrude

Set the extrusion parameters as below.

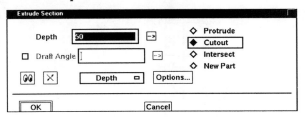

 Select **OK** to extrude-cut the section

Select the **Isometric View** icon to show the part as in Figure 7.48.

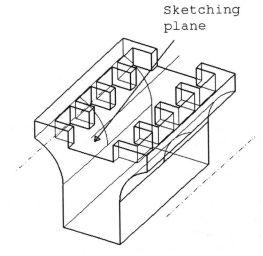

Sketching plane

Figure 7.48

### Step 7. Create a section for revolving. Use Figure 7.48 as reference.

Select the **Sketch in place** icon,

then pick the step surface as sketching plane as shown in Figure 7.48

Select the **Top (XZ) View** icon to display the model as in Figure 7.49

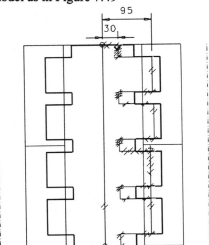

Figure 7.49

Create a section as shown in Figure 7.49

7-30

## Step 8. Revolve-cut the section.

Sequentially pick the entities to form a closed section as shown in Figure 7.50

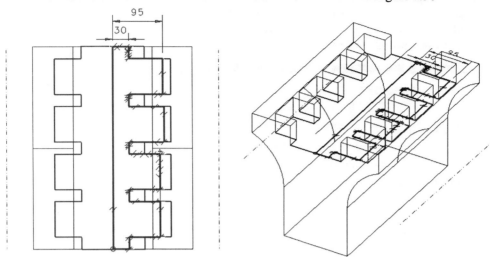

Figure 7.50

Select the **center line** (on the sketch plane) as the axis to rotate about
Set the revolving parameters as below.

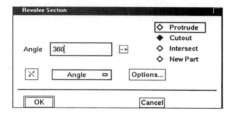

Select **OK** to revolve-cut the section
The new part shown in isometric view should look like Figure 7.51.

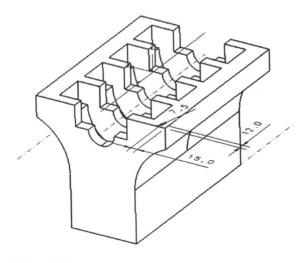

Figure 7.51a

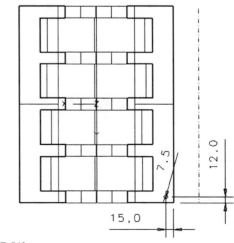

Figure 7.51b

# Patterning Features

**Step 9.** **Add a cylinder feature. Use Figure 7.51 as reference.**

Select the **top surface** as the sketching plane then create a circle as shown in Figure 7.51
Add two dimensions and modify them to correct values as shown
Extrude the circle using the following extrusion parameters.
(The extrusion arrow must point downward.)

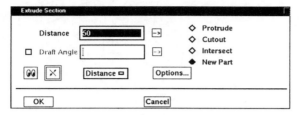

Select **OK** to create the feature as in Figure 7.52

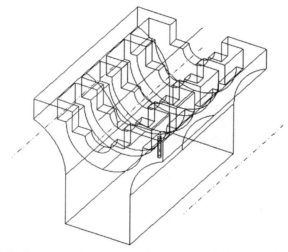

Figure 7.52

**Step 10. Copy the cylinder to nine locations using rectangular pattern function.**

 Select the **Rectangular Pattern** icon,
then pick the cylinder just created as the part to be the pattern
Select the top surface of the cylinder (**F1**) as the patterning plane
The initial patterning layout should resemble Figure 7.53.

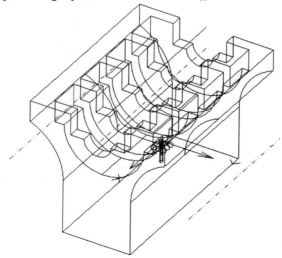

Figure 7.53

7-32

# Patterning Features

Set the patterning parameters as below.

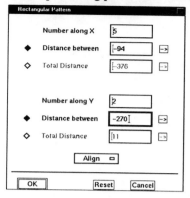

Select **OK** to copy the cylinder to nine locations as shown in Figure 7.54

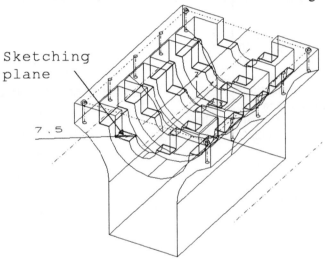

Sketching
plane

7.5

Figure 7.54

**Step 11.  Cut the cylinders from the part.**

 Select the **Cut** icon
Pick the **cylinder pattern** as the cutter part
Pick the **main part** as the part to cut
The two parts are joined as one and cylinders have become holes,
  you can see the hole features from the shaded display mode.

**Step 12.  Create a cylinder feature. Use Figure 7.54 as reference.**

 Select the **Sketch in place** icon, then select the step face as the sketching plane
Create a circle and add dimensions as shown in Figure 7.54.
 The circle center must be located at the center of selected step face.
Select the **Extrude** icon, then pick the circle as the entity to extrude

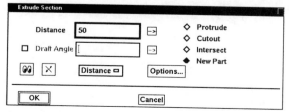

# Patterning Features

Select **OK** to create a cylinder as a separate part as in Figure 7.55.

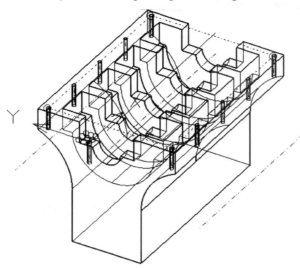

Figure 7.55

**Step 13. Copy the cylinder to nine locations.**

Select the **Rectangular Pattern** icon, pick
the cylinder just created as the part to pattern
Pick the top face (**F1**) on the cylinder
as the patterning plane
The initial patterning layout appears
as in Figure 7.55.
Set the patterning parameters as here.

| Rectangular Pattern | | |
|---|---|---|
| Number along X | 5 | |
| ◆ Distance between | 94 | ⊡ |
| ◇ Total Distance | 376 | ⊡ |
| Number along Y | 2 | |
| ◆ Distance between | -90 | ⊡ |
| ◇ Total Distance | 11 | ⊡ |
| Align ▭ | | |
| OK | Reset | Cancel |

Select **OK** to copy the cylinder to nine locations as in Figure 7.56

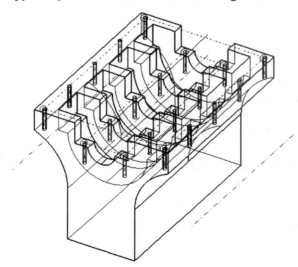

Figure 7.56

Mastering I-DEAS,
Scholars International Publishing Corp., 1999

## Patterning Features

**Step 14. Cut the cylinder pattern from the part.**

 Select the **Cut** icon
Pick the **cylinder pattern** just created as the cutter part
Pick the **main model** as the part to cut from

**Step 15. Rotate the part 180 degrees about Z axis.**

 Select the **Rotate** icon, then pick any element on the part to select the entire part
Pick the **lower front-right corner** as the pivot point
Select **About Z** from the list
Enter angle about Z: **180**
The new orientation of the part appears as in Figure 7.57.

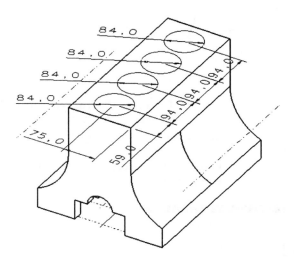

Figure 7.57

**Step 16. Create four circles on the top surface. Use Figure 7.57 as reference.**

 Select the **Sketch in place** icon, then pick the top surface as the sketching plane
Create four circles and modify their dimensions as shown in Figure 7.57

 Select the **Extrude** icon, then pick these four circles as entities to extrude
Set the extrusion parameters as below.

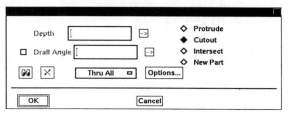

Select **OK** to complete the extrusion cut

# Patterning Features

The four holes are added as in Figure 7.58.

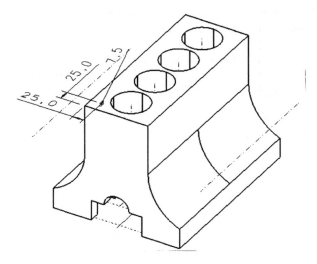

Figure 7.58

**Step 17. Create a cylinder feature on the top surface. Use Figure 7.58 as reference.**

 Select the **Sketch in place** icon, then pick the top face as the sketching plane
Create a circle, add two dimensions, and modify them to their correct values
as shown in Figure 7.58
Select the **Extrude** icon, then pick the circle just created as the entity to extrude
Set the extrusion parameters as below (direction arrow must point downward).

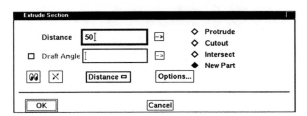

Select **OK** to complete the cylinder feature as in Figure 7.59 (shown in Line mode)

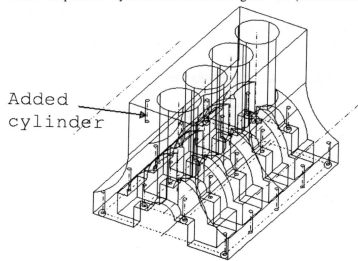

Added
cylinder

Figure 7.59

Mastering I-DEAS,
Scholars International Publishing Corp., 1999

# Patterning Features

## Step 18. Copy the cylinder feature to nine locations using rectangular pattern.

 Select the **Rectangular Pattern** icon, then pick the cylinder just created as the part to pattern
Pick the top face of the cylinder (**F1**) as the patterning plane
Set the patterning parameters as below. (Distance between in X must be −81,−94,−94,−81.)

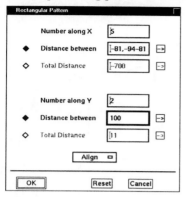

Select **OK** to complete the rectangular pattern as in Figure 7.60

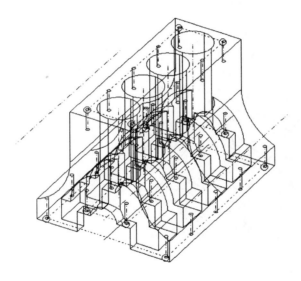

Figure 7.60

## Step 19. Cut the cylinder pattern from the part.

 Select the **Cut** icon
Pick the **cylinder pattern** as the cutter part
Pick the **main part** as the part to cut
Delete a redundant line at the bottom

# Patterning Features

Figures 7.61, 7.62 and 7.63 show various modes and orientations of the complete part model.

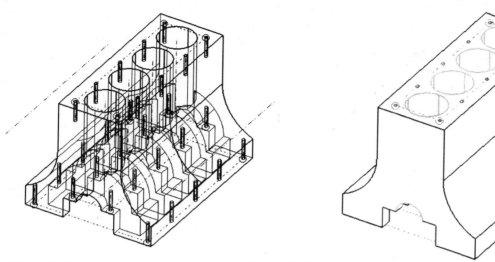

Figure 7.61                                    Figure 7.62

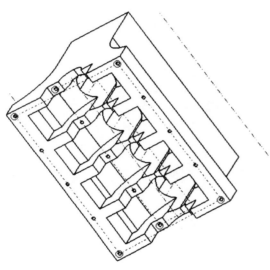

Figure 7.63

**Step 20. Check the part into library.**

 Select the **Check In** icon
Pick the part to check in
Enter "**engine-body**" into the Name field of the Name menu
Set the check-in parameters as below.

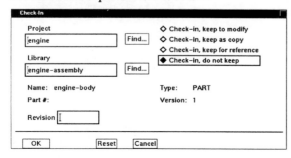

Select **OK** to check the part into library

Mastering I-DEAS,
Scholars International Publishing Corp., 1999

# 7.3 Circular Patterns

A circular pattern is created by duplicating a pattern leader onto a specified number of locations around a circle. There are two types of circular patterns; **rotate pattern** and **translate pattern**. A rotating pattern rotates the lead feature about the center of the circle (Figure 7.64). In other words, the feature orientation of duplicated instances changes with the location. In a translate pattern, the instances are produced along the circumference of a circle, but their feature orientation remains the same as the lead feature (Figure 7.65).

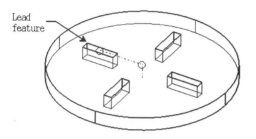

Figure 7.64          Figure 7.65

The circular pattern parameters menu is shown here. The five main parameters for defining a circular pattern are (Figure 7.66):

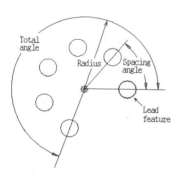

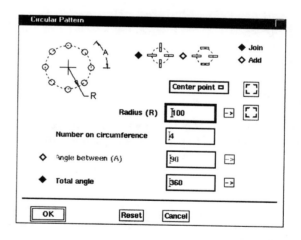

Figure 7.66

**Feature orientation:** controls the orientation of instances in the pattern.
**Radius of reference circle:** specifies the radius of reference circle on which the instances located.
**Number of instances:** indicates the number of instances to be created.
**Spacing angle:** specifies the spacing angle between two instances.
**Total angle:** specifies the total angle span from the lead feature to last instance.

# Selecting Patterning Plane

The selection of patterning plane dramatically affects
the orientation of the patterns. A rectangular block is
used as the pattern leader to create a circular pattern.
Figure 7.67 shows the pattern orientation when the top
surface is selected as the patterning plane. The pattern
is located on the top view. When the right side surface
is selected as the patterning plane, the pattern orientation
is in the right side view (Figure 7.68). Figure 7.69 shows
the pattern orientation for the patterning plane is selected
at the front vertical surface.

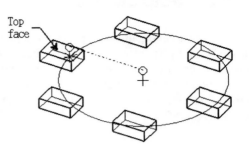

Figure 7.67

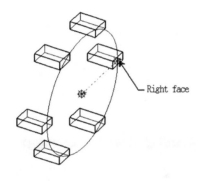

Figure 7.68

Figure 7.69

Cylindrical features only have two planar surfaces for you to choose as the patterning plane. The
orientation is limited to one direction (Figure 7.70).

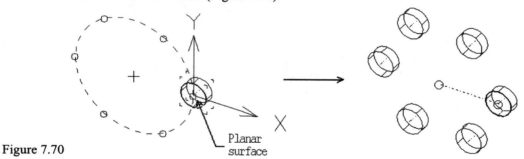

Figure 7.70

We need to take an extra step to define a plane to serve as the patterning plane if the existing planar
surfaces are **not** used.

 **Follow these steps to define a patterning plane.**

After selecting the lead feature to be patterned:

1. Click the right mouse button to open the options menu

Mastering I-DEAS,
Scholars International Publishing Corp., 1999

# Patterning Features

2. Select Axis Planes from the list
3. Select ZX Plane from the plane list
4. Enter distance (0.0) = 0
5. Pick the part to associate this plane to
6. Pick the coordinate system origin as the center point of the circular pattern (Figure 7.71a)

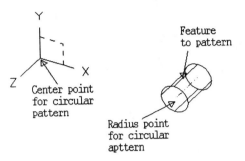

Figure 7.71a

7. Pick the center of the front face of the part as the radius point
8. Set the circular pattern parameters as below:

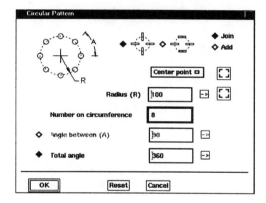

9. Select OK.

The circular pattern is shown in Figure 7.71b.

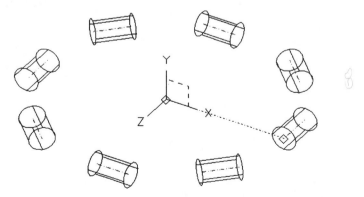

Figure 7.71b

## Patterning Features

Figures 7.72 and 7.73 show the circular pattern results of using the XY plane and YZ plane, respectively.

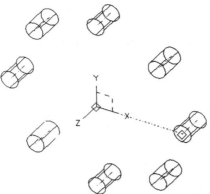

Figure 7.72

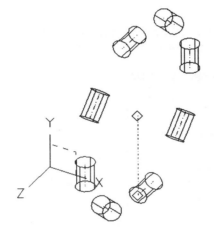

Figure 7.73

# Creating a Circular Pattern in Radial Orientation

Applications of hole patterns around the circumference of cylinders are found very often in mechanical parts (Figure 7.74).

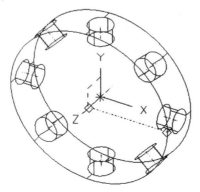

Figure 7.74a

Mastering I-DEAS,
Scholars International Publishing Corp., 1999

# Patterning Features

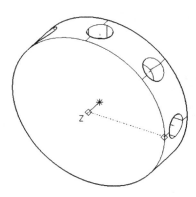

Figure 7.74b

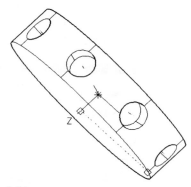

Figure 7.74c

 **The procedure for creating a circular pattern in Radial orientation is:**

 1. Create a coordinate system

> Select the coordinate systems icon.
> Pick the active work plane to reference
> Select Done to complete the coordinate system in Figure 7.75

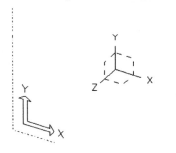

Figure 7.75

2. Create a circle on the XY plane.

> Select the Sketch in place icon
> Pick the XY-plane as the sketch plane
> Select the Center-Edge icon
> Press RMB, then select Focus from the list
> Pick the origin as the entity to focus
> Pick the origin as the center and another point to create a circle
> Modify its diameter to 100
> The circle is shown in Figure 7.76

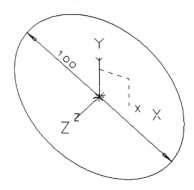

Figure 7.76

# Patterning Features

3. Extrude the circle in two directions by a total distance of 25.

 Select the Extrude icon, then pick the circle to extrude

Set the extrude parameters as below:

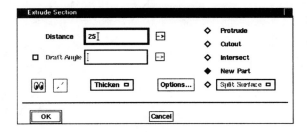

Select OK

The Extrude feature is created as in Figure 7.77.

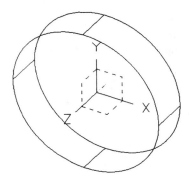

Figure 7.77

4. Create a circle on the YZ-plane

 Select the Sketch in place icon, then pick the YZ plane

Create a circle and modify its diameter to 15 as shown in Figure 7.78 below.

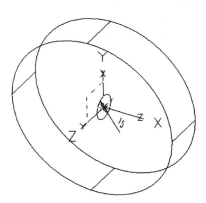

Figure 7.78

Mastering I-DEAS,
Scholars International Publishing Corp., 1999

# Patterning Features

5. Move the circle to a new location

 Select the Move icon
Pick the circle to move
Enter translation coordinates X,Y,Z: 0, 0, 50
The circle is moved to a new location as Figure 7.79.

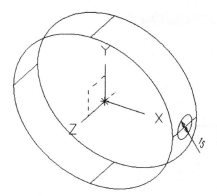

Figure 7.79

6. Extrude the circle as a new part.

 Select the Extrude icon, then pick the circle to extrude
Make sure the extrusion parameters are set as below:

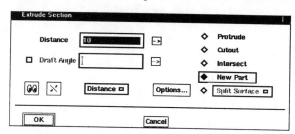

Select OK
The extruded feature is added as in Figure 7.80

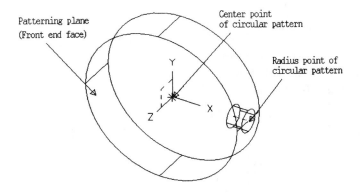

Figure 7.80

7. Create a circular pattern. Use Figure 7.80 as a reference.

Select the Circular pattern icon

# Patterning Features

Pick the small extrude feature as the part to pattern
Pick the front end face as the patterning plane
Pick the coordinate system origin as the center point of the circular pattern
Pick the center point of the right end face as the radius point
Set the parameters as below:

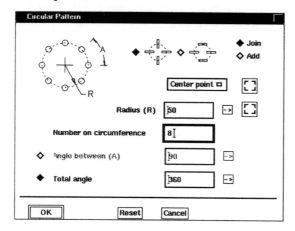

Select **OK**
The circular pattern is added as in Figure 7.81.

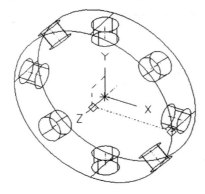

Figure 7.81

8. Perform the Boolean-cut function

Select the Cut icon
Pick the circular pattern as the cutter part
Pick the larger feature as the part to cut
The new model appears as in figure 7.82.

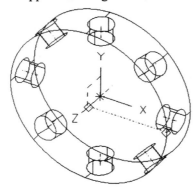

Figure 7.82

7-46

9. Show the model in different modes.

Figure 7.83a and b show the model in different orientation and mode, respectively.

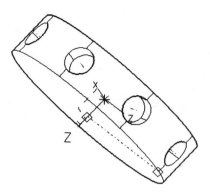

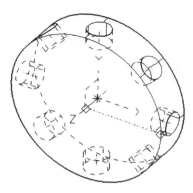

Figure 7.83a

Figure 7.83b

# Aligning a Circular Pattern to the Part

The feature as the pattern leader for creating a circular pattern is normally created as a new part. When it is a new part, a Boolean function must be used to join the pattern to a part. Aligning a circular pattern to the part is similar to the procedure used for rectangular patterns. In addition, we sometimes need to add an angular relations constraint to fully align the circular pattern to the part. The example below is presented to show how to align a circular pattern to a part.

 **The procedure for aligning a circular pattern to a part (Figure 7.84).**

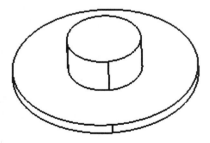

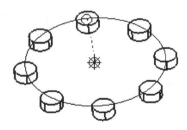

Figure 7.84

 1. Select the "Cut" command icon
2. Press the right mouse button to open the Options menu
3. Select "Turn Relations On" from the Options menu
4. Pick the top end surface of any instance on the pattern
5. Pick the top planar surface of the base on the revolved feature

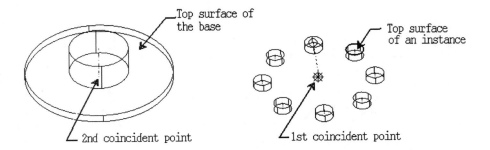

Figure 7.85

    6. Select "Coincident Points" from the Options menu
    7. Pick the center point of the circular pattern
    8. Pick the center point of the top surface of the base
    9. Select "Done" from options list
    10. The new model becomes Figure 7.86

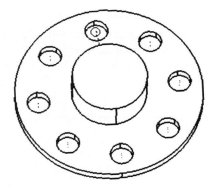

Figure 7.86

Mastering I-DEAS,
Scholars International Publishing Corp., 1999

# Project 4.
# Creating a Fan-wheel part

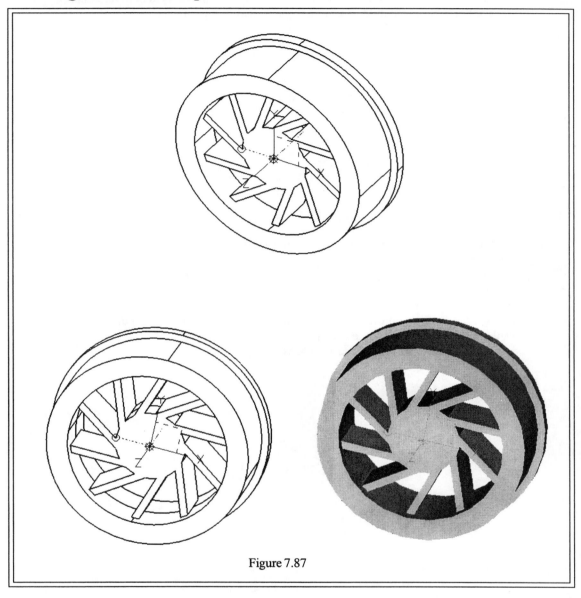

Figure 7.87

This project creates a fan wheel model that consists of three features and one rotational pattern (Figure 7.87). A coordinate system is created to facilitate the making of the rotational pattern of the fan blade. The base feature is the wheel hub. Fan blades are the added extrude features. One fan blade is created by extruding a rectangle. This blade feature is then copied to nine locations using the circular pattern function. The two features, base feature and pattern feature are then joined as one part. The hub feature is created by revolving a section about a center line. The blade part and rim part are joined to form the final part model.

# Patterning Features

**Step 1. Create a coordinate system.**

 Select the **Coordinate Systems** icon,
   then pick the default work plane as the entity for the coordinate system to reference
The coordinate system should appear on the screen as in Figure 7.88
Select **Done** to complete the process of creating a coordinate system

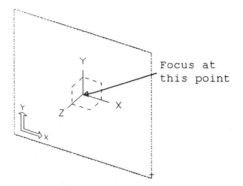

Focus at
this point

Figure 7.88

**Step 2. Create a circle. Use Figures 7.88 and 7.89 as reference.**

 Select the **Sketch in place** icon,
   then pick the XY-plane on the coordinate system as the sketching plane

 Select the **Circle – Center Edge** icon
   Click the **right mouse button,** then select **Focus** from the list
Pick the origin of the coordinate system as the focus point as shown in Figure 7.88
Use the focus point as the circle center,
   then click the other point to create a circle as in Figure 7.89

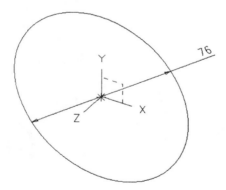

Figure 7.89

Modify the diameter to **76** as shown

**Step 3. Extrude the circle by 50.**

 Select the **Extrude** icon and pick the circle as the curve to extrude
Set the extrusion parameters as below (direction arrow must point inward).

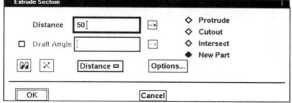

Select **OK** to complete the base feature as in Figure 7.90

Mastering I-DEAS,
Scholars International Publishing Corp., 1999

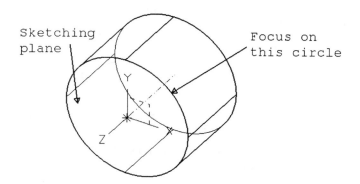

Figure 7.90

**Step 4.** **Create a rectangle. Use Figures 7.90 and 7.91 as reference.**

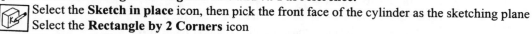 Select the **Sketch in place** icon, then pick the front face of the cylinder as the sketching plane
Select the **Rectangle by 2 Corners** icon
Click the **right mouse button** and select **Focus** from the list
Pick a point on the front circle as the entity to focus (Figure 7.90)
Pick two points to create a rectangle as in Figure 7.91

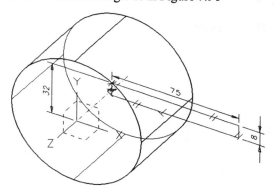

Figure 7.91

Select the **Dimension** icon and add a dimension between the center point
and the top horizontal line of the rectangle
Modify three dimensions to their correct values as shown in Figure 7.91

**Step 5.** **Extrude the rectangle by 50 to create a new part.**

Select the **Extrude** icon and pick the rectangle as entities to extrude
Set the extrusion parameters as below (make direction arrow pointing inward).

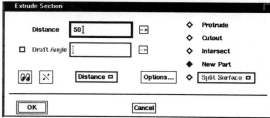

Select **OK** to create the feature as in Figure 7.92

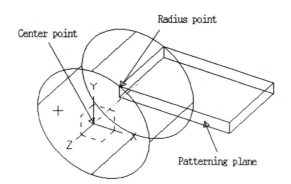

Figure 7.92

**Step 6. Copy the blade to nine locations using circular pattern function. Use Figure 7.92 as reference.**

Select the **Circular Pattern** icon
Select the **rectangular blade** as the part to make as the pattern
Select the **front face** of the blade as the patterning plane (Figure 7.92)
Pick the coordinate system **origin** as the center point
Pick the **upper left corner** of the blade as the radius endpoint
Set the circular pattern parameters as below:

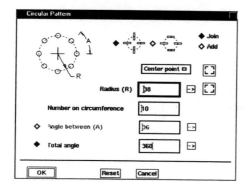

Select **OK**
The circular pattern is added as in Figure 7.93.

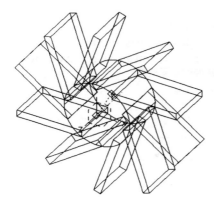

Figure 7.93

Mastering I-DEAS,
Scholars International Publishing Corp., 1999

# Patterning Features

### Step 7.  Join the two parts.

 Select the **Join** icon
(Click the right mouse button to make sure that "Turn Relations On" appears on the list)
Pick the 1st part to join:  **pick the fan blade pattern**
Pick the 2nd part to join:  **pick the extrude cylinder**
The two parts are joined as one (Figure 7.94).

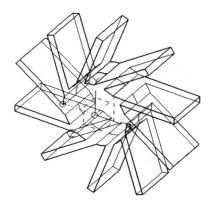

Figure 7.94

### Step 8.  Create a section and a line.

 Select the **Sketch in place** icon,
then pick the XY-plane of coordinate system as the sketching plane

 Select the **Front (XY) View** icon to show the model in the front view
Create a section and a line as shown in Figure 7.95.

Figure 7.95

Modify the dimensions to their correct values as shown in Figure 7.95

### Step 9.  Revolve the section about the line.

 Select the **Revolve** icon
Pick the **section** as entities to revolve
Pick the **horizontal line** as the axis of revolution

# Patterning Features

Set the revolving parameters as below.

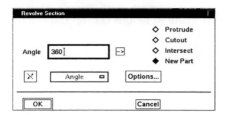

 Select **OK** to complete the revolve feature

Select the **Isometric View** icon to show the model as in Figure 7.96

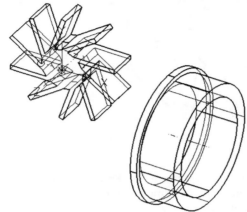

Figure 7.96

**Step 10. Rotate the revolve feature by –90 degrees about the Y axis.**

Select the **Rotate** icon and pick the revolve feature as the part to rotate

Pick the **center point** of the right end face of the revolve feature as the pivot point

Select **About Y** from the list

Enter angle about Y:  **-90**

The new orientation of the revolve feature appears as in Figure 7.97.

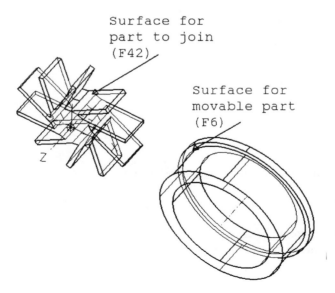

Surface for
part to join
(F42)

Surface for
movable part
(F6)

Figure 7.97

7-54

**Step 11. Join two parts. Use Figure 7.97 as reference.**

Select the **Join** icon

(Make sure "Turn Relations Off" appears in options list)

Click the **right mouse button** then select **Filter** from the list

Pick "**Surface**" from Selection Filter menu, then select the **Pick Only** button

Pick the second planar surface from the inside (F6) of the rim feature
 as the planar surface for the movable part (Figure 7.97)

Click the **right mouse button** again and select **Filter** from the list

Select **Surface** from the list then select the **Pick Only** button

Pick the back vertical face (**F42**) of the blade feature as the planar surface of the part to join

The two parts should move into their new positions as in Figure 7.98.

Figure 7.98

Select **Coincident Points** from the list

Pick the center point of the front face of the blade as the first point

Pick the center point of the front face of the rim as the second point

Select **Done** from the options list to complete the join function

The final part should look likes Figure 7.99.

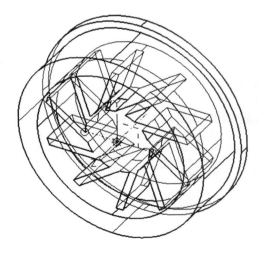

Figure 7.99

# Patterning Features

Figures 7.100, 7.101a and 7.101b show different display modes and orientation of the model.

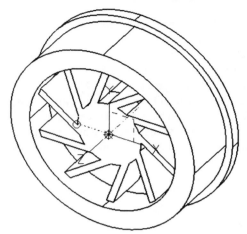

Figure 7.100

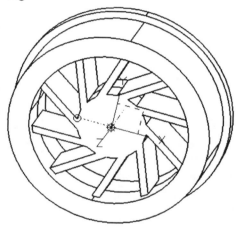

Figure 7.101a

Figure 7.101b

## Step 12. Check the part into library.

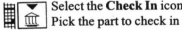 Select the **Check In** icon
Pick the part to check in
Enter **"fan-wheel"** into the Name field in Name menu
Set the check-in parameters as below.

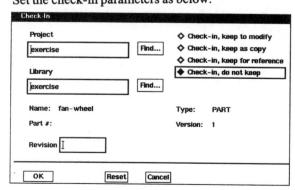

Select **OK** to check the part into library

# Chapter 7. Review Questions

1. What are the pattern leaders and instances?

2. Describe the benefits of using patterns.

3. What are the two types of patterns?

4. Use drawings to describe the unidirectional pattern and bidirectional pattern.

5. Explain how the selection of patterning plane affects the orientation and location of patterned instances.

6. List the eight methods of defining reference planes that can be used as the patterning planes.

7. Use drawings to illustrate the three basic pattern orientations.

8. Use a drawing to describe the patterning parameters for rectangular patterns.

9. What are the two ways for specifying the spacing between instances?

10. Explain how to join a pattern to a part.

11. What are the two types of circular patterns? Describe their differences.

12. Use a drawing to define the circular patterning parameters.

13. Use drawings to show how the selection of patterning plane affects the orientation of circular patterns.

# Chapter

**8**

# Variables and Equations

---

## Highlights of the Chapter

- Dimension variables and engineering variables
- Creating engineering variables
- Arithmetic operators
- Creating equations
- Specifying units for variables
- Creating conditional equations
- Using the spline function to create involute curves

---

## Overview

A variable is a symbolic quantity that may have a number of different values. There are two types of variables used in I-DEAS; **dimension variables** and **engineering variables**. Dimension variables are quantities that measure the lengths, widths, heights, radii, diameters, and angles of sketches, features, or parts. Engineering variables are any variables other than dimension variables. They are not directly associated with geometry. Variables can be related by a set of equations. I-DEAS provides the **Equations function** to define equations from which certain relationships among variables can be obtained. Equations can be applied to both wireframe sketches or feature parameters. I-DEAS uses **If** and **Then commands** to define conditional equations for performing logic decisions in creating part features.

I-DEAS has a special way of specifying units for variables in equations. The default units use the SI units system. You need to specify the proper units to convert them from SI to the Inch (English) unit system. I-DEAS provides a spline function that enables us to create spline curves based on the points generated from math functions. This is a very useful tool for creating any form of splines and involute curves when creating a tooth profile in gears.

# 8.1 Dimension and Engineering Variables

A variable is a measurable quantity whose value may change. The two types of variables used in I-DEAS are dimension variables and engineering variables. Dimension variables are measures of length, width, depth, radii, diameters, and angles of geometry. They are used to define the size and shape of the features or parts. Figure 8.1 shows dimension variables of a wireframe sketch, while Figure 8.2 shows dimension variables of a part feature, draft angle and extrude distance.

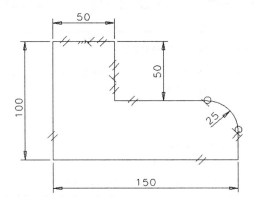

Figure 8.1

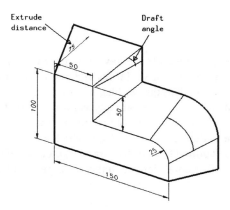

Figure 8.2

Engineering variables used in this text are any variables other than dimension variables. They are not used to describe the geometry of the part, instead, they are the measures of physical properties of the part. Typical engineering variables include area, volume, density, temperature, linear velocity, angular velocity, acceleration, etc. You can also define special variables to meet your specific needs. For example, a variable "Scale" can be created to enlarge or reduce the size of the part. I-DEAS uses the "Part Equations" command to define engineering variables and specifies their relationships with other variables. Directions on how to use the "Part Equations" command are presented in following sections.

# 8.2 Arithmetic Operators

I-DEAS uses common arithmetic operators to describe relationships among variables and equations. Some of commonly used arithmetic operators are listed below:

| Operator | Description | Example |
|---|---|---|
| + | Addition | D1 + D2 |
| - | Subtraction | D1 - 30 |
| * | Multiplication | D1 * 2 |
| / | Division | length / 3 |
| < | Less than | hole_diameter < 20 |
| =< | Less than or equal | hole_diameter =< 20 |
| > | Greater than | length > 150 |
| => | Greater than or equal | length => 200 |
| == | Equal to | arc_radius = 50 |
| != | Not equal to | area != 250 |
| and, && | Logical 'AND' operator | A && B |
| or, \|\| | Logical 'OR' operator | A or B |
| sin( ) | Sine (radians) | sin(1.57) |
| cos( ) | Cosine (radians) | cos(1.57) |
| tan( ) | Tangent (radians) | tan(1.57) |
| asin( ) | Arc Sine (radians) | asin(0.5) |
| acos( ) | Arc Cosine (radians) | acos(0.5) |
| atan( ) | Arc Tangent (radians) | atan(-0.25) |
| log10( ) | Common log, base 10 | log10(2) |
| log( ); ln( ) | natural log, base e | ln(1) |
| exp( ) | Exponentiation, e to power | exp(3) |
| ^, power( ), pow( ) | Power (base, exponent) | power(3) |
| sqrt( ) | Square root | sqrt(A) |
| fabs( ), abs( ) | Absolute value | abs(A) |
| sinh( ) | Hyperbolic | sinh(angle) |
| cosh( ) | Hyperbolic | cosh(angle) |
| tanh( ) | Hyperbolic | tanh(angle) |
| Round( ) | Rounds off double precision number to integer | Round(A) |
| Truncate( ) | Truncates double precision number to integer | Truncate(A) |

# 8.3 Creating Equations

Equations express relationships between variables. Arithmetic operators are used to relate variables to form such desired relations. Labels can be added to dimension variables for easy identification.

**The procedure for creating equations:**

1. Select the **Part Equations** icon

The dimensions and feature parameters of the active model should appear on the Equations menu as shown below (Use the part feature in Figure 8.2).

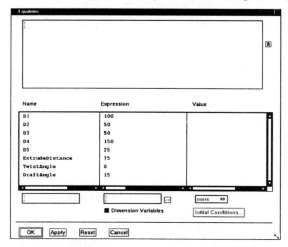

2. Enter equations into the equation window as shown below.

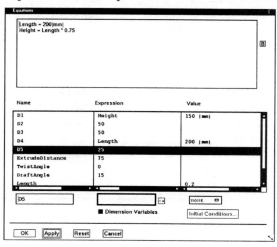

3. Select **OK** to exit the Equations menu
4. Select **Update** to reflect the change

made from the equations

Figure 8.3 displays the part model after the change.

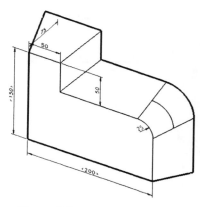

Figure 8.3

Mastering I-DEAS
Scholars International Publishing Corp., 1999

## Variables and Equations

The Equations function can be used in sketches and part features. Typical tasks performed using equations include:

> Assigning labels to dimension variables
> Relating dimension variables in a definite relationship
> Relating feature parameters in a part

# Assigning Labels to Variables

The sketch shown in Figure 8.4 is used to show how to use the Equations function.

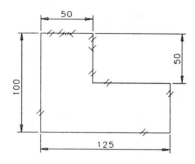

Figure 8.4

**The procedure for assigning labels to dimension variables:**

1. Select **Part Equations**
2. Pick any dimension on the sketch to open the Equation menu as shown below.

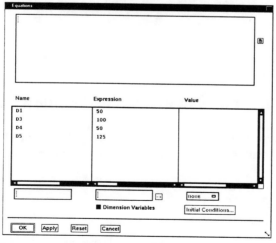

3. Click the selected variable from the list to highlight it
      (The selected dimension will be shown in white on the graphic view)
4. Enter the label "**step_height**" in the first column and dimension value "**30**" in the second column
5. Select "**Apply**" to accept the label and the new dimension

# Variables and Equations

6. Repeat the same procedure for the remaining three variables as shown below.

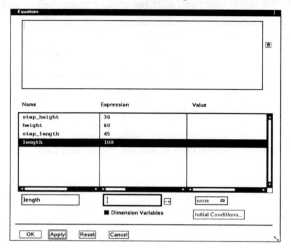

7. Select **OK** to exit the Equations menu

The sketch with the new dimension values appears in Figure 8.5.

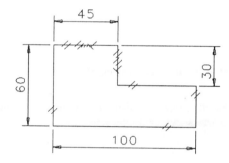

Figure 8.5

## Showing Variable Labels in a Graphic Window

Place the cursor on the selected dimension, the dimension will be highlighted in white and its label will appear as in Figure 8.6. The label will disappear when the cursor is not on the dimension.

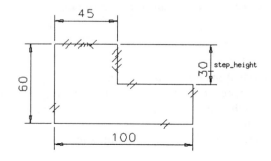

Figure 8.6

8-6

# Relating Dimensions in a Section

I-DEAS allows the use of mathematical expressions to relate dimensions in the cross sections.

**The procedure for defining mathematical expressions:**

1. Select the **Part Equations** icon, then pick any dimension to open the Equations menu as below.

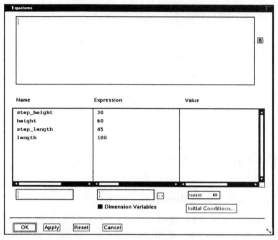

2. Pick the dimension from the Equations menu that you want to control with an equation
   (step_height in this case)
3. Enter the governing equation in the Expression column ( height /2 in this case),
   then select **Apply**
4. Repeat the same procedure to define the governing equation for step-length as "length /3"

5. The two equations for step_height and step_length with their value are shown in
   the Equations menu as below.

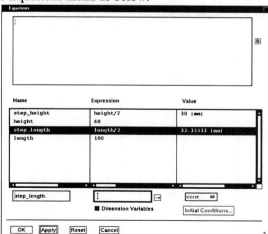

6. Select **OK** to exit the Equations menu

---

*Note* that the two dimensions governed by equations are enclosed by < > to indicate that they are dependent variables as shown in Figure 8.7.

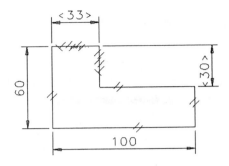

Figure 8.7

## Changing Independent Dimension Values

**The procedure for changing independent dimension values:**

1. Click the dimension whose value you want to change (height in this example)
2. Select the **"Modify Entity"** icon to open the Modify Dimension menu as below.

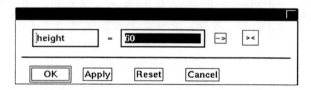

3. Change this value to **150**, then select **OK**
   The new cross section becomes Figure 8.8.

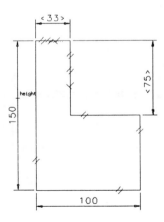

Figure 8.8

4. Repeat the same procedure to change the length dimension to 150

Mastering I-DEAS
Scholars International Publishing Corp., 1999

The change in length is reflected onto the cross section as shown in Figure 8.9.

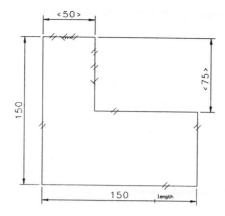

Figure 8.9

# Relating Feature Parameters in a Part

The feature parameters are added to the part every time you extrude or revolve a cross section. The following three parameters are added for extruding a feature:

> ExtrudeDistance
> TwistAngle
> DraftAngle

The following three parameters are added for revolving a cross section:

> RevolveAngle
> DeltaRadius
> AxialTrans

⊠ **Example:** Create an extrude feature using a cross section with two equations. The extrude distance is set to 50. The extrude feature should appear as in Figure 8.10.

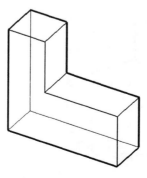

Figure 8.10

# Variables and Equations

1. Select the "**Part Equations**" icon
2. Pick the extrude feature to open the Equations menu as below.

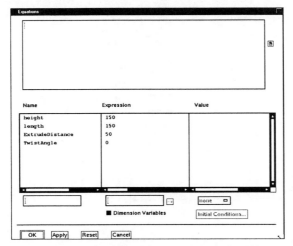

3. Enter "(height + length) / 5" to the Extrude Distance parameter as below.

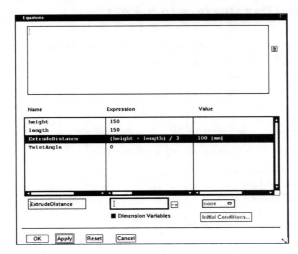

4. Select **OK** to exit Equations menu
5. Select the **Update** icon to update the change as in Figure 8.11.

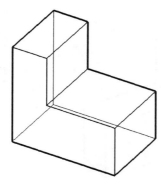

Figure 8.11

# 8.4   Creating Condition Equations

I-DEAS allows the use of condition equations to make decisions. The condition equations follow this format:

**If (condition 1) then [(equation 1) (equation 2) . . .]**
**elseif (condition 2) then [(equation 3) (equation4) . . .]**

"If" is the required word. It must be entered first with a space following it. The word "then" is optional.

**Examples:**     if (length < 100 |mm|) then (step_length = length / 2)
            if (length => 100 |mm|) then (step_length = length /3)

# 8.5   Unit conventions

I-DEAS has assigned the default in SI units. Variables can be specified in units other than the default units. Units are expressed between two vertical bars. The valid units are listed below:

| | |
|---|---|
| Angle unit | \|deg\| or \|degree\| |
| Inch system | \|in\| or \|inch\| <br> \|ft\| or \|feet\| <br> \|in sq\| or \|inch sq\| <br> \|ft sq\| or \|feet sq\| |
| Metric system | \|mm\| or \|millimeter\| <br> \|cm\| or \|centimeter\| <br> \|m\| or \|meter\| <br> \|mm sq\| or \|millimeter sq\| <br> \|cm sq\| or \|centimeter sq\| <br> \|m sq\| or \|meter sq\| |

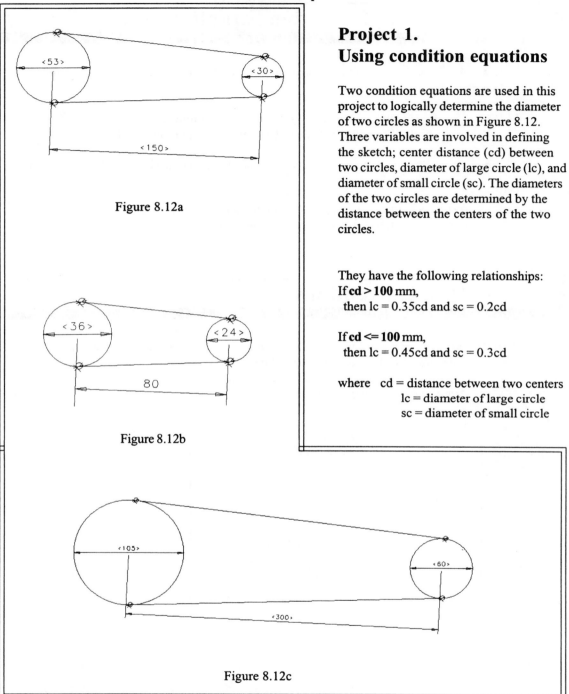

Figure 8.12a

Figure 8.12b

Figure 8.12c

# Project 1.
# Using condition equations

Two condition equations are used in this project to logically determine the diameter of two circles as shown in Figure 8.12. Three variables are involved in defining the sketch; center distance (cd) between two circles, diameter of large circle (lc), and diameter of small circle (sc). The diameters of the two circles are determined by the distance between the centers of the two circles.

They have the following relationships:
If **cd > 100** mm,
   then lc = 0.35cd and sc = 0.2cd

If **cd <= 100** mm,
   then lc = 0.45cd and sc = 0.3cd

where   cd = distance between two centers
           lc = diameter of large circle
           sc = diameter of small circle

**Step 1.**   **Create the sketch shown in Figure 8.13.**
Create two circles and two tangent lines as shown
Add a horizontal dimension between the centers of the two circles
Use "**Tangent**" constraint to constrain four locations between circles and lines

Mastering I-DEAS
Scholars International Publishing Corp., 1999

# Variables and Equations

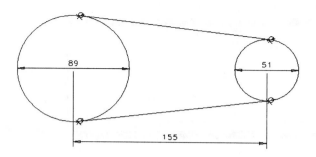

Figure 8.13

**Step 2.  Initiate the part equations function.**

Select the **Part Equations** icon,

then pick any dimension from the sketch to open Equations menu as below.

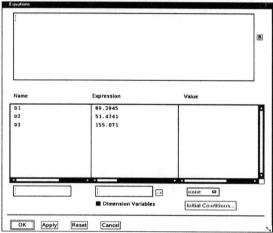

**Step 3.  Define the condition equations and variables.**

Enter the condition equations and define the variables as below.

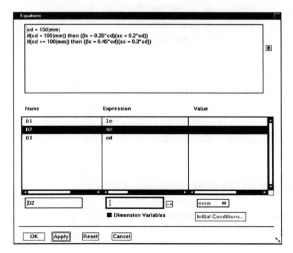

# Variables and Equations

Select the **Apply** button to execute condition equations
The result is shown on the Equations menu as below.

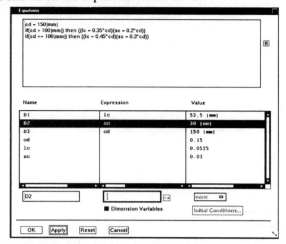

The sketch is redefined to reflect the new values from equations as in Figure 8.14.

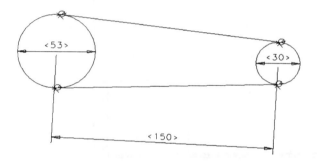

Figure 8.14

## Step 4. Change the parameter units.

Click variable "**cd**" to highlight its row
Click the **unit button**, "none" appears near the bottom right of the menu to open the list,
then select "**mm**" from the list
Repeat this procedure for two remaining variables "**lc**" and "**sc**"
The units are added to three variables are shown below.

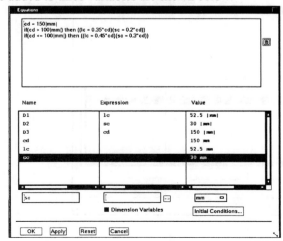

Mastering I-DEAS
Scholars International Publishing Corp., 1999

# Variables and Equations

**Step 5.** **Change the value of variable "cd" to 300.**

Change the value of variable "**cd**" to **300** in the Equations menu

Select the **Apply** button to execute this change

The new set of variable values appears as below.

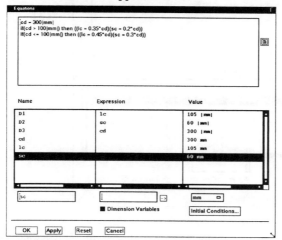

The new sketch becomes Figure 8.15.

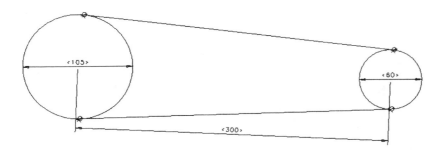

Figure 8.15

**Step 6.** **Change the value of variable "cd" to 80.**

Change the value of "**cd**" to **80** in the Equations window

Click "**D3**" in the variable window to highlight its row, then enter "**80**" as shown below.

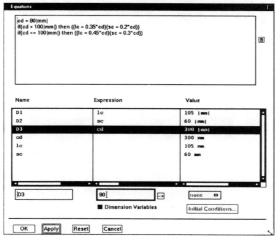

# Variables and Equations

Click the "**Apply**" button to execute the change
The new set of variable values appears as below.

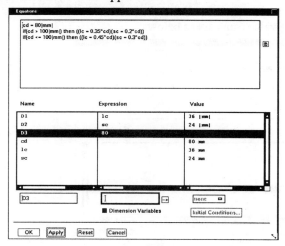

The new sketch based on the new center distance value of **80**mm becomes Figure 8.16.

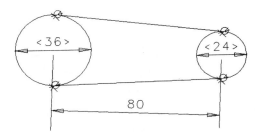

Figure 8.16

**Step 7.    Exit the Equations menu.**
Select **OK** to exit Equations menu

# 8.6 Spline Function

A spline is the smooth curve that passes through a set of points. The control points of a spline can be defined mathematically in I-DEAS. The **Function Spline** function allows the creation of spline curves from algebraic equations. The equations used in defining function splines use an independent (input) variable, **u**. Variables X, Y, and Z are dependent (output) variables that are required to be defined. The equations are used to relate the three dependent variables to the independent variable by math functions. The independent variable **u** can be the time, angle, distance, or some other variable.

The units of angle values used for trigonometric functions in I-DEAS are radians. Use the following expression to convert the angle units from degrees to radians:

$$A = 2*pi*u/360$$

where    A = the angle in radians
pi = 3.1416
u = the input variable (angle in degrees in this example)

⊠**Example:** Creating a spiral curve. This is an example showing the principle and procedure for using the Function Spline function. A spiral curve is created by varying the radius, X, and Y variables in relation to the input variable, angle. The equations to define a spiral curve are listed below:

$$R = u/15$$
$$A = 2*pi*u/360$$
$$X = R*cos(A)$$
$$Y = R*sin(A)$$
$$Z = 0$$

where    R = radius
u = input angle in degrees
A = angle in radians
X, Y, and Z are coordinate values of a given point

The radius variable R can be scaled by any factor (ex. u/15). Using a larger denominator will result in a smaller radius increment per cycle. A smaller denominator produces a larger radius increment per cycle. Figure 8.17 shows two spiral curves having two rounds and four rounds.

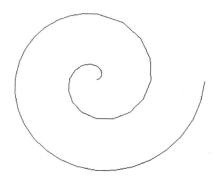

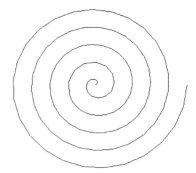

Figure 8.17a Two-round spiral curve        Figure 8.17b Four-round spiral curve

# Variables and Equations

**The procedure for using the Function Spline function is:**

1. Select the **Function Spline** icon to open the "Function Manager" menu as below.

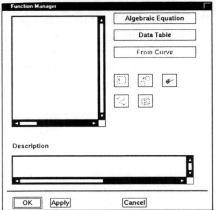

2. Select the "**Algebraic Equation**" button from the Function Manager to open the "Algebraic Equation Editor" as below.

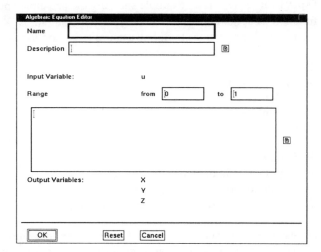

3. Enter data into equation editor as below.

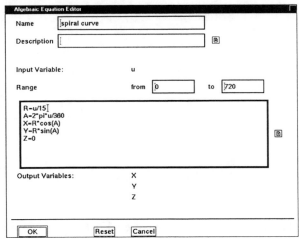

Mastering I-DEAS
Scholars International Publishing Corp., 1999

4. Select **OK** to return to Function Manager menu as shown below.

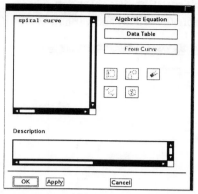

5. Select the **OK** button to generate the curve as shown in Figure 8.18

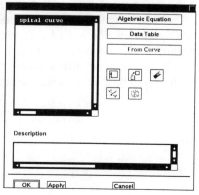

Figure 8.18

6. Select **Cancel** to exit the Function Spline function

# Modifying Spline Equations

The function spline equations can be rerun and modified to create new curves. Follow these steps to modify and rerun the spiral spline.

 **The procedure for modifying spline equations:**

 1. Select the **Function Spline** icon to open the "Function Manager" menu as below.

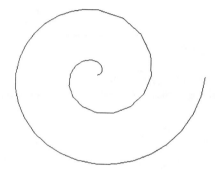

# Variables and Equations

2. Click on "**spiral curve**" from the list to highlight it
3. Click the "**Modify**" icon to open the "Algebraic Equation Editor" menu
4. Modify the range of input variable (from 0 to 1800) and variable R (R=u/30) as below.

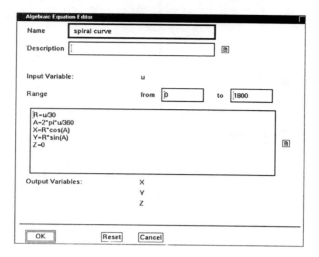

5. Select **OK** to return to the Function Manager menu
6. Select **OK** from the Function Manager menu to create a new spiral curve as in Figure 8.19

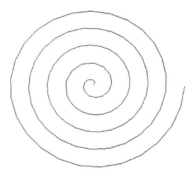

Figure 8.19

Four tutorial projects are presented in this section. The first tutorial, project 2, shows how to create a sine function curve using the Function Spline function. The remaining three projects create involute curve, spur gear, and helical gear. In project 3, the Function Spline function is used to create an involute curve as the basic gear form. Other geometry entities are added to the involve curve to form the tooth profile. Project 4 extrudes the tooth profile to form a gear tooth. The circular pattern function is then used to copy the gear tooth to create the gear. Project 5 uses the tooth profile to create a helical gear.

Mastering I-DEAS
Scholars International Publishing Corp., 1999

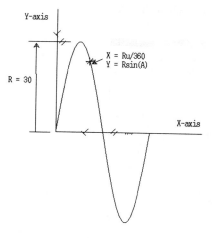

Figure 8.20

# Project 2.
# Creating sine function curves

This project illustrates the use of the Function Spline to create sine function curves. Figure 8.20 shows the derivation of defining variables. The Y-coordinate of control points is defined by the sine function. The variable R is the amplitude of the sine function. The X-coordinate of the control points is defined by a relation equation using the input variable u and amplitude R. The input variable u represents the angle in this case. A complete sine wave cycle is 360 degrees.

The basic set of equations is listed below. Modify the values for amplitude, input range, and scale factor for X to produce different sine curves. Figure 8.21 shows three sine curves created in this project.

$$R = 50$$
$$A = 2*pi*u/360$$
$$X = R*u/720$$
$$Y = R*sin(A)$$
$$Z = 0$$

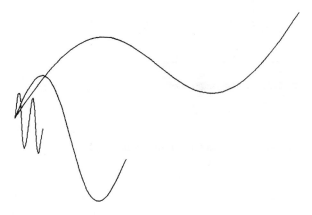

Figure 8.21

**Step 1.  Initiate the Function Spline function.**

 Select the **Function Spline** icon to open the Function Manager menu
Click on the **"Algebraic Equation"** button to open the Algebraic Equation Editor menu

# Variables and Equations

Enter name, input range, and equations to the editor menu as below.

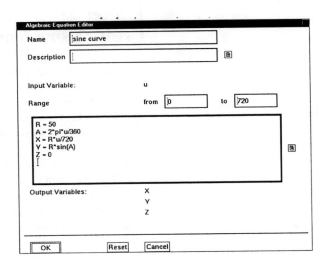

Select **OK** to return to the Function Manager menu
The "sine curve" appears in the list as shown below.

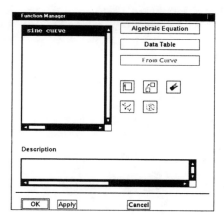

Select **OK** to generate the sine curve as shown in Figure 8.22

Figure 8.22

**Step 2.   Modify the existing equations.**

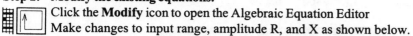

Click the **Modify** icon to open the Algebraic Equation Editor
Make changes to input range, amplitude R, and X as shown below.

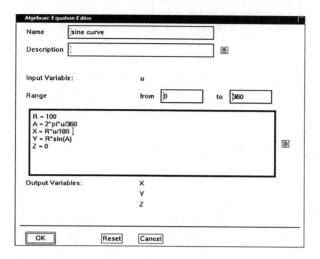

| Algebraic Equation Editor | |
|---|---|
| Name | sine curve |
| Description | |

Input Variable:       u

Range       from 0   to 360

```
R = 100
A = 2*pi*u/360
X = R*u/180
Y = R*sin(A)
Z = 0
```

Output Variables:       X
                        Y
                        Z

OK      Reset      Cancel

Select **OK → OK** to generate another sine curve as in Figure 8.23

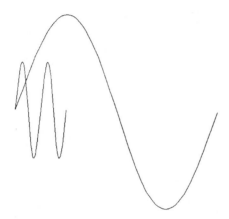

Figure 8.23

**Step 3.   Add Z-dimension to the curve.**

Click on the **Modify** icon again to open the Algebraic Equation Editor menu

# Variables and Equations

Change the equation for Z to (-500*u/360) as below.

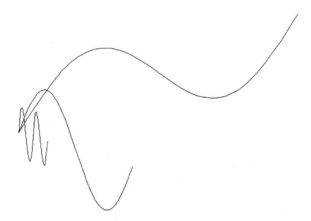

Select **OK** → **OK** to generate the third sine curve as in Figure 8.24

Figure 8.24

Select **Cancel** to exit the Function Spline function

# 8.7  Involute Curves as a Gear Tooth Profile

If gears are to operate smoothly with a minimum of noise and vibration, the curved surface of the tooth profile must be of a definite geometric form. The most common form in use today is the involute curve. The portion of the profile from the base circle to the addendum circle can be drawn as the involute of the base circle (Figure 8.25). That part of the profile below the base circle is drawn as a radial line that terminates in the fillet at the root circle. The fillet should have a radius equal to one and one-half times the clearance.

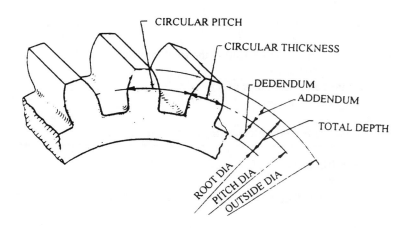

Figure 8.25

An **involute** is defined as the path of a point on a string, as the string unwinds from a circle (Figure 8.26). A circle may be regarded as a polygon with an infinite number of sides. The involute is constructed by dividing the circles' circumference into a number of equal segments, drawing a tangent at each division point, setting off along each tangent the length of the corresponding circular arc (Figure 8.27) and drawing the required curve through the points set off on the several tangents.

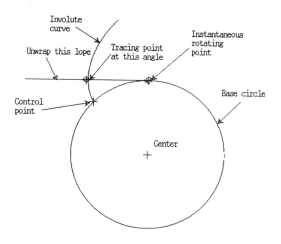

Figure 8.26

<h1 style="text-align:center">Variables and Equations</h1>

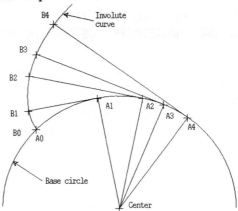

Figure 8.27 Construction of an Involute curve

We need the following information to construct the tooth profiles:

> **DP** (diametral pitch)
> **N** (number of teeth on a gear)
> **PA** (pressure angle)

The following equations are used to calculate the gear geometry:

| | |
|---|---|
| **Pitch Diameter** | $PD = N/(DP)$ |
| **Base Circle Diameter** | $BD = PD*COS(PA)$ |
| **Addendum** | $ADD = 1/(DP)$ |
| **Outside Diameter** | $OD = PD + 2(ADD)$ |
| **Dedendum** | $DED = (1.157)/(DP)$ |
| **Root Diameter** | $RD = PD - 2(DED)$ |

⊠ **Example:** Find the diameter values of the base circle, outside circle and root circle of a gear that has 24 teeth, diametral pitch of 5 and pressure angle of 20 degrees.

Solution:

$DP = 5, \quad N = 24$
$PD = N / DP = 24/5 = 4.8$

$PA = 20$
Base Circle Diameter $(BD) = PD*COS(PA) = 4.8 * COS(20) = 4.5105$

Addendum $(ADD) = 1/DP = 1/5 = 0.2$

Outside Diameter $(OD) = PD + 2(ADD) = 4.8 + 2(0.2) = 5.2$

Dedendum $(DED) = 1.157/DP = 1.157/5 = 0.2314$

Root Diameter $(RD) = PD - 2(DED) = 4.8 - 2(0.2314) = 4.3372$

Mastering I-DEAS
Scholars International Publishing Corp., 1999

# Variables and Equations

The point coordinates on the involute curves can be algebraically derived below (Figure 8.28):

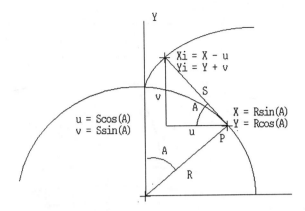

Figure 8.28

The coordinates of any point on the base circle can be expressed as:
$$X = R \sin(A)$$
$$Y = R \cos(A)$$

The arc length encompassed by the angle (A) is:
$$S = RA \quad \text{(A is in radians)}$$

Calculating from the right triangle PQB, we can find the distances for two adjacent sides of the right angle as below:
$$u = S \cos(A)$$
$$v = S \sin(A)$$

From the geometry relationship in Figure 8.28 we can derive the following two equations to calculate the X and Y coordinate values for points on involute curves:

$$X_i = X - u \qquad\qquad\qquad Y_i = Y + v$$
$$\text{or} = R\sin(A) - RA\cos(A) \qquad \text{or} = R\cos(A) + RA\sin(A)$$

We can use the I-DEAS' Function Spline command to create the involute curves. The program shown below can be used to create any type of involute curves:

**Independent variable, u, ranging from 0 to 60 (from 0 degree to 60 degrees)**

```
R = 1                        (the radius of the base circle)
A = 2*pi*u/360               (the angle in radians)
X = R*sin(A)-R*A*cos(A)      (x-coordinate of the involute point)
Y = R*cos(A)+R*A*sin(A)      (y-coordinate of the involute point)
Z = 0
```

How to use this program:

1. Determining the radius of the base circle (R).
2. Independent variable u is the angle parameter which may range from 0 to 60 degrees.

# Project 3.
# Creating an Involute Curve

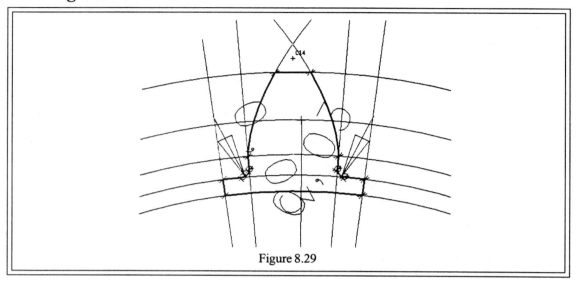

Figure 8.29

This project creates an involute curve using the following gear data:

Root circle radius = 2.1686          Base circle radius = 2.2553
Pitch circle radius = 2.4            Outside circle = 2.6
The number of teeth is 24

The curve is mirrored about a radial line to obtain the involute curve of the other side. Figure 8.29 shows the completed gear tooth profile. Save this profile as "involute". This profile will be used later to create a spur gear in project 4 and a helical gear in project 5.

**Step 1.   Set the units to inch and set display border size.**

Select **Options** → **Units** → **Inch (pound f)**

Select **Workplane Appearance**
Set the X and Y for Min. and Max, values as below:

| X | Y | |
|------|------|------|
| -2.0 | -2.0 | Min. |
| 2.0 | 2.0 | Max. |

Select **OK** to exit the Workplane Attributes menu

**Step 2.   Create a coordinate system and name it coord1.**
Select the **Coordinate Systems** icon, then pick the workplane as the entity to reference
Select **Done**
Select the **Name Parts** icon, then pick the coordinate system as the part to name
Enter "**coord1**" into the name field, then select **OK**

**Step 3.   Create an involute curve.**
Select the **Sketch in place** icon, then pick **XY-plane**
Select the **Function Spline** icon to open the Function Manager menu
Click the "**Algebraic Equation**" icon to open the Algebraic Equation Edit

Mastering I-DEAS
Scholars International Publishing Corp., 1999

## Variables and Equations

Enter the name, range, and equations to the equation editor as below.

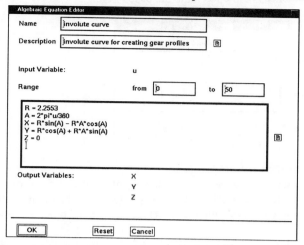

Select **OK** to return to Function Manager menu as below.

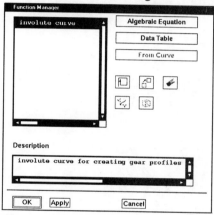

Select **OK** to generate the involute curve as shown in Figure 8.30.

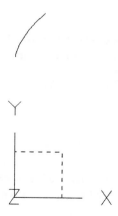

Figure 8.30

**Step 4.   Create four circles.**

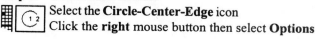 Select the **Circle-Center-Edge** icon
Click the **right** mouse button then select **Options**

# Variables and Equations

Set the circle parameters as below to create the base circle.

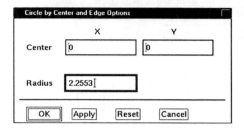

Select **Apply** to create the base circle
Change the Radius value to "**2.1686**", then select **Apply** to create the root circle
Change the Radius value to "**2.4**", then select **Apply** to create the pitch circle
Change the Radius value to "**2.6**", then select **OK** to create the outside circle

The four circles are added as in Figure 8.31.

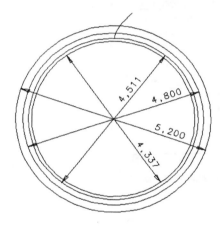

Figure 8.31

**Step 5. Create a 3-D point at the intersection of the base circle and the involute curve.**

 Select **3-D Points**, then click the **right** mouse button and select "**Intersection**" from the list
Pick the involute curve as the 1ˢᵗ entity to intersect
Pick the second circle from outside as the 2ⁿᵈ entity to intersect
The point is added to the drawing.

**Step 6. Create a line.**

 Select the **Lines** icon
Pick the **origin** as the start point
Click the **right** mouse button, then select **Focus** and pick the 3-D point just created
Pick the **focused point** as the second point to create the line as shown in Figure 8.32.

 Select **Constrain & Dimension** → **Fix Angle**
Pick the line just created to fix it at the current location

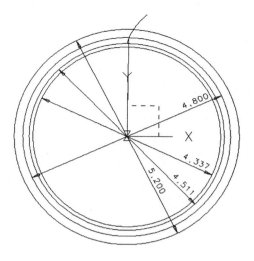

Figure 8.32

**Step 7. Create a vertical line.**

Pick the **origin** as the start point and a **point** on the vertical line

 Select the **Constraint and Dimension** icon to open the Constrain panel
Select the **Vertical Ground** icon, then pick the vertical line just created
The new drawing becomes Figure 8.33.

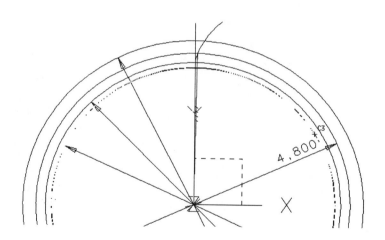

Figure 8.33

**Step 8. Add another line.**

Select the **Lines** icon
Create a line from the origin to the right side of the Y-axis as in Figure 8.34
Select **Constrain & Dimension → Angular**

# Variables and Equations

Add an angular dimension between two lines and change its value to 3.75 as in Figure 8.34.

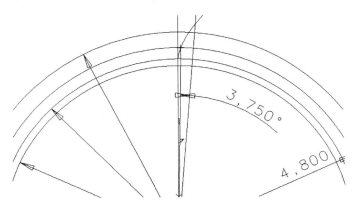

Figure 8.34

**Step 9. Build a section.**

 Select the **Build Section** icon
Press **RMB**, then select options from
the list
Toggle Stop at intersection to **ON**
Select **OK**
Pick curve segments to form
a section as shown in Figure 8.35.

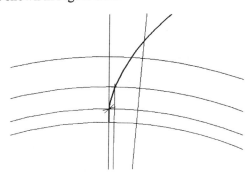

Figure 8.35

**Step 10. Rotate the section.**

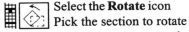 Select the **Rotate** icon
Pick the section to rotate
Press **Enter** to accept the origin as the default rotation center
Select **About Z → Align Vector**
Pick the right radian line as the vector to rotate from (The direction arrow points upward.)
Select **Yes** to "Is the direction OK?"
Pick the vertical line as the vector to rotate to (Direction arrow points upward.)
Select **Yes** to "Is the direction OK?"

# Variables and Equations

The profile has been rotated to a new position as in Figure 8.36.

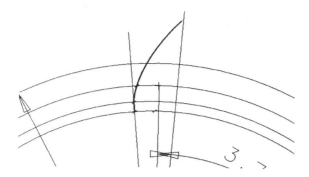

Figure 8.36

**Step 11. Mirror the section about the YZ-plane.**

 Select the **Reflect** icon
Pick the section to reflect
Click the **right** mouse button, then select **Axis Plane → YZ Plane**
Enter distance (0.0): **0**
Select **Keep Both**
A section is created as in Figure 8.37.

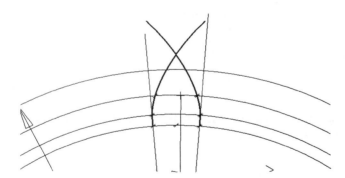

Figure 8.37

**Step 12. Create three radian lines.**

Create three radian lines as shown in Figure 8.38. The middle line must be a vertical line and constrained vertically. Change angles to correct values.

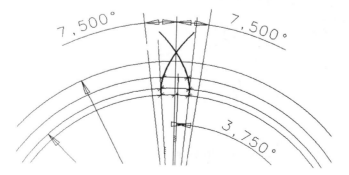

Figure 8.38

**Step 13. Delete two section curves.**

 Select the **Delete** icon
Delete two section curves (curve geometries still remain)

**Step 14. Add two fillets. Use the pick points in Figure 8.39.**

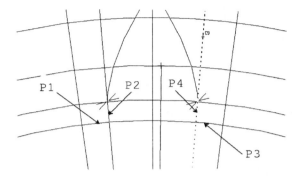

Figure 8.39

 Select the **Fillet** icon
Pick the root circle **P1** and the radian line **P2**
Set the fillet parameters as below.

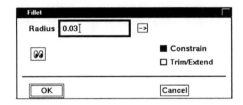

Select **OK**
Pick **P3** and **P4** to select two entities, then select **OK** to complete the second fillet
The two fillets are added as in Figure 8.40.

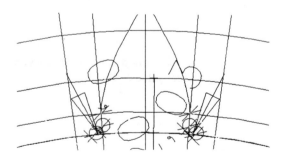

Figure 8.40

**Step 15. Add a circle.**

 Select the **Circle – Center Edge** icon
Click the **right** mouse button, then select **Options**

# Variables and Equations

Set the circle parameters as below:

| Center | X0 | Y0 |
|--------|-----|-----|
| Radius | 2.1 | |

The circle is added to the model.

## Step 16. Build a section.

 Select the **Build Section** icon

Pick all segments that form the section as shown in Figure 8.41.

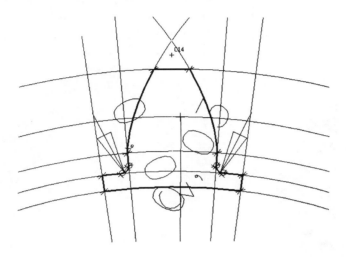

Figure 8.41

## Step 17. Save the section as involute.

Select **File → Save As**

New model file name: **D:\Ideas\Ms7\involute.mf1**

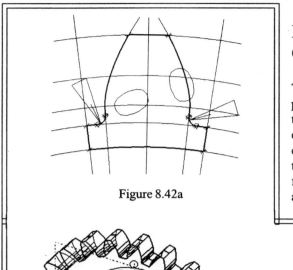

Figure 8.42a

# Project 4.
# Creating a Spur Gear

This project uses the gear tooth profile created in project 3 to create a spur gear. Figure 8.42 shows the tooth profile and gear. The tooth profile is extruded by a distance of 0.5" to form a tooth. The circular pattern function is used to copy the gear tooth to produce a gear of 24 teeth. A revolve feature is created as the gear hub. The gear and hub are joined to form a part.

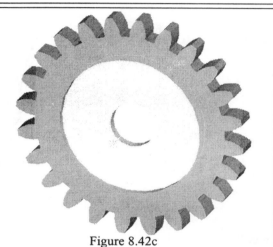

Figure 8.42b

Figure 8.42c

**Step 1.** **Open the involute profile ( unless it is already open)**

Select **File → Open**

Filename: **involute.mf1**

The involute profile appears as in Figure 8.43.

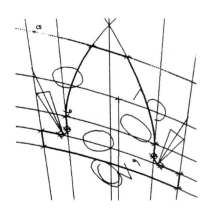

Figure 8.43

8-36

### Step 2. Extrude the gear profile.

Click on the **Isometric View** icon
Select the **Extrude** icon, then pick the gear profile section
Make the direction arrow point toward the **inside** and set the Distance to **0.5**
The gear tooth is created as in Figure 8.44.
Delete the remaining circle.

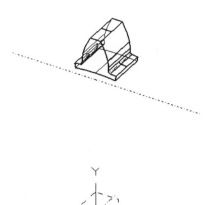

Figure 8.44

### Step 3. Create a circular pattern for the tooth.

Select the **Circular Pattern** icon
Pick the tooth as the part to make as the pattern
Pick the front face of the tooth as the patterning plane
Pick the coordinate origin as the center point
Pick the lower front corner of the teeth feature as the radius point
Set the circular pattern parameters as below:

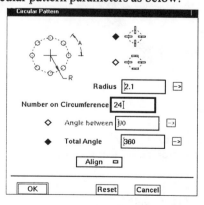

The initial circular pattern is shown in Figure 8.45.

# Variables and Equations

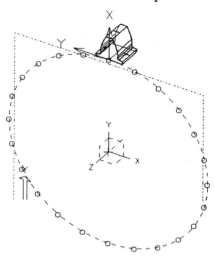

Figure 8.45

Select **OK** to complete the patterning of tooth as in Figure 8.46.

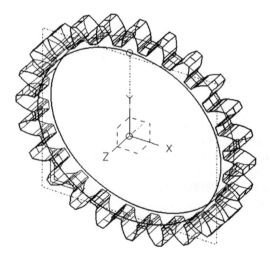

Figure 8.46

**Step 4.  Create a new coordinate system "coord2".**

Select the **Coordinate Systems** icon
Pick the reference plane (in blue) as the entity to reference
Select **Origin**, then click the **right** mouse button and select **Key In**
Enter **(5,0,0)** to define the origin location
Select **Done**
The new coordinate system is added as in Figure 8.46.

**Step 5.  Name the new coordinate system as "coord2".**

Select the **Name Parts** icon
Pick the new coordinate system as the part to name
Enter **"coord2"** into the Name field in the Name menu, then select **OK**

**Step 6. Create a section using XY-plane of coord2 as the sketch plane.**

Select the **Sketch in place** icon, then select **XY-plane** in the right coordinate system
Select the **Front View** icon

Use the Polylines command to create a section and a horizontal line aligning with the X axis as shown in Figure 8.47

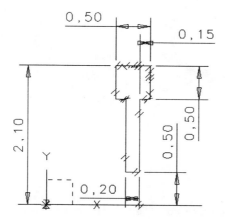

Figure 8.47

**Step 7. Create a revolve feature.**

Select the **Isometric View** icon
Select the **Revolve** icon

Pick the **section** as the revolving section, and pick the **horizontal line** as the revolving axis
Set the revolving parameters as below.

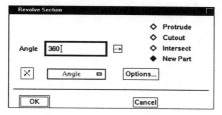

The revolved feature appears as in Figure 8.48.

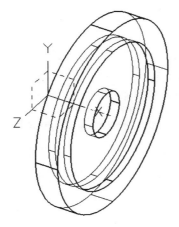

Figure 8.48

**Step 8. Join two features. Use Figure 8.49 as reference.**

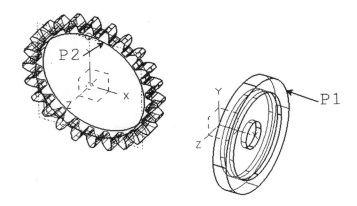

Figure 8.49

 Select the **Join** icon
Click the **right** mouse button to make sure "Turn Relations ON" is on
Pick the right end face **P1** as the planar surface of the movable part
Pick the front face **P2** as the planar surface of the part to join
The two parts are temporarily placed as in Figure 8.50.

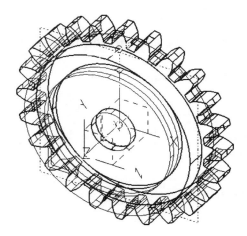

Figure 8.50

Select **Surface Operations → Offset Surfaces**
Pick **CP1** of the gear part as the first point in Figure 8.50
Pick **CP6** of the revolved part as the second point
Select **Switch direction** from the list to make the direction arrow point inward
Enter distance between points: **0**
Select **Done** to complete the join operation

# Variables and Equations

The new part appears as in Figure 8.51.

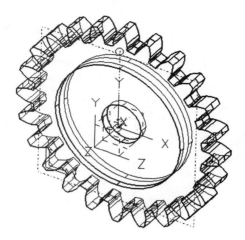

Figure 8.51

Figure 8.52 shows the shaded model of the gear.

Figure 8.52

**Step 9.** **Check in the gear wheel.**

 Select the **Check in** icon
Enter the part name as **"spur gear"**
Set the check-in parameters as below:

> Project: **Exercise**
> Library: **gear**
> **Check in, do not keep**

Select **OK**

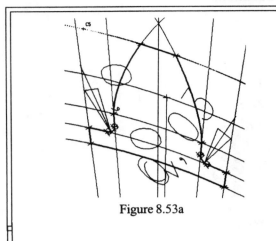

Figure 8.53a

# Project 5.
# Creating a helical gear

This project extrudes the tooth profile in a vector direction of (0.5,0,-1) to produce a helical gear. The circular pattern function is then used to copy the tooth to the other 23 locations. Figure 8.53 shows the tooth profile and the gear.

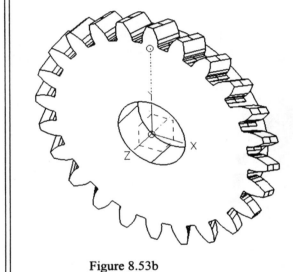

Figure 8.53b

Figure 8.53c

**Step 1. Open the section "involute".**

Select **File → Open**

File name: **D:\Ideas\Ms7\involute.mf1**

(or the name you saved the involute file)

Select the **Isometric View** icon

The involute section appears as in Figure 8.54.

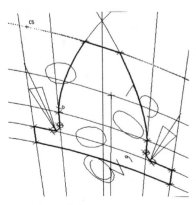

Figure 8.54

Mastering I-DEAS
Scholars International Publishing Corp., 1999

### Step 2. Extrude the section.

Select the **Extrude** icon, then pick the section
Set the distance parameter to "**0.5**"
Click the **Options** button to open the Extrude Options menu
Set the Along Vector as below.

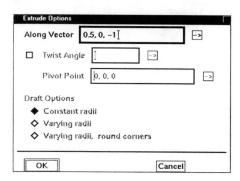

Select **OK** → **OK** to complete the tooth as in Figure 8.55.

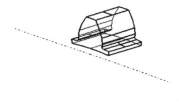

Figure 8.55

### Step 3. Create a circular pattern.

Select the **Circular Pattern** icon
Pick the **tooth just created** as the part to make a pattern of
Pick the **front end face** of the tooth as the patterning plane
Pick the **origin** of the coordinate system as the pattern center
Pick the **lower-right corner** of the gear profile as the radius point
Set the circular pattern parameters as below:

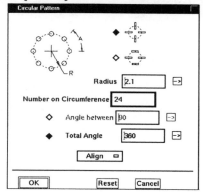

Select **OK** to complete the circular pattern as in Figure 8.56.

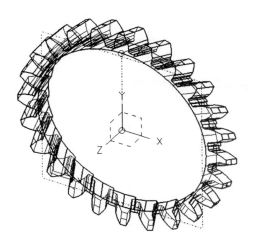

Figure 8.56

**Step 4.   Create two circles for extrusion. Use Figure 8.57 for reference.**

  Select the **Sketch in place** icon, then pick the XY-plane as the sketch plane
Select the **Circle – Center Edge** icon
Create two concentric circles as in Figure 8.57 (use Focus function to create a point at the origin)
Change the circle diameters to their correct value as shown

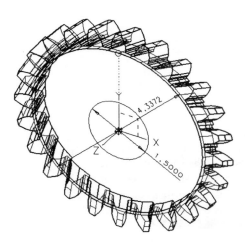

Figure 8.57

**Step 5.   Extrude the feature.**

  Select the **Extrude** icon
Pick two circles to extrude

Mastering  I-DEAS
Scholars International Publishing Corp., 1999

# Variables and Equations

Set the extrude parameters as below (with the extrude arrow pointing inward).

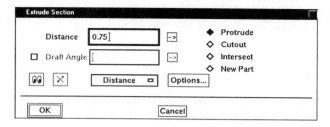

Select **OK** to complete the extrude-cut as shown in Figure 8.58.

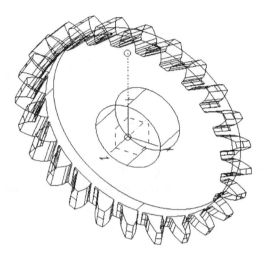

Figure 8.58

Figure 8.59 shows the rendering model of the gear.

Figure 8.59

**Step 6. Name the part and check it into the library.**

Select the **Name Parts** icon
Pick the part to name, then enter **"helical-gear"** in the Name field
Select the **Check In** icon
Pick the gear part to check in
Set the Check-In parameters as below.

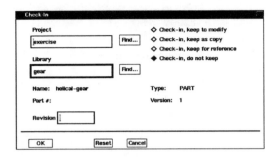

Select **OK**

# Chapter 8. Review Questions

1. What are variables?

2. What are the two types of variables? Describe them.

3. What are equations?

4. How do we relate variables to form desired relations in I-DEAS.

5. Explain how to create labels to dimension variables and feature parameters.

6. What are typical tasks performed in using equations?

7. How do we show variable labels in a graphic window?

8. Describe the format of condition equations.

9. What is a spline?

10. Describe how to create a spline curve using the Function Spline function.

11. What are input and output variables used by the Function Spline function?

12. Explain how to convert the angle unit from degrees to radians.

13. Describe how to modify existing algebraic equations in the Function Spline function.

# Chapter 9

# I-DEAS Data Management System

**Highlights of the Chapter**
- Data management system in I-DEAS
- Name parts
- Put away
- Get
- Manage bins
- Check in
- Check out
- Managing libraries

## Overview

I-DEAS provides a very powerful data management system for you to manage and control project data. I-DEAS data management concepts are analogous to an office space. I-DEAS has a data hierarchical structure to store part information. It consists of data installation, projects, model files, libraries, and catalogs. Data ownership can be set to one of two modes; administrator mode and user mode. It is set at the data installation parameter. A part model contains five types of information including topology, display attributes, physical properties, history tree, and metadata. The first four types are the part data and metadata is the data about part data. Metadata contains such information as names of the parts, where they are located, who created, relationships, etc. A project is a container for model files, libraries, and catalogs. It resembles a work cubicle in office. A model file contains everything you create during a work section. It is analogous to a desk with the workbench on top of several drawers. Drawers are referred to as bins in I-DEAS. A library is a permanent storage area like a bookshelf where you place data to share with others. A catalog is similar to a library where you store standard parts and features to be used by other users.

Parts you create can be checked in to libraries or catalogs. There are four check-in options to save a part file to the library; keep to modify, keep as copy, keep for reference, and do not keep. The selection of check in option greatly affects who has the ownership of the part model and who can make modification to the original model. I-DEAS provides three check-out options for getting a part from the library; reference, check-out, and copy. To be effectively using the I-DEAS data management system, it is essential to know how these check-in and check-out options affect the original part ownership. This chapter covers essential concepts of managing data files in I-DEAS.

# 9.1    I-DEAS Data Structure

I-DEAS Data Management (IDM) system keeps track of the files that the system creates for you. It uses the containers concept for data storage. Figure 9.1 shows the data structure used in I-DEAS. It has the following three layers; **Data installation**, **Projects**, and **Model file, library, and catalog**

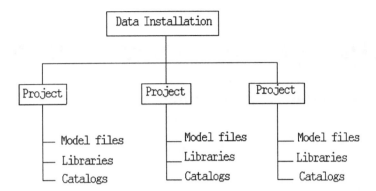

Figure 9.1

## Data Installation

The data installation concept is separate from the software installation. A data installation is all of the projects that are visible to users in the software. By default, there is one data installation for each software installation. However, it is possible to divide up the installation into multiple data installations. It is also possible to have multiple software installations share a common data installation. A data installation decides two important factors in managing data; **data ownership** and **data storage**.

### Data Ownership
I-DEAS allows data files to be shared by a team of users. The question of "who will own the files that I-DEAS creates?" must be addressed. The file ownership can be set to one of two modes; **administrator mode** and **user mode.**

#### Administrator mode
The I-DEAS administrator will own all I-DEAS data files. This mode prevents users from deleting files tracked by the I-DEAS data management at the operating system level. The users can only use commands and utilities in I-DEAS to delete items. This mode provides a higher level of data security and is recommended in most cases.

#### User mode
The users own their data files. This mode allow users to easily delete all of their own I-DEAS data files at the operating system level after a project is finished. This option is useful in training/education installations, or stand-alone installations where data is not normally shared between users.

### Data storage
There are five types of information that define a part in I-DEAS; **topology**, **display attributes**, **physical attributes**, **history tree**, and **data management metadata** (Figure 9.2).

Mastering I-DEAS,
Scholars International Publishing Corp., 1999

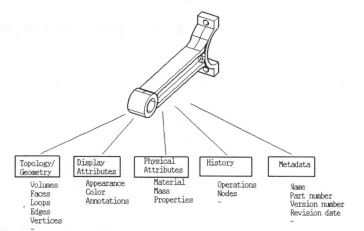

Figure 9.2

### Topology

I-DEAS part models contain a topology representation that describes the part geometry. Topology defines how volumes of the solid are defined by faces, how faces are defined by loops, how loops are defined by edges, and how edges are connected at vertices. The geometry of these topological elements is defined by **locations of vertices** and **equations for edges and surfaces**. Each of these topological elements is tracked in the I-DEAS software by ID labels (Figure 9.3). Features use these topological ID labels to keep track of relations between mating faces and edges.

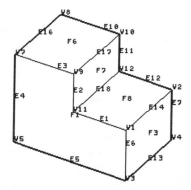

Figure 9.3

### Display attributes

Each surface of a part has display attributes such as color, glossiness, and transparency. Each feature you add uses a different color to differentiate its surfaces from the rest of the part.

### Physical properties

Mass properties of a solid part can be computed and listed. They include surface **area**, **volume**, **mass**, **center of gravity location**, and **moments of inertia**.

### History tree

The history tree of a part contains the **parts**, the **construction steps** in creating the final part, and the **rules defining the design intent** at each construction operation. The history tree is described by **nodes** and **leaves**, where the leaves are the features used and the node is the operation performed on the leaves, such as joining two features together (Figure 9.4).

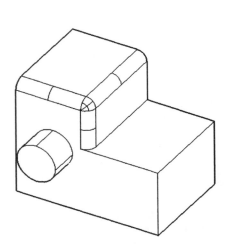

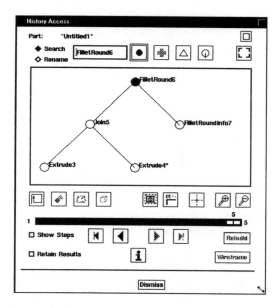

Figure 9.4a                                    Figure 9.4b

**Metadata**

I-DEAS uses the concept of "data about data" to store information about the data files. These information include:

| | |
|---|---|
| **Names of the files** | **Where they are located** |
| **Type of information in files** | **Who created the files** |
| **When they were created** | **Part number** |
| **Version number** | **Revision number** |
| **Relationships** | |

The project name you gave when you enter the I-DEAS software is the container for the project metadata. The part data and metadata are stored in different locations. Your part data is first created in your model file. When you name a part, the software creates the metadata describing that part. The part itself is in your model file, the metadata about that part is stored in a central project file. When you check your part into a library, the metadata is still stored in the project file, but the part data is now stored in the library file.

# Projects

A project is a container for model files, libraries, and catalogs. It is designed to make it convenient for a group of people working on the same design to share information, much the way you would share office space with people working in your design group. Individual work cubicles are analogous to projects (Figure 9.5). Projects contain **model files**, **libraries** and **catalogs**. The parts can be stored in two main areas; model files and libraries/catalogs. Initially, parts are temporarily created in the model file. Then they are stored in libraries or catalogs to share with others.

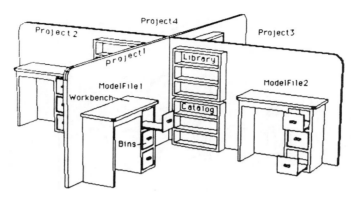

Figure 9.5 Courtesy of SDRC (from "I-DEAS Master Series Student Guide", 1999)

## Model file

A model file is made up of a workbench and any number of bins (Figure 9.6). It contains everything you create or generate during a work session for all I-DEAS applications. A model file is used for storing work-in-progress. Parts in the model file can be temporarily put away into bins in the model file, much like storing your work in a drawer in your desk.

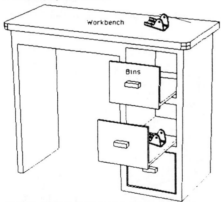

Figure 9.6   Courtesy of SDRC (from "I-DEAS Master Series Student Guide", 1999)

## Library

A library can be regarded as a permanent storage area, like a bookshelf, where you place data to share with others in your group (Figure 9.7). The advantages of using libraries include:

- **Share your work with other users**
- **Automatically update your work**
- **Control concurrent access**
- **Provide version control**
- **Provide a safe storage area for your work**

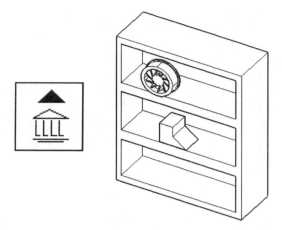

Figure 9.7

## Catalog

Catalogs contain standard parts and features that will be used by all users at a site (Figure 9.8). Only those parts and features that are not likely to change should be stored in a catalog. You can get copies of the items from a catalog. The system notifies you if the original item changes, however, it can not automatically update your copy with changes to the original item. Parts can be placed in a catalog as a parameterized part that lets the user change key parameters. Parts can also be placed into the catalog as a part family that contains a table with variable parameters for defining a series of similar parts.

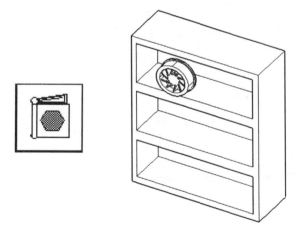

Figure 9.8

# 9.2  Naming a Part

After a part has been created on the workbench, you may want to give it a unique name and/or number. The "**Name Part**" command is used to name a part. You can name a part in one of the following two ways:

- **Name a part while you are still working on it**
- **Name a part while putting the part away**

**The procedure for naming a part while you are still working it is:**

1. Select the "Name Part" icon
2. The system prompts to pick a part to name:  pick the part
   The name menu appears as below.

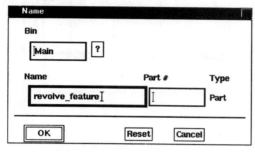

The three parameters in the name menu are:

**Bin:**     specifies the bin in which you want to put the part.
**Name:**   specifies the name of the part.
**Part #:**  specifies the part number associated with the item.

4. Select **OK** to name the part

**The procedure for naming a part while putting the part away is:**

1. Select the "Put Away" icon
2. The system will prompt to pick the part to put away:  pick the part
   The put away menu will appear as below for you to specify the name and part number for the part to put away.

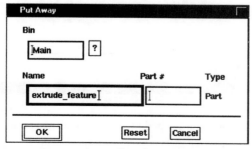

3. Enter the proper name and part # to the put away menu, then select OK to put away the part

# 9.3 Getting An Item from A Bin

This is the reverse process of putting away a part. Use the "Get" function to get an item out of the bin and place it on the workbench.

**The procedure for putting away a part is:**

1. Select "Get" to open the get menu which displays the names of the items in the bin as below.

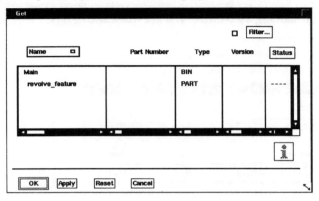

2. Pick the name from the list of items in the bin, then select OK
   The part appears on the screen as in Figure 9.9.

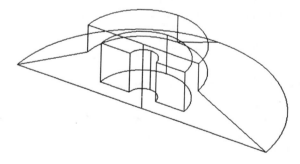

Figure 9.9

# 9.4 Managing Bins

Parts temporarily stored in bins can be managed in a variety of ways by using the "Manage Bin" menu as shown below.

# I-DEAS Data Management System

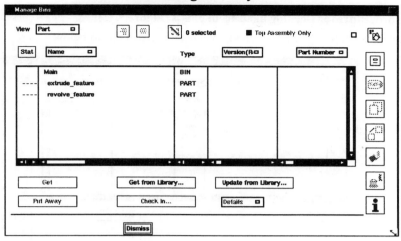

| Get: | get a selected item to the workbench. |
|---|---|
| **Get from library:** | get a item stored in the library. |
| **Put away:** | remove an item from the workbench and place it in a bin. |
| **Check in:** | check an item into a library or catalog. |
| **Update from library:** | update a library item to latest version. |
| **Create bin:** | create a new bin in the model file. |
| **Rename part:** | rename an item in the model file. |
| **Copy items:** | copy items in the model file. |
| **Move items:** | move items from one bin to another. |
| **Delete items:** | delete an item. |
| **Change library status:** | change library status of an item. |

Deleting parts are one of most commonly used functions in managing data files. There are two ways to delete a part; **deleting parts from workbench** and **deleting parts from bins**.

  **The procedure for Deleting parts from workbench is (Figure 9.10):**

1. Click on the "Delete" icon
2. The system will prompt "Pick entity to delete": pick the entity you want to delete
3. The system prompts "Parts have been selected for deletion. OK to delete these parts?": select OK

The part will be deleted from the workbench.

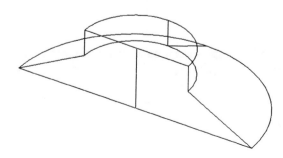

Figure 9.10

**The procedure for Deleting parts from bins is (Figure 9.11):**

1. Select the "Manage Bins" icon to open the manage menu as below.

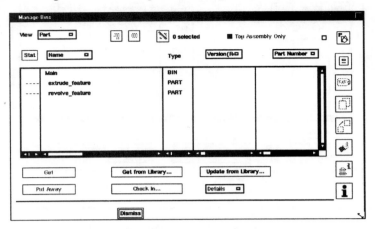

2. Select the item (bin, part, assembly, etc.) to highlight it
3. Select "Delete" icon in the manage menu to delete it

The Delete dialog box appears as below:

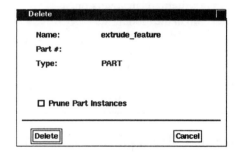

4. Select Delete

The part has been deleted from the Manage Bins as below.

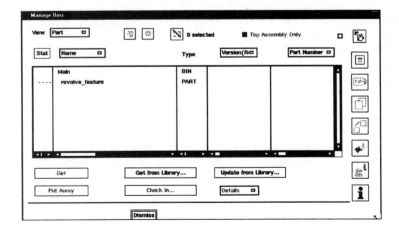

Mastering I-DEAS,
Scholars International Publishing Corp., 1999

# 9.5 Checking Parts into Libraries

After parts are created, they can be checked into libraries to share with someone else. There are four check in options you can choose from. They are explained in the table below.

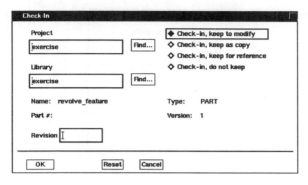

## Table 9.1 Four Check-in Options

| Check-In Option | Description | When to Use |
|---|---|---|
| Keep to modify | Place a new version of the in the library for others to reference or copy, but still have the original item in your model file and only you can modify it. | Want to keep working on a part, yet want to make it available to others. |
| Keep as copy | Place the original item in the library and keep a copy of it in your model file. You can not update your copy with changes made to the original item. You can request to be notified when the original changes. | Want to keep a copy without associativity to the part checked into the library. |
| Keep for reference | Place the original item in the library and keep a copy of it in your model file. You will be notified if someone changes the part in the library. | When a part is completed and want to be notified if others change it. |
| Do not keep | Place the original item in the library and completely remove the part from the model file. | When a part is completed and do not want to keep the part for reference or to modify. |

**The procedure for checking a part into the library (Figure 9.11):**

1. Select the "Check In" icon
2. Pick the pick to check in
3. Specify the library name and check-in option from the check-in menu as below.

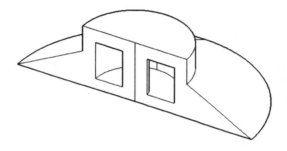

4. Select OK to complete the check-in procedure

Figure 9.11

The part is checked in to the library and has disappeared from the workbench.

# 9.6   Getting Parts from Libraries

Parts stored in the libraries can be readily checked out and become available for use.

**The procedure of checking out parts from libraries is:**

1. Select "Get From Library" icon to open the get from library menu as below.

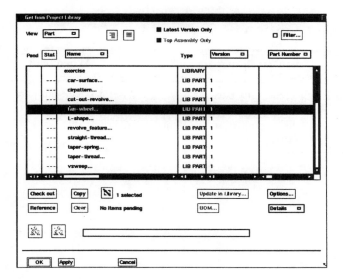

2. Highlight the part or entity to get from the list
3. Select the "Copy" option at the bottom the menu
4. Select "Apply" or "OK"
5. Select Get icon to open its dialog box
6. Select "fan-wheel" as below.

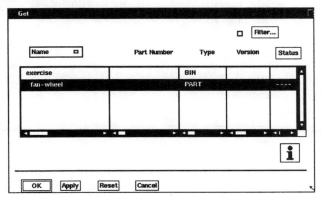

7. Select OK

The part is shown in Figure 9.12.

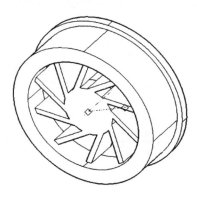

Figure 9.12

The three check-out options to choose from are described in the table below.

## Table 9.2 Check Out Options

| Check-out Option | Description | When to use |
| --- | --- | --- |
| Reference | Bring a read-only part into the model file and leave the original part in the library. You can not modify the reference part. | When a check out part is not intended to be modified. |
| Check-out | Place the original part in your bin and retain a read-only part in the library. | When a check-out part is expected to be modified. |
| Copy | Bring a copy of the part in your bin and leave the original part in the library. The copy can be modified and checked in to the library under a different part name. It can not be checked in as a version of the original. | When you want to create a new part by modifying the existing one in the library. |

# 9.7 Managing Libraries

I-DEAS provides five functions for you to manage data in data management system. They are:

| | |
| --- | --- |
| **Update from library:** | updates a library item to latest version. |
| **Manage items:** | accesses and modifies item details. |
| **Manage libraries:** | finds, displays, accesses, and modifies item details. |
| **Manage projects:** | accesses and modifies project details. |
| **Manage catalogs:** | finds, displays, accesses, and modifies catalog item details. |

Mastering I-DEAS,
Scholars International Publishing Corp., 1999

# Manage items

Click on the "Manage Items" icon to open the items menu as below.

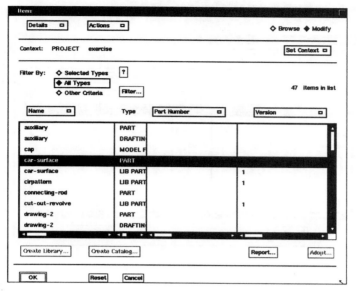

## Details

This parameter allows selection of the type of information to be displayed. You can select the one of following eight types:

| | |
|---|---|
| **Details:** | display the detail information of the libraries. |
| **Name:** | display the name information of the selected part. |
| **File:** | display the file information of the part. |
| **User attr:** | display the attribute labels and value of the selected part. |
| **Appl. Attr:** | display the application attributes of the selected part. |
| **History:** | display the construction history of the selected part. |
| **Access:** | display the ownership of the selected part. |
| **Related items:** | display the related information of the selected part. |

## Item Actions

This parameter performs a selected action on the selected items. Those actions may include the following:

| | |
|---|---|
| **Approve:** | approve the default state of new items. |
| **Copy:** | copy a selected part to a new file name. |
| **Delete:** | delete selected items and associated operating system files and relationships. |
| **Move:** | move a selected file to a new directory. |
| **Move Related:** | move a related file to a new directory. |
| **Rename:** | rename a selected file to a new name. |
| **Reconnect File:** | reconnect associated files. |
| **View File:** | view the associated files of selected part. |
| **Lock/Unlock:** | set or remove access for imported library items, or remove check out lock. |
| **Purge:** | purge a selected item. |
| **Create New Version:** | create a new version of the selected item. |
| **Update in Library:** | update the selected item to its latest in the library. |

# Manage projects

The managing projects dialog box appears as below.

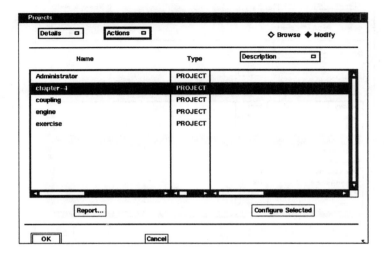

# Manage libraries

The manage libraries dialog box appears as below.

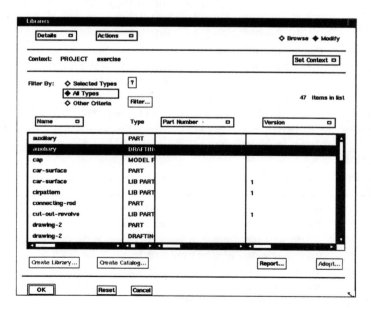

Mastering I-DEAS,
Scholars International Publishing Corp., 1999

## Manage catalogs

The manage catalogs dialog box appears as below.

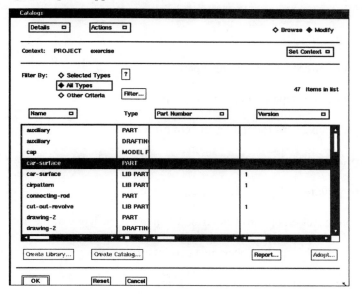

![Catalogs dialog box]

# Chapter 9. Review Questions

1. Use a drawing to describe the three layers of I-DEAS data management system.

2. What is a data installation?

3. What two factors in managing data are affected by the data installation?

4. List the two modes of file ownership and describe what they are.

5. What are the five types of information that define a part in I-DEAS?

6. How I-DEAS uses topology representation to describe the part geometry.

7. What are the mass properties that can be computed from a solid model?

8. What is the history tree?

9. What is the metadata?

10. What is a project?

11. What is a model file?

12. What is a library?

13. What is a catalog?

14. Describe the procedure steps for naming a part.

15. Describe the procedure steps for putting away a part.

16. Describe the procedure steps for getting an item from a bin.

17. Describe the procedure steps for deleting parts from the workbench.

18. Describe the procedure steps for deleting parts from bins.

19. What are the four check-in options? Describe when to use each one of them.

20. Describe the procedure steps for checking a part into the library.

21. Describe the procedure steps for getting parts from the library.

22. What are the three check-out options? Describe when to use each one of them.

Mastering I-DEAS,
Scholars International Publishing Corp., 1999

# Chapter

**10**

# Catalogs and Family Tables

## Highlights of the Chapter

- Using catalogs
- Creating Parameterized parts
- Adding parameterized parts to catalogs
- Creating family tables

## Overview

Many mechanical parts have similar features and shapes, yet have different dimensions and minor details. Typical examples of families of parts manufactured by a company include threads, screws, washers, blocks, cylinders, sphere, and tubes. I-DEAS uses **catalogs** and the **family table** function to quickly create those commonly used parts or features. A catalog contains a list of parts along with the major characteristics of each part represented by parameters or variables. By changing the values of the variables, we can readily define a new part or feature without stepping through the entire part creating process. Parts, features, sections, and surfaces can be defined and stored in catalogs.

Family tables are great tools to create a group of parts that are similar in shape. We need to create only a single part model, and then create a family table from this part to generate many other parts that differ in size. The part model used to create a family table is referred to as the **generic model**. All part models generated from the family tables are called **instances**. Dimensions and parameters can be included in the family table. Dimensions are numerical variables. Changing a numerical value in a dimension variable results in size variation. A greater flexibility comes with using patterns in family tables. Using patterns in family tables allows us to produce part families that can vary the number of identical features in instances. The number of fan blades in a wheel varying in instances is an example of using patterns in family tables. This chapter presents essential concepts and techniques for checking parts and adding features into catalogs, as well as how to retrieve parts from catalogs to regenerate a part or feature of desired size. The procedure for creating a family table is also covered.

# 10.1 Catalogs

A catalog is a list of standard parts or features stored in the system ready to be used. I-DEAS provides a variety of catalog functions to store parts, features, surfaces, sections, and fasteners in the system. The benefits of using catalog functions are:

- No need to recreate those parts, features, surfaces, sections that are often used in design.
- The components are parameter-driven from which values can be easily changed to redefine a new part to meet your needs.
- Saves time during the creation of standard mechanical elements such as fasteners.

I-DEAS provides the following catalog functions:

| | |
|---|---|
| **Parts:** | get parts from catalog. |
| **Features:** | get features from catalog. |
| **Surface features:** | get surface features from catalog. |
| **Sections:** | get sections from catalog. |
| **Fasteners:** | open the fastener icon subpanel to select fasteners. |
| **Modify catalog:** | define the part parameters, create a family table, check in entities, and create a catalog. |

A feature or part must be **parameterized** before a catalog can be created for it. The procedures for creating a parameterized part and "check it in" for creating a catalog are presented in this section.

## Creating a Parameterized Part

I-DEAS uses variables to control the shape and size of features or parts. These variables can be assigned as parameters. These values can be changed to generate a new feature or part. The process of assigning parameters to selected variables is referred to as "Parameterized" in I-DEAS.

Follow these steps in the parameterized procedure; they are presented like a project.

1. Create a part to be parameterized (Figure 10.1).

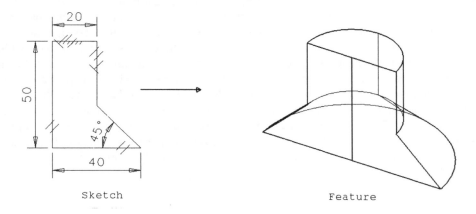

Sketch                              Feature

Figure 10.1

2. Select the **Modify Entity** icon, then pick the part to modify.

3. Select **Show Dimensions** from the options list, the dimensions of the part should appear on the screen.(Figure 10.2)

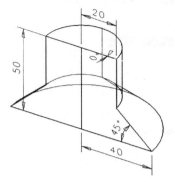

Figure 10.2

 4. Select **Catalogs** → **Modify Catalogs** to open the Catalog menu as shown here.

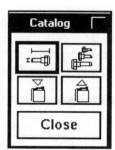

5. Select **Parameters** from the Catalog menu.
6. Pick the part to parameterize.

The Parameters menu appears with six variables of a revolved feature as below.

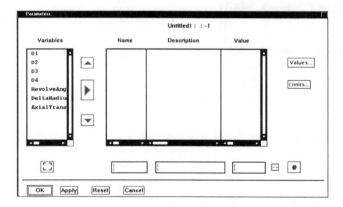

7. Select those variables to be assigned as parameters: select all six variables and then click the **Move** button.

# Catalogs and Family Tables

The new Parameters menu appears as below.

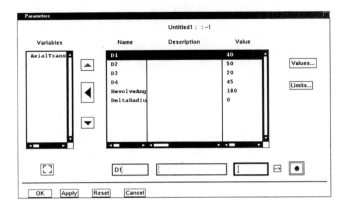

8. Assign parameter names to each name field: use the name field to change the name of four  parameters to "height", "top_radius", "base_radius", and "slope_angle", respectively. The new parameters menu becomes as below.

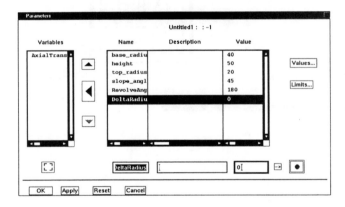

9. Select **OK** to exit the Parameters menu

# Check In Entities and Create Catalogs

After the part is parameterized, we need to "check it in" and create a catalog for it.  A parameterized part can be checked in and created as a part catalog or feature catalog. The difference between the part catalogs and feature catalogs is that features from catalogs are features only and they need to be joined to other parts by a Boolean operation.  The parts taken from part catalogs are treated as separate parts and do not need to reference to another part. Follow these steps to create a catalog for a parameterized part.

**The procedure for creating a part catalog for a parameterized part:**

1. Select "Check In" function from Catalog menu.
2. Pick the part to check in.

3. Define the name parameters as below:

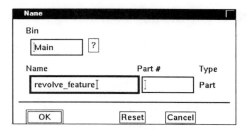

Select **OK**

4. Select **Catalog Part** from the options list and define the Check-In parameters as shown on the next page.

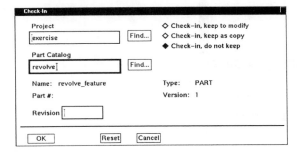

Select **OK**

5. Select **OK** to "New Catalog will be created".

The procedure for checking in a parameterized part as a feature catalog is same as checking in as a part catalog except the following two points:

4. Select **"Catalog Feature"** from options list.
5. Select one of **Boolean functions**; join, cut, or intersect for defining the feature relation

# 10.2 Getting Parts from Catalog

Commonly used parts can be defined as a parameterized part and stored in the catalog. There are two types of parts in a catalog; **primitives** and **user-defined**.

## Getting User-Defined Parts from Catalogs

The procedure for getting a user-defined part from catalogs is listed next. We use the revolved feature just created as an example.

**The procedure for getting a user-defined parts from catalogs:**

1. Select **Catalogs → Parts** to open the Part catalog menu as below.

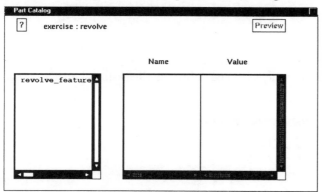

2. Click on "revolve feature" from the list to open its parameters as below.

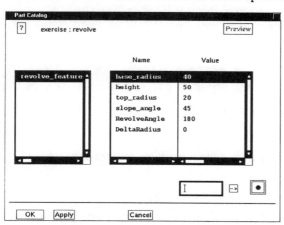

3. Modify the parameter values as shown in the next screen menu.

Mastering I-DEAS
Scholars International Publishing Corp., 1999

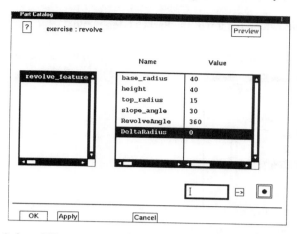

Select OK to generate the new part as shown in Figure 10.3

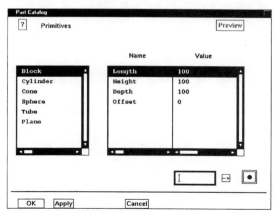

Figure 10.3

## Getting the Primitive Parts from the Catalog

Primitive parts include block, cylinder, cone, sphere, tube, and plane. They are defined by a group of dimensional variables. Table 10.1 summarizes the six primitive parts from catalogs.

 **The procedure for getting a primitive part from part catalogs:**

1. Select **Catalogs → Parts.**

The Part Catalog menu appears as below (Your menu may differ from the one shown here).

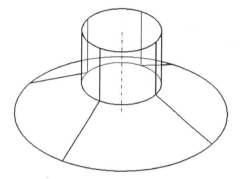

# Catalogs and Family Tables

2. Select **"Primitives"** if it is not shown on the top of the Part Catalog menu.

3. Select **Block** from the list, then define the four parameters to the new values as below.

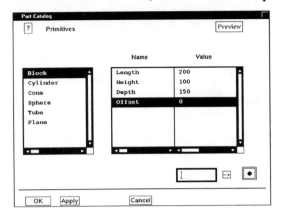

4. Select **OK** to exit the Part Catalog menu and create a block feature as shown here.

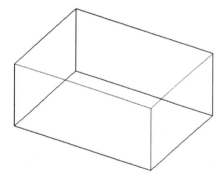

# Table 10.1 Six primitive parts from catalogs

| Primitive | Part Dimension Variables | Illustration |
|---|---|---|
| Block | Length<br>Height<br>Depth<br>Offset | |
| Cylinder | Radius<br>Height<br>Offset | |
| Cone | Bottom_Radius<br>Top_Radius<br>Height<br>Offset | |
| Sphere | Radius<br>Offset | |
| Tube | Inner_Radius<br>Outer_Radius<br>Height<br>Offset | |
| Plane | X-Dimension<br>Y-Dimension | |

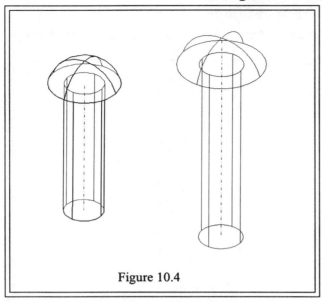

Figure 10.4

# Project 1.
# Creating a parameterized part and saving as a part in catalog

This project creates a round-head screw model. Its five dimensions are defined as parameters and each assigned a name for easy recognition. It is then checked in as a part catalog with a file name "screw-round". This catalog part is then checked out with a different set of variable values. Figure 10.4 shows the initial part and the check out part with new dimension values.

**Step 1. Create a sketch. Use Figure 10.5 as reference.**

 Use **Polylines** and **Three Points On** commands to create a section as shown in Figure 10.5.

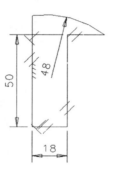

Figure 10.5

**Step 2. Add three dimensions to the section. Use Figure 10.6 as reference.**

Delete the vertical dimension

 Select **Dimension**, then add these three dimensions

        **Total height, Head height, Distance from center to outer edge of head**

*Note:* The dimension values should not be exactly as shown here.

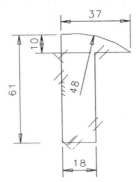

Figure 10.6

10-10

### Step 3. Create a revolved feature.

 Select **Revolve**
Pick the section to be revolved and select the **left vertical line** as the axis of revolution
Set the revolve angle to **360** to complete the feature as shown in Figure 10.7.

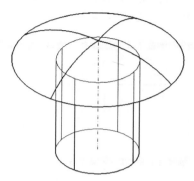

Figure 10.7

### Step 4. Show the dimensions.

 Select **Modify Entity**, then pick the revolve feature to modify
Select **Show Dimensions** from the options list
The five dimensions of the feature should appear on the screen as Figure 10.8.

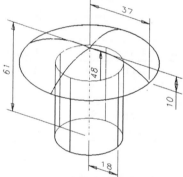

Figure 10.8

### Step 5. Open Modify Catalogs function.

 Select **Modify Catalogs** to open the Catalog menu
Select **Parameters** from the catalog menu
Pick the revolve feature to parameterize
The Parameters menu should appear as below.

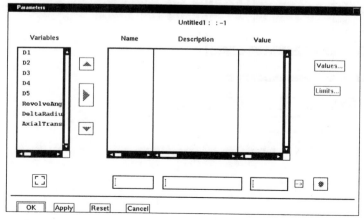

**Step 6. Assign a name to each of five variables.**

Select **D1** under the Variables column,

then select the **Move** icon to move this variable to right si ̇ ̇

Repeat this process until the remaining seven variables all go to the right side

The new Parameters menu should appear as below.

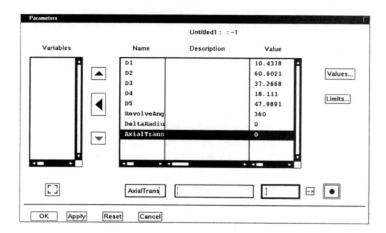

Change the name and value of **D1 - D5** variables to the following:

| Original name | New name | Value |
|---|---|---|
| D1 | Head_height | 4.5 |
| D2 | Total_height | 30 |
| D3 | Total_radius | 5.8 |
| D4 | Thread_radius | 3.2 |
| D5 | Head_radius | 6 |

The new parameters menu should appear as below.

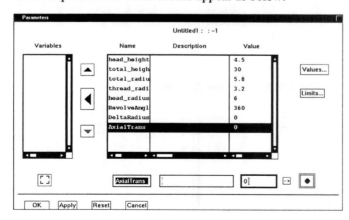

Select **OK** to exit the Parameters menu

Mastering I-DEAS
Scholars International Publishing Corp., 1999

**Step 7. Update the part.**

 Select the **Update** icon to update the changes of variable values to the part
The revolved feature should appear as Figure 10.9.

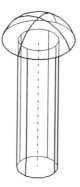

Figure 10.9

**Step 8. Create a catalog "screw-round".**

 Select **Modify Catalogs** → **Check In**
Pick the revolve feature just created
Define the Name menu as below.

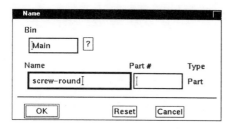

Select **OK**

 Select **Catalog Part** from the options list
Set the **Check-In** parameters as below.

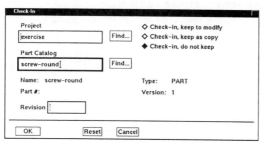

Select **OK**
Select **OK** to "New Catalog will be created"

### Step 9. Check out the catalog part "screw-round".

 Select **Parts**

Click the button next to "Primitives" to open Project: Catalog menu as below if necessary.

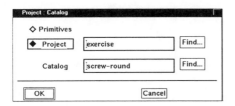

Click the **Project** button and the **Find...** button to the right
Select **exercise** from the Project Selection menu, then select **OK**
Click the **Find...** button for the Catalog field
Select "**screw-round**" from the Catalog Selection menu
Select **OK** to return to Project: Catalog menu
Select "**screw-round**" from the list
The screw-round catalog menu should appear as below.

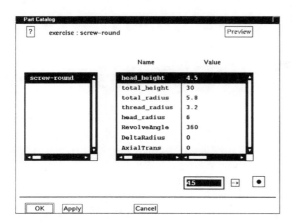

Select **OK**
The part is retrieved from the catalog as shown in Figure 10.10.

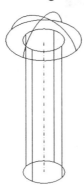

Figure 10.10

### Step 10. Put the part away.

 Select the **Put Away** icon
Pick the screw to put away
The screw is removed from the screen

10-14

**Step 11. Retrieve the part with the new dimension values.**

Repeat step 9 to check out the same part with the following new set of dimension values:

| | |
|---|---|
| Head_height | 6 |
| Total_height | 45 |
| Total_radius | 8 |
| Thread_radius | 4 |
| Head-radius | 8 |

The part is retrieved from the catalog with new dimensions as shown in Figure 10.11.

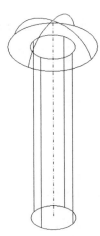

Figure 10.11

# 10.3 Creating Family Tables

In mechanical systems, we often use families of parts that are available in different sizes or have slightly different detailing features. For example, machine screws come in a variety of sizes, but they all perform the same function and look somewhat alike. I-DEAS uses family tables to generate a family of parts from a single part model. These families of parts are referred to as **table-driven parts** because they are created by using the variables from a table.

The part model used to generate the family table is called **generic model**. All family parts generated from the family table are referred to as **instances** (Figure 10.12). You can regard the generic part as the parent part and the instances as the child parts. They bear a parent-child relationship.

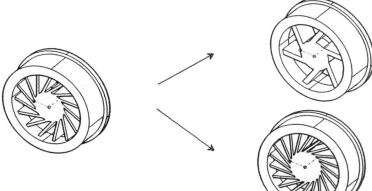

Figure 10.12

# Catalogs and Family Tables

A family table contains columns and rows as shown in Figure 10.13. It includes the following items: **Variables, Names, Dimensions** and **Variable values**.

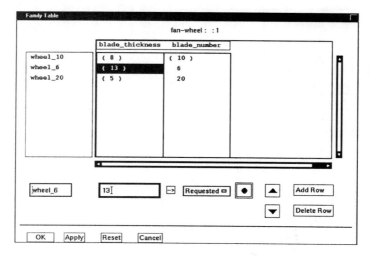

Figure 10.13

The advantages of using a family table are:

- Provide a simple and compact way of creating and storing a large number of parts
- Promote the use of standardized components
- Represent the actual part inventory on I-DEAS
- Facilitate interchangeability of parts and sub-assemblies in an assembly

There are two groups of dimensions in the generic model; **common dimensions** and **varying dimensions** (Figure 10.14). Common dimensions are those that have the same values in all instances. In other words, those dimensions remain the same from one instance to another. Varying dimensions are those dimensions whose values change from one instance to another instance. A family table does not require that all dimensions in the part model be included. Only varying dimensions need to be included in the family table.

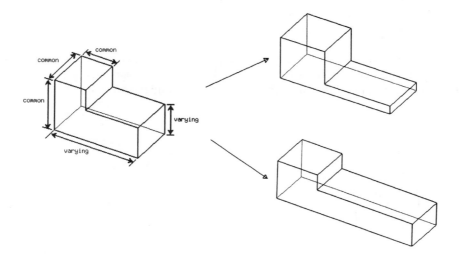

Figure 10.14

10-16

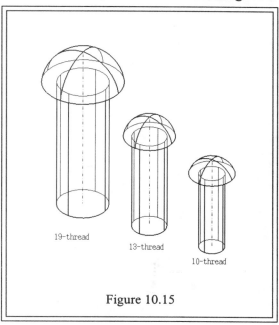

19-thread

13-thread

10-thread

Figure 10.15

## Project 2.
## Creating a family table for the round screw

This project uses the parameterized part "screw-round" created in project 1 of this chapter to create a family table. The family table consists of the generic part and three instances. Each of these three instances has a different set of dimension values for three instances that are tabulated below.

| Instances | Head height | Total radius | Total height | Thread radius | Head radius |
|-----------|-------------|--------------|--------------|---------------|-------------|
| G-thread  | (4.5)       | (5.8)        | (30)         | (3.2)         | (6)         |
| 10-thread | 6.5         | 8.5          | 40           | 4.8           | 9           |
| 13-thread | 9           | 9.5          | 50           | 6.4           | 10.3        |
| 19-thread | 14          | 15           | 70           | 9.5           | 15.9        |

The three instances are shown in Figure 10.15 above.

**Step 1. Retrieve the part "screw-round" from the Catalog.**

 Select **Parts**

Select the part to bring up the Catalog menu shown below.

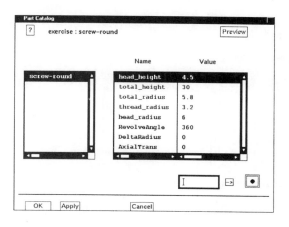

Select **OK** to open the screw part as in Figure 10.16.

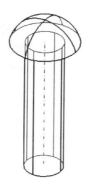

Figure 10.16

## Step 2. Parameterize the part.

Select the **Parameters** icon
Pick the part to parameterize
Set the parameters as below.

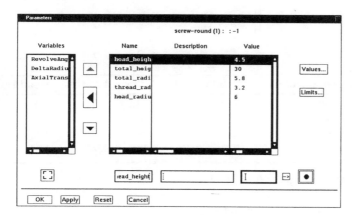

## Step 3. Initiate the family table function.

Select **Modify Catalogs** to open the Catalog menu
Select the **Family Table** icon

Pick the screw (parameterized part)
The family table menu should appear as below.

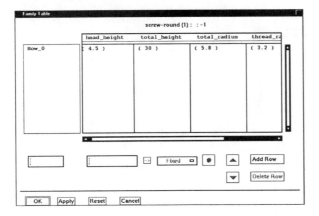

**Step 4.   Add three rows to the family table.**

Select the **Add Row** button three times to add three rows as shown below.

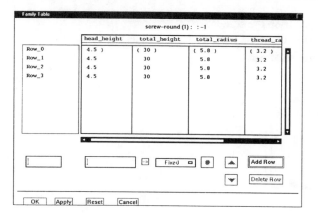

**Step 5.   Rename the instance names and define the parameter valuesas below.**

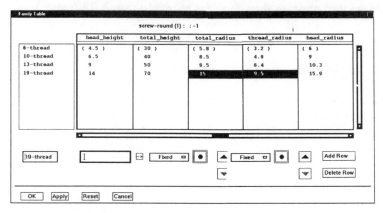

Select **OK** to complete the family table

**Step 6.   Check in to create a catalog.**

Select "**Check In**" from the Catalog menu
Pick the part to check in
Select **Catalog Part** from the options list
Define the check-in parameters as below.

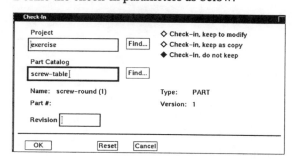

Select **OK**
Select **OK** to "New Catalog will be created"

**Step 7. Get the thread catalog just created.**
Select **Catalogs** → **Parts**
The part catalog menu should appear on the screen.
Click "screw-round" from the list to open the part catalog menu as shown below.

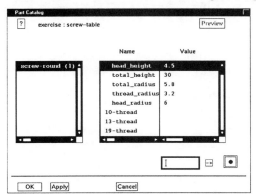

Scroll the vertical bar to the bottom to show three instances (10-thread, 13-thread, and 19-thread) appear

**Step 8. Select "19-thread" instance.**
Click on the **"19-thread"** instance, then select **OK**
The 19-thread instance should appear on the screen as in Figure 10.17.

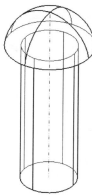

Figure 10.17

**Step 9. Generate the other two instances "10-thread and 13-thread".**
Repeat step 7 to open the other two instances "10-thread" and "13-thread"
These two instances should appear as in Figure 10.18.

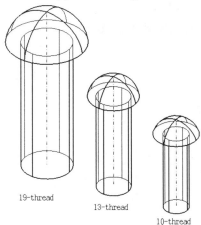

19-thread

13-thread

10-thread

Figure 10.18

10-20

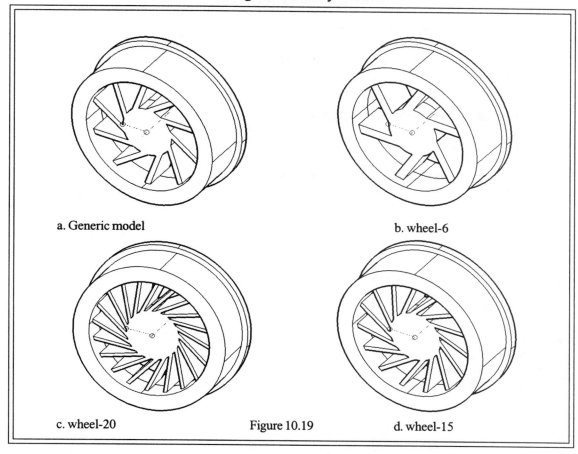

a. Generic model

b. wheel-6

c. wheel-20

Figure 10.19

d. wheel-15

# Project 3. Creating a family table with a circular pattern

The family table created in project 2 involves only dimension parameters. I-DEAS allows pattern parameters to be used in the family tables. This capability facilitates the number of features in the instances to be changed easily. This project adds a family table to a wheel model which is created using the circular pattern function introduced in chapter 7. Two variables are included in the family table; blade thickness and blade number. Figure 10.19 shows the generic model and three instances created from the family table. The instance values of the family table for this project are given below.

| Instances | Blade-thickness | Blade-number |
|---|---|---|
| wheel 10 (generic) | (8) | (10) |
| wheel-6 | 18 | 6 |
| wheel-20 | 5 | 20 |

Figure 10.19d shows an instance created by using the generic model with different values for the two parameters. The blade number is 15 and the blade thickness is 6.

**Step 1. Check out the part "fan-wheel" from the library.**

Select **Get** from the Library to open the Get menu
Select the part from the library as shown next

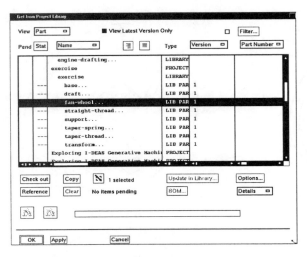

Select "fan-wheel" from the list
Click on **"Copy"** near the bottom of the menu
Select **OK** to get the part

**Step 2.** **Get the part from the bin.**

 Select **"Get"** to open the Get menu
Select **"fan-wheel"** from the part list.
Select **OK** to bring the part to the workbench as shown in Figure 10.20.

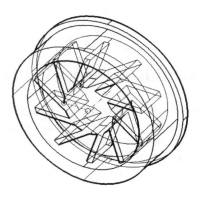

Figure 10.20

**Step 3. Show dimensions.**

 Select **Front (XY) view**
Select the **Modify Entity** icon
Pick on the part to select the entity to modify
 Select **Show Dimensions** from the options list
The dimensions of the part should appear as in Figure 10.21.

10-22

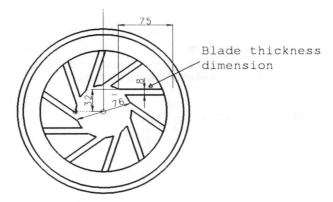

Blade thickness
dimension

Figure 10.21

## Step 4.  Initiate parameterize function.

 Select **Modify Catalogs → Parameters**
Pick the part to parameterize
The Parameters menu should appear as below.

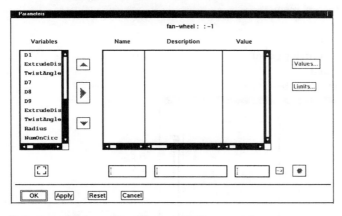

## Step 5.  Select variables using Figure 10.21 as a reference.

Click on the **"pick dimensions from screen"** icon,
then pick the blade thickness dimension **"D8"** from the part model (Figure 10.21)
Select **OK**
Click on the **Move** button
Click **"NumOnCir"** from the Variables list, then click on the **Move** button
The Parameters menu becomes as below.

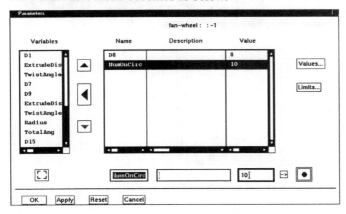

**Step 6.** **Change two variable names.**

Click in the "**D8**" row

Place the cursor on Name field "**D8**" and change it to "blade_thickness"

Click on the **NumOnCirc** row, then enter "blade_number" into the name field

The two new variable names appear on Parameters menu as below.

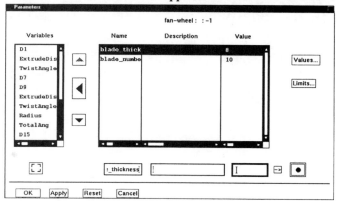

Select **OK** to exit the Parameters menu

**Step 7.** **Initiate the family table function.**

 Select **Family Table** from the Catalog panel

Pick the part just parameterized

The Family Table menu appears as below.

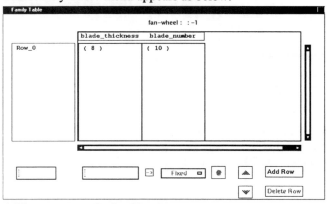

**Step 8.** **Add two rows to the family table.**

Click the **Add Row** button twice (it is located at lower right corner of the family table)

This will add two instances to the family table as below.

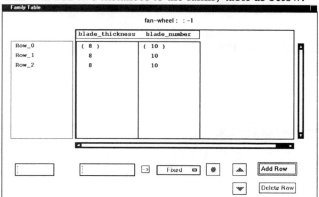

Mastering I-DEAS
Scholars International Publishing Corp., 1999

**Step 9. Change instance names and their parameter values.**

Click **Row_0**, then click the row field and change its content to **"wheel_10"**
Change the row field,
and two parameters to proper names and values for row_1 and row_2 as below.
Select **"Requested"** for entering the blade thickness parameter.

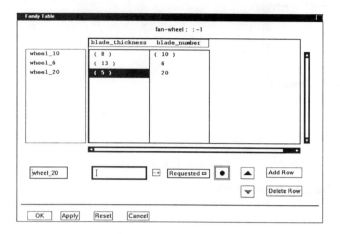

Select **OK** to complete the family table

**Step 10. Check it in to create a catalog.**

 Select **Check In** from the Catalog menu
Pick the part to check in
Select **Catalog Part** from the options list
Define the Check-In parameters as below.

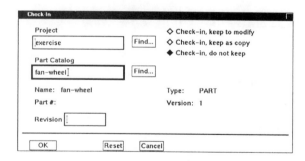

Select **OK**
Select **OK** to "New Catalog will be created"
Select **Close** to close the Catalog menu

**Step 11. Get a catalog part just created.**
Select **Parts** → **OK**

# Catalogs and Family Tables

The Part Catalog menu should appear as below.

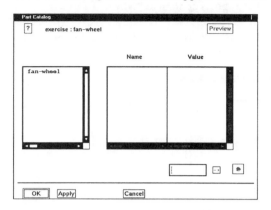

Click on the **"fan wheel"** to bring up more information as below.

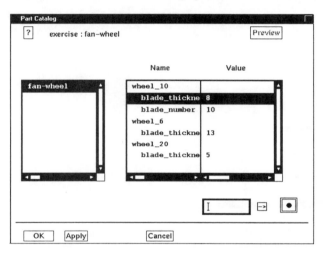

**Step 12. Select an instance "wheel_6" from the part catalog.**

Click wheel_6 from Part Catalog

Select **OK**

The instance should appear as in Figure 10.22.

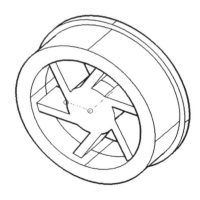

Figure 10.22

**Step 13. Put away the instance.**

Select the **Put Away** icon
Pick the instance part just generated

**Step 14. Generate the instance "wheel_20".**

Select **Parts** to open the Part Catalog menu
Select **fan-wheel** from the part catalog
Select **wheel_20"** from the instance list
Select **OK**
The instance should be generated as in Figure 10.23.

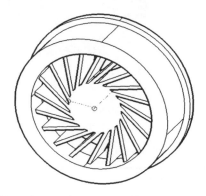 

Figure 10.23

**Step 15. Put away the instance.**

Select the **Put Away** icon
Pick the part to put away

---

| **Note:** | You can change the values to the parameters in the main (generic) part to generate a new part. We will assign a different value for each parameter for generating an instance. |
|---|---|

**Step 16. Generate a new part from the generic part.**

Select **Parts**
Select **fan-wheel** from the part catalog to open parameters and instances
Assign new values: wheel_10  blade_thickness = **6** and blade_number= **15** as below.

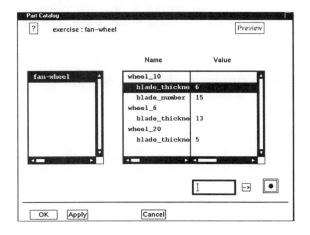

Select **OK**

The new instance appears as in Figure 10.24.

Figure 10.24

# Chapter 10. Review Questions

1.  What is a catalog?

2.  List the benefits of using catalog functions.

3.  What is parameterized in I-DEAS?

4.  Describe the procedure to parameterize a part.

5.  Describe the difference between the part catalogs and feature catalogs.

6.  Describe the "check in" procedure for a parameterized part and creating a catalog.

7.  What are the two types of parts in catalogs?

8.  What are primitive parts in catalogs?

9.  Describe the procedure for creating a part using primitive catalogs.

10. What are the six primitive parts in catalogs?

11. What are family tables?

12. Describe the benefits of using family tables.

13. Describe the relationship between generic part and instances.

14. Describe the procedure for creating a family table.

10-28

# Chapter

# Creating Assemblies

## Highlights of the Chapter

- Degrees of Freedom
- Acquiring parts and assemblies for assembly
- Defining assembly hierarchy
- Placement constraints
- Basic concepts of assembling parts
- Exploded assembly
- Modifying an assembly

## Overview

Most parts created in I-DEAS are used to form a sub-assembly or an assembly. An **assembly** is the process of constraining the degrees of freedom of component parts for building up a complete unit. This chapter covers the basic principles of creating an assembly. They include degrees of freedom, acquiring parts for assembly, defining assembly hierarchy, placement constraints, modifying assemblies, and exploded assemblies. The chapter concludes with three assembly projects. The first project is a simple coupling assembly that consists of only three components. This simple project is intended for you to practice the basic assembly procedure and lay the groundwork for creating larger assemblies in the second and third projects.

# 11.1 Degrees of Freedom and Constraints

Without being constrained, a part can move freely in space. There are two types of movements; **translational** and **rotational**. An object can move with six degrees of freedom (DOFs) including three translational DOFs and three rotational DOFs. Translational DOFs allow a part to move in the specified axis direction, and rotational DOFs allow it to rotate about the specified axis (Figure 11.1).

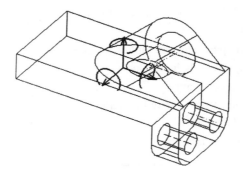

Figure 11.1

A **constraint** eliminates one degree of freedom of rigid body motion. A fully constrained rigid body can not move in any direction. I-DEAS uses six constraint commands to constrain instances in the assemblies. They are **parallel, perpendicular, tangent, coincident and collinear, dimension,** and **fix**. These six constraint commands are presented in the following sections.

# 11.2 Assembly

An **assembly** is an entity that organizes instances into a spatial and logical hierarchy. **Instances** can be any collection of parts from the workbench, bins, catalogs, or libraries. Instances can also be other assemblies. The assemblies that are used as instances to form another assembly are referred to as **subassemblies**. Figure 11.2 shows an assembly that consists of several instances.

## Assemblies can be used to:

1. Perform the analysis of configuration creation, physical properties, interference checking, or a visual check through animation.
2. Investigate the modification of a part, since assemblies can reflect changes.
3. Define relationships between parts, specifically their position and dimensional relationships.

Mastering I-DEAS
Scholars International Publishing Corp., 1999

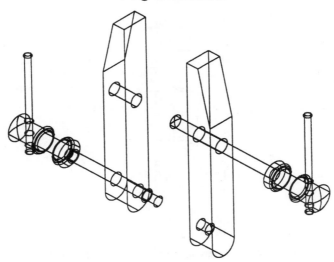

Figure 11.2

## Relationship of parts, part instances, and assembly instances

A **part** is the actual part model created using various modeling functions. A **part instance** is the duplicated copy of the part model that can be used in assembly, testing, etc. The instances used in the assembly are referred to as assembly instances. Parts and their instances bear a definite relationship. The changes made to a part will be automatically reflected to its instances. However, the changes made to an instance can not reflect back to the part.

## Assembly and subassemblies

When the number of instances used in an assembly has become very large, we can organize part instances into several subassemblies. Then we assemble subassemblies to form the final assembly. Subassemblies are regarded the same as instances. This means we can check an assembly into a library, then retrieve this assembly to the workbench and constrain it as a subassembly to the current assembly model. In this way we can easily handle very large assembly systems.

## Assembly hierarchy

The first step in creating an assembly is to set up its assembly hierarchy (or structure) that outlines the structure of assembly and subassemblies. After an assembly hierarchy is created, we can add instances to assembly and subassemblies. The assembly hierarchy functions are shown next.

| | |
|---|---|
| **Hierarchy:** | manages the hierarchy and display the workbench assembly. |
| **Add to assembly:** | adds a part instance or assembly. |
| **Remove from assembly:** | removes the selected part instance or subassembly. |
| **Replace instance:** | replaces the selected part instance or subassembly. |
| **Duplicate instance:** | duplicates the selected part instance or subassembly. |
| **Make unique:** | creates a new part or assembly and adds it to the assembly. |

The Hierarchy function manages the hierarchy and display of the workbench assembly. We can arrange the assemble structure using this function. Click this icon to open the Hierarchy menu as shown next.

# Creating Assemblies

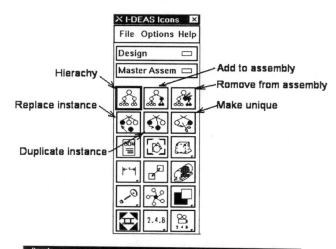

Hierarchy
Add to assembly
Remove from assembly
Replace instance
Make unique
Duplicate instance

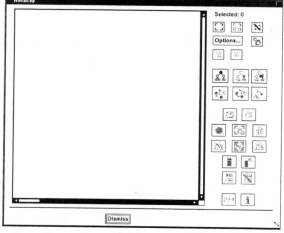

**The procedure for using the Hierarchy function:**

1. Create the top-level assembly for the workbench.
   Click the "**Top-level assembly**" icon to open the "Name" menu
   Define the name for bin, assembly name, and part # as below.

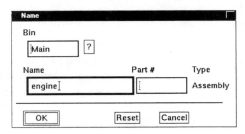

The "engine" is added to the Hierarchy menu

2. Add subassemblies.
   Click "**engine**" from Hierarchy menu
   Select the "**Add an empty subassembly**" icon
   The Name menu should appear again for you to enter a subassembly name.
   Enter "**block**" into the name field.
   The subassembly "block..." is added as shown next.

11-4

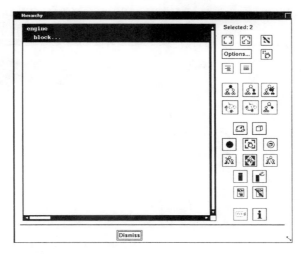

3. Add another subassembly "piston".
    Select the "**Add an empty subassembly**" icon
   Add "**piston**" to the name filed in Name menu
   The "piston" subassembly is added as below.

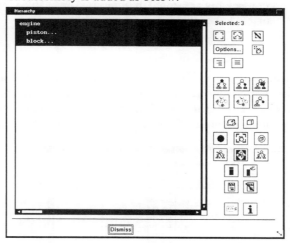

# 11.3 Get Parts for Assembly

Parts used in the assembly can be acquired from the following sources:
Workbench
Libraries
Catalogs

## Getting parts from the workbench

The parts already in the workbench can be readily used in the assembly. Select the "Add instance" icon in the assembly menu to allow the parts selected from the workbench to be added to the assembly. There are three parts currently in the workbench (Figure 11.3). We add these three parts to the assembly using the "Add instance" function.

The assembly hierarchy should appear as below after these three parts are added.

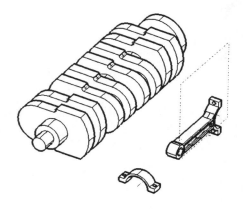

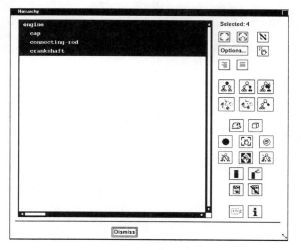

Figure 11.3

# Get parts from libraries

Most parts used to create a larger assembly are stored in libraries. They can be retrieved from libraries to the workbench and become available to be included in the assembly.

**The procedure for getting parts from libraries:**

1. Select the "**Get from Library**" icon to open the "**Get from Project Library**" menu
2. Select the "**engine**" project and "**engine-assembly**" Library to further list the library parts
3. Select two parts "**connecting-rod**" and "**cap**" under the engine-assembly menu
4. Select the "**Copy**" option after selecting each part. The menu should appear as below.

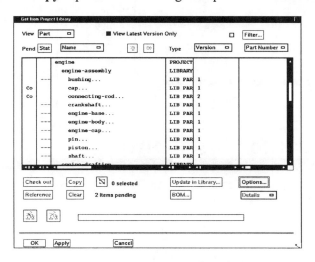

5. Select the "**OK**" to exit the Get from the Library menu
6. Select the "**Get**" icon to open the Get menu as below.

# Creating Assemblies

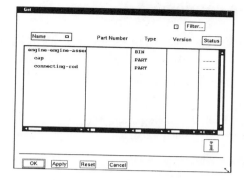

7. Select "**cap**" and "**connecting-rod**" from the list, then select OK
   The two parts are retrieved and appear on the screen as in Figure 11.4.

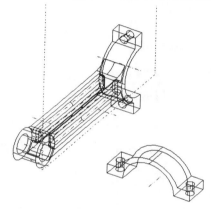

Figure 11.4

 8. Select the "**Add a part instance to assembly**" icon
   The system will prompt you to enter the assembly name if it is not available yet.
   Enter "**engine**" if necessary.
   If an active assembly is available,
    pick the middle mouse button to open the "**Hierarchy Selection**" menu.
9. Select the "**piston...**" from the list, then select **OK**
10. Pick two components from the screen to add to the selected subassembly
 11. Click the "**Hierarchy**" icon to open the Hierarchy menu to show the two instances under
    the "piston" subassembly as below.

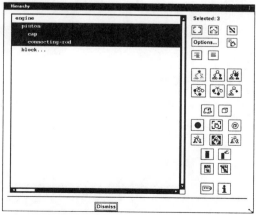

12. Select **Dismiss** to return back to graphic mode

# Getting parts from catalogs

Standard parts and user-defined parts in catalogs can be retrieved as instances for assembly.

**The procedure for getting parts from catalogs:**

1. Select **Catalogs → Part**
2. Enter the part name to get from the catalog menu as below
   (you may not have this part in your library).

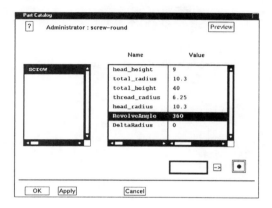

3. Select **OK** to add the part to the workbench as in Figure 11.5.

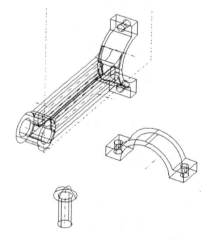

Figure 11.5

# 11.4 Constraining Instances in Assemblies

I-DEAS uses various constraint functions to constrain instances to the assembly. These functions are organized in the Constrain panel as shown below.

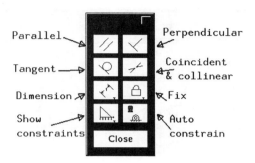

The constraint functions are briefly described below:

**Parallel:** constrains two entities being parallel to each other.
**Perpendicular:** constrains two entities being perpendicular to each other.
**Tangent:** constrains an entity being tangent to something curved.
**Coincident and collinear:** constrains entities being coincident, collinear or coplanar.
**Dimension:** creates a linear, angular, or radial dimension.
**Fix:** a group of functions to fix or maintain their relative positions of the entities.
**Show constraints:** shows free geometry, effects of constraints, and constraints.
**Auto constrain:** automatically constrains wireframe sections.

Assembly constraints are labeled by a symbol and a name. Table 11.1 displays the constraint symbols.

## Table 11.1 Constraint symbols and names

| Constraint Type | Symbol |
|---|---|
| Parallel | // |
| Perpendicular | |
| Tangent | ⟨ |
| Coincident and Collinear | ⚲ |
| Dimension | ⤢ |
| Fix | ⤢ |

# Parallel constraint

This function constrains two entities as parallel to each other. These two entities can be lines and planar surfaces. It can have a combination of line-line, line-face, and face-face. Table 11.2 illustrates the three cases using the parallel constraint.

## Table 11.2  Parallel constraints

| Entity Types | Description | Illustration |
|---|---|---|
| Line-line | The two selected lines from two instances are parallel to each other. | |
| Line-face | The selected line in one instance is parallel to the selected face in another instance. | |
| Face-face | The two selected faces from two instances are parallel to each other. | |

If two selected faces have been parallel, yet not aligned, the instances will not move (Figure 11.6a). If two selected faces are not parallel yet, the parallel constraint will cause one of the instances to move into having a parallel relation (Figure 11.6b).

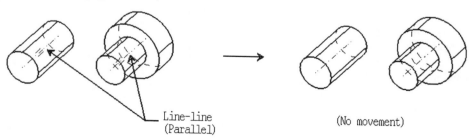

Line-line
(Parallel)

(No movement)

Figure 11.6a.  Already parallel

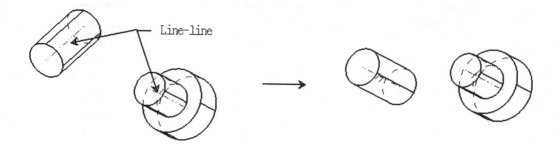

Figure 11.6b  Not parallel yet

If neither of the two selected entities has been locked, the first picked entity will move to retain the parallel relation, while the second picked entity will remain in the same position (Figure 11.7). If one of two selected entities has been locked, then the unlocked entity always moves to retain the parallel relation with the locked one, disregarding the picking order (Figure 11.8).

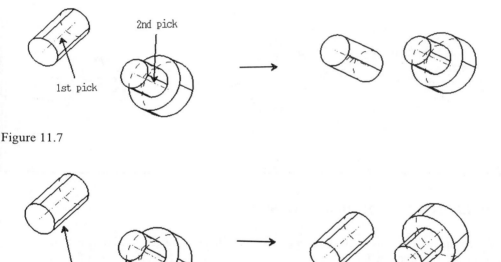

Figure 11.7

Figure 11.8

## Perpendicular constraint

This function constrains two entities perpendicular to each other. It can be used to constrain between two faces, two lines, or one line and one face. Table 11.3 illustrates the three cases using perpendicular constraint.

## Table 11.3  Perpendicular constraints

| Entity Type | Description | Illustration |
|---|---|---|
| Line-line | The two selected lines from two instances are perpendicular to each other. | |
| Line-face | The selected line is perpendicular to the selected face from the other instance. | |
| Face-face | The two selected faces from two instances are perpendicular to each other. | |

# Coincident and Collinear Constraint

This function constrains two entities coincident, collinear or coplanar. It can be used to constrain two faces, two lines, or one line and one face as coincident. Table 11.4 illustrates three cases of coincident and collinear constraint.

## Table 11.4  Coincident and collinear constraint

| Entity Type | Description | Illustration |
|---|---|---|
| Line-line | Two selected lines from two instances that are collinear to each other. | |

Mastering I-DEAS
Scholars International Publishing Corp., 1999

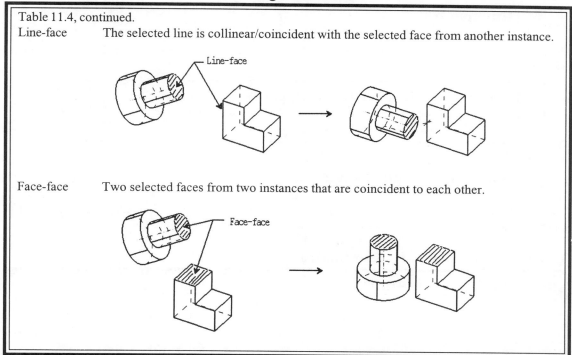

Table 11.4, continued.

Line-face    The selected line is collinear/coincident with the selected face from another instance.

Face-face    Two selected faces from two instances that are coincident to each other.

## Tangent constraint

This function constrains a selected entity tangent to a curved entity. It requires one curved entity and one face (Figure 11.9).  No two curved entities or two faces are allowed. You can use the "Flip" option in the Assembly Relations Browser to change the tangent side between two instances (Figure 11.10).

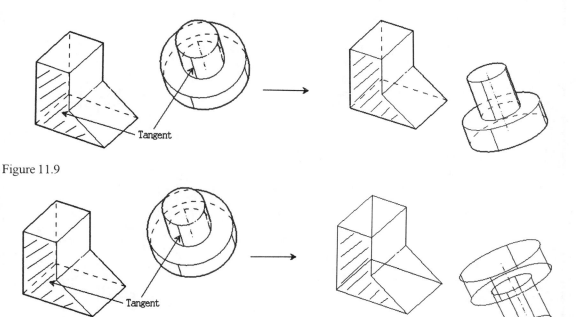

Figure 11.9

Figure 11.10

# Dimension

Dimensions are often used to constrain instances in an assembly. The following three dimension types are used in I-DEAS:

| | |
|---|---|
| **Linear:** | add a linear dimension to constrain two instances. |
| **Angular:** | add an angular dimension to constrain two instances. |
| **Radial:** | add a radial dimension to constrain instances. |

## Linear dimension constraint

The eligible entity types to be used for applying linear dimension constraints include points, lines, and planar surfaces. Table 11.5 illustrates the five possible combinations of entity types.

### Table 11.5  Five types of linear dimension constraints

| Entity Combination | Description | Illustration |
|---|---|---|
| Point-line | A linear dimension is added between a point in one instance and a line in another instance. | |
| Point-surface | A linear dimension is added between a point in one instance and a planar surface in another surface. A text plane is required to place the dimension text. The text plane should be perpendicular to the selected planar surface. | |
| Line-line | A linear dimension is added between two lines from two instances. The two lines must be parallel. | |

Mastering I-DEAS
Scholars International Publishing Corp., 1999

Table 11.5, continued

Line-surface A linear dimension is added between a line in one instance and a planar surface in another instance. The line and surface should be parallel.

Surface-surface A linear dimension is added between two planar surfaces from two instances. The two surfaces must be parallel.

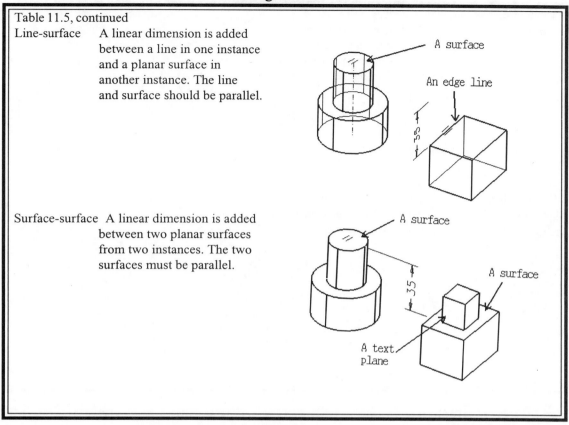

## Angular dimension constraint

The available entity types for adding angular dimension between two instances are lines and planar surfaces. Table 11.6 shows examples of three possible combinations of entity types for angular dimensions.

**Table 11.6  Three types of angular dimension constraints**

| Entity Combination | Description | Illustration |
|---|---|---|
| Line-line | Add an angular dimension between two lines from two instances. The two selected lines must lie in the same plane. | |

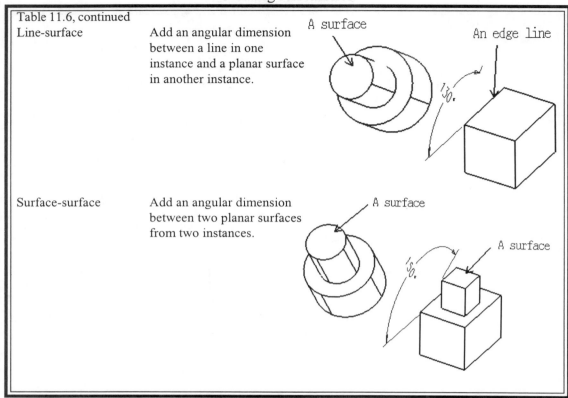

| Table 11.6, continued | | |
|---|---|---|
| Line-surface | Add an angular dimension between a line in one instance and a planar surface in another instance. | |
| Surface-surface | Add an angular dimension between two planar surfaces from two instances. | |

## Fix Functions

I-DEAS provides a group of six functions for fixing an entity at the specified location, orientation, etc. They are summarized in Table 11.7.

**Table 11.7  Entity fixing functions**

| Fixing Function | Description | Illustration |
|---|---|---|
| Anchor | Geometry will not be movable by constraints or dimensions. | |
| Fix Angle | Fix the angular orientation of a line. | |

Mastering I-DEAS
Scholars International Publishing Corp., 1999

Table 11.7, continued

| | | |
|---|---|---|
| Horizontal Ground | Constrain a line or surface so that it will be horizontal. | Horizontal ground symbol |
| Vertical Ground | Constrain a line or surface so that it will be vertical. | Vertical ground symbol |
| Lock | Constrain two instances to maintain their relative position. | Lock symbols |
| Fuse | All instances will maintain their relative position. | Fuse symbol |

# 11.5 Modifying Constraints

After a constraint is applied to two instances, the constraint symbol should appear on the two constrained entities. Constraint symbols are shown below.

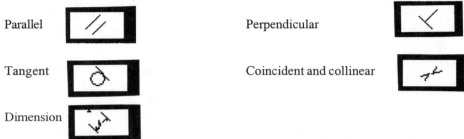

Parallel

Perpendicular

Tangent

Coincident and collinear

Dimension

All constraints are labeled with a GC followed by a number (ex. GC1, GC2, etc.). It is possible to modify constraints after they are created. I-DEAS uses "Assembly Relations Browser" functions to modify constraints. Follow this procedure to initiate the"Assembly Relations Browser" menu (Figure 11.11):

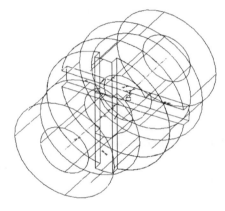

Figure 11.11

 **Procedure for Modifying constraints:**

 1. Select the **"Browse Relations"** icon
2. Pick any instance in the assembly to display constraint relations
3. The "Assembly Relations Browser" menu will appear as below.

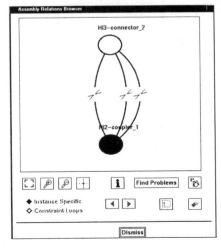

The browser menu shows assembly instances and their constraint relations. You can use this browser to perform the following operations:

## Graphically display the entities that are constrained in instances.

Click the constraint symbol on the browser menu, the constrained entities on two instances should be highlighted on the graphic window.

## Modifying constraints

The selected constraint can be disabled and/or flipped.

**The procedure for Modifying Constraints is:**

1. Click the constraint symbol in the browser menu
2. Select the Modify icon in the browser menu
   to open the "Modify Options" menu as below.

```
Disable
Flip
Backup
Cancel
```

---

**Disable:** disable the selected constraint. A parentheses is added to the disabled constraint in the browser. It can be enabled again by selecting the "Enable" option.

**Flip:** change the orientation of instances for coincident/collinear constraint and the side of tangency. The Flip option is only available with the "Coincident and collinear" and "Tangent" constraint types. Figure 11.12 shows the effect of using Flip on the coincident constraint and tangent constraint.

---

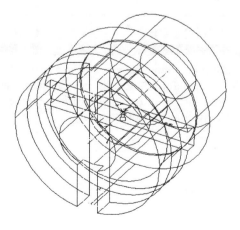

Figure 11.12

## Delete constraints

The Delete option removes the selected constraint from instances. (Figure 11.13):

**The procedure to Delete Constraints:**

1. Click the constraint to be deleted from the browser menu
2. Select the **Delete** icon from the browser menu
3. Select **OK** to "OK to delete the selected relation?"

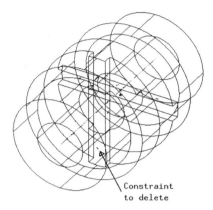
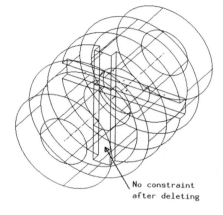

Figure 11.13

The other method for deleting constraints is to use the regular "Delete" function. This delete mode is not operated from the "Assembly Relations Browser" menu.

**The procedure for using the regular Delete function:**

1. Select the **Delete** icon
2. Pick the assembly symbol to delete, then click the middle mouse button
3. The system prompts "OK to delete 1 constraint (Yes)": select "**Yes**" to confirm it

# 11.6  Moving Instances Without Constraints

I-DEAS offers the five transform functions that are used in Master Modeler for moving instances in the assembly mode. These five transform functions move instances to new locations without constraining them. They are used to move instances to proper locations before applying constraining functions. Table 11.8 summarizes these five transform functions.

Mastering I-DEAS
Scholars International Publishing Corp., 1999

## Table 11.8  Five transform functions for moving instances

| Transform Function | Description | Illustration |
|---|---|---|
| Move | Moves entities from one location to another. | Move to here |
| Rotate | Rotates selected entities by three angles about three principal axes or a vector about a pivot point. | Rotate about x-axis for a -45 degrees |
| Align | Aligns two planar surfaces from two instances face-to-face. | Align these two surfaces |
| Drag | Dynamically moves and sizes wireframe. This function is only applied to the wireframe geometries, not for features. | Dynamically drag and move to this new location |
| Dynamic Orient | Dynamically moves and rotates parts and instances. | Dynamically rotate with respect to this pivot point |

# 11.7  Assembly Equations

I-DEAS uses equations to express the mathematical and functional relationships between dimensional variables in the assemblies. Equations are very useful when certain relationships must be maintained between instances. Figure 11.14 shows an example using an assembly equation to control the distance between two faces in two instances by a linear dimension. Equations can also be used to create various configurations for animation. Assembly equations have the following four functions:

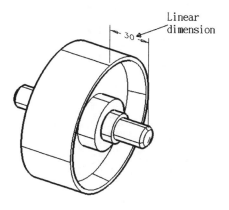

Figure 11.14

| | |
|---|---|
| **Create:** | create a new assembly equation. |
| **Modify:** | modify an existing assembly equation. |
| **List:** | list all existing assembly equations. |
| **Delete:** | delete selected assembly equations. |

## Creating Assembly Equations

Eligible variables which can be used in assembly equations are assembly dimensions. You must add asembly dimensions to the assembly before assembly equations can be defined. The assembly dimensions are normally labeled as Hil_D1, Hil_D2, Hi2_D5, etc. Place the cursor on an assembly dimension, its dimension label will be displayed on the screen.

  **The Procedure for creating an Assembly Equation is (Figure 11.15):**

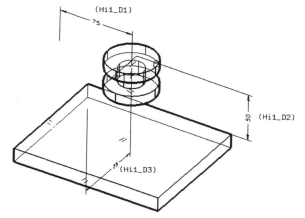

Figure 11.15

Mastering  I-DEAS
Scholars International Publishing Corp., 1999

# Creating Assemblies

1. Add a parallel constraint.
   Make the bottom face of the revolved instance and the top face of extruded instance parallel.

2. Add three linear dimensions.
   a. Add a linear dimension Hi1_D1 between the left end surface and the center line as shown.
   b. Add a linear dimension Hi1_D2 between the two parallel horizontal surfaces as shown.
   c. Add a linear dimension Hi1_D3 between the front end face and the center line as shown.

3. Open the Assembly Equations menu.
   Select the Assembly Equations icon, then select Create

4. Define the assembly equation (Hi1_D2 = Hi1_D1/2).
   . Pick dimension to drive:  pick the vertical dimension "Hi1_D2"
   Enter Expression:  enter  Hi1_D1/2
   Pick dimension to drive:  pick the depth dimension "Hi1_D3"
   Enter Expression:  enter  Hi1_D1

5. List the assembly equation.
   Select the "Assembly Equations" icon, then pick List
   Two equations "Hi1_D2=Hi1_D1/2" and "Hi1_D3=Hi1_D1" appear in the I-DEAS window.
   Select Cancel to exit the list mode

6. Verify the assembly equation just created.
   Select the "Modify Entity" icon
   Pick "Hi1_D1" dimension, then enter "100" as the new value
   Select OK to change the vertical dimension as shown in Figure 11.16.

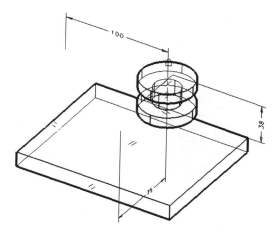

Figure 11.16

| Note: | The horizontal dimension has not changed yet. We need to update its change. |
|---|---|

 7. Update the change.
   Select the Update icon
   The horizontal dimension has been updated to reflect the relation governed by the
   assembly equation as shown in Figure 11.17.

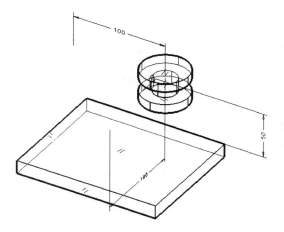

Figure 11.17

## Modifying assembly equations

Existing assembly equations can be modified. Follow this procedure to modify an assembly equation (Figure 11.18):

 **The procedure to modify an assembly equation is:**

1. Select Assembly Equations → Modify
2. Pick dimension to drive:   pick "Hi1_D2"
3. Enter expression (Hi1_D1/2):   enter  Hi1_D1*1.25
4. Select Update to reflect the change in assembly equation

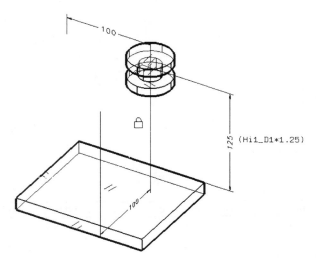

Figure 11.18

## Deleting Assembly Equations

**The procedure for deleting an assembly equation is:**

1. Select Assembly Equations → Delete
2. Pick assembly equation to deletepress the right mouse button to open the options menu
   Two options that are often very useful are "Invalid Equations" and "All Equations".
   Select "All Equations" from the list in this case.

# 11.8  Explode Assemblies

      Assemblies can be exploded for creating design presentations, catalogs, and sales literature. They show all the parts of an assembly and how they fit together. I-DEAS provides two modes to create exploded assemblies; explode linearly and explode radially. The "Undo Explode" function is used to bring exploded assemblies back to their original form.

## Explode linearly

This function repositions instances by exploding them linearly (Figure 11.19).

**The procedure for Exploding Linearly is:**

1. Select the "Explode Linearly" icon
2. Pick the assembly to explode
   The options menu should appear as here.

| X Direction |
| Negative X |
| Y Direction |
| Negative Y |
| Z Direction |
| Negative Z |
| Backup |
| Cancel |

Select the axis/direction option, then enter a distance value to explode the assembly

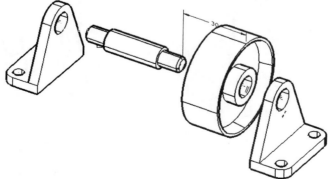

Figure 11.19

## Creating Assemblies

Figure 11.20 shows the assembly exploded in various axis/direction combinations.

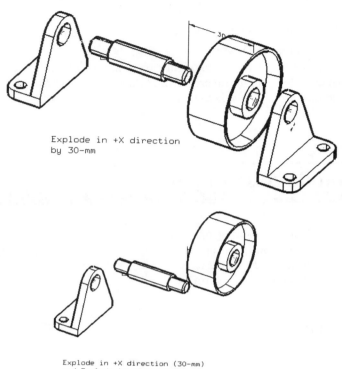

Explode in +X direction
by 30-mm

Figure 11.20a

Explode in +X direction (30-mm)
and Explode in +Y direction
by 10-mm

Figure 11.20b

## Undo explode

The "Undo Explode" function cancels a previous explode command and returns the assembly back to its original configuration (Figure 11.21).

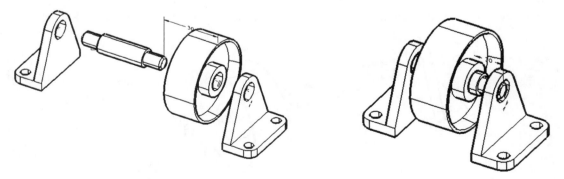

Figure 11.21

11-26

## Explode radially

This function repositions instances by exploding them radially (Figure 11.22).

**The procedure for Exploding Radially is:**

1. Select the "Explode Radially" icon
   The options menu should appear as here.

| Other Assembly |
| Spread Point |
| Continue |
| Backup |
| Cancel |

2. Select "Spread Point" from the menu
3. Pick a point as the center point for spread
4. Select "Continue" from the menu
5. Enter spread radius (110.00): 100
   The assembly will be exploded as in Figure 11.22.

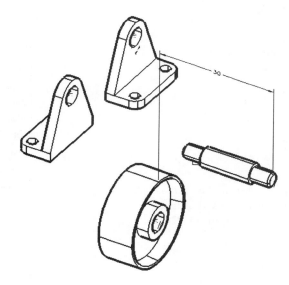

Figure 11.22

# 11.9   Suppressing Instances

Assembly instances can be suppressed from the assembly. Suppressing an instance temporarily removes the selected instance from the display of the assembly. This reduces the number of instances displayed in the workstation to facilitate the adding of other instances to the assembly. It also reduces the processing time for the system to regenerate the model.

**The procedure for suppressing instances is (Figure 11.23):**

1. Select the "Suppress" icon
2. Pick assembly node to suppress:  pick the instance to suppress
   The selected instance is graphically removed from the assembly.
3. Continue to pick those instances to be suppressed if necessary.

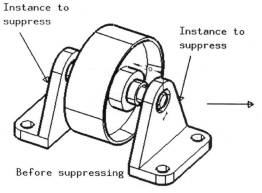

Figure 11.23

Those suppressed instances can be unsuppressed. Click the "Unsuppress" icon to open an options menu as below to allow you to select instances to be unsuppressed.

| |
|---|
| sample 0 |
| shaft 1 |
| wheel–assembly 2 |
| support 3 |
| support2 4 |
| Visible |
| Label |
| Hierarchy... |
| Done |
| Backup |
| Cancel |

Select the instances to be unsuppressed from the options list, then select Done and Cancel.  The unsuppressed instances return to the graphic window as shown in Figure 11.24.

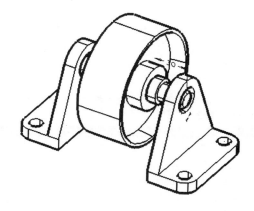

Figure 11.24

Mastering  I-DEAS
Scholars International Publishing Corp., 1999

# 11.10    Changing Instances' Color

Each instance has a default color. The color can be changed to one of your choice.

**The procedure of changing the color of instances is:**

1. Select the "Color Code" icon
2. Pick assembly node to color code:  pick an instance
3. Select "Directory" from the options list to open the color list as below.

| BLACK |
|---|
| BLUE |
| GRAY BLUE |
| LIGHT BLUE |
| CYAN |
| DARK OLIVE |
| DARK GREEN |
| GREEN |
| YELLOW |
| GOLDEN ORANGE |
| ORANGE |
| RED |
| MAGENTA |
| LIGHT MAGENTA |
| PINK |
| WHITE |
| Backup |
| Cancel |

4. Select a color (ex. Yellow)
    The color of selected instance will be changed to yellow. Repeat the above process to continue to pick instances and assign a color.

    Use the "Reset Color" icon to reset the color back to the default color.

**The procedure for resetting color is:**

1. Select the "Reset Color" icon
2. Pick an instance to reset color, then select Done

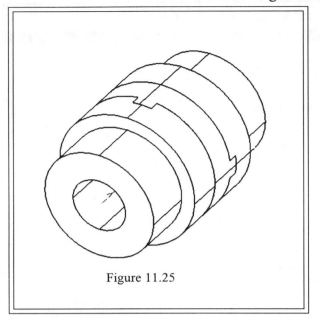

Figure 11.25

# Project 1.
# Creating a simple assembly project

This project assembles three instances to form a coupling (Figure 11.25). Two instances are created from the same coupler part. Lock the connector instance to fix it in the assembly. The two coupler instances are rotated by –90 degrees and 90 degrees about the X axis, respectively to place them in the proper orientation for assembling. Assemble the first coupler to the connector using three coincident constraints. Suppress the coupler in the assembly to make it invisible from the assembly model. Use three coincident constraints to fully constrain the second coupler to the assembly. Unsuppress the first coupler to display the entire assembly model. Finally, explode the assembly (Figure 11.26).

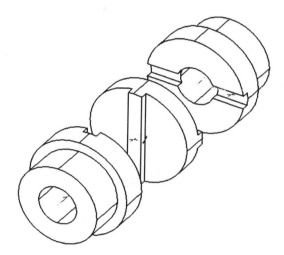

Figure 11.26

**Step 1. Open the Master Assembly program.**
Select **Master Assembly** from the task menu to open the assembly program.

**Step 2. Get two instances from the library.**
 Select the "**Get from Library**" icon to open the library menu as shown next (your menu may appear differently).

Mastering I-DEAS
Scholars International Publishing Corp., 1999

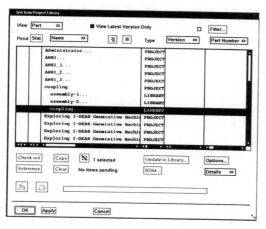

Change View to "**Part**"

Double click "**Coupling**" or "**assembly-1**" to make two parts under it appear on the menu as below.

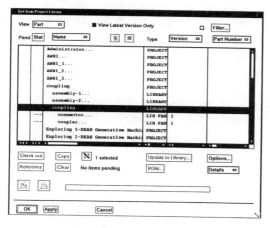

Select "**connector**" from the list, then select "**Copy**" near the bottom of the menu
Select "**coupler**" from the list, then select "**Copy**"
Select "**OK**" to exit the library

### Step 3.   Get the instances.

Select the "**Get**" icon to open the Get menu as below.

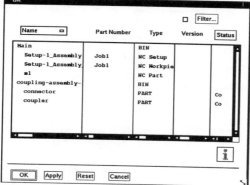

Select "**connector**" to highlight it,
   then select "**Apply**" to make it appear on the graphics window
Select "**coupler**",
   then select "**OK**" to make it appear on the graphics window and exit Get menu

 Click the "**Isometric view**" icon to display the two instances as in Figure 11.27.

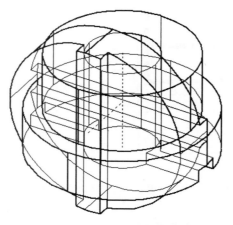

Figure 11.27

**Step 4.   Move the coupler instance to the right of the screen.**

 Select the "**Move**" icon
Pick the coupler instance to move
Enter translation X,Y,Z:   **100,0,0**
The coupler has been moved to a new location as shown in Figure 11.28.

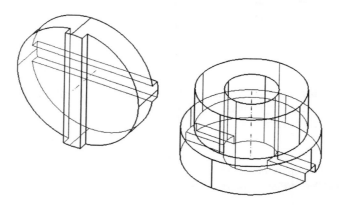

Figure 11.28

**Step 5.   Create the assembly hierarchy.**

 Select the "**Hierarchy**" icon to open the hierarchy menu as shown next.

Mastering I-DEAS
Scholars International Publishing Corp., 1999

# Creating Assemblies

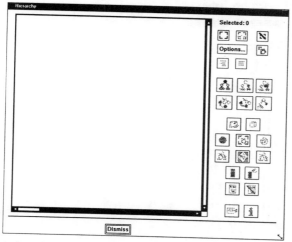

Select the "**Top-level assembly**" icon to open the Name menu
Enter "**coupling**" into the Name field as below.

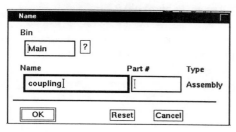

Select **OK**
The coupling is added to the Hierarchy menu as below.

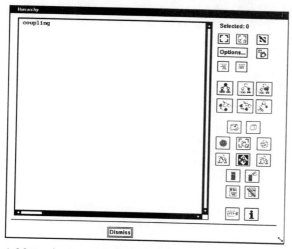

**Step 6.**  **Add two instances to the assembly.**

Click "**coupling**" in the hierarchy menu to highlight it
Select the "**Add a part instance**" icon from the hierarchy menu
Pick the coupler part from the graphics window
The coupler instance is added to the hierarchy list
Select the "**Add a part instance**" icon again
Pick the connector instance to add to the assembly list

# Creating Assemblies

The two instances are added to the assembly list as below.

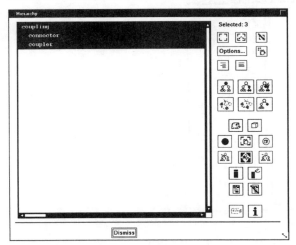

### Step 7.  Copy the coupler instance.

Click the "**coupler**" instance from the hierarchy menu to highlight it
Select the "**Duplicate part instance**" icon
Pick the assembly to add instance to (Hierarchy...):   pick any instance in the graphics window
Hold the left mouse button and drag the coupler to the upper right corner to a new location
The second coupler instance is added to the hierarchy menu
Select the "**Dismiss**" icon to exit the hierarchy menu
The three instances in the assembly appear as in Figure 11.29.

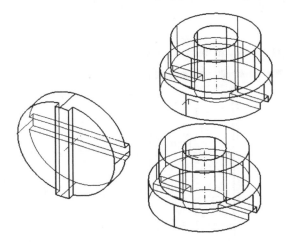

Figure 11.29

### Step 8.  Lock the connector instance.

Select the "**Constrain & Dimension**" to open Constrain subpanel
Select the "**Lock**" icon

Pick the connector instance as the first part to constrain
Click the right mouse button, then select "**Hierarchy**" from the options list
Select "**coupling**" from the hierarchy selection menu to select the assembly
  as the second instance to constrain
Select **OK** to exit the hierarchy menu

Mastering  I-DEAS
Scholars International Publishing Corp., 1999

# Creating Assemblies

The lock constraint symbol is added as in Figure 11.30.

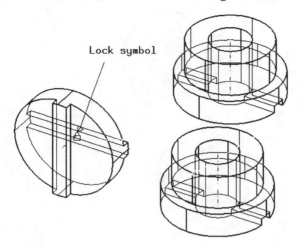

Lock symbol

Figure 11.30

**Step 9.   Rotate a coupler by 90 degrees about the X axis.**

Select the "**Rotate**" icon

Pick the front coupler as the entity to rotate

Pick a point near the bottom of the base of the left coupler as the center to rotate about

Select **About X** from the options list

Enter rotation angle:  **90**

The coupler is rotated to a new orientation as in Figure 11.31.

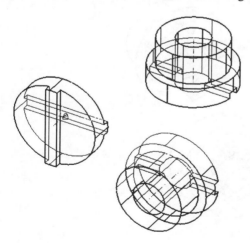

Figure 11.31

**Step 10. Rotate the other coupler by -90 degrees about the X axis.**

Select the "**Rotate**" icon

Pick the upper right coupler as the entity to rotate

Pick a point near the bottom of the base in the upper right coupler as the center to rotate about

Select **About X** from the options list

Enter rotation angle:  **-90**

The new drawing becomes Figure 11.32.

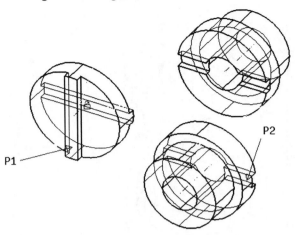

Figure 11.32

**Step 11. Apply the first constraint between the first coupler and the connector.**
 **Use Figure 11.32 as reference.**
Select the **"Coincident & Collinear"** icon
Pick the front flat face of the flange in the connector (**P1**) as the first entity to constrain
Pick the flat bottom face of groove feature in the coupler (**P2**) as the second entity to constrain
The coupler instance has moved to a new location as shown in Figure 11.33.

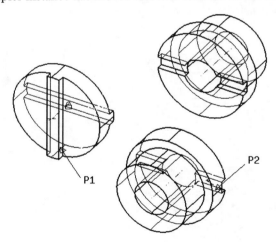

Figure 11.33

**Step 12. Add the second constraint. Use Figure 11.33 as reference.**
Pick the right vertical edge of the front flange in the connector (**P1**) as the first entity
Pick the lower side face of the slot in the coupler (**P2**) as the second entity
The coupler instance rotates to a new constraint location as in Figure 11.34.

11-36

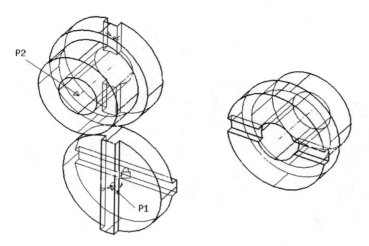

Figure 11.34

**Step 13. Apply the third constraint. Use Figure 11.34 as reference.**
Pick the center line of the connector (**P1**) as the first entity
Pick the center line of the coupler (**P2**) as the second entity
The two instances are fully constrained as in Figure 11.35.

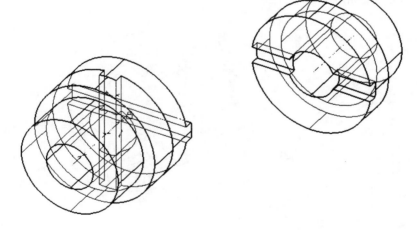

Figure 11.35

**Step 14. Suppress the coupler from the assembly.**

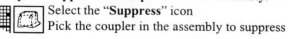 Select the "**Suppress**" icon
Pick the coupler in the assembly to suppress

The selected coupler instance becomes invisible in the assembly as in Figure 11.36.

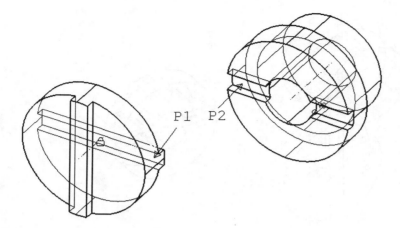

Figure 11.36

**Step 15. Apply the first constraint between the connector and the second coupler.**
 **Use Figure 11.36 as reference.**
Select the **Coincident** icon
Select the bottom flat face of the other flange of the connector (**P1**) as the first entity
Select the bottom flat face of the slot in the coupler (**P2**) as the second entity
The new drawing becomes Figure 11.37.

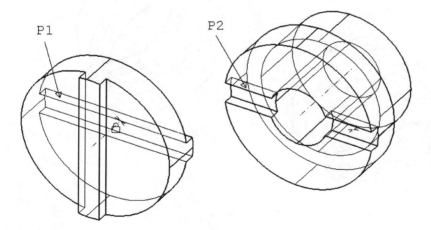

Figure 11.37

**Step 16. Add the second constraint to these two instances. Use Figure 11.37 as reference.**
Pick the top side face of the back flange in the connector (**P1**) as the first entity
Pick the top side face of the slot in the coupler (**P2**) as the second entity
The new assembly becomes Figure 11.38.

11-38

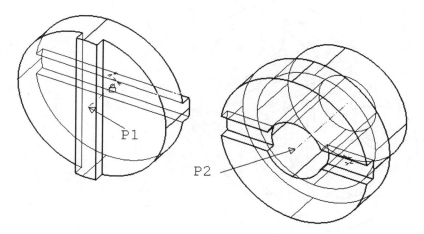

Figure 11.38

**Step 17. Add the third constraint between two centerlines. Use Figure 11.38 as reference.**
Pick the center line of the connector (**P1**) as the first entity
Pick the center line of the coupler (**P2**) as the second entity
The two instances are fully constrained as shown in Figure 11.39.

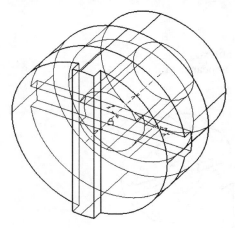

Figure 11.39

Select **Close** to exit the constrain subpanel

**Step 18. Unsuppress the first coupler.**
Select the **Unsuppress** icon
Select "**coupler 1**" from the options list,
  then select **Done** to make the suppressed coupler becomes visible as in Figure 11.40.

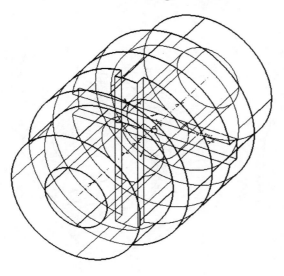

Figure 11.40

Select **Cancel** from the options list

**Step 19. Explode the assembly.**

 Select the **Explode Linearly** icon
Pick the assembly to explode
Select the **Z Direction** from the list
Enter minimum distance between entities:   **50**
The exploded view of the assembly appears as Figure 11.41.

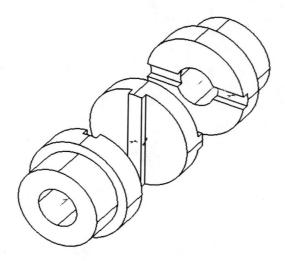

Figure 11.41

**Step 20. Render the model.**

 Select the "**Shade Hardware**" icon

Mastering I-DEAS
Scholars International Publishing Corp., 1999

# Creating Assemblies

The shade assembly model appears as in Figure 11.42.

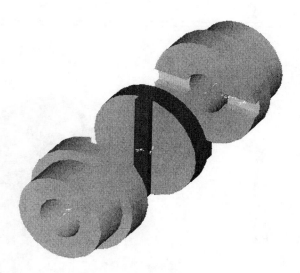

Figure 11.42

## Step 21. Check the assembly into the library.

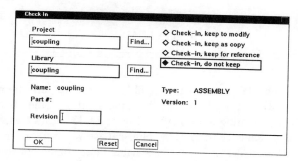
Select the "**Check In**" icon to open the check-in menu
Set the parameters for check-in menu as below.

| Check In | |
|---|---|
| Project | ◇ Check-in, keep to modify |
| coupling          Find... | ◇ Check-in, keep as copy |
| | ◇ Check-in, keep for reference |
| Library | ◆ Check-in, do not keep |
| coupling          Find... | |
| Name:  coupling | Type:     ASSEMBLY |
| Part #: | Version:  1 |
| Revision [ | |
| OK          Reset      Cancel | |

Select **OK** to check in the assembly

# Project 2.
# Creating a wheel assembly

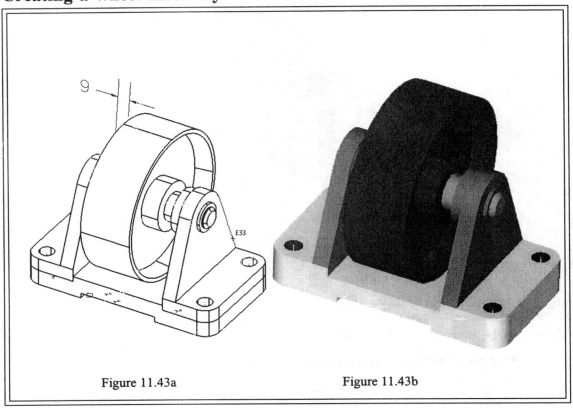

Figure 11.43a                          Figure 11.43b

This project uses five parts created in previous chapters to form an assembly. These five parts are named base, support, bushing, shaft, and wheel-assembly. We need to check those parts out from the library and use the Get command to make them available for creating the assembly. Figure 11.43 shows these five parts and their assembly drawing. The assembly sequence follows the physical assembly steps. The base is locked first to make it fixed. A support is fully constrained to the base using three coincident constraints in three mutually perpendicular surfaces. A bushing is inserted into the support by using two coincident constraints to constrain a surface and the centerline. The shaft is constrained by using two coincident constraints in a surface and the center line. The wheel is inserted into the shaft next. The Coincident & Collinear constraint is used to align the center lines of shaft and wheel. A linear dimension is used to position the wheel in the desired location along the shaft. The bushing is next inserted into the right side of the shaft by constraining its centerline and left end face. The support at the right side is the last instance to be constrained. The Coincident & Collinear is used three times to constrain three surfaces to the assembly model.

**Step 1.  Entering Master Assembly program.**
> Click the **Task** button, then select **Master Assembly** from the list

**Step 2.  Check five parts out from the library.**
> Select the **Get from Library** icon to open the Get menu as below
> (Your menu may differ from what is shown here)

Mastering  I-DEAS
Scholars International Publishing Corp., 1999

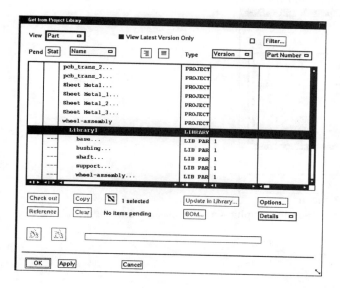

Click the **View** button, then select **Part** from the list
Click on **Library1** to show the parts under this library
The Get menu should look like the menu shown above

**Step 3.** **Check five parts out as copies.**
Click these five parts (press the Shift key to continuously pick parts)
They are highlighted as shown below and indicated "5 selected"

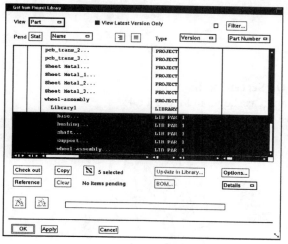

Select the **Copy** button located near the bottom of the menu, then select **OK**
The system will return back to Master Assembly mode

**Step 4.** **Get these five parts from the Get menu.**

Select the **Get** icon to open Get menu as below.

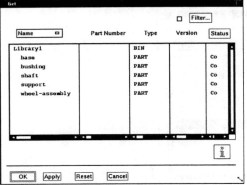

Select all five parts from the menu,
then select **OK** to get those parts to the graphic window as shown in Figure 11.44.

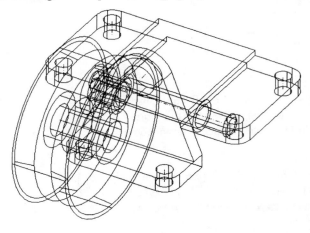

Figure 11.44

**Step 5.** **Move parts apart from each other.**

Select the **Move** icon
Pick the **wheel**, then select "**Slide On Screen**" from the list
Move the wheel to upper right location as shown in Figure 11.45
Repeat the same procedure to move the other three parts (support, shaft, and bushing) to
locations as shown

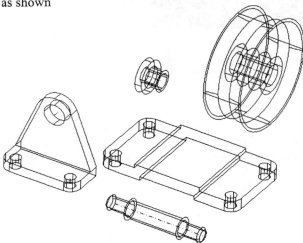

Figure 11.45

11-44

# Creating Assemblies

### Step 6. Create the assembly hierarchy.

Click **Hierarchy** icon to open the Hierarchy form
Click on the "**Top level assembly**" icon to open the Name menu
Enter "**wheel-assembly**" into the Name field, then select **OK**
The wheel-assembly should be added to the Hierarchy menu as below.

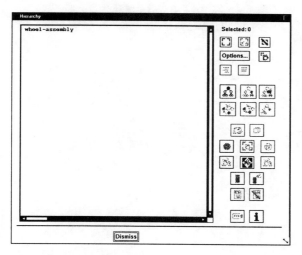

### Step 7. Add instances to the assembly.

Click "**wheel-assembly**" from the Hierarchy menu to highlight it
Click on the "**Add a part instance**" icon from the Hierarchy menu
Pick the "base" as the part to add, then press Enter to add instance
Repeat the above process to add all five parts to the Hierarchy menu as shown below.

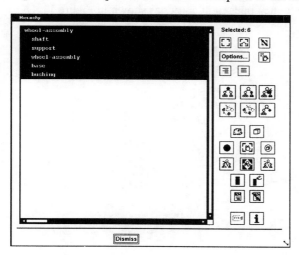

### Step 8. Duplicate the support instance.

Click the "**support**" instance from the Hierarchy menu to highlight it
Select the "**Duplicates the selected part instance**" icon
Press **Enter** to accept Hierarchy as the assembly to add instance
The Hierarchy Selection menu will appear
Select "**wheel-assembly**" from the menu to highlight it, then select **OK**

Move the second support instance to the right side of the base as shown in Figure 11.46.

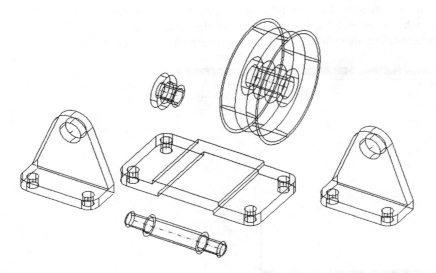

Figure 11.46

**Step 9.  Duplicate the bushing instance.**

Click **"bushing"** from the Hierarchy menu to highlight it
Click **"Duplicates the selected part instance"** icon
Press **"Enter"** to accept Hierarchy as the assembly to add instance to
Click **"wheel-assembly"** from the Hierarchy Selection menu, then select **OK**
Drag the second bushing instance to the upper right corner as shown in Figure 11.47.

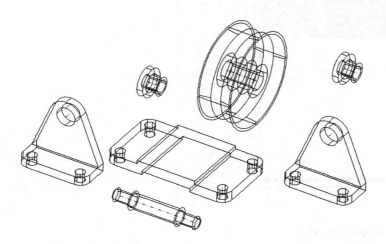

Figure 11.47

11-46

# Creating Assemblies

The system will return to Hierarchy menu as shown here.

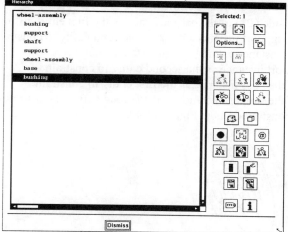

Select **Dismiss** to return to the graphic mode

**Step 10.** **Lock the base instance to the assembly hierarchy.**

Select the **Constrain & Dimension** icon to open constrain panel
Select the **Lock** icon
Pick the base instance as the first part to constrain
Click the right mouse button, then select Hierarchy from the list
Click "**wheel-assembly**" from the Hierarchy Selection menu to select the entire list
Select **OK** to return to graphic window
Select **Close** to close the Constrain panel

**Step 11.** **Rotate the support and bushing instances at the left side by 90 degrees about Y axis.**

Select the **Rotate** icon, then pick the support instance at the left side as the entity to rotate
Pick the back right corner on the bottom face as the pivot point
Select **About Y** from the list
Enter angle about Y:  **-90**
The part is rotated to the new position as in Figure 11.48.
Pick the bushing instance at the left side as the entity to rotate
Pick the left end point of the center line as the pivot point
Enter angle about Y (90.0):  **180**
The new drawing should resemble Figure 11.48.

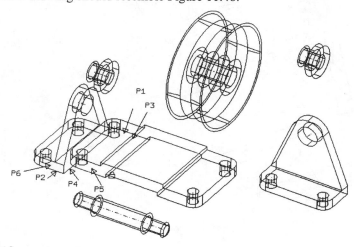

Figure 11.48

**Step 12. Constrain the left support instance to the base. Use the pick points in Figure 11.48.**

 Select **Constrain & Dimension → Coincident & Collinear**

Pick the top flat surface at the left side (**P1**) of the base instance as the first entity to constrain

Pick the bottom surface of the left support instance (**P2**) as the second entity to constrain

Pick the edge line (**P3**) of the base instance as the first entity to constrain

Pick the edge line (**P4**) of the support instance as the second entity to constrain

Pick the front end surface (**P5**) of the base instance as the first entity to constrain

Pick the front end surface (**P6**) of the support instance as the second entity to constrain

The left support instance is fully constrained as in Figure 11.49.

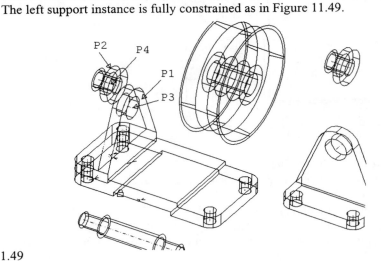

Figure 11.49

**Step 13. Constrain the left bushing instance to the assembly. Use the pick points in Figure 11.49.**

Pick the right vertical face (**P1**) of the left support instance as the first entity to constrain

Pick the left vertical face of the step (**P2**) in the left bushing instance as the second entity to constrain

Pick the center line of the left support (**P3**) as the first entity to constrain

Pick the center line of the left bushing (**P4**) as the second entity to constrain

The left bushing is fully constrained to the assembly as in Figure 11.50.

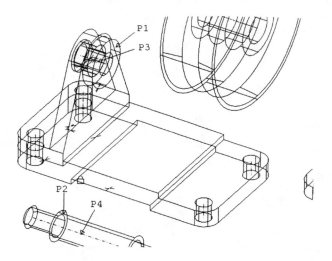

Figure 11.50

11-48

**Step 14. Constrain the shaft to the assembly. Use the pick point in Figure 11.50.**

 Select the **Coincident & Collinear** icon

Pick the right face of the bushing (**P1**) as the first entity to constrain

Pick the left side of the step face in the shaft (**P2**) as the second entity to constrain

Pick the center line of the bushing (**P3**) as the first entity to constrain

Pick the center line of the shaft (**P4**) as the second entity to constrain

The shaft is fully constrained to the assembly as in Figure 11.51.

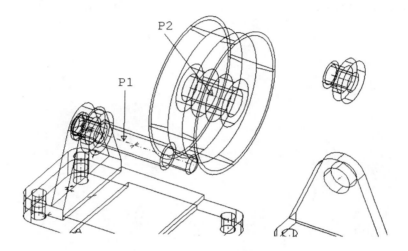

Figure 11.51

**Step 15. Constrain the wheel to the assembly. Use the pick points in Figures 11.51 and 11.52.**

Select the **Coincident & Collinear** icon

Pick the center line of shaft (**P1**) as the first entity to constrain (Figure 11.51)

Pick the center line of wheel (**P2**) as the second entity to constrain (Figure 11.51)

The new drawing becomes Figure 11.52.

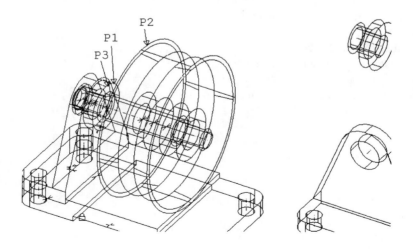

Figure 11.52

Select the **Linear Dimension** icon

Pick the right end face of the bushing (**P1**) as the first entity to dimension

Pick the left end face of the wheel (**P2**) as the second entity to dimension

Click the right mouse button, then select **On Curve** from the list

Pick the outer circle of the right end face of bushing as the curve

Pick a point to make the plane closer to vertical direction (**P3**) to define the plane

Pick a location to place the dimension text

Select **Close** to close the constrain panel

Select the **Modify Entity** icon, then pick the linear dimension to modify

Enter **9** to the Hi1_D1 dimension

The wheel is assembled as in Figure 11.53.

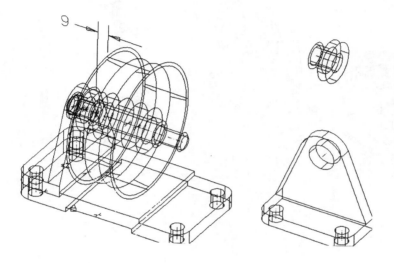

Figure 11.53

**Step 16. Rotate the support and bushing instances.**

Select the **Rotate** icon

Pick the right support instance as the entity to rotate

Pick the right bottom corner as the pivot point

Select **About Y** from the list

Enter angle about Y (90.0): **90**

The support instance is rotated to the new location

Pick the bushing instance as the entity to rotate

Pick the right end point of the center line as the pivot point

Enter angle about Y (90.0): **180**

The new drawing becomes Figure 11.54.

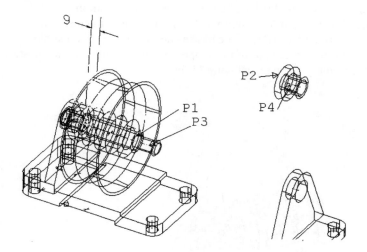

Figure 11.54

**Step 17. Constrain the bushing instance. Use Figure 11.54 as reference.**

 Select the **Coincident & Collinear** icon

Pick the right step face (**P1**) of the shaft as the first entity to constrain
Pick the left end face of the bushing (**P2**) as the second entity to constrain
Pick the center line (**P3**) of the shaft as the first entity to constrain
Pick the center line (**P4**) of the bushing as the second entity to constrain
The bushing is constrained as in Figure 11.55.

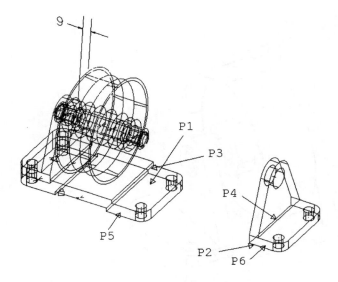

Figure 11.55

**Step 18. Constrain the right support instance. Use Figure 11.55 as reference.**

Select the right top face (**P1**) of the base as the first entity to constrain

Select the bottom face (**P2**) of the support as the second entity to constrain

Select the edge line (**P3**) on the base as the first entity to constrain

Select the edge line (**P4**) on the support as the second entity to constrain

Select the front vertical face (**P5**) of the base as the first entity to constrain

Select the front vertical face (**P6**) of the support as the second entity to constrain

The complete assembly is shown in Figure 11.56.

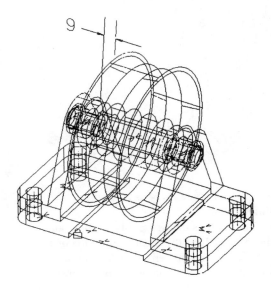

Figure 11.56

**Step 19. Show the assembly in different modes.**

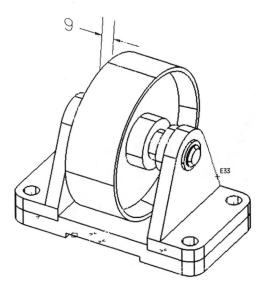

Figure 11.57

Mastering I-DEAS
Scholars International Publishing Corp., 1999

Figure 11.58

**Step 20. Check the assembly into the library.**

 Select the **Check In** icon
Set the Check-In parameters as below.

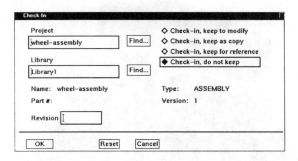

Select **OK** to check the assembly into the library

# Project 3.
# Assembling the engine

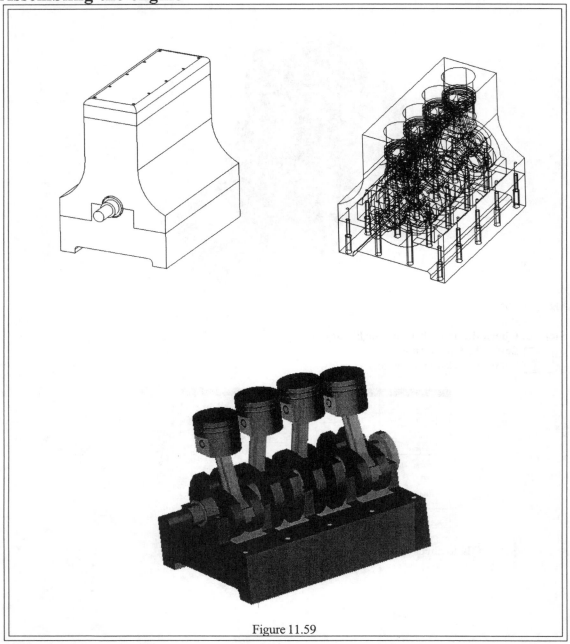

Figure 11.59

This project provides step-by-step instructions for assembling the engine. We use a sub-assembly approach to simplify the process. Pistons and bushings have four identical instances. They are ideal cases to use as sub-assemblies. We only need to assemble for one instance, then make three instance copies. Figure 11.59 shows various views of the final assembly. The animation of this assembly is presented in Chapter 12.

Mastering I-DEAS
Scholars International Publishing Corp., 1999

# Creating Assemblies

**Step 1. Check the engine components out from the library.**

 Select the **"Get from Library"** icon to open Get from Project Library menu

Click **View** icon to select the "Part" from the list

Click the **"engine"** project name,

then double click **"engine**-assembly" library to list all components as below.

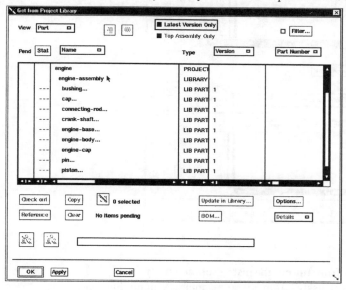

Select the following **nine parts** (pressing Shift key) to highlight them

**Bushing**
**Cap**
**Connecting-rod**
**Crankshaft**
**Engine-base**
**Engine-body**
**Engine-cap**
**Pin**
**Piston**

Select the **Copy** button to check out the copy of parts

Select **OK** to exit Get menu

**Step 2.  Create the piston sub-assembly.**

 Select the **"Hierarchy"** icon from the Master Assembly to create a new assembly

Select the **"Add to parent"** icon

 Select the **"engine assembly"** bin

# Creating Assemblies

Enter "**piston sub assly**" to the name field as shown below.

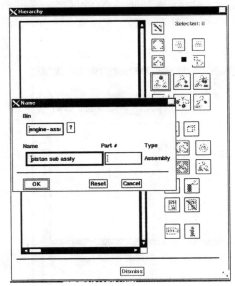

Select **OK**

**Step 3.** **Add four parts from the bin the piston sub-assembly.**

Click "**piston sub assly**" from Hierarchy menu to highlight it
Select the "**Add to Assembly**" icon from Hierarchy menu
Click the right mouse button and select "**From Bin**" at the pop up window
Highlight the following four parts from "engine assembly" bin
(Press the control key to pick more than one part)

**Cap**
**Connecting-rod**
**Pin**
**Piston**

Select **OK**
Click the **Deselect** icon
Dismiss the Hierarchy window
The parts appear as shown in Figure 11.60.

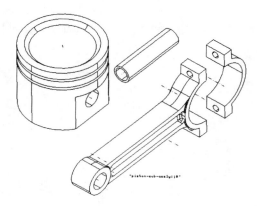

Figure 11.60

**Step 4. Lock the piston instance to the piston sub-assembly.**

Select the "**Constrain & Dimension**" icon from the Dimension pull down menu
Select the "**Lock**" icon from the constrain window

Click the right mouse button then select "**Hierarchy**" from the options list
Highlight "**piston sub assly**" as the first instance to constrain
Select **OK**
Click the piston instance to constrain
Click the middle mouse button to accept the instance
The lock symbol is added to the model as shown in Figure 11.61.

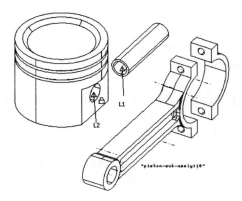

Figure 11.61

**Step 5. Constrain the pin to the piston. Use the pick points in Figures 11.61 and 11.62.**

Select the **Coincident & Collinear** icon from the constrain window
Click the right mouse button then select **Filter**
Select **Centerline → Pick only**
Pick the centerline **L1** of the piston pinhole
Pick the centerline **L2** of the pin
The pin is moved to a new location as in Figure 11.62.

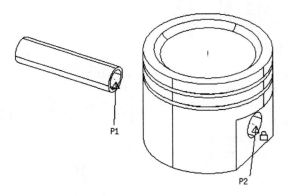

Figure 11.62

Select the **Coincident & Collinear** icon
Click the right mouse button then select **Filter**
Select **Center-point → Pick only**
Pick the center point **P1** of the pin
Pick the center point **P2** of the piston

# Creating Assemblies

The new assembly becomes Figure 11.63.

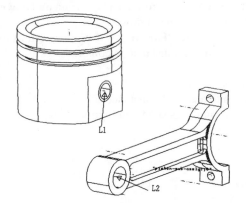

Figure 11.63

**Step 6.** **Constrain the connecting rod to the piston. Use the pick points in Figures 11.63 and 11.64.**

Select the **Coincident & Collinear** icon

Click the right mouse button then select **Filter**

Select **Centerline → Pick only**

Pick the centerline **L1** of the piston pinhole (make sure you select the right instance, otherwise press F8 key to reconsider)

Pick the centerline **L2** of the eye of connecting rod

The rod is moved to a new location as in Figure 11.64.

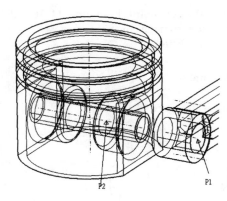

Figure 11.64

Select the **Coincident & Collinear** icon

Click the right mouse button then select **Filter**

Select **Center-point → Pick only**

Pick the center point **P1** of the connecting rod

Pick the center point **P2** of the piston pinhole

Click on the **Rotate** icon,

   then pick all parts to rotate

Specify **90-degree** about the centerline of the eye

The assembly now appears as Figure 11.65.

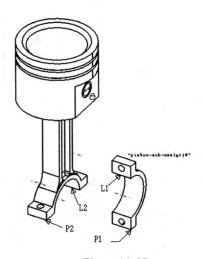

Figure 11.65

Mastering I-DEAS
Scholars International Publishing Corp., 1999

**Step 7.** **Constrain the cap to the connecting rod. Use the pick points in Figure 11.65.**

Select the **Coincident & Collinear** icon

Pick the inner edge **L1** of the cap

Pick the inner edge **L2** of the connecting rod

Pick the outer corner **P1** of the cap

Pick the outer corner **P2** of the connecting rod

Select the **front display view**

The piston sub-assembly should appear as Figure 11.66.

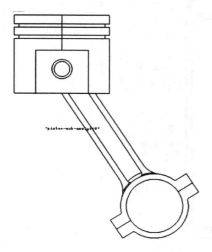

Figure 11.66

**Step 8.** **Put away the piston sub-assembly into the bin.**

Select the **Put Away** icon

Pick the **piston assembly** to put away

**Step 9.** **Create a bushing sub-assembly.**

Select the **Hierarchy** icon from Master Assembly to create a new assembly

Select the **Add to parent** icon

Select the **"engine assembly"** bin

Enter **"bushing-sub-assly"** to the name field as shown below.

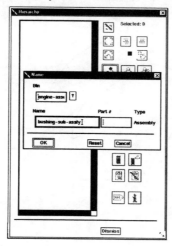

Select **OK**

**Step 10. Add the part bushing to the hierarchy.**

Click the top level assembly "**bushing-sub-assly**" from the Hierarchy menu to highlight it

 Select the **Add to Assembly** icon

Click the right mouse button and select "**From Bin**" at the pop up window

Highlight the part "**bushing**" from the "engine assembly" bin

Select **OK**

The hierarchy window appears as below.

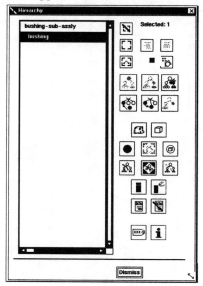

**Step 11. Duplicate the bushing instance.**

Highlight the **bushing instance** in the Hierarchy window

 Pick the **Duplicate** icon

Click the middle mouse button to accept default option (Hierarchy)

Click on the "**bushing-sub-assembly**" as the assembly to add the instance to

Select **OK**

Place the cursor on the bushing on the workbench

Hold the left mouse button and drag the duplicate instance to a new location
as shown in Figure 11.67

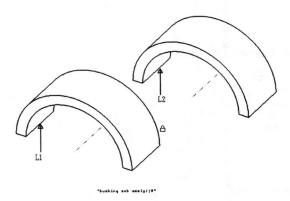

Figure 11.67

Click on the **Deselect all** icon
Dismiss the Hierarchy window

11-60

**Step 12. Lock a bushing instance.**

Select the **Constrain & Dimension icon,** then select the **Lock** icon
Click the right mouse button and select **Hierarchy** from the options list
Highlight "**bushing-sub-assly**" as the first instance to constrain
Select **OK**
Click the **bushing** from the workbench to constrain
Click the middle mouse button to accept the instance

**Step 13. Constrain the inner edges of the two bushings. Use the pick points in Figure 11.67.**

Select the **Coincident & Collinear** icon
Pick edges **L1** and **L2** from two bushings
If the bushings **do not** face each other, follow this procedure to modify:

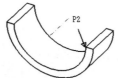
       Select the **Modify** icon
       Click the right mouse button then select **Filter**
       Select **Asm constrain → Pick only**
       Pick any of the constrain edges
       Choose **Flip** from the pop up menu
The bushings look like Figure 11.68.

Figure 11.68

**Step 14. Constrain the inner corners of the bushings. Use the pick points in Figure 11.68.**

Select the **Coincident & Collinear** icon
Click the inner vertex **P1** of the first bushing
Click the inner vertex **P2** of the second bushing
The assembly becomes Figure 11.69.

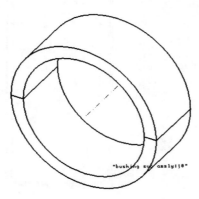

Figure 11.69

# Creating Assemblies

**Step 15. Put away the bushing sub-assembly.**

Click the **Put Away** icon

Pick the assembly to place it into the bin

**Step 16. Create the main engine assembly.**

Select the **Hierarchy** icon from Master Assembly to create a new assembly

Select the **Add to parent** icon

Choose the "**engine assembly**" bin

Enter "**engine**" to the name field as below.

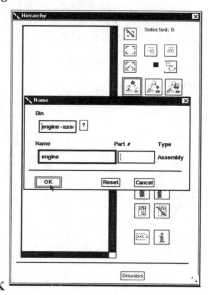

Select **OK**

**Step 17. Add two sub-assemblies and four parts to the hierarchy.**

Click the parent assembly "**engine**" from the Hierarchy menu to highlight it

Select the **Add to Assembly** icon from Hierarchy menu

Click the right mouse button and select "**From Bin**" at the pop up window

Highlight the following parts and sub-assemblies from the "**engine assembly**" bin

> **Bushing-sub-assly**
> **Piston-sub-assly**
> **Engine cap**
> **Engine body**
> **Engine base**
> **Engine shaft**

Select **OK**

The hierarchy window appears as here.

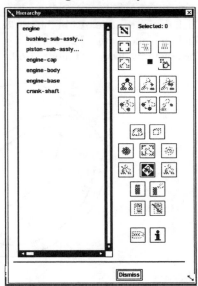

### Step 18. Reposition the instances to their proper locations.

 Use the **Move** command to rearrange the instances on the workbench
 to appear as in Figure 11.70.

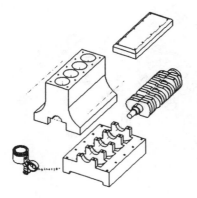

Figure 11.70

### Step 19. Copy all sub-assembly configurations into the main assembly "engine".

Select the **Manage Configuration** icon
Highlight the top-level "**engine**" assembly
 Select the **Unuse All** icon to copy all subassembly configurations into "engine" as shown below.

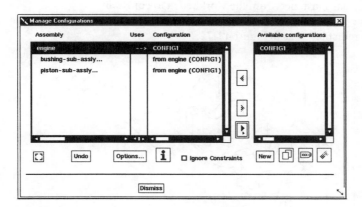

   Select **Dismiss**

### Step 20. Copy piston sub-assembly and bushing sub-assembly four times each.

 Select the **Hierarchy** icon
Highlight "**bushing-sub-assly**"
 Select the **Duplicate** icon
Click the middle mouse button to accept the default as Hierarchy
Highlight the top level assembly
Select **OK**
Hold the left mouse button on the "bushing-sub-assly" instance
Drag the new instance to a new location on the workbench
Repeat the above procedures to create the three remaining bushing sub-assembly instances
 and four piston sub-assembly instances

# Creating Assemblies

Move and rearrange the instances on the workbench to appear as shown in Figure 11.71.

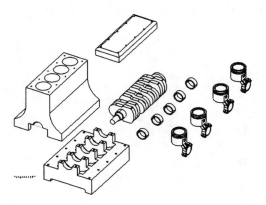

Figure 11.71

**Step 21. Lock the engine base.**

Select the **Constrain & Dimension** icon
Select the **Lock** icon
Click the right mouse button then select the **Hierarchy** option from the pop up menu
Highlight the "**engine**" then select **OK**
Click the engine base instance from the workbench to constrain
Click the middle mouse button to accept the instance
The drawing is redisplayed as in Figure 11.72.

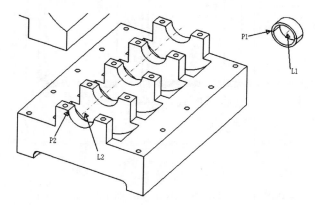

Figure 11.72

**Step 22. Constrain the bushing sub-assembly to the engine base. Use the pick points in Figure 11.72.**

Select the **Coincident & Collinear** icon
Select **Filter → Centerline → Pick only**
Pick the centerline **L1** of the bushing sub-assembly
Pick the centerline **L2** of the engine base
Select the **Coincident & Collinear** icon
Select **Filter → All Non Pickable items → vertex**
Click the vertex **P1** of the bushing sub-assembly
Click the vertex **P2** of the engine base

# Creating Assemblies

(Make sure that you are selecting the centerline and the vertex L1 and P1 from the same bushing of the bushing sub-assembly, otherwise, the constrain may be invalid)

Repeat the above procedure to constrain the remaining three bushing sub-assemblies to the engine-base

The new assembly appears as shown in Figure 11.73.

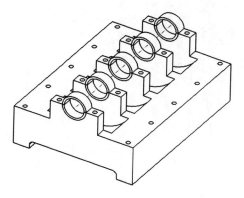

Figure 11.73

**Step 23. Suppress all the instances on the workbench except the crank shaft and the engine base.**

 Select the **Suppress** icon

Pick the five bushing sub-assemblies to suppress

The new drawing becomes Figure 11.74.

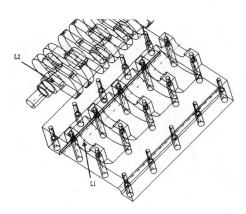

Figure 11.74

**Step 24. Constrain the crank shaft to the engine base. Use the pick points in Figure 11.74.**

 Select the **Coincident & Collinear** icon

Click the right mouse button

Select **Filter → Centerline → Pick only**

Pick the centerline **L1** of the engine base

Pick the centerline **L2** of the crank shaft

# Creating Assemblies

The new drawing may appear as in Figure 11.75.

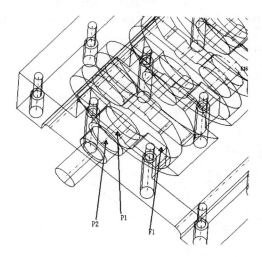

Figure 11.75

Select the Dimension icon
Click the right mouse button
Select **Filter → Centerpoint → Pick only**
Pick the centerpoint **P1** of the engine base baring cavity as shown in Figure 11.75
Pick the centerpoint **P2** of the crank shaft bearing surface
Pick the face **F1** as the plane to place the dimension on
A linear assembly dimension is added.

 Select the **Modify** icon
Pick the assembly dimension just created
Enter **3** in the dimension dialog box (use negative sign if necessary for proper orientation)
Select **OK**
The new assembly appears as in Figure 11.76.

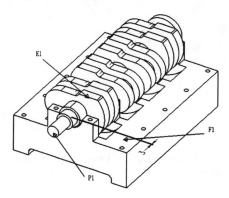

Figure 11.76

**Step 25. Rotate the crank shaft about its axis. Use the pick points in Figure 11.76.**

 Select the **Rotate** icon
Pick the crank shaft as the entity to rotate
Pick the center point **P1** of the crank shaft axis
Select **About Z** from the pop up menu as the axis of rotation
For the angle of rotation enter **25**

11-66

**Step 26. Add an angular dimension between the crank shaft and the engine base.**

Select the **Angular Dimension** icon

Click the right mouse button

Select **Filter → Edge → Pick Only**

Select the edge **E1** of the crank shaft as the first entity to dimension

Click the right mouse button

Select **Filter → All Non Selectable Item → Move to Right icon → Surfaces → Pick only**

Select the face **F1** of the engine base as the second entity to dimension

Drag the mouse to place the text at the appropriate position

Select the **Modify** icon

Pick the angular dimension just created and enter **30**

The new assembly appears as shown in Figure 11.77.

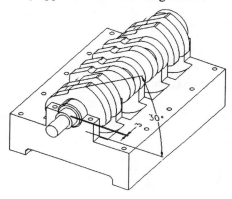

Figure 11.77

**Step 27. Constrain the engine body to the engine base. Use the pick points in Figure 11.78.**

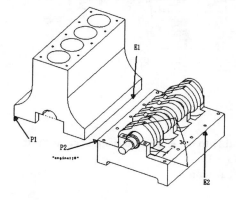

Figure 11.78

Select the **Coincident & Collinear** icon

Select **Filter → Edge → Pick only**

Pick the edge **E1** of the engine body

Pick the edge **E2** of the engine base

Select the **Coincident & Collinear** icon

Select **Filter → All Non Pickable items → Vertex → Pick only**

Pick the vertex **P1** of the engine body

Pick the vertex **P2** of the engine base

The assembly model becomes Figure 11.79.

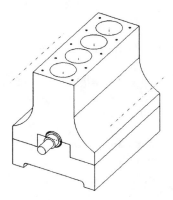

Figure 11.79

**Step 28. Change to side view and wireframe display mode.**

 Select the **Side view** icon

Select the **Wireframe** icon

 The new drawing becomes Figure 11.80.

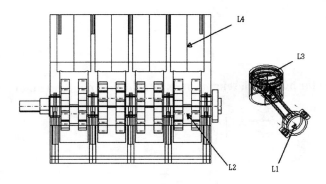

Figure 11.80

**Step 29. Constrain the piston sub-assembly to the engine body and crank shaft.**
      **Use the pick points in Figure 11.80.**

 Select the **Coincident & Collinear** icon

Click the right mouse button

Select **Filter → Centerline → Pick only**

Pick the centerline **L1** of the crank pin of the crank shaft

Pick centerline **L2** of the connecting road

Select the **Coincident & Collinear** icon

Pick the centerline **L3** of the piston of the piston sub-assembly

Pick the centerline **L4** of the cylinder of the engine body

 Click the **Front view** icon

# Creating Assemblies

The assembly appears as in Figure 11.81.

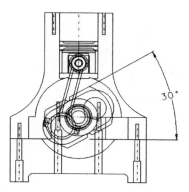

Figure 11.81

**Step 30. Assembly the three remaining piston sub-assemblies.**

Repeat the steps 27-29 to constrain the remaining three piston sub-assemblies

The assembly appears as shown in Figure 11.82 (side view), Figure 11.83 (front view), and Figure 11.84 (isometric view) without showing the engine body.

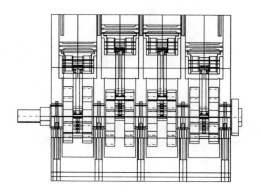

Figure 11.82

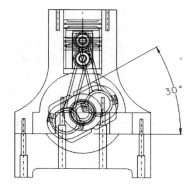

Figure 11.83

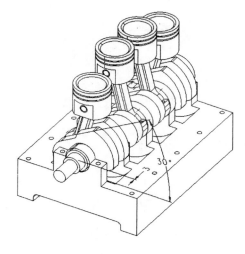

Figure 11.84

**Step 31. Constrain the engine cap to the engine body. Use the pick points in Figure 11.85.**

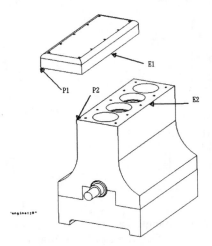

Figure 11.85

Select the **Coincident & Collinear** icon
Select **Filter → Edge → Pick only**
Pick the edge **E1** of the engine body
Pick the edge **E2** of the engine base
Select the **Coincident & Collinear** icon
Select **Filter → Vertex → Pick Only**
Pick the vertex **P1** of the engine body
Pick the vertex **P2** of the engine base
The complete assembly appears as shown in Figure 11.86.

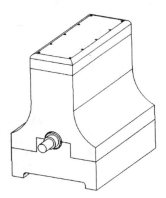

Figure 11.86

**Step 32. Show the assembly model in the wireframe mode.**
 Select the **Wireframe** icon

# Creating Assemblies

The assembly model shown in wireframe mode appears as in Figure 11.87.

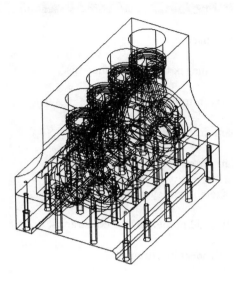

Figure 11.87

**Step 33. Check the assembly to the library.**

 Select the **Check in** icon
Pick the assembly to check in
Enter the name "**engine_assembly**"
Define the check in parameters as below.

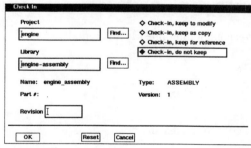

Select **OK**

# Chapter 11. Review Questions

1. List three ways an assembly can be used.

2. Write a short description of each of the six hierarchy functions.

3. Describe how to get assembly parts from the Workbench.

4. Describe how to get assembly parts from the Libraries.

5. Describe how to get assembly parts from the Catalogs.

6. List the six constraint types and sketch their symbols.

7. What are the three types of parallel and perpendicular constraints.

8. What are the five combinations of Linear constraints?

9. List the six types of Fix functions.

10. Explain how you would use a Fix function.

11. Explain the proper use of the Flip option when modifying constraints.

12. Explain how to remove a selected constraint from an instance.

13. List the five transform functions that are used to move instances.

14. Describe the process of creating an Assembly Equation.

15. Use a sketch to explain the differences between exploding linearly and radially.

16. What does it mean to "suppress an instance"?

17. List the benefits of suppressing an instance.

18. Briefly describe the process of changing the color of an instance.

Mastering I-DEAS
Scholars International Publishing Corp., 1999

# Chapter

**12**

# Analyzing and Animating Assemblies

## Highlights of the Chapter
- Checking interference
- Generating mass properties
- Creating configurations
- Animating a stored sequence

## Overview

After an assembly is created, we can analyze the assembly by checking interference between instances, generating mass properties, and animating the motion of moving instances. Checking interference determines whether instances or subassemblies interfere. It also examines whether instances touch. I-DEAS can generate a list of mass properties including surface area, volume, average density, mass, center of gravity, inertial properties, radius of gyration, and gyration axes. I-DEAS uses the concept of configurations and sequence to animate the motion of moving instances of the assembly. A configuration is a stored positional data of instances in various orientations. A sequence is the user-defined ordered list of configurations. I-DEAS can animate a selected sequence for you to visually check on interference and mating assemblies.

# 12.1 Checking Interference

I-DEAS uses the "Interference" command to determine whether an assembly of two or more instances occupies the same volume. This command allows the user to check whether instances or subassemblies interfere, and if not, whether they touch. Interference generates a list of data on the interference.

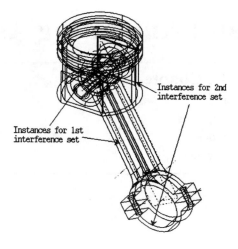

Instances for 2nd interference set

Instances for 1st interference set

Figure 12.1

**The procedure for performing interference checking is (Figure 12.1):**

1. Select the "Interference" icon
2. The system prompts "pick instances for the first interference set": pick the instance

**Note:** Continue to select more instances to be included in the first set of instances if needed, otherwise press Enter key to terminate the selection of instances in the first set)

3. Select the instances in the second set, then press Enter key
   The interference check menu should appear as below.

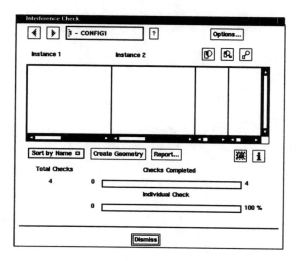

The **three interference check options** are briefly described below:

| | |
|---|---|
| **Interference volume:** | the system checks for interference between the selected instance sets. |
| **Clearance and volume:** | the system calculates both interference and clearance between selected instances. |
| **Clearance:** | the system checks for clearance between the selected instance sets. |

## Options

I-DEAS provides options to specify numeric results for the interference check. Click on the "Options" button to open the "Interference check Options" dialog box as below:

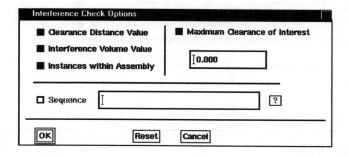

| | |
|---|---|
| **Clearance distance value:** | specifies numeric results of the clearance distance for the interference check. |
| **Interference volume value:** | specifies the interference volume value for the interference check. |
| **Instances within assembly:** | indicates the interfered instances in the selected assembly. |
| **Maximum clearance of interest:** | specifies the maximum clearance distance of the selected instances. |

Three other parameters in the "Interference Check" dialog box are described below:

### Sort

There are two options; **sort by name** and **sort by result**. Sort by name sorts the instance sets alphabetically. Sort by result lists according to the check results.

### Create geometry

This parameter creates part geometry for the interference volume or curve. This helps in visualizing the interference results.

### Report

The Report parameter creates a default report for the current interference check. Click on the "Report" button to open the view report menu as shown next.

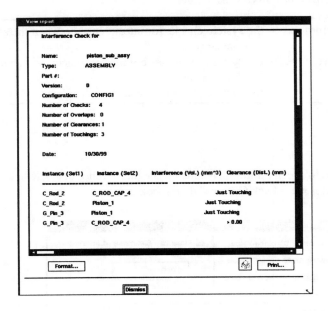

# 12.2 Material

A part model must be assigned a material type and its physical properties before it can be used for further engineering analyses. You can assign an existing material in the database to the model, or define a new material and assign it to the part model.

**The procedure for creating a material is:**

1. Select the Materials icon to open its dialog box as below.

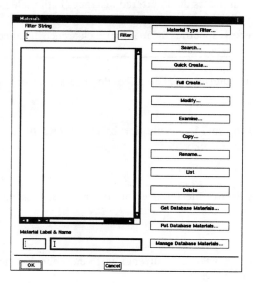

# Analyzing and Animating Assemblies

The main parameters in material dialog box are summarized below:

| | |
|---|---|
| **Material type filter:** | filter and display materials according to material type. |
| **Search:** | select materials according to criteria. |
| **Quick create:** | create a new material using default properties. |
| **Full create:** | create a new material with general properties. |
| **Modify:** | modifies materials and their data. |
| **Examine:** | displays materials and their data. |
| **Copy:** | make a copy of a material. |
| **Rename:** | change the name of a material. |
| **List:** | display material data. |
| **Delete:** | remove a material from the model file database. |
| **Get database materials:** | copy materials from material databases. |
| **Put database materials:** | copy materials from external material databases. |
| **Manage database materials:** | let you work with materials in external databases. |

2. Select the Quick Create button to open its dialog box as below.

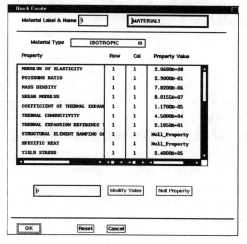

3. Click Material Type button to open the material types list as below on the left.
4. Select the desired material type "ISOTROPIC" from the list and enter label and name as below on the right.

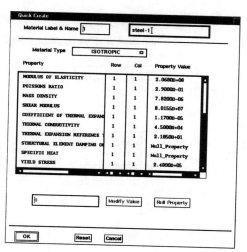

5. Select **OK** to exit Quick Create mode

The material just defined is added to the Materials list as below.

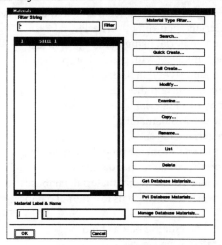

6. Select **OK** to exit Materials dialog box

# 12.3  Physical Properties

Each part or assembly model can be evaluated to find its physical properties. There are two groups of physical properties; **geometry properties** and **inertial properties**. Geometry properties include **solid surface area, open surface area, volume**, and **center of gravity**. Inertial properties include **density, mass, weight**, and **various moments of inertial of mass**.

  **The procedure for calculating physical properties is:**

 1. Select the Properties icon

2. Pick the entity for property calculation

The physical properties menu should appear as below.

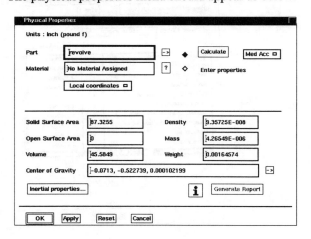

Mastering I-DEAS,
Scholars International Publishing Corp., 1999

3. Click "?" button next to "Material" parameter to open the materials menu as below.

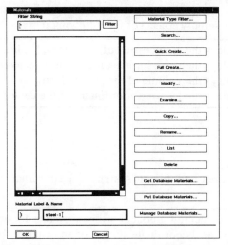

4. Select a desired material or enter the material label and name (steel-1)
5. Select **OK** to exit the materials menu to return back to physical properties menu as below.

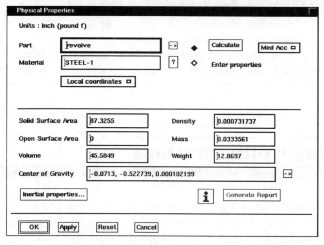

6. Click "Initial Properties" button to calculate first- and second-order inertial properties as below.

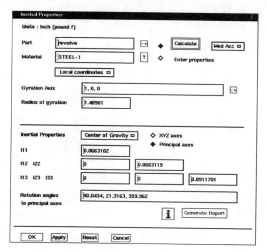

## Geometry Properties

The geometry properties of a part or an assembly consist of the following items:

| | |
|---|---|
| **Solid surface area:** | displays the surface area of the selected solid. |
| **Open surface area:** | displays the open surface area of the selected entity. |
| **Volume:** | displays the volume of the selected entity. |
| **Center of gravity:** | displays the location coordinates of the center of gravity. |

## Inertial Properties

The calculation of inertia properties requires a coordinate system. The coordinate system can be selected from one of following three options:

| | |
|---|---|
| **Global coordinates:** | use the default global coordinate system for analysis. |
| **Local coordinates:** | use a local coordinate system of an instance for analysis. |
| **User coordinates:** | use a user defined coordinate system for analysis. |

The inertial properties of a part or an assembly include the following items:

| | |
|---|---|
| **Gyration axis:** | specifies the direction for the axis of gyration. |
| **Radius of gyration:** | displays the radius of gyration. |
| **Inertial properties:** | specifies the reference point of the inertial properties. |
| **Rotation angles to principal axes:** | displays the values for the moments and products of inertia. |

# 12.4 Creating Configurations

Most assemblies consist of moving instances. The change of location and orientation in one instance affects other instances due to its assembly constraints. It is very useful to examine the position and orientation of each instance and their relationships in an assembly at various cases. A configuration is a stored orientation of instances in an assembly. Multiple configurations can be used to store the information in various orientations (Figure 12.2).

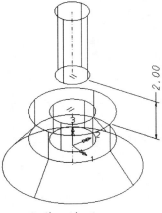

Configuration 1

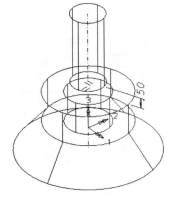

Configuration 2

Figure 12.2

Mastering I-DEAS,
Scholars International Publishing Corp., 1999

# Analyzing and Animating Assemblies

A configuration can be used for **(1) showing different orientations of the same assembly, (2) checking interference between instances**, and **(3) animating the assembly. A sequence is a collection of user-defined ordered configurations**. Any configurations included in a sequence can be created by modifying a linear or an angular dimension when using the "Modify Entity" icon.

**The procedure for modifying a linear or angular dimension:**

 1. Select the Modify Entity icon, then pick the assembly dimension to be modified. The modify dimension dialog box should appear as below.

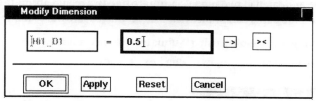

The parameters of the modify dimensions are briefly described below:

| | |
|---|---|
| **Equations (→):** | open an options list. The list dialog appears here: |

> **Reference**
> **Constant**
> **Measure**
> **Animate**

| | |
|---|---|
| **Reference:** | specifies the dimension being a reference dimension. |
| **Constant:** | specifies the dimension being a constant dimension. |
| **Measure:** | measures the distance between two selected entities and assigns this value to the dimension. |
| **Animate:** | animates the selected dimension between a distance range. |

2. Click on the Equations (→) button, then select Animate to open the animate dimension dialog box as below.

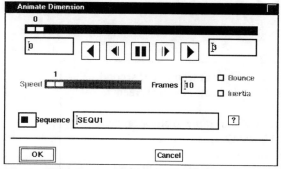

The animate parameters are summarized as below:

| | |
|---|---|
| **Start:** | specify the start dimension of the animation which is the linear or angular dimension of the first frame. |
| **End:** | specify the end dimension of the animation which is the linear or angular dimension of the last frame. |
| **Frame:** | specify the number of steps between the start and end dimensions. |
| **Sequence:** | save the animated frames in the specified sequence name that can be animated using the Animate Hardware or Animate Software command. |

3. Click on the Forward button to continuously animate the dimension frame by frame
4. Select **OK** to exit the Animate dimension dialog box
5. Select **OK** to exit the Modify Entity dialog box

## Animating a Sequence

A sequence of configurations can be animated in two modes: **animate hardware** and **animate software**. Only those computers with good graphic cards can implement the "Animate Hardware" mode.

 **The procedure for animating an assembly using Animate Software mode is:**

 1. Select the Animate Software icon to open its dialog box as below.

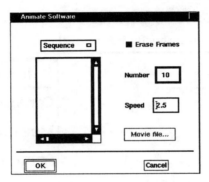

Two animate software parameters are described below:

| | |
|---|---|
| **Number:** | controls the number of configurations in a sequence. |
| **Speed:** | controls the number of frames per second displayed. |

## Animation options

Click the right mouse button to open the options list as to the side.

| | | |
|---|---|---|
| **Rate:** | specifies the number of frames per second. | Rate |
| **All frames:** | specifies show all frames on the screen (Figure 12.3). | All frames |
| **Frame:** | specifies a selected frame to show on the screen (Figure 12.4). | Frame |
| **Reset:** | resets the animation. | Reset |
| **Continue:** | makes the system to continuously animate frame by frame. | Continue |
| **Faster:** | increases the animation speed. | Faster |
| **Slower:** | decreases the animation speed. | Slower |
| **Single step:** | animates a single step at a time. | Single step |
| **End:** | ends the animation. | End |

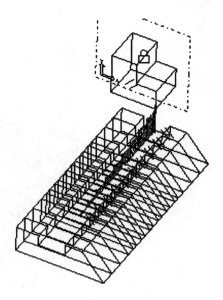

Figure 12.3

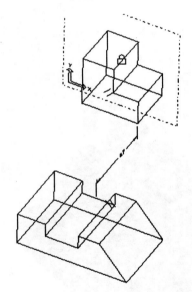

Figure 12.4

# Project 1.
# Animating engine assembly

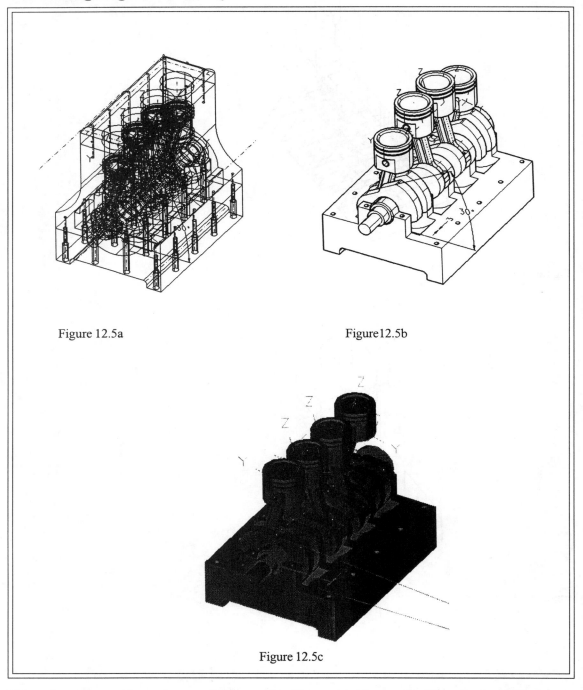

Figure 12.5a                    Figure 12.5b

Figure 12.5c

This project animates the engine assembly created in Chapter 11. The angular dimension is modified to create the animation sequences. The sequence has ten steps and is saved as "engine assly seq". Engine cap and engine body instances are pruned from the assembly for providing a better view of the animation. Figure 12.5 shows a number of display modes of engine assembly animation.

Mastering I-DEAS,
Scholars International Publishing Corp., 1999

**Step 1. Check out the engine assembly.**

 Select the **Get from Library** icon

Set the check out parameters as below.

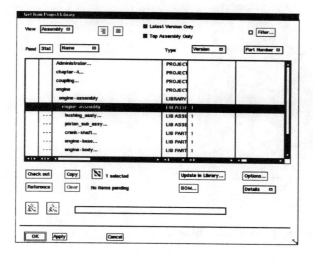

Select **OK**

**Step 2. Get the assembly from the bin.**

 Select the **Get** icon

Select "**engine – assembly**" as shown below.

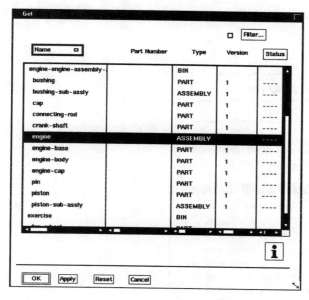

Select **OK** to bring the engine assembly to workbench

The engine assembly should appear as Figure 12.6.

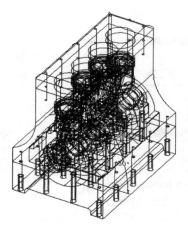

Figure 12.6

### Step 3.   Define the display filters and assembly display filters.

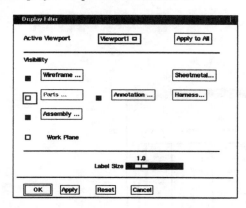

Select the **Display Filter** icon
Set the display filter parameters as below.

Click on the "**Assembly**" button to open its dialog box
Set the assembly display filter parameters as below.

Select **OK**

Select the **Front View (XY)** icon
The assembly shown in front view should look like Figure 12.7.

Mastering I-DEAS,
Scholars International Publishing Corp., 1999

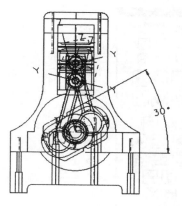

Figure 12.7

**Step 4.   Modify an angular dimension.**

 Select the **Modify Entity** icon

Pick the **30° angular dimension** to open the modify dimension dialog box

Click the **Equation (→)** button to open the options list as below

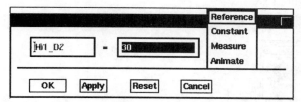

Select "**Animate**" from the list to open the animate dimension dialog box

Set its parameters as below

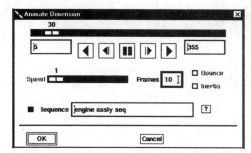

Select the **Forward** button to create the sequence

Select **OK** to exit the animate dimension dialog box

Select **OK** to exit the modify dimension dialog box

**Step 5.   Prune engine cap and engine body instances from the assembly.**

 Click on the **Hierarchy** icon to open its dialog box

Select the **engine-cap** and then press the **Ctrl key** to Select the engine-body instances as displayed on the Hiearchy menu

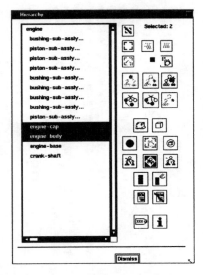

Select the **Prune** icon to prune these two instances
Select the **Dismiss** button to exit the dialog box
The new drawing becomes Figure 12.8.

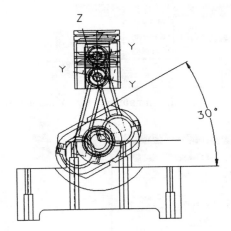

Figure 12.8

## Step 6.  Show in isometric view.

Select the **Isometric View** icon
Select **Options** and set its parameters as below.

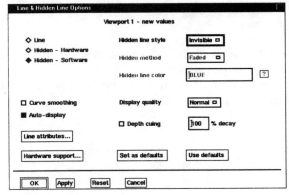

Mastering I-DEAS,
Scholars International Publishing Corp., 1999

Select **OK**

The new assembly view becomes Figure 12.9.

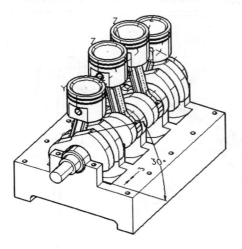

Figure 12.9

## Step 7. Animate the motion.

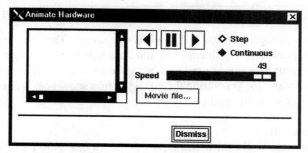

Select the **Animate Hardware** icon
Set the animate hardware parameters as below.

Click on the **"Forward Animation"** button to animate the motion on the screen

| *Note:* | You can simulate the animation with the line mode or hidden line mode. With the hidden line mode, your assembly may be tilted. Change to line mode if this problem happens. |
| --- | --- |

Select **Dismiss** to exit the animation

# Project 2.
# Creating a four-bar linkage assembly and animation

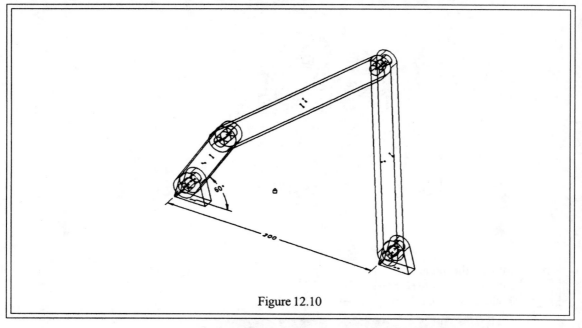

Figure 12.10

The four-bar linkage assembly shown in Figure 12.10 consists of five instances. The two base-support instances are identical. The long link is used for the floating bar and right side bar. Therefore we need to model only three parts. The Modify entity function is used to modify the angular dimension between the short link instance and the horizontal plane for generating the configuration sequence. We use the animate software function to run animation in this project.

**Step 1.  Create the section for base support.**
      Create a section and add dimensions for the base support as shown in Figure 12.11

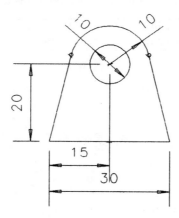

Figure 12.11

**Step 2.  Create a section and add dimensions for the short link.**
      Create a section and add dimensions to constrain it as shown in Figure 12.12.

Mastering I-DEAS,
Scholars International Publishing Corp., 1999

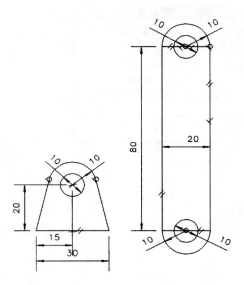

Figure 12.12

**Step 3. Create a section and add dimensions for the long link.**

Create a section and add dimensions to constrain it as shown in Figure 12.13.

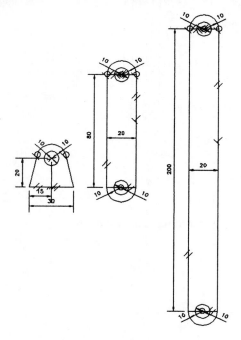

Figure 12.13

**Step 4. Create three extrude features using the three sections just created.**

Extrude three sections separately to obtain three features as shown in Figure 12.14.
The extrusion distance is **10** for all three features.

The extrude parameters are shown below for all three features.

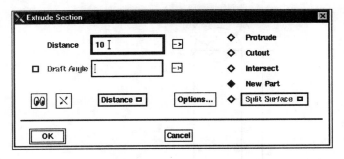

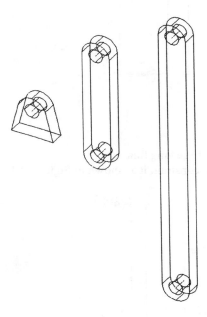

Figure 12.14

**Step 5.** **Name these three parts.**
 Select the **Name Parts** icon
Pick each part and give its name according to the list below.
> **Base-support**
> **Short-link**
> **Long-link**

**Step 6.** **Save the file as "linkage".**
Select **File → Save As**
File name: **linkage**

**Step 7.** **Change to Master Assembly program.**
Click on the "**Master Assembly**" program

**Step 8.** **Create an assembly hierarchy.**
 Select the "**Hierarchy**" icon to open the hierarchy menu
Select the "**Add Parent**" icon from hierarchy menu

Mastering I-DEAS,
Scholars International Publishing Corp., 1999

Enter "**Linkage**" into the Name field as below.

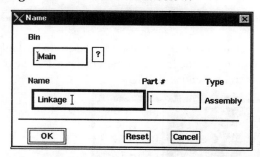

The "Linkage" should appear on the hierarchy menu as below.

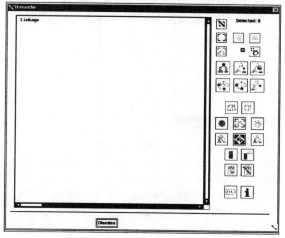

**Step 9. Add part instances.**

Click on "**Linkage**" from the list to highlight it for making various assembly functions active

Select the "**Add to**" icon, then pick the **base support part**

The base support appears on the hierarchy menu now

Select the "**Add to**" icon again, then pick the **short link part**

Select the "**Add to**" icon, then pick the **long link part**

The three instance names are listed on the hierarchy menu as shown below.

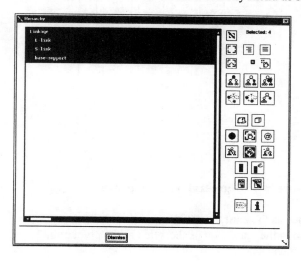

**Step 10. Duplicate the instances.**

In this project, two base-support instances and two long-link parts are needed. We need to duplicate them.

Select the "**Add to**" icon, then pick the **base support part** that needs to be duplicated

Select the "**Add to**" icon again, then pick the **long link part** that needs to be duplicated

The five instances appear in hierarchy menu as below.

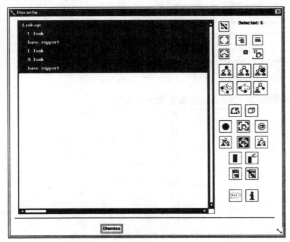

You now only see three instances on the screen. To see all five instances, Select the "Move" icon, pick the base support instance as the entity to move on screen and drag it to a new location. Similarly, move the long link instance. Now you can see five instances all show on screen as in Figure 12.15.

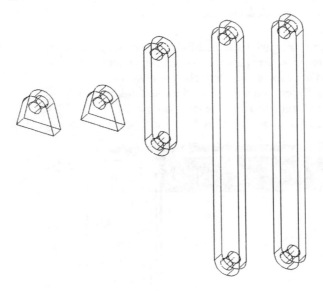

Figure 12.15

**Step 11. Rotate the short link instance by 30 degrees about its upper end.**

 Select the "**Rotate**" icon.

Pick the **short link instance** as the entity to rotate

Pick the **front center point** at the upper end of short link as the pivot point

Select "**About Z**" from the menu list

Enter angle about Z (90.0): **-30**

Mastering I-DEAS,
Scholars International Publishing Corp., 1999

The short link instance has been rotated to the new orientation as in Figure 12.16.

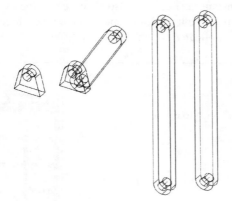

Figure 12.16

**Step 12. Rotate one of the long link instances by 45 degrees about the Z axis.**

 Select the "**Rotate**" icon

Pick the **left long link** instance as the entity to rotate

Pick the **front center point** of the axis line at the upper end as the pivot point

Select "**About Z**" from the options list

Enter angle about Z (90.0): **-45**

The long link instance is rotated to a new location as in Figure 12.17.

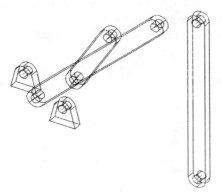

Figure 12.17

**Step 13. Change to top view.**

Select the **Top view (ZX-view)** to show the drawing view as in Figure 12.18

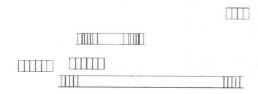

Figure 12.18

**Note:** Your drawing view may appear differently from what was shown in Figure 12.18 due to different creating and moving locations of instances. You may also observe that the two duplicated instances, base support and long link, are out of alignment with the other three original instances. This means that the two duplicated instances have a different Z-coordinate value from the three original instances.

**Step 14. Ground a base support instance.**

Change to **isometric view.**
Select the "**Constrain & Dimension**" icon to open
the constrain menu shown here

Select "**Lock**",
then select the **base support instance** located at the left side as the first part to constrain
Click the right mouse button, then select "**Hierarchy**" from options list
Click "**Linkage**" from assembly menu, then select **OK** to lock the base support instance

**Step 15. Assemble the short ink to the left base support.**

Select the "**Coincident & Collinear**" icon
Pick the **center line** of the left base support instance as the first entity, then pick the **center line** at the lower end of the short link instance as the second entity.
The short link instance has moved to coincident with the base support as in Figure 12.19.

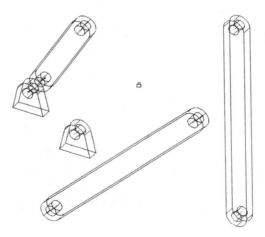

Figure 12.19

Select the "**Coincident & Collinear**" icon
Pick the **front face** of left base support instance as the first entity
Pick the **real face** of the short link instance as the second entity.
The rear face of the short link instance has moved to be coincident with the front face of the base support as in Figure 12.20.

12-24

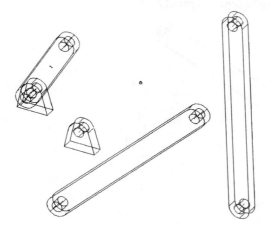

Figure 12.20

## Step 16. Add an angular dimension constraint.

 Select the "**Angular**" dimension icon
Pick the **horizontal face** of the support base as the first entity to dimension
Pick the **right flat face** of the short link instance as the second entity to dimension
Pick **a point** to locate the text
The angular dimension between two instances is added as in Figure 12.21.

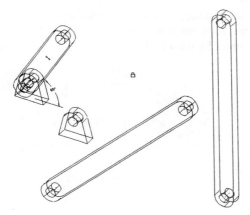

Figure 12.21

## Step 17. Assemble the floating link.

 Select the "**Coincident & Collinear**" icon
Pick the **centerline** at the upper end of the short link
Pick the **centerline** at the lower end of sloped long link instance
Select "**Coincident & Collinear**"
Pick the **front face** of the short link instance
Pick the **real face** of the long link instance

The new assembly drawing becomes Figure 12.22.

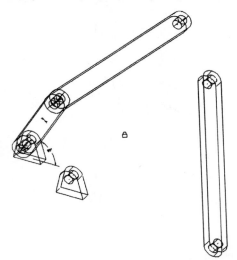

Figure 12.22

**Step 18. Assemble the third link.**

 Select "**Coincident & Collinear**"

Pick the **centerline** at the upper end of the long link instance with slope angle, then
  pick the centerline at the upper end of vertical long link instance
Select "**Coincident & Collinear**"
Pick the **rear face** of the long link instance with slope angle, then
  pick the front face of the vertical long link instance.
The new assembly drawing becomes Figure 12.23.

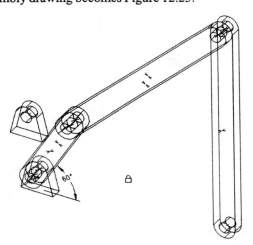

Figure 12.23

**Step 19. Assembly the other base support.**

Select "**Coincident & Collinear**"
Pick the **centerline** at the lower end of the vertical long link instance and then
  pick the  **centerline** of the other base support instance
Select "**Coincident & Collinear**"
Pick the **real face** of the vertical long link instance and
  the **front face** of the base support instance

12-26

The new assembly drawing becomes Figure 12.24.

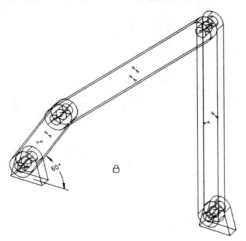

Figure 12.24

**Step 20. Constrain the horizontal face of two base support instances.**

Select "**Coincident & Collinear**"
Pick the **horizontal face** of the left base support instance and the **other** one's.
The new assembly drawing becomes Figure 12.25.

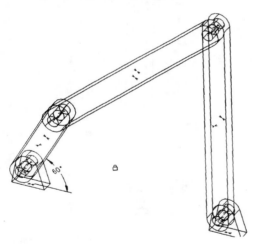

Figure 12.25

**Step 21. Add a dimension between two base support instances.**

Select the **Linear dimension** icon from the constrain menu
Pick the **left** (or right) **line** of the left base support instance's vertical face as the first entity to dimension and pick the **left** (or right) **line** of the right base support instance's vertical face as the second entity to dimension
Pick **a point** to locate the text

# Analyzing and Animating Assemblies

The Linear dimension between two base support instances is added as in Figure 12.26.

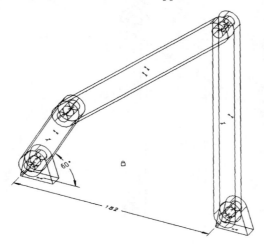

Figure 12.26

You can modify this dimension to 200mm as shown in Figure 12.27.

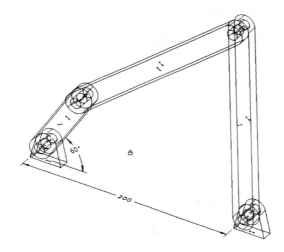

Figure 12.27

## Step 22. Create animation sequence.

Click on **angular dimension**, then select the "**Modify Entity**" icon
The Modify Dimension dialog box should appear as below.

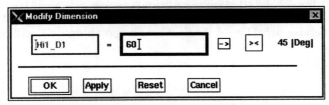

Clicks on the "**Equations**" icon and select "**Animate**"

# Analyzing and Animating Assemblies

The "**Animate Dimension**" menu should appear and set the parameters as below.

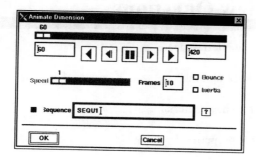

Select **OK**

## Step 23. Run the animation.

 Select the "**Animate Software**" icon and set its parameter settings as below.

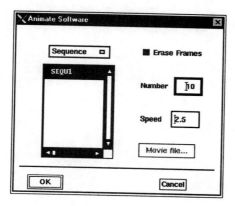

Change speed to **5** (5 frames per second)

Select **OK** to start animation on the screen

---

**Note:** If you want to change the speed rate or stop the animation, press the right bottom and select what you want.

# Chapter 12.  Review Questions

1. Describe the procedure for checking interference.

2. What are the three interference check options?

3. Describe the procedure for creating a new material.

4. What are the two types of physical properties?

5. What is a configuration?

6. Describe the use of a configuration.

7. Describe how to use the "Modify Entity" function to generate a sequence of configurations.

8. What are the two modes of animating a sequence of configurations?

Mastering I-DEAS,
Scholars International Publishing Corp., 1999

# Chapter

**13**

# Creating Surfaces

---

## Highlights of the Chapter

- Surface types
- Three approaches to modeling surfaces
- Creating extruded and revolved surfaces
- Creating loft surfaces
- Creating sweep surfaces
- Creating surfaces by boundaries
- Creating meshes of curves
- Creating surfaces through points

---

## Overview

A surface is the shape representation of a part's skin defined by mathematical equations. A surface normally consists of many sections or patches that are smoothly blended together to form an entity. Due to the increased computer power and new surface modeling techniques, today's surface modeling in CAD/CAM systems can accurately and completely describe a complex part shape.

This chapter covers important surfacing techniques used in I-DEAS. Three basic approaches to modeling surfaces and seven methods of creating surfaces are presented. Useful hints are provided to help in your understanding of the principles and procedures of the surfacing techniques.

Surfaces represent only the shape of a part's skin without thickness and volume. We can use the "material side" function to indicate which side of the skin should get the added material. Next, the shell function is used to add thickness to the surface. The three Boolean operation functions: **join**, **cutout** and **intersect,** join the surfaces to the existing part model. In this way, the features of a complex shape can be added to parts.

# 13.1  Surface Types

Surface modeling is widely used to describe complex objects such as a car, ship, and airplane body components, as well as their part dies and molds. The data of surface models can be used to perform the following engineering, design, and manufacturing functions:

- Part geometric design and representation
- Mass properties calculation
- Interference checking between mating parts
- Cross-sectioned views generation
- Finite element meshes generation
- NC tool paths generation

I-DEAS provides the following **seven methods for creating a surface**:

| | |
|---|---|
| **Extrude:** | extrudes a section along a specified vector direction to create a surface. |
| **Revolve:** | revolves a section about a line by a given angle to create a surface. |
| **Sweep:** | sweeps a section along a path to create a surface. |
| **Loft:** | smoothly blends a series of sections to form a surface. |
| **Mesh of curves:** | smoothly blends a series of sections and curves to form a surface. |
| **Surface by boundary:** uses a set of connected curves or edges as boundary to create a surface. | |
| **Fit surface to point:** uses a set of points to create a surface though them. | |

**Three basic approaches** to modeling surfaces in I-DEAS are solids-based surfacing, open surfacing, and hybrid. They are described below:

| | |
|---|---|
| **Solids-based surfacing:** | uses the same solid modeling techniques such as extrude, revolve, loft, and sweep to create dimension driven surfaces. |
| **Open surfacing:** | uses a set of curves or points to create planar surfaces or patches. The available surfacing techniques include surface by boundary, fit surface to points, and mesh of curves. |
| **Hybrid:** | uses a combination of solids-based surfacing and open surfacing methods. In this approach, we model the majority of a part with simple "solid modeling" techniques, then extract edges and define additional curves to create open surfaces. This is the most effective approach. |

The seven surface methods are presented in the following seven sections, respectively.

# 13.2  Creating Surfaces from Extrusion

The procedure for creating surfaces from extrusion is the same as those used to create solids from extrusion. The only difference is that you need to use **open sections** for creating surfaces and use **closed sections** for generating solid features. When an open section is used in extrusion, the system will issue a message "Section containing an open loop was extruded". Figure 13.1 shows an example of using an open section to create an extruded surface.

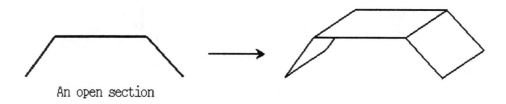

An open section

Figure 13.1

When a closed section is used, we can create a solid or a surface depending on the choice of endcaps status. With the endcaps "On", a solid feature is created and the feature becomes a surface if the endcaps is turn to "Off". Figure 13.2 shows the effect of "endcaps" on the features created from the same closed section.

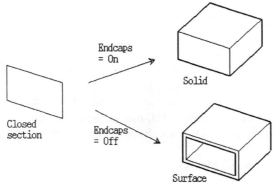

Figure 13.2

  **The procedure for creating an extruded surface is (Figure 13.3):**

1. Create an open section
2. Select Extrude function
3. Select the open section
4. Define extrude parameters

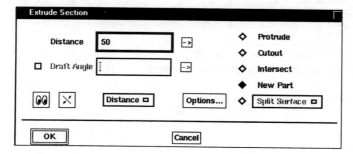

5. Select Preview to display the surface
6. Select **OK** from the Extrude Sections menu to complete the surface

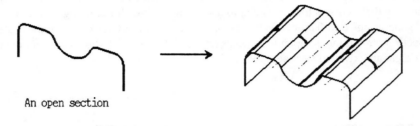

An open section

Figure 13.3

# Project 1.
# Creating an extrude surface with an open section

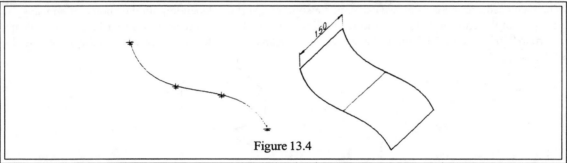

Figure 13.4

This project extrudes a spline curve by a distance of 150-mm to form a surface as shown in Figure 13.4. The spine is created from four points on the XY-plane. Save the surface model file as "surface-extrude".

**Step 1.    Create a four-point spline on XY plane.**

 Select the **Spline** icon
Press the **right mouse button** and select **Option** from the list
Enter the coordinate values for the first point as below.

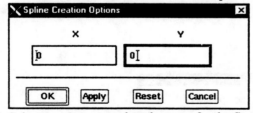

Select **Apply** to complete the entry for the first point
Enter the following three additional sets of point coordinates:

**(60, -65)**
**(120, -80)**
**(180, -130)**

Press **MMB** to end the spline

Mastering I-DEAS,
Scholars International Publishing Corp., 1999

# Creating Surfaces

Choose the Through Point in Spline Constraint Control form as below.

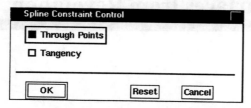

Select **OK** to create the spline as shown in Figure 13.5

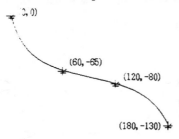

Figure 13.5

**Step 2.  Extrude the spline by a distance of 150.**

 Select the **Isometric View** icon

Select the **Extrude** icon

 Pick the spline as the curve to extrude

Set the extrude section parameters as below.

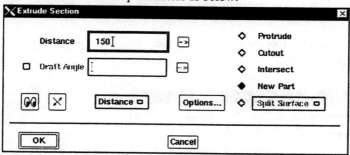

Select **OK** to create the surface as shown in Figure 13.6

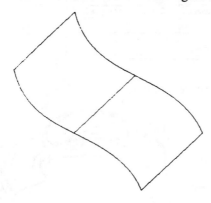

Figure 13.6

**Step 3.  Save the surface model as "surface-extrude".**

# 13.3  Creating Surfaces from Revolution

Creating a "Surface from Revolution" uses the same principle as for extrusion. When a closed section is used, the revolved feature becomes a solid. The revolved feature becomes a surface of revolution when an open section is used. Figure 13.7 shows the comparison between a revolved solid and a revolved surface using similar sections.

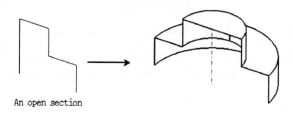

An open section

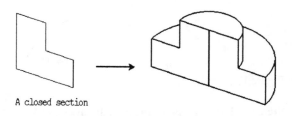

A closed section

Figure 13.7

**The procedure for creating a surface from revolution is (Figure 13.8):**

1.  Create an open section
2.  Select Revolve function
3.  Select the open section and define the axis of revolution
4.  Define the revolve parameters

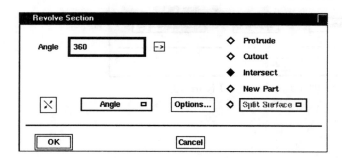

5.  Select OK to complete the surface of revolution

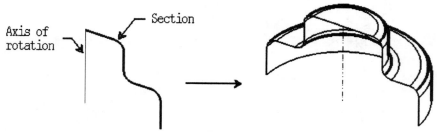

Figure 13.8

Mastering I-DEAS,
Scholars International Publishing Corp., 1999

# Project 2.
# Creating a surface of revolution

Revolving an arc about a vertical axis creates the revolved surface shown in Figure 13.9. The arc is created by using the "three through points" option. Save the surface model as "surface-revolve".

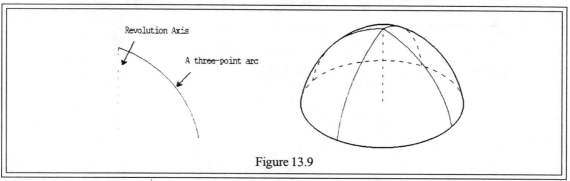

Figure 13.9

**Step 1.   Create a three-point arc on XY plane.**

 Select the **Three Point On** icon
Press the **right mouse button** and select **Option** from the list
Enter the coordinate values of three points as below.

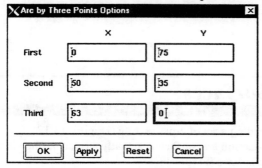

Select **OK** to create the arc as in Figure 13.10

Figure 13.10

**Step 2.   Revolve the arc by an angle of 360-degree.**

 Select the **Isometric View** icon
Select the **Revolve** icon
 Pick the arc as the curve for revolving
Press the **right mouse button** and select **Heading,** then **Y Axis** as the axis to revolve about
Press **MMB** to complete the axis selection

Set the revolve section parameters as below.

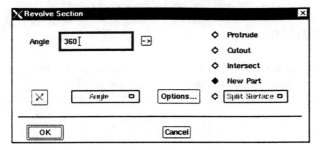

Select **OK** to create the surface as in Figure 13.11

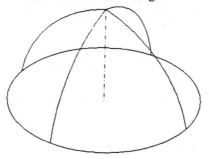

Figure 13.11

**Step 3.** **Save the surface model file as "surface-revolve".**

# 13.4   Creating Loft Surfaces

A loft surface is created by smoothly blending a set of cross sections (Figure 13.12). It requires at least two sections to form a loft surface. A two-section loft surface is actually a ruled surface in which the two sections are connected by a series of straight lines (Figure 13.13).

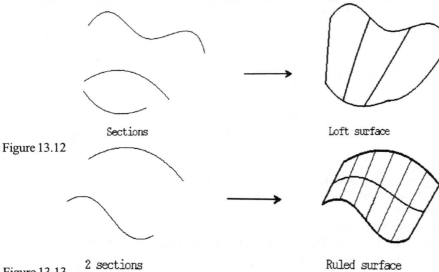

Figure 13.12

Figure 13.13

# Creating Surfaces

The cross sections used for creating loft surfaces can be open or closed loops of connected curves. They can be one of the following types:

- Edges of existing surfaces as the curves
- Sections from existing surface
- Non-planar sections
- A single point

Those sections used in creating a loft surface can have a different number of sides. The system will connect the starting point of the section and automatically determine how to connect those sides in the sections. Figure 13.14 shows an example of connecting one four-side section and one three-side section to form a loft surface. Figure 13.15 illustrates the loft surface created from a four-side section and a one-element section.

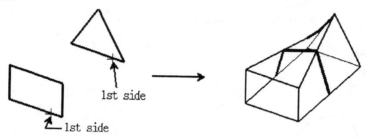

Figure 13.14

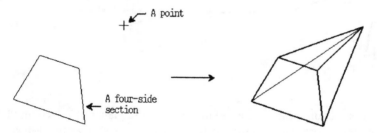

Figure 13.15

The shape and orientation of a loft surface are also determined by three parameters: **starting point**, **starting element**, and **lofting direction**. The location you pick on the section determines the above three parameters. I-DEAS uses the element you pick on the section as the starting element. The starting point is snapped to the closer end point of the starting element. The lofting direction starts from the start point and points to the other end of the starting element (Figure 13.16). Make sure that the starting point and lofting direction are properly defined for all lofting sections. Figure 13.17 shows an example in which the starting points in a section are not properly selected. Figure 13.18 illustrates how the change of lofting direction alters the loft surface.

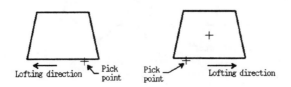

Figure 13.16

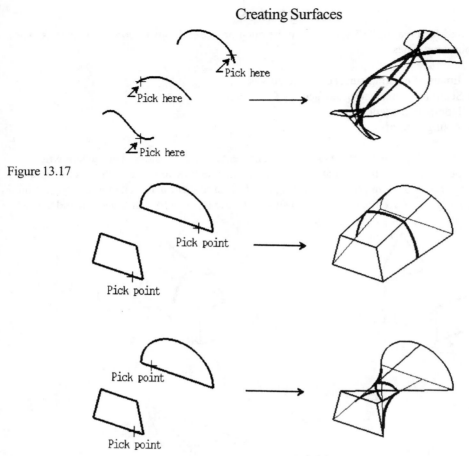

Figure 13.17

Figure 13.18

The picking order of a cross section must be selected in the correct sequence. The system blends the sections according to the picking order of the cross sections. Figure 13.19 shows two loft surfaces that result from different picking orders on the same sections.

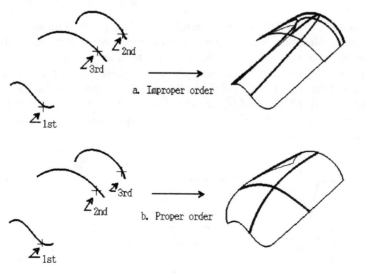

Figure 13.19

13-10

# Preparing Cross-Section Curves

Cross-section curves used in creating loft surfaces can be **edges** or **sections** of existing features and independent curves. Curves are created in a sketch plane, which have a single Z-depth. They need to be moved to other desired locations. To do that you need to do two things:

- Converting curves into sections
- Using Move and/or Rotate commands to relocate the sections to desired locations

### Converting curves into sections

I-DEAS uses sections to create loft surfaces. A section is a chain of connected entities. Entities are treated as separate elements before they are formed as a section. We can use the "**Build Section**" function to trace a section from a set of wireframe geometry. This is a very useful function in preparing sections to be used in creating surfaces.

### Translating sections into desired locations

Use the **Move function** to move a selected section to a new position by entering its translation distance in X, Y, and Z directions, respectively. Figure 13.20 shows an example of moving the middle section by the distances (0,0,-50) and outer section by the distances (30,0,-100).

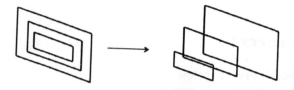

Figure 13.20

The **Rotate function** allows the designer to rotate a section about three axes at a point on the section. I-DEAS provides The following **six ways** to define the rotation angles about principal axes:

| | |
|---|---|
| **Default 3-axis angles:** | Enter rotation angles about three principal axes (Figure 13.21). |
| **About X:** | Rotate about X-axis only (Figure 13.22). |
| **About Y:** | Rotate about Y-axis only (Figure 13.23). |
| **About Z:** | Rotate about Z-axis only (Figure 13.24). |
| **About Vector:** | Rotate about the angular direction defined by a vector (Figure 13.25). |
| **Align Vectors:** | Rotate the orientation defined by two vectors (from vector and to vector) (Figure 13.26). |

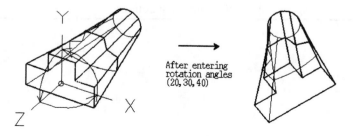

After entering rotation angles (20, 30, 40)

Figure 13.21

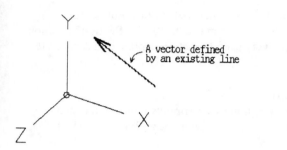

Figure 13.22          Figure 13.23          Figure 13.24

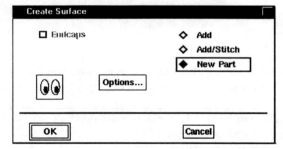

Figure 13.25                    Figure 13.26

## Lofting parameters

The loft surface dialog box should appear as below.

The five parameters in loft surface dialog box are summarized as below:

| | |
|---|---|
| **Endcaps:** | add caps to top and bottom of the surface model (Figure 13.27). |
| **Add:** | add the surface to be created to the existing part. |
| **New Part:** | create a new part. |
| **Surface preview:** | display a temporary wireframe view of the surface. |
| **Options:** | specify the surface defining options. |

Figure 13.27

13-12

# Creating Surfaces

**The procedure for creating a loft surface is:**

1. Create wireframe geometries that to be formed as sections (Figure 13.28).

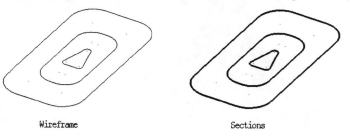

Wireframe          Sections

Figure 13.28

2. Use the "Build Section" function to convert wireframe geometries to sections.
3. Use the transform functions such as Move, Rotate, and/or Drag to position the cross section at proper locations (Figure 13.29).

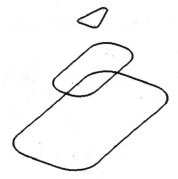

Figure 13.29

4. Select the Loft surface function.
5. Pick the cross sections in the order of the lofting direction (Figure 13.30).

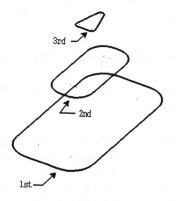

3rd

2nd

1st

Figure 13.30

6. Define the loft surface parameters (Figure 13.31).

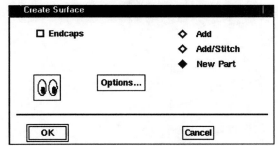

Figure 13.31

7.  Pick Preview to verify the surface (Figure 13.32).

Figure 13.32

8.  Select **OK** to complete the loft surface (Figure 13.33).

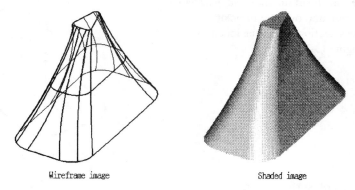

Wireframe image          Shaded image

Figure 13.33

## Modifying Loft Surfaces

After a loft surface is created, you can modify its section dimensions and feature parameters to redefine the loft surface.

### Modifying section dimensions

Click the "**Modify**" command icon and pick the loft surface to modify. Select "**Show Dimensions**" from the options list. The dimensions should appear on the sections of the surface (Figure 13.34). Select the dimension to be modified, the system will prompt for new dimension values. Select the "**Update**" icon to update the model for dimension changes (Figure 13.35).

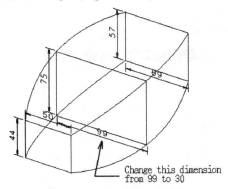

Change this dimension
from 99 to 30

Figure 13.34

13-14

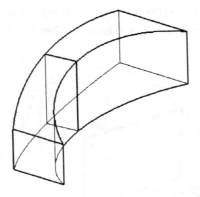

Figure 13.35

### Modifying feature parameters

I-DEAS allows access to the **Surface Options menu** to redefine the surfacing parameters. After selecting the surface to be modified, select "**Feature Parameters**" from the options list to open the Surface Options menu as below.

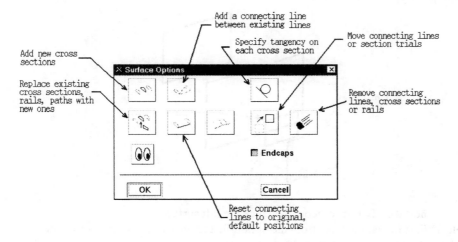

The modifying parameters are listed below and the first two have procedure steps described in detail on the next page.

- Add new cross section
- Replace existing cross sections, rails, paths with new ones
- Add a connecting line between existing lines
- Reset connecting lines to original, default positions
- Specify tangency on each cross section
- Move connecting lines or section triads
- Create a temporary wireframe view of the geometry
- Removes connecting lines, cross sections, or rails

### Adding new cross sections

Any number of cross sections can be added to the existing loft surface to redefine the surface.

**The procedure for adding a new cross section to a loft surface is:**

1. Create the section wireframe geometry to be added (Figure 13.36).

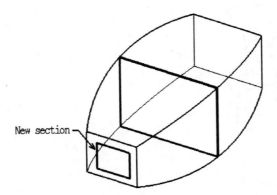

New section

Figure 13.36

2. Select the "Build Section" icon to convert the wireframe geometry to section.
3. Select the "Move" icon, then pick the section just created and move it to a new location (Figure 13.37).

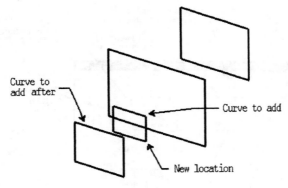

Curve to
add after

Curve to add

New location

Figure 13.37

4. S elect the "Modify Entity" icon, then pick the loft surface.
5. Select "Feature Parameters" from the options list to open Surface Options menu.
6. Select "Add new cross sections".
7. Pick cross-section curve to add before: pick the 2nd cross section
8. Pick cross-section curve to add: pick the new section just created
9. Click the middle mouse button to complete the adding section.
10. Select **OK** to complete the surface modification.

The final surface becomes Figure 13.38.

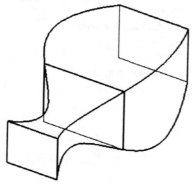

Figure 13.38

13-16

## Replacing existing cross sections

The cross sections used to define a loft surface can be replaced by a new cross section. The new section must be placed in the desired location.

 **The procedure for replacing a cross section for a loft surface is:**

1. Create a cross section wireframe geometry,
   then convert it to a cross section
   (Figure 13.39).

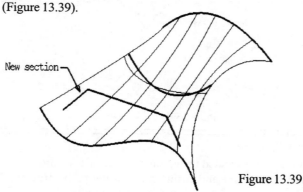

New section—

Figure 13.39

 2. Use the "Move" command to translate the new
   section to the desired location
   (Figure 13.40).

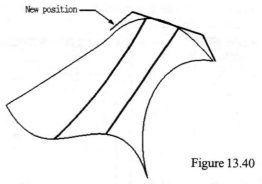

New position—

Figure 13.40

 3. Select the "Modify" icon, and then select the loft surface to modify.
4. Select "Feature Parameters" from the options list.
5. Select "Replace existing cross sections".
6. Pick the cross-section to replace:
   pick the fourth section
7. Pick the new cross-section:
   pick the section just created
8. Click the middle mouse button,
   and then select **OK** from
   the Surface Options menu.
   The new surface becomes Figure 13.41.

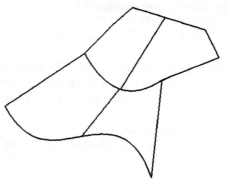

Figure 13.41

# Project 3.
# Creating a loft surface using three curves

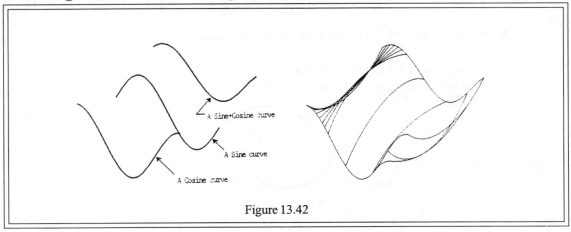

Figure 13.42

The loft surface shown in Figure 13.42 is created using three curves. These three curves are a cosine curve, a sine curve and a combination of sine and cosine curve. Refer to the previous chapter sections on creating sine and cosine curves. Save the surface model file as "surface-loft".

**Step 1.   Create a cosine curve suing function spline function.**
Select the **Function Spline** icon
Select the **Algebraic Equation** from the Function Manager form to open the editor
Enter the equation and its information as below.

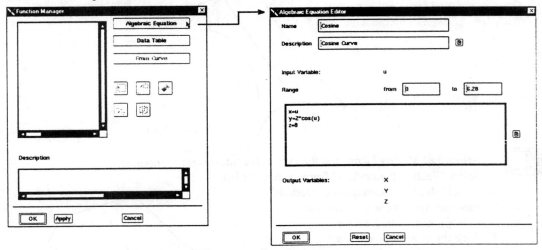

Select **OK** to exit the Algebraic Equation Editor form
Select **OK** in the Function Manager form to create the cosine curve
A cosine curve should appear on the screen

**Step 2.   Create a sine curve.**
Select **Algebraic Equation** again and enter the data as shown next.

Algebraic Equation Editor  ☒

| | |
|---|---|
| **Name** | Sine |
| **Description** | Sine Curve  ▣ |

**Input Variable:**      u

**Range**      from 0   to 6.28

```
x=u
y=2*sin(u)
z=-1
```
▣

**Output Variables:**      x
           Y
           Z

[ OK ]    [Reset]   [Cancel]

Select **OK** to exit the Algebraic Equation Editor form
Select **OK** to create the sine curve

**Step 3.** **Create a curve from a combination of sine and cosine functions.**
Select the **Algebraic Equation** again
Enter the data for the new curve as below.

Algebraic Equation Editor

| | |
|---|---|
| **Name** | Sine+Cosine |
| **Description** | Sine plus Cosine Curve  ▣ |

**Input Variable:**      u

**Range**      from 0   to 6.28

```
x = u
y = sin(u) + cos(u)
z = 0
I
```
▣

**Output Variables:**      X
           Y
           Z

[ OK ]    [Reset]   [Cancel]

Select **OK** to exit the Algebraic Equation Editor form
Select **OK** to create the third curve
Select **Cancel** in the Function Manager to exit the form
Select **Isometric View** and **Zoom All** icons to display the curve as in Figure 13.43

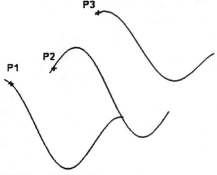

Figure 13.43

**Step 4. Create a loft surface using these three curves. Use the pick points in Figure 13.43.**

 Select the **Loft** icon

Pick **P1** then press **MMB** to end the selection for the first curve

Pick **P2** then press **MMB** to end the selection for the second curve

Pick **P3** then press **MMB** to end the selection for the third curve

Press **MMB** to end the selection

Set the Create Surface parameters as below.

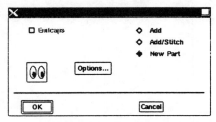

Select **OK** to create the loft surface as in Figure 13.44

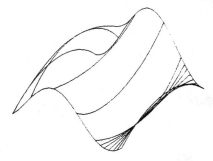

Figure 13.44

**Step 5. Save the surface model file as "surface-loft".**

# 13.5  Creating Sweeping Surfaces

Sweeping sections or curves along a path (Figure 13.45) creates a sweep surface. I-DEAS provides two sweep surfacing techniques: **sweep** and **variational sweep**. This section presents sweep surfaces. Variational sweep surfaces are covered in next section.

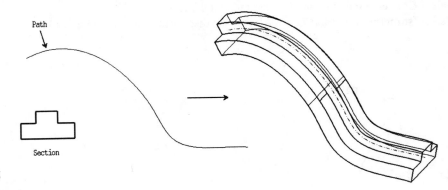

Figure 13.45

Mastering I-DEAS,
Scholars International Publishing Corp., 1999

Valid geometry for creating sweep surfaces and some helpful hints in preparing sections and paths are summarized below:

- Has at least has a smooth, continuous path and one cross section.
- Path and cross sections may be planar or non-planar.
- The path must be open type, while cross sections may be open or closed type.
- Sweep surface sections can not include holes.
- There is no limit to the number of curves (elements) per section. However, it is easier to control a sweep if the sections have the same number of curves.
- Path and cross sections may be created from wireframe curves, edges or faces of a part.

## Sweep Options

I-DEAS provides the following **four options** to control how the sections are oriented along the path and functional cross-sections:

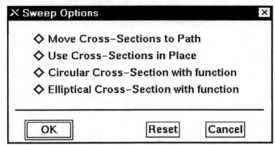

| | |
|---|---|
| **Move Cross - Sections to Path:** | The cross-sections are moved to path locations and evenly distributed along the path. |
| **Move Cross-Sections in Place:** | The cross-sections stay in where they are while the path curve moves. |
| **Circular Cross-Section with function:** | Create a function to define the radius of the cross section by the length of the path. |
| **Elliptical Cross-Section wit function:** | Create a function to define a cross section ellipse along a path. |

After you select the "Sweep" function, then click the right mouse button to open the Options list. Select "Sweep Options" from the list to open the "Sweep Options" menu.

## Move Cross-Sections to Path

This option uses the path as the controlling element to define the location and orientation of the sweep surface. The path stays where it is while the cross sections moves to path locations (Figure 13.46). When multiple cross sections are used, the cross sections are evenly distributed along the path.

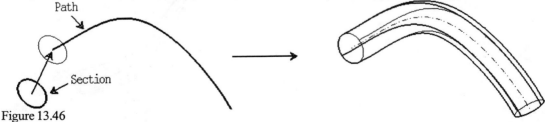

Figure 13.46

# Use Cross-Sections in Place

This option uses the cross-sections to control the location and orientation of the sweep feature.

**The following two requirements are needed for successfully creating a sweep feature of this type:**

1. The cross-sections and path curve must not be in the same plane. It must have at least an angle between the two elements. Figure 13.47 shows an example in which the path and the cross section are created on the same plane. It can not successfully create a sweep surface using the "Use cross-sections in place" option. The example shown in Figure 13.48 has the cross section on a sketch plane that is 45 degrees with the sketch plane for the path. The sweep surface using "Use cross-sections in place" is successfully completed.

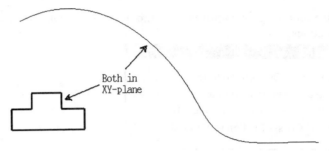

Figure 13.47

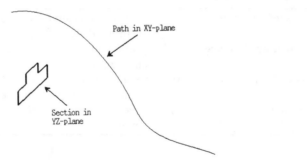

Figure 13.48

2. The plane of each cross-section must intersect the path curve (Figure 13.49). You can use Move and Rotate functions to move sections to locations for intersecting the path curve.

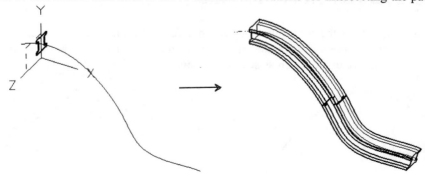

Figure 13.49

Mastering I-DEAS,
Scholars International Publishing Corp., 1999

# Section Options

The sections used in defining sweep surfaces can be planar or non-planar type. This is controlled by two parameters in the Section Options menu. After selecting the Sweep function, click the right mouse button and select "Section Options" from the options list. The Section Options menu should appear as below.

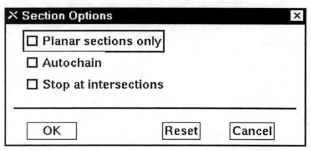

There are **three parameters** used to set the section orientation type that can be accepted in creating sweep surfaces. They are:

| | |
|---|---|
| **Planar sections only:** | It limits the section type to planar sections. |
| **Autochain:** | Automatically traces around contiguous wireframe geometry. |
| **Stop at intersections:** | Stops tracing at intersections. |

# Section Definition

The simplest definition of a sweep surface is a section swept along a path (Figure 13.50). It is used in most sweep surfaces. I-DEAS allows multiple sections to be used in sweep surfaces. When two sections are used, the first section is placed at the start of the path and the second section at its end, and the surface will transition the entire length of the path (Figure 13.51).

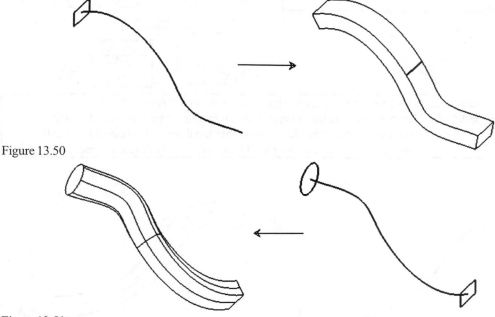

Figure 13.50

Figure 13.51

When three or more sections are used, the first section is placed at the start of the path, the last section at its end, and the others are equally spaced along the path (Figure 13.52).

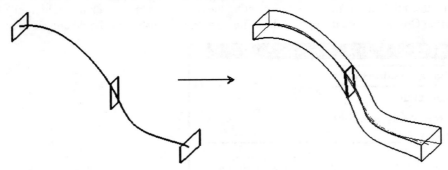

Figure 13.52

# Controlling Section Orientation

I-DEAS provides three options to control the section orientation in sweep surfaces. The Z-axis of the section coordinate system lies tangent to the path curve at the connection location.

These three options are:

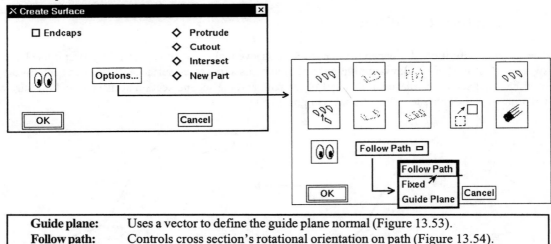

| | |
|---|---|
| **Guide plane:** | Uses a vector to define the guide plane normal (Figure 13.53). |
| **Follow path:** | Controls cross section's rotational orientation on path (Figure 13.54). |
| **Fixed:** | Uses a vector to define the fixed orientation direction (Figure 13.55). All sections in the surface lie parallel to a previously defined plane. |

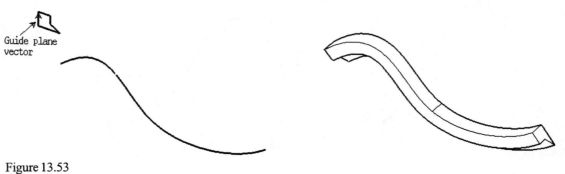

Figure 13.53

13-24

Figure 13.54

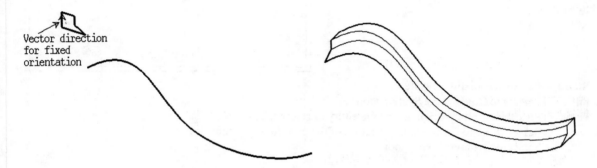

Figure 13.55

## Project 4.
## Creating a swept surface

Sweeping a cross section along a path creates the surface shown in Figure 13.56. A coordinate system is created first. The cross section is created on the YZ-plane and the sweeping path on the XY-plane. The sweeping path consists of three lines and two fillets.

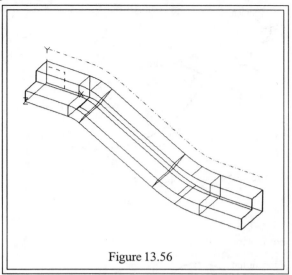

Figure 13.56

**Step 1.   Create a coordinate system.**

 Select the **Coordinate System** icon
Pick the current work plane as the entity to reference
Select **Done** to complete the creation of the coordinate system
Select the **Isometric view** icon

**Step 2.   Create a cross section of six lines on YZ-plane.**

 Select the **Sketch in place** icon, and then pick the YZ-plane as the sketch plane
Select the **Right View** icon
 Select the **Polyline** icon
Create six line segments as shown in Figure 13.57.

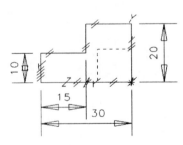

Figure 13.57

Select the **Modify Entity** icon
Modify four dimensions to their proper values as shown in Figure 13.57

**Step 3.   Create a sweeping path.**

 Select the **Isometric view** icon
Select the **Sketch in place** icon, and then pick XY-plane as the sketch plane
Select the **Front view** icon
Use the **Polyline function** to create three lines and modify four dimensions to their
   correct value as in Figure 13.58a
(You may need to use Focus and anchor commands to fix the starting point on the Y-axis)

13-26

# Creating Surfaces

Use the **Fillet function** to add two fillets of radius 50 as in Figure 13.58b

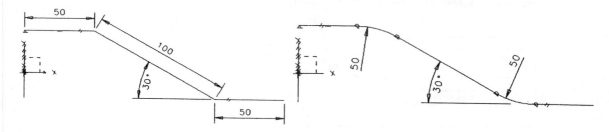

Figure 13.58a                                    Figure 13.58b

**Step 4.**   **Create a sweep surface.**

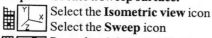 Select the **Isometric view** icon

Select the **Sweep** icon

Press the **right mouse button** then select **Section Options**
Set the section options parameters as below.

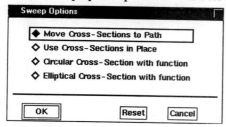

Select **OK**

Press the **right mouse button** then select **Sweep Options**
Set the Sweep options parameters as below.

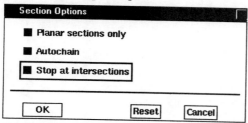

Select **OK**

Pick anywhere on the curve to select the path curve
Press **Enter** to complete the path selection
Pick anywhere on the section then press **Enter** key
Set the sweep parameters as below.

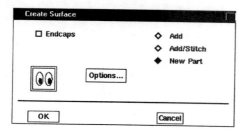

**Click on Options**

Set the surface options parameters as in Figure 13.59.

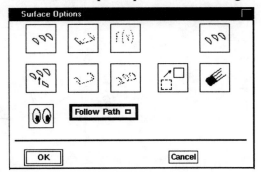

Figure 13.59

Select **OK** to create the sweep surface as in Figure 13.60.

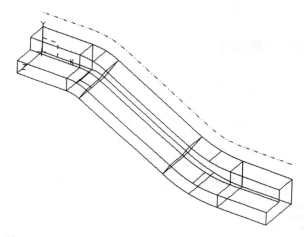

Figure 13.60

Mastering I-DEAS,
Scholars International Publishing Corp., 1999

# Project 5.
# Creating a sweep surface with multiple cross-sections

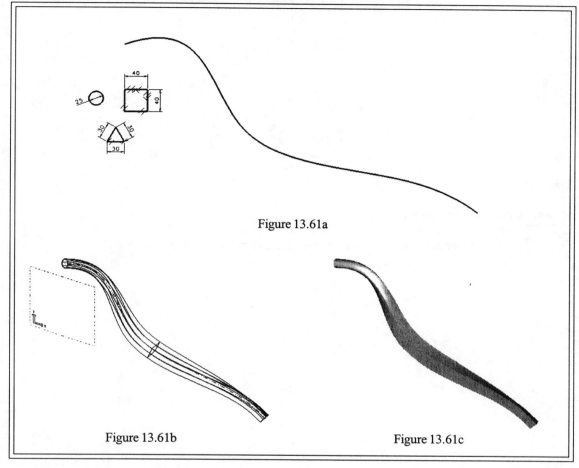

Figure 13.61a

Figure 13.61b

Figure 13.61c

Three sections are used to create a sweep surface (Figure 13.61) in this project. These three sections include a circle, a rectangle, and a star. The sweep path is a spline curve.

**Step 1.  Create a circle.**

 Select the **Center Edge** icon
Pick two points to create a circle
 Select the **Modify Entity** icon then change the diameter value to **25**

**Step 2.  Create a rectangle.**

 Select the **Rectangle by 2 Corners** icon
Pick two points to create a rectangle
Select the **Modify Entity** icon to change all two dimensions to **40**

**Step 3.  Create a triangle.**

 Select the **Polylines** icon
Create three lines to form a triangle
Use the **Modify Entity** function to change all three dimensions to **30**
The three sections look like Figure 13.62.

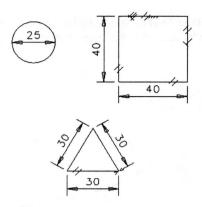

Figure 13.62

**Step 4. Create a spline curve.**

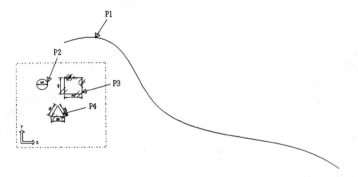

Select the **Splines** icon
Pick a number of points on the screen to create a spline resembling the one in Figure 13.63

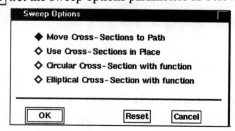

Figure 13.63

**Step 5. Create a sweep surface. Use the pick points in Figure 13.63.**

Select the **Isometric view** icon
Select the **Sweep** icon
Press the **right mouse button** then select **Sweep Options**
Set the sweep options parameters as below.

| Sweep Options |
|---|
| ◆ Move Cross-Sections to Path |
| ◇ Use Cross-Sections in Place |
| ◇ Circular Cross-Section with function |
| ◇ Elliptical Cross-Section with function |
| OK    Reset    Cancel |

Select **OK**
Press the **right mouse button** then select **Sections Options**

Mastering I-DEAS,
Scholars International Publishing Corp., 1999

# Creating Surfaces

Set the section options parameters as below.

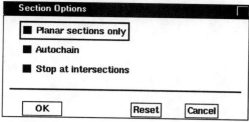

Select **OK**

Pick **P1** then hit **Enter** to complete the path selection
Pick **P2** then hit **Enter** to select the first cross-section curve
Pick **P3** then hit **Enter** to select the second cross-section curve
Pick **P4** then hit **Enter** to select the third cross-section curve
Press **Enter** again to complete the cross-sections selection
Set the create surface parameters as below.

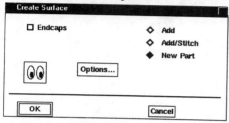

Click the **Options** button to open the surface options dialog box
Define the surface options parameters as below.

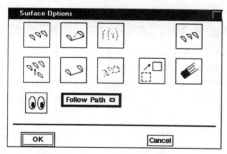

Select **OK → OK**

The sweep surface with multiple cross-sections is created as in Figure 13.64.

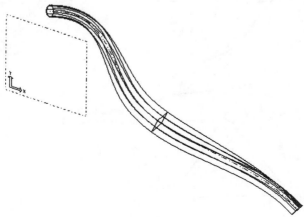

Figure 13.64

Mastering I-DEAS,
Scholars International Publishing Corp., 1999

### Step 6.   Shade the model.

 Select the **Shaded Software** icon
The shaded model is shown in Figure 13.65.

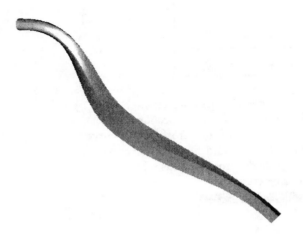

Figure 13.65

# 13.6   Variational Sweep Surfaces

The variational sweep function acts similar to the sweep function. It sweeps wireframe geometry varying sections along a path (Figure 13.66). The cross sections used in variational sweep surfaces must be normal to the path. You need to use the "Sketch on path" function to define the sketch planes for creating cross sections. The plane of the variational sweep cross section must intersect the path (Figure 13.67).

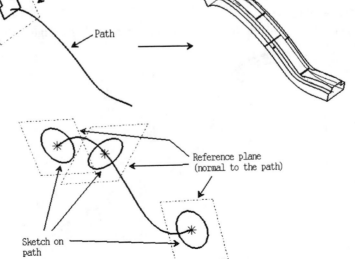

Figure 13.66

Figure 13.67

13-32

# Extent of Variational Sweep

The variational sweep feature can be extended by the following three methods:

| | |
|---|---|
| **Extend path:** | extends the sweep path to desired locations at both ends (Figure 13.68). |
| **Path length:** | limits the sweep surface to the length of defining path (Figure 13.69). |
| **From/To:** | limits the sweep surface between two selected points on the defining path (Figure 13.70). |

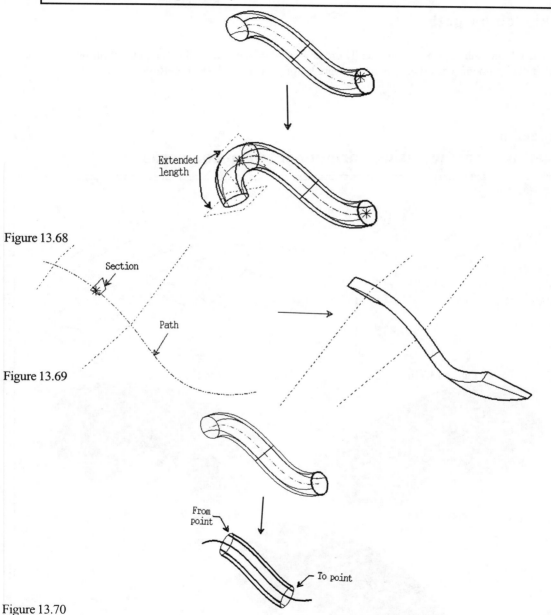

Extended length

Figure 13.68

Section

Path

Figure 13.69

From point

To point

Figure 13.70

Variational sweep creates surfaces based on a path and one or more rails. It allows the 2D cross-section to vary as it sweeps along the path. Paths and rails can be either wireframe or edges.

**The paths and rails must satisfy the following requirements:**
- They can't have sharp bends
- Wireframe geometries must first be converted to a reference curve before they can be used as paths or rails

## Sketch on path

The "Sketch on Path" option automatically creates a sketch plane normal to the path. "Follow curve" is the default alignment. The other two methods are **hinge method** and **fixed method**.

# Project 6.
# Creating a surface using variational sweep command

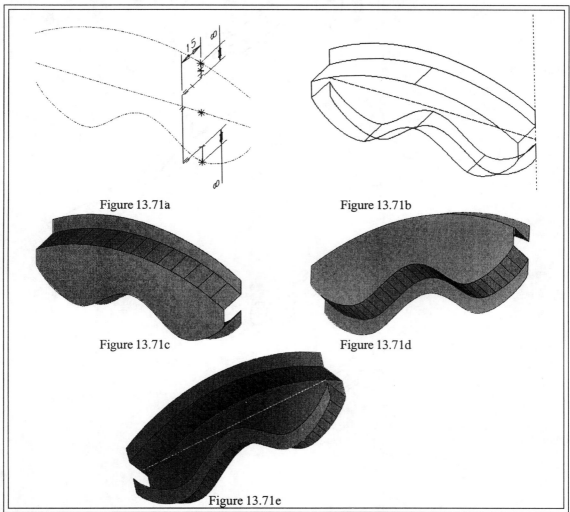

Figure 13.71a

Figure 13.71b

Figure 13.71c

Figure 13.71d

Figure 13.71e

Mastering I-DEAS,
Scholars International Publishing Corp., 1999

# Creating Surfaces

Figure 13.71 shows a variational sweep surface that is created using a path and two rails. Save the surface file as "surface-vsweep".

**Step 1. Crate an arc.**

 Select the **Three Points On** icon
Press **RMB**, then select **Options**
Enter the coordinate values of three points as below.

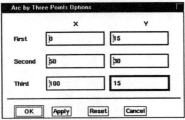

Select **OK** to create an arc
The arc is shown in Figure 13.72.

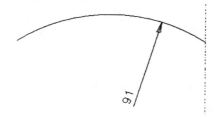

Figure 13.72

**Step 2. Create a line.**

 Select the **Lines** icon
Press **RMB**, then select **Options**
Enter the coordinate values of two points as below.

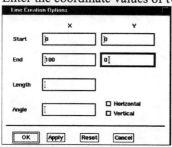

Select **OK**
The line is added as in Figure 13.73.

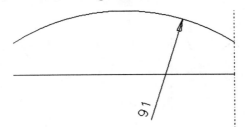

Figure 13.73

**Step 3. Create a spline curve.**

 Select the **Spline** icon

Press **RMB,** then select **Options** to open the spline creation options dialog box

Enter **(0, -10)** to the X and Y fields as below.

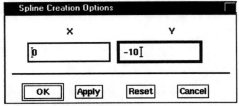

Select **Apply** then **Reset**

Enter the following eight sets of point coordinates

    **(10, -21)**
    **(25, -25)**
    **(35, -18)**
    **(50, -10)**
    **(65, -18)**
    **(75, -25)**
    **(90, -21)**
    **(100, -10)**

Select **OK**

Press the **Enter** key to complete the spline curve as in Figure 13.74.

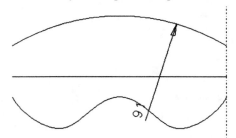

Figure 13.74

**Step 4. Create reference curves for all three curves.**

 Select the **Isometric view** icon

Select the **Reference Curves** icon

Pick all three curves then press **Enter** to complete the selection

Figure 13.75 shows three reference curves.

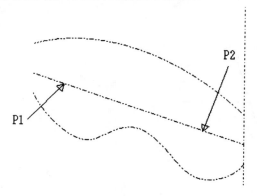

Figure 13.75

Mastering I-DEAS,
Scholars International Publishing Corp., 1999

# Creating Surfaces

**Step 5.** **Create a reference plane using the pick points in Figure 13.75.**

Select the **Sketch in place** icon
Press **RMB,** then select the **Sketch on Path** option
Pick **P1** to select the curve
Pick **P2** to pick the point on curve to position the reference plane
The reference plane is created as in Figure 13.76.

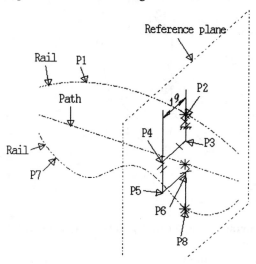

Figure 13.76

> **Note:** sketch a wireframe shape as shown. It does not matter if the dimensions are different from what are shown. However, we need to apply the intersect option to create points (P2 and P8) where the rail intersects the sketch plane.

**Step 6.** **Create a master section using the pick points in Figure 13.76.**

Select the **Polylines** icon
Press **RMB,** than select the **Intersect** option
Pick **P1** to select the curve
Pick **P2,** the intersect point, as the start point of the curve
Sequentially pick **P3 – P6** (all lines must be perpendicular and aligned to each other)
Press **RMB** and select the **Intersect** option
Pick **P7** to select the curve
Pick **P8** to select the point
Press the **Enter** key to end the polyline creation
The new drawing should appear as Figure 13.77.

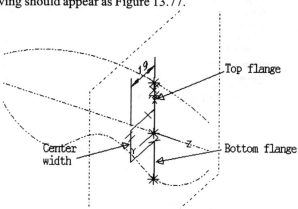

Figure 13.77

**Step 7.** **Add two dimensions for top flange and bottom flange and change to their correct value.**

  Select the **Dimension** icon then add two dimensions for top flange and bottom flange

 Select the **Modify Entity** icon then change three dimensions to the values as shown in Figure 13.78

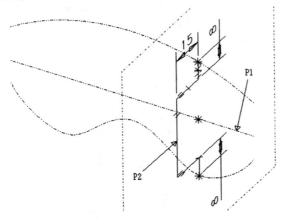

Figure 13.78

**Step 8.** **Create a variational sweep surface using the pick points in Figure 13.78.**

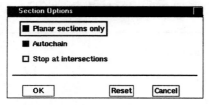 Select the **Variational Sweep** icon

Pick **P1** to select the line as the path curve

Press **MMB** to end the path curve selection

Press **RMB,** then select the **Section Options**

Set the section options dialog box as below.

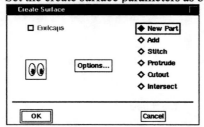

Select **OK** to exit the dialog box

Pick **P2** to select the cross-section curve

Press **Enter** to end the cross-section curve selection

Set the create surface parameters as below.

Select **OK** to create the surface as in Figure 13.79.

Mastering I-DEAS,
Scholars International Publishing Corp., 1999

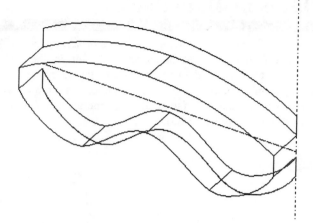

Figure 13.79

### Step 9. Shade the surface model.

 Click the **Shade Software** icon

Figure 13.80 shows three different shaded views of surface.

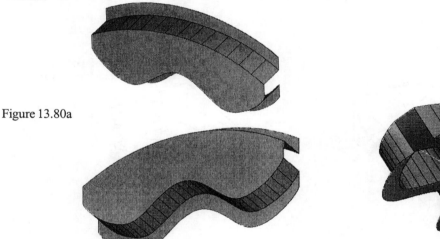

Figure 13.80a

Figure 13.80b                                Figure 13.80c

### Step 10. Check in the model file as "vsweep-surface".

 Select the **Check In** icon

Pick the surface for check in

Enter "**vsweep-surface**" to the Name field, and then select **OK**

Set the check-in parameters as below.

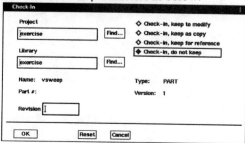

Select **OK** to check in the surface model

# 13.7   Surfaces by Boundaries

This function creates a surface that is bounded by curves or surface edges. The curves or surface edges used as the boundaries must be contiguous, and not intersect themselves or be coincident. In other words, the boundaries must form a closed loop of wireframe geometry. The minimum number of curves is three. You can use any number of curves as surface boundaries. Four curves render the best results (Figure 13.81). Three curves produce a surface with a degenerate side (Figure 13.82). Five or more curves result in multiple surfaces (Figure 13.83).

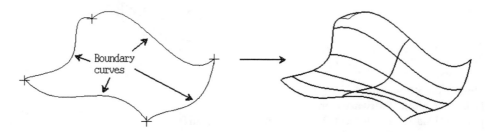

Figure 13.81

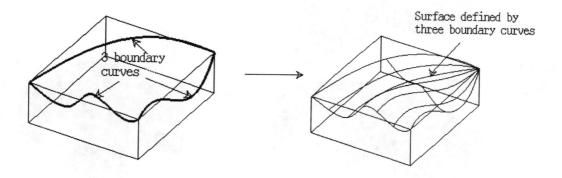

Figure 13.82

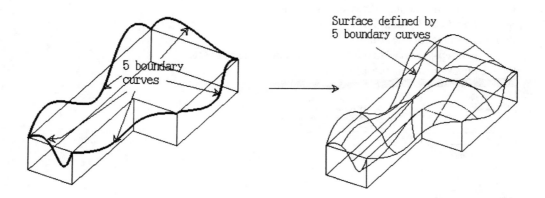

Figure 13.83

Mastering I-DEAS,
Scholars International Publishing Corp., 1999

# Options

Click the right mouse button to open the Options menu as below.

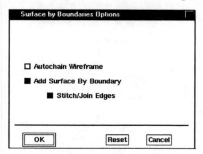

Select Options from the list to open the Options dialog box that consists of two parameters:
- Stitch/Join Edges
- Autochain wireframe

### Stitch/Join Edges

This parameter is used to automatically stitch and join together those edges that are shared by two surfaces during the surface creating process. The surface is associative to the part model when this parameter is turned On.

### Autochain wireframe

The parameter automatically builds the largest contiguous section that it can from your defined wireframe.

 **The procedure for creating a surface by boundaries is (Figure 13.84):**

1. Create curves for boundaries
2. Select the Surface – Surface by Boundaries icon
3. Sequentially pick curves in proper sequence as the boundaries
4. Preview the surface
5. Modify the curves if necessary
6. Accept the surface

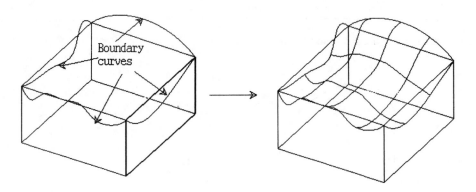

Figure 13.84

# Project 7.
# Creating a surface by four boundaries

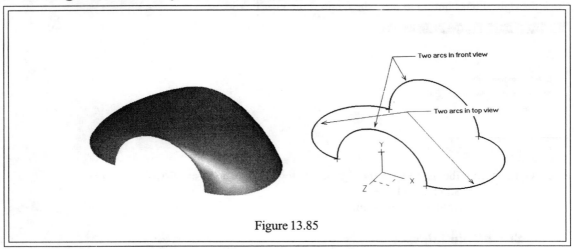

Figure 13.85

A surface is created using four arcs as its boundaries (Figure 13.85). Two arcs are created in the front view and the other two arcs in the top view. In order to use the top view as the sketch plane for creating two arcs, we need to create a coordinate system, then use its ZX-plane as the sketch plane.

**Step 1.   Create arcs in the front-view.**

 Select **Arc — Start End 180**
Click the **right mouse button**, and then select **Options** to open the coordinate input menu
Set start and end point coordinate values of the arc as below.

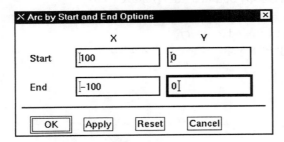

Select **OK** to create the arc as shown in Figure 13.86.

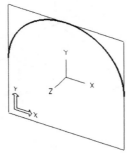

Figure 13.86

Mastering I-DEAS,
Scholars International Publishing Corp., 1999

**Step 2. Move the arc by a distance of 200 in -Z direction.**

 Select the **Move** icon

Pick the arc, and then click the middle mouse button

Enter translation X,Y,Z:  enter **0,0,-200**

The arc is translated to the new location as in Figure 13.87.

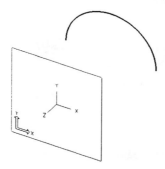

Figure 13.87

**Step 3. Create another arc in the front view.**

 Select the **Start End 180** icon

Click the **right mouse button**, and then select **Options** to open the coordinate input menu

Set the start and end point coordinates for the arc as in step 1

Select **OK** to complete the second arc

The two arcs are shown in Figure 13.88.

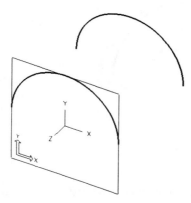

Figure 13.88

**Step 4. Create a coordinate system.**

 Select the **Coordinate Systems** icon

Pick the **blue coordinate frame** as the entity for coordinate system to reference

Select **Done** from the options list

A coordinate system is added as in Figure 13.89.

# Creating Surfaces

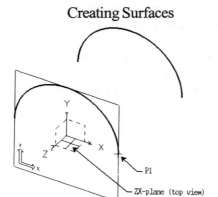

Figure 13.89

**Step 5.   Select the top view as the sketch plane.**

 Select the **Sketch in Plane** icon

Select **ZX-plane** from the coordinate system just created

**Step 6.   Create two arcs.**

 Select **Arc — Start End 180**

Click the **right mouse button**, and then select **Focus**

Pick **P1** to define a focus point

Repeatedly use the **Focus function** three times to create another three points at the end points of two arcs

The four focus points appear on the drawing as in Figure 13.90.

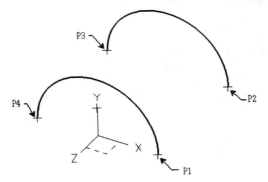

Figure 13.90

Pick **P1** as the start point and **P2** as the end point to complete the first arc

Pick **P3** as the start point and **P4** as the end point to complete the second arc

The two arcs are added as in Figure 13.91.

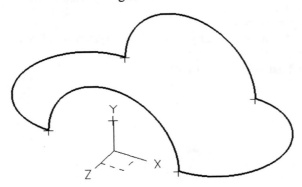

Figure 13.91

Mastering I-DEAS,
Scholars International Publishing Corp., 1999

**Step 7.  Create a surface using the Surface by Boundary function.**

 Select **Surface — Surface by Boundary**
Sequentially pick four curves as the surface boundaries
Select **Preview** from the options list
The surface will temporarily display on the screen as Figure 13.92.

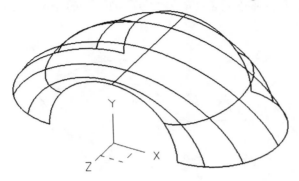

Figure 13.92

Select **Yes** from the options list to accept the surface

**Step 8.  Shade the surface image.**

 Click the **Shade Software** icon to shade the surface image as in Figure 13.93.

Figure 13.93

# 13.8  Creating Surfaces Using Mesh of Curves

This function uses a set of sections and rails to interpolate a surface (Figure 13.94). There is no limitation on how many sections and rails can be used. The two outside cross-section curves and two outside rail curves must be connected to each other (Figure 13.95). The remaining cross-section curves and rail curves do not have to touch.

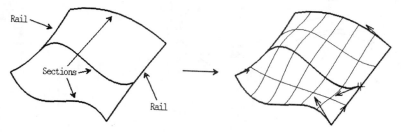

Figure 13.94

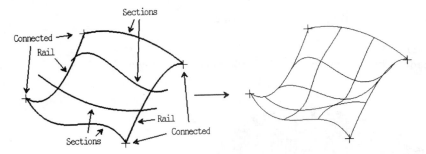

Figure 13.95

 **The procedure for creating a surface using mesh of curves function (Figure 13.96):**

1. Create curves for cross-sections and rails.
2. Select Surface — Mesh of Curves icon.
3. Sequentially pick the sections.
4. Sequentially pick the rails.
5. Preview the surface.
6. Modify the curves if necessary.
7. Accept the surface.

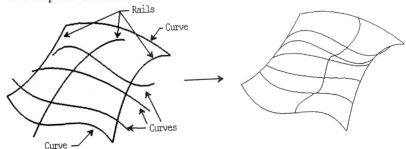

Figure 13.96

Mastering I-DEAS,
Scholars International Publishing Corp., 1999

# Project 8.
# Creating a car body surface model using mesh of curve command

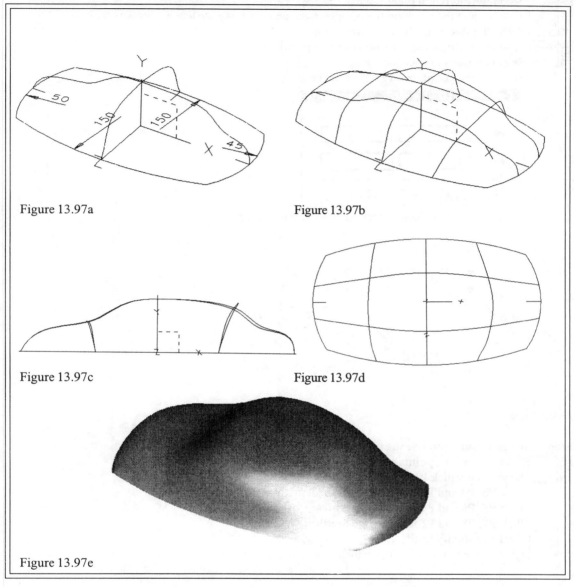

Figure 13.97a

Figure 13.97b

Figure 13.97c

Figure 13.97d

Figure 13.97e

The model car shown in Figure 13.97 is a surface created by using the mesh of curve command. It uses a total of six curves; three for cross-section curves and other three for rail curves. Save the surface model file as "surface-mesh".

**Step 1.  Create a coordinate system.**

Select the **Coordinate Systems** icon

Pick the work plane as the entity for the coordinate system to reference

Select **Done** from the options list to create a coordinate system

Creating Surfaces

**Step 2.  Create a rectangle on the XY-plane.**

 Click the **Isometric View** icon

Select the **Sketch in place** icon,

      and then pick on the XZ-plane on the coordinate system as the sketch plane

Select the **Rectangle by 2 Corners** icon

Press the **right mouse button** to open the options list

Select **Options** to open the dialog box

Set the point coordinate values as below.

| Rectangle by Two Points Options | | |
|---|---|---|
| | **X** | **Y** |
| **First** | [-25 | [-50 |
| **Second** | 25 | 50 |

| OK | Apply | Reset | Cancel |

Select **OK** to complete the rectangle as in Figure 13.98

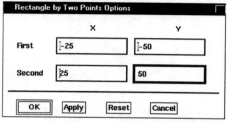

Figure 13.98

**Step 3.  Create four arcs. Use the pick points in Figure 13.98.**

Select the **Three points on** icon

Sequentially pick **P1**, **P2** and **P3** to create the first arc

Pick **P3**, **P4** and **P5** to create the second arc

Pick **P5**, **P6** and **P7** to create the third arc

Pick **P7**, **P8** and **P1** to create the fourth arc

Click the **Modify Entity** icon

Change the four radius dimensions of arcs as in Figure 13.99

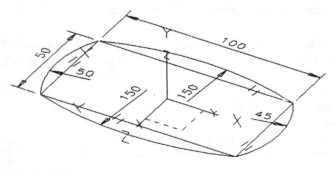

Figure 13.99

Mastering I-DEAS,
Scholars International Publishing Corp., 1999

**Step 4. Delete the four sides of rectangle.**

Click on the **Delete** icon
Press the **Shift** key and pick the four sides of rectangle
Press the **Enter** key then select **Yes** from the options list
The new drawing becomes Figure 13.100.

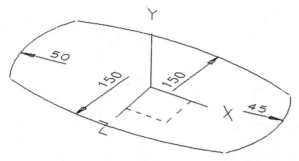

Figure 13.100

**Step 5. Select YZ-plane as the sketch plane.**

Select the **Sketch in place** icon
Pick the **YZ-plane** as the sketch plane
The new drawing becomes Figure 13.101.

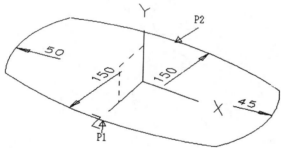

Figure 13.101

**Step 6. Create a spline curve. Use the pick points in Figure 13.101.**

Select the **Splines** icon
Click the **right mouse button** then select **Focus**
Pick **P1** to select the entity to focus
Pick the location near the middle of the curve to pick the middle point as the start point
Click the **right mouse button** then select **Options** to open the Spline Creation Options dialog box
Enter (**10, 30**) to the X and Y fields as below.

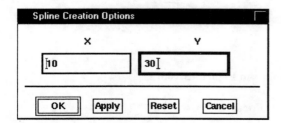

## Creating Surfaces

Click on the **Apply** button then **Reset** button to complete the point entry
        (Do not click **OK** button)
Continuously enter the following eight sets of point coordinates:

$\qquad$ **(17, 27)**
$\qquad$ **(22, 20)**
$\qquad$ **(24, 10)**
$\qquad$ **(25, 0)**
$\qquad$ **(24, -10)**
$\qquad$ **(22, -20)**
$\qquad$ **(17, -27)**
$\qquad$ **(10, -30)**

Select **OK**
Click the **right mouse button** then select **Focus**
Pick **P2** to select the arc
Pick the location near the middle of the curve to pick the middle point
Press the **Enter** key twice to create a spline as Figure 13.102

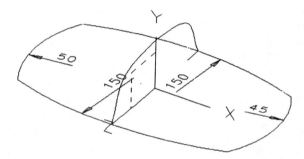

Figure 13.102

**Step 7.  Select XY-plane as the sketch plane.**
 Select the **Sketch in place** icon
Pick the **XY-plane** as the sketch plane
The new drawing becomes Figure 13.103.

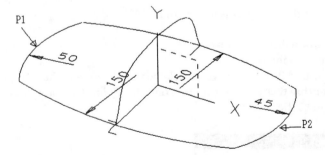

Figure 13.103

**Step 8.  Create a spline curve. Use the pick points in Figure 13.103.**
 Select the **Splines** icon
Click the **right mouse button** then select **Focus**
Pick **P1** to select the entity to focus
Pick the location near the middle of the curve to pick the middle point

13-50

Click the **right mouse button** then select **Options**

Follow the instructions in step 6 to enter the following 13 sets of point coordinates:

> **(-45, 11)**
> **(-35, 12.5)**
> **(-25, 15)**
> **(-20, 18.5)**
> **(-10, 24)**
> **(0, 25)**
> **(10, 25)**
> **(25, 24)**
> **(30, 23)**
> **(35, 21)**
> **(40, 16)**
> **(45, 12.5)**
> **(50, 11)**

Select **Apply** → **OK** to exit the dialog box

Click the **right mouse button** then select **Focus**

Pick **P2** to select the entity to focus

Pick a location near the middle point to select the middle point

Press **Enter twice** to complete the spline curve as in Figure 13.104

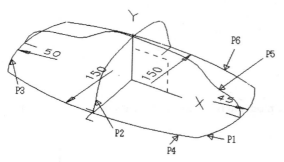

Figure 13.104

**Step 9.** **Create a surface using the mesh of curves command. Use the pick points in Figure 13.104.**

 Select the **Mesh of curves** icon

Click the **right mouse button** then select **Section Options**

Set the section options parameters as below.

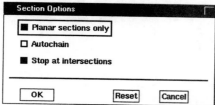

Select **OK**

Pick **P1** to select the first cross-section curve, then press the **Enter** key

Pick **P2** to select the second cross-section curve, then press the **Enter** key

Pick **P3** to select the third cross-section curve, then press **Enter** twice

Pick **P4** to select the first rail curve, then press **Enter**

Pick **P5** to select the second rail curve, then press **Enter**

Pick **P6** to select the third rail curve, then press **Enter** twice

# Creating Surfaces

Click on the **Preview** button from the Create Surface dialog box
The surface model is displayed as in Figure 13.105.

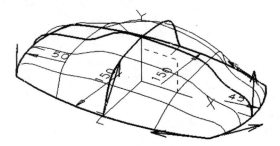

Figure 13.105

Click the **OK** button to create the surface as in Figure 13.106.

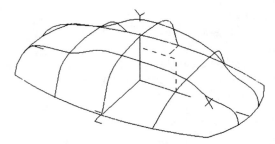

Figure 13.106

## Step 10. Show the model in three views.

Figure 13.107 shows the surface model in front, top, and right side views, respectively.

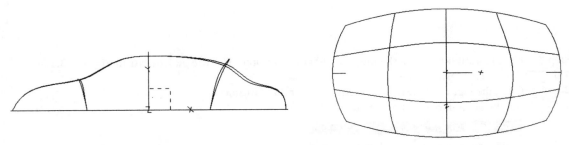

Figure 13.107a                    Figure 13.107b

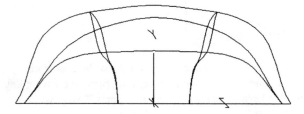

Figure 13.107c

13-52

### Step 11. Shade the surface model.

 Select the **Shaded Software** icon
The shaded model appears as in Figure 13.108.

Figure 13.108

### Step 12. Check in the model to library.

 Use the following information to check the car surface into the library.

        Project: **exercise**
        Library: **exercise**
        File name: **car-surface**

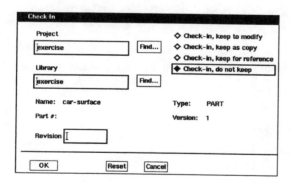

# 13.9 Creating Surfaces Through Points

I-DEAS can create a surface from a set of points. These points can be created in the following two methods:

**3D Points:** Creates points independently of the workplane.
**Points on Curve:** Creates a specified number of points along a curve.

## 3D Points

I-DEAS provides the following seven methods to define 3D points:

| | |
|---|---|
| **Screen location:** | locates the point at the picked screen position. |
| **Key in:** | locates the point by the specified X, Y, and Z coordinates. |
| **Intersect:** | locates the point at the intersection between two entities. |
| **Between:** | locates the point along the direction between two selected points. The exact location is measured in percentage of distance between two points. |
| **Translated:** | locates a point by translating a selected point by specified distances in X, Y, and Z directions. |
| **On curve:** | locates a point at any selected location on a curve. |
| **On surface:** | locates a point at any selected location on a surface. |

## Points on curve

This method allows for creating a set of points along a selected curve. Pick a curve and the system will open a Points On Curves menu as below.

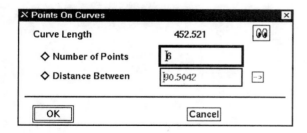

Two points on curve options are described below:

| | |
|---|---|
| **Number of points:** | specifies the total number of points evenly created along the curve. The system will automatically calculate the spacing distance. |
| **Distance between:** | specifies the spacing distance between two points. The system will calculate the number of points to create. |

**The Procedure for creating a surface through points (Figure 13.109):**

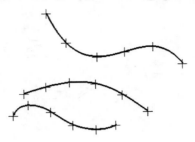

Figure 13.109

1. Create a set of points.
2. Select the "Fit Surface to Points" icon.

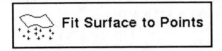

3. Click the right mouse button, and then select "Matrix of Points" from the list.
4. Pick all points of the first row for surface to fit: select the first point, then press the "Shift" key to sequentially pick the remaining five points, finally click the middle mouse button to complete the point selection for row 1.
5. Pick all six points of row 2 for surface to fit: select the first point in row 2, then press the "Shift" key to continuously select the remaining five points.
6. Pick all 6 points of row 3 for surface to fit: select the first point in row 3, then press the "Shift" key to continuously select the remaining five points.
7. Pick all 6 points of row 4 for surface to fit: click the middle mouse button to terminate point selection

The surface is created as shown in Figure 13.110.

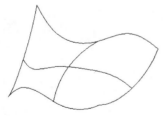

Figure 13.110

You must follow these guidelines in order to pick the points successfully for defining a surface:

1. There must have the same number of points in each row.
2. The picking direction of each row must be consistent. Figure 13.111 shows the result of using an inconsistent row direction in the second point row.

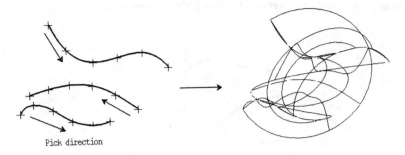

Figure 13.111

3. Selecting points for the first row affects the number of rows and their direction. The example shown in Figure 13.112 shows the two directions of selecting points for the first row. Selecting the six points along the X direction produces three rows of points. Selecting the three points along the Y direction produces six rows of points.

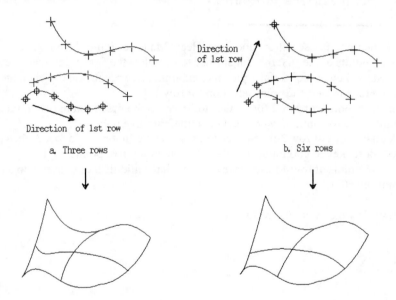

Figure 13.112

Mastering I-DEAS,
Scholars International Publishing Corp., 1999

# Project 9.
# Creating a fan model

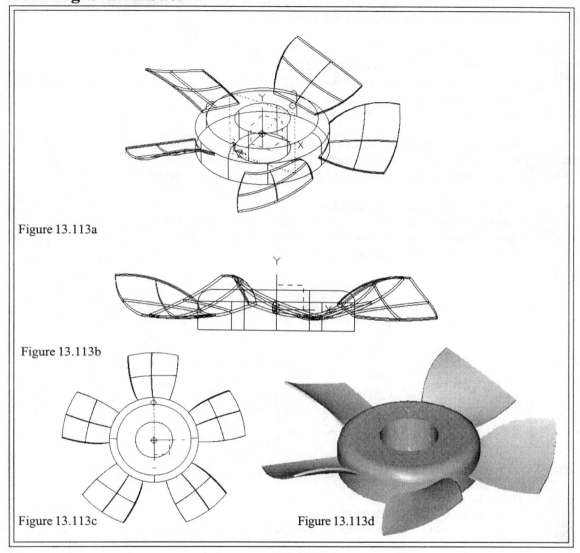

Figure 13.113a

Figure 13.113b

Figure 13.113c

Figure 13.113d

The fan model shown in Figure 13.113 consists of five blades with a hub. Using the loft function from three arcs creates the shape of the blade. Use the shell function to add 3-mm thickness to the loft surface. The blade is then copied to four locations using the circular pattern function. The hub is created from extruding two circles. The outer edges of blades are trimmed to a circular curve. This is accomplished by extruding a circle with the "Intersect" operation. Save the surface model as "fan-surface".

Some hints of creating curves are given below:

1.   Use a rectangle to aid the construction of an arc using three points on function. The rectangle locates the start point and end point of the arc and their locations with respect to the origin of the coordinate system.

2.   Three arcs are created on the same sketch plane. Then they are moved to their desired locations.

# Creating Surfaces

3.  Use the XZ-plane as the patterning plane. Align the X-axis of the coordinate system as the Y-axis for the patterning layout. This orients the circular pattern in the proper direction. The origin of the coordinate system is first used as the key point of the pattern. This key point is then translated by (0,0,-80) to the desired location.

**Step 1.   Set the units system to inch.**

Select **Options → Units → Inch** (pound f)
Select the **Coordinate Systems** icon,
  and then pick the default workplane as the entity for reference
Select **Done** to create the coordinate system

**Step 2.   Assign the name "coord1" to the coordinate system.**

Select the **Name Parts** icon, then pick the coordinate system
Enter "**coord1**" to the Name field in the Name menu, and then select **OK**

**Step 3.   Create a rectangle using the XY-plane.**

Select the **Sketch in place** icon, and then pick **XY-plane** as the sketch plane
Create a rectangle and add dimensions as shown in Figure 13.114.
Focus the origin for adding dimensions

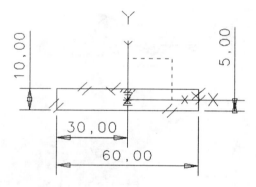

Figure 13.114

**Step 4.   Create an arc.**

Select the **Arc – Three Points On** icon
Create an arc and change the radius value to **125** as shown in Figure 13.115.

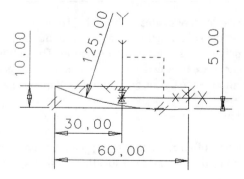

Figure 13.115

Mastering I-DEAS,
Scholars International Publishing Corp., 1999

**Step 5.** **Delete the rectangle.**

 Select the **Delete** icon, then delete the rectangle
The new drawing becomes Figure 13.116.

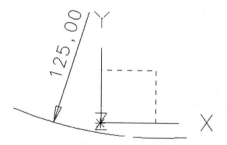

Figure 13.116

**Step 6.** **Create another rectangle and an arc.**

Create another rectangle and add dimensions as shown in Figure 13.117.

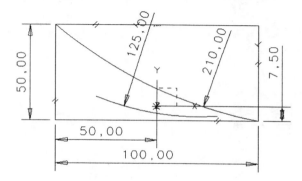

Figure 13.117

Create an arc with the arc radius as shown

**Step 7.** **Delete the rectangle.**

Delete the four sides of the rectangle
The new drawing becomes Figure 13.118.

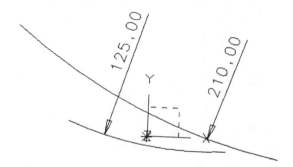

Figure 13.118

**Step 8.   Create a rectangle and a curve.**

Create a rectangle and a curve with the dimensions given in Figure 13.119.

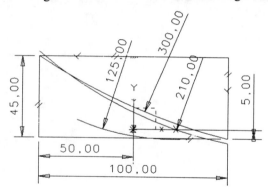

Figure 13.119

Delete the rectangle to make the drawing as in Figure 13.120.

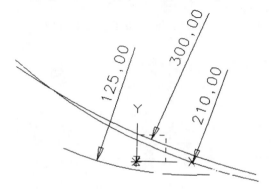

Figure 13.120

**Step 9.   Move the three curves by Z-80, Z-170, and Z-190, respectively.**

 Select the **Move** icon

Pick the **first arc** (R125) as the entity to move

Enter translation X, Y, Z:  **0,0,-80**

Pick the **second arc** (R210) as the entity to move

Enter translation X, Y, Z:  **0,0,-170**

Pick the **third arc** (R300) as the entity to move

Enter translation X, Y, Z:  **0,0,-190**

Select **Isometric View** icon to show the drawing as in Figure 13.121.

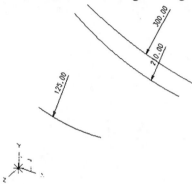

Figure 13.121

13-60

# Creating Surfaces

## Step 10. Create a loft surface.

Select the **Loft** icon

Sequentially pick **three curves** (press Done after picking each curve)

Select the "**Add**" option in the Create Surface menu, and then select **OK**

Pick the coordinate system as the part to be protruded to

The loft surface is created as in Figure 13.122.

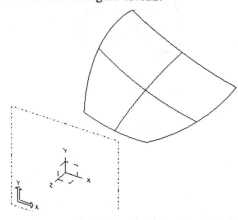

Figure 13.122

## Step 11. Shell the surface to produce the thickness.

Select the **Shell** icon

Pick the surface as the part to shell

Enter "**3**" to the Thickness field in the Shell menu, then select **OK**

The thickness is added to the surface as in Figure 13.123.

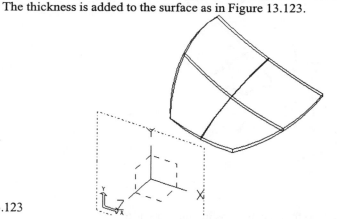

Figure 13.123

## Step 12. Copy the blade to four locations using circular pattern command.

Select the **Circular Pattern** icon

Pick the **blade** as the part to make into a pattern

Pick the **XZ-plane** as the patterning plane

Set the circular pattern parameters as here.

Select **Align → Y Axis**

Pick the **X-axis** of the coordinate system as new Y-axis

If the default arrow direction is pointing to right,
   select No to reverse it to left

Select **Yes** to accept the direction

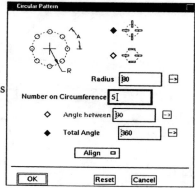

# Creating Surfaces

Select **Align** → **Key Point**
Pick the origin of the coordinate system as the new key point
The new patterning layout becomes Figure 13.124.

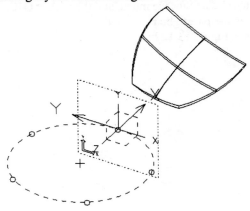

Figure 13.124

Select **Align** → **Key Point**
Press the **right mouse button,** and then select **Translated**
Pick the **origin** as the point to translate from
Enter translation X,Y,Z:   **0,0,-80**
The new patterning layout becomes Figure 13.125.

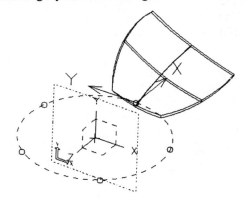

Figure 13.125

Select **OK** to copy the blade to four locations as in Figure 13.126.

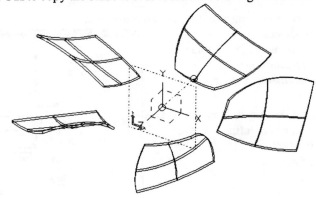

Figure 13.126

13-62

### Step 13.  Add two concentric circles in XZ-plane.

 Select the **Sketch in place** icon, and then select **XZ-plane**
Create two concentric circles having the origin as the center (Use Focus to locate the origin)
Change dimensions to their values as in Figure 13.127.

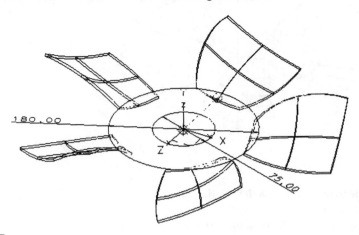

Figure 13.127

### Step 14.  Extrude the two circles.

 Select the **Extrude** icon
Pick the two circles as the sections to extrude
Set the Protrude parameters as below.

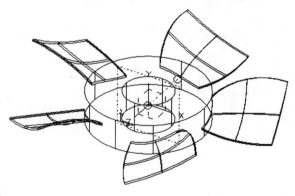

Select **OK** to complete the extrude feature as in Figure 13.128.

Figure 13.128

### Step 15.  Create a circle as shown in Figure 13.129.

 Select the **Sketch in place** icon, and then select **XZ-plane**
Create a circle having its center at the origin
Change its diameter to desired value (370)

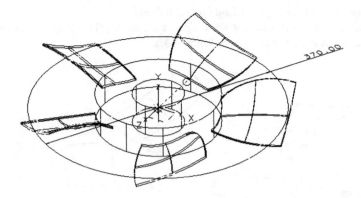

Figure 13.129

**Step 16. Extrude the circle to intersect with the existing model.**

 Select the **Extrude** icon
Pick the circle just created as the section to extrude
Set the Extrude Section parameters as below.

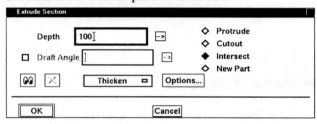

Select **OK** to protrude the circle
The new drawing becomes Figure 13.130.

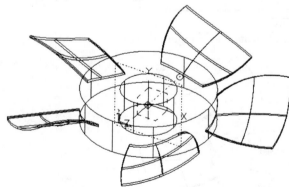

Figure 13.130

**Step 17. Add a fillet the rim of the model.**

 Select the **Fillet** icon
Pick the top circle on the rim as the edge to fillet
Enter radius for selected edges: 15
The fillet is added as in Figure 13.131.

13-64

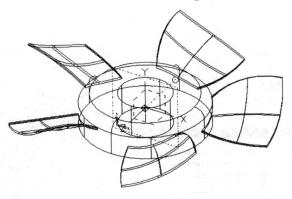

Figure 13.131

Figures 13.132 and 13.133 show the model in different modes.

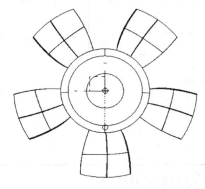

Figure 13.132

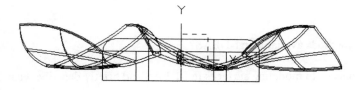

Figure 13.133

**Step 18. Shade the model.**

 Select the **Shaded Software** icon
Figure 13.134 shows the shaded model of the fan.

Figure 13.134

**Step 19. Check the model into the library.**

 Select the **Name Parts** icon
Pick the model to name
Enter "**fan-surface**" into the Name field
Select the **Check In** icon
Pick the **model** as the part to check in
Set the check in parameters as below.

```
Check-In
    Project                      ◇ Check-in, keep to modify
    [Administrator]  [Find...]   ◇ Check-in, keep as copy
                                 ◇ Check-in, keep for reference
    Library                      ◆ Check-in, do not keep
    [surface]        [Find...]

    Name:  fan-surface           Type:    PART
    Part #:                      Version:  1

    Revision [I]

    [ OK ]        [Reset]  [Cancel]
```

Select **OK** to check the part into the library

# Chapter 13. Review Questions

1. What is a surface?

2. List the seven surfacing methods available in I-DEAS?

3. What are the three approaches to modeling surfaces in I-DEAS and briefly describe what they are?

4. Explain how the parameter "endcaps" affects the type of feature created from using a closed section.

5. Describe, with the aid of a drawing, how to create a loft surface.

6. What are the three parameters that determine the shape and orientation of a loft surface?

7. Use a drawing to show how the picking order of cross sections affects the loft surface.

8. What is a section?

9. Explain how to convert a set of connected wireframe entities into a section.

10. What is a sweep surface?

11. What are the two sweep surfacing techniques? Describe their differences.

Mastering I-DEAS,
Scholars International Publishing Corp., 1999

# Creating Surfaces

12. Describe, with the aid of a drawing, how the "Move cross-sections to path" option affects the surface.

13. Describe, with the aid of a drawing, how the "Use cross-section in place" option affects the surface.

14. What are the two requirements for using "Use cross-sections in place" option in creating sweep surfaces?

15. Describe how I-DEAS handles multiple sections in creating a sweep surface.

16. List three options of controlling section orientation in creating sweep surfaces.

17. What are the requirements for boundaries used in the "Surfaces by boundaries" technique?

18. What are the curve requirements for creating surfaces using mesh of curves?

# Chapter

**14**

# Editing Surfaces

---

### Highlights of the Chapter

- Creating curves
- Creating offset surfaces
- Trimming surfaces
- Creating new surfaces from existing surfaces
- Exploding surfaces
- Creating free or unstitched edges
- Extending surfaces
- Stitching surfaces

---

## Overview

The basic surface creation techniques are presented in chapter 13. In this chapter, we cover a variety of techniques that are used to edit existing surfaces. These techniques require one or more existing surfaces to work with. Typical applications of surface editing are creating curves on surfaces, creating offset surfaces, trimming and extending surfaces, exploding surfaces, stitching surfaces, and evaluating surface properties.

## 14.1  Creating Curves

I-DEAS provides various methods to create curves. Splines, elliptical curves, and conics are curves that can be created without using existing surfaces or solids. The techniques to create these type of curves have been presented in chapter 3.

This section presents the curves that are created using existing surfaces. We refer to this group of curves as derived curves. They include:

| | |
|---|---|
| **Project curve:** | a curve is created by projecting a curve onto a surface. |
| **Surface intersection:** | a spline is created along the intersection of two surfaces. |
| **ISO curve:** | a curve is created along iso-parametric curve on a surface. |
| **Through points:** | a spline is created through points on a surface. |
| **Silhouette curve:** | a curve shows the outline of the feature |

## Creating Project Curves

The Project Curve function projects an entity onto a selected surface to create a curve (Figure 14.1). The direction that is perpendicular to the sketch plane of the projecting entity is normally used as the default projection direction. I-DEAS provides the following two ways to define the projection direction or vector:

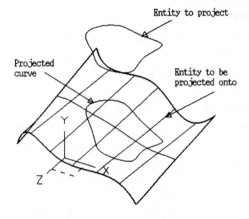

Figure 14.1

| | |
|---|---|
| **Normal to surface:** | specifies the projection direction is perpendicular to the selected surface (Figure 14.2). |

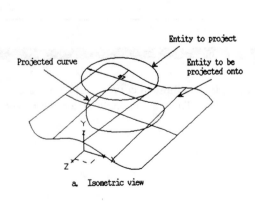

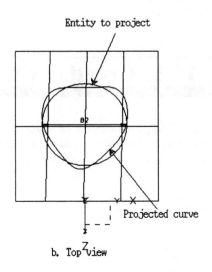

a. Isometric view

b. Top view

Figure 14.2

Mastering I-DEAS,
Scholars International Publishing Corp., 1999

| **Projection vector:** | specifies the projection direction in the given direction. It has nine methods of specifying the projection vector. Click the right mouse button to open the options list. The nine options are shown below. |
| --- | --- |

Key In
Angle
Point to Point
Between
Normal to Plane
Normal to Surface
Heading
Intersection
Curve Tangent

These nine options are briefly described below:

| **Keyin:** | specifies the X, Y, and Z vector value of the projection vector (Figure 14.3). |
| --- | --- |

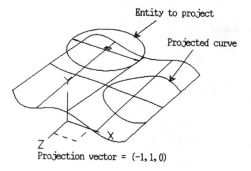

Projection vector = (-1, 1, 0)

Figure 14.3

| **Angle:** | specifies the projection direction by an angle with the X axis of the current sketch plane (Figure 14.4). |
| --- | --- |

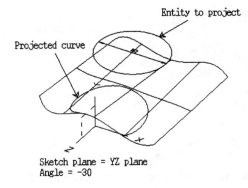

Sketch plane = YZ plane
Angle = -30

Figure 14.4

| **Point to point:** | specifies the projection direction by two points (Figure 14.5). |
|---|---|

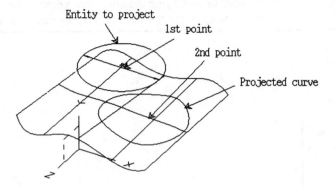

Figure 14.5

| **Between:** | specifies the projection direction between two vectors and the weight of the first vector (Figure 14.6). |
|---|---|

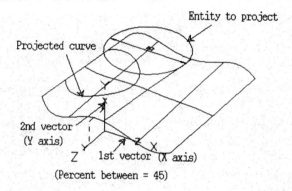

Figure 14.6

| **Normal to plane:** | specifies the projection direction being perpendicular to the sketch plane of the entity to project (Figure 14.7). |
|---|---|

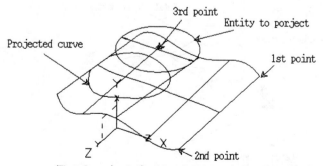

Figure 14.7

Mastering I-DEAS,
Scholars International Publishing Corp., 1999

| **Heading:** | specifies the projection direction by a starting axis and two axes to move toward as well as two angles (Figure 14.8). |
|---|---|

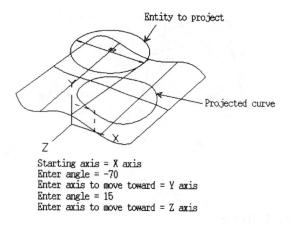

```
Starting axis = X axis
Enter angle = -70
Enter axis to move toward = Y axis
Enter angle = 15
Enter axis to move toward = Z axis
```

Figure 14.8

| **Intersection:** | specifies the projection direction being the intersection line between two planes. |
|---|---|
| **Curve tangent:** | specifies the projection direction being the tangent direction at a point on the selected curve (Figure 14.9). |

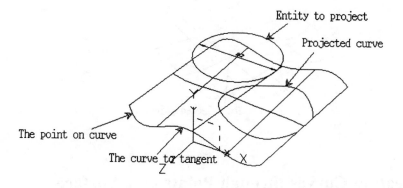

Figure 14.9

You can only project one entity to the surface at one time. When a section with more than one entity is to be projected, you can use "Build Section" function to make a section out of the entities. In this way, you are able to project the section to the surface simultaneously.

## Creating a Curve at Surface Intersection

This function creates a curve at the intersection between two surfaces. The system will prompt "Pick surface 1" and "Pick surface 2", then the curve will be created (Figure 14.10). If two surfaces are separate parts, the system will issue "Surfaces to be intersected belong to different parts.

The two parts will be merged to allow history support for the intersection curve." You can select the Yes or No option.

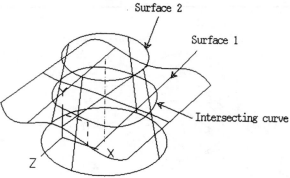

Figure 14.10

## Creating ISO Curves

Curves can be readily created along the isoparametric curves on a selected surface. The system will prompt to pick a surface and a point on the surface. The system will display two isolines at the selected point (Figure 14.11). You can select either one of the ISO curves or keep both.

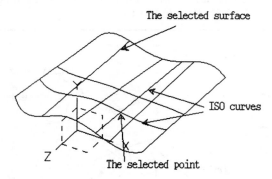

Figure 14.11

## Creating Curves through Points on a Surface

A curve can be created by fitting a set of points on a surface.

   **The procedure for creating a curve through points on a surface is (Figure 14.12):**
1. Select a surface
2. Sequentially pick a series of points
3. Click the middle mouse button to terminate the selection of point

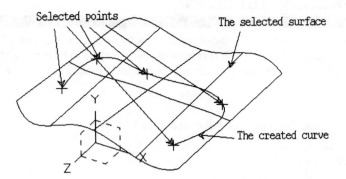

Figure 14.12

# Creating Silhouette Curves

Silhouette curves can be created from a given surface.

 **The procedure for creating silhouette curves (Figure 14.13):**

1. Select a surface
2. Define the Silhouette parameters in terms of view direction and angle from view direction

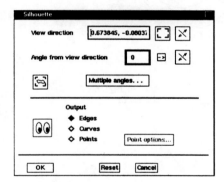

3. Select the output type to be edges, curves, or points

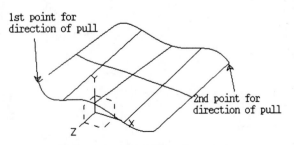

a. Before creating silhouette curves

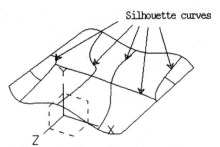

b. After creating silhouette curves

Figure 14.13

# 14.2  Trimming Surfaces

The Trim Surface function is used to remove material along selected boundaries. The trimming curves must be laid on the surface to be trimmed. It is possible for a surface to be trimmed to more than one boundary. The system prompts "pick point on region" to indicate which side to keep after trimming for each trimming boundary.

**The procedure for trimming a surface follows (Figure 14.14):**

1.  Select Trim at Curve icon
2.  Pick a surface to trim
3.  Pick trimming curve, edge or section
4.  Pick point on region:  pick a point to indicate region(s) of surface to keep
5.  The surface has been trimmed to the selected boundary as shown in Figure 14.14

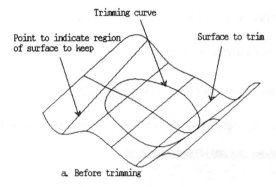

a. Before trimming

Figure 14.14a

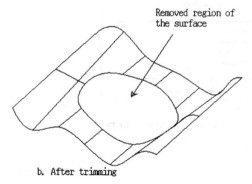

b. After trimming

Figure 14.4b

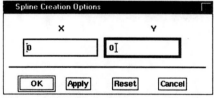

Figure 14.15a

## Project 1.
## Trimming a surface using curves

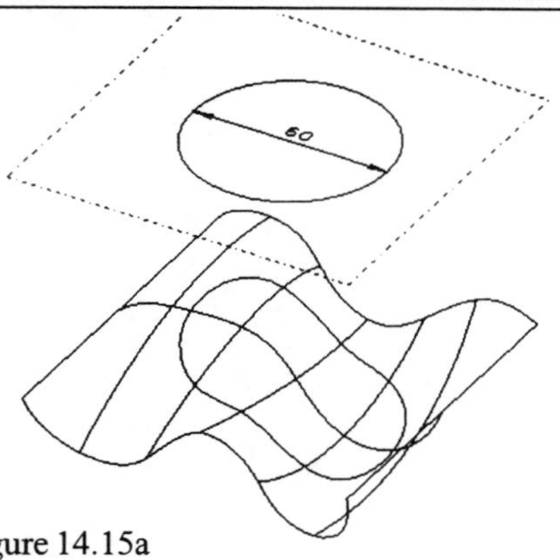

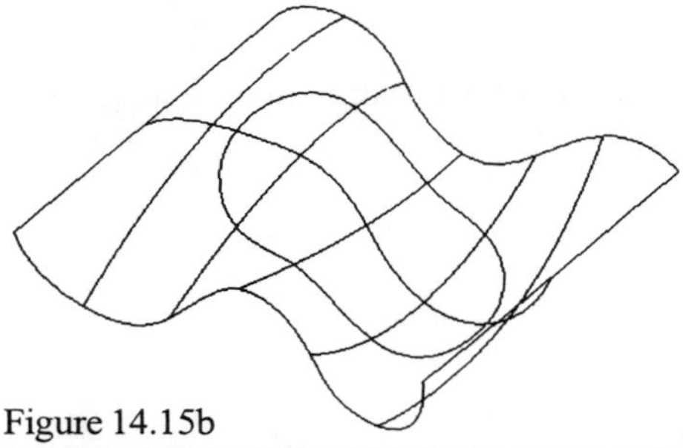

Figure 14.15b

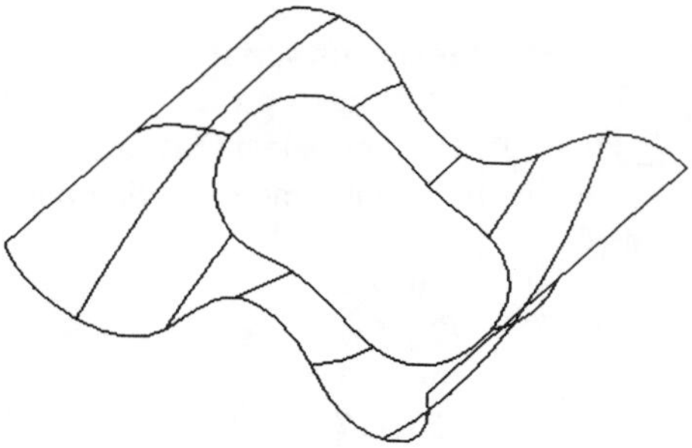

Figure 14.15c

This project involves creating a project curve on a loft surface from a circle. The loft surface is created from using three spline curves. The project curve is then used to trim the surface. Figure 14.15 shows the surface before and after trimming.

**Step 1.  Create a spline curve.**

 Select the **Splines** icon

Press RMB, then select **Options** from the list

Enter **0** and **0** to the two coordinate fields as below.

| Spline Creation Options | |
|---|---|
| **X** | **Y** |
| 0 | 0 |
| OK   Apply   Reset   Cancel | |

Select **Apply** then **Reset** for entering more sets of coordinate values

Sequentially enter the following nine sets of coordinate values:

> **(10, -10)**
> **(35, -10)**
> **(45, 0)**
> **(55, 7)**
> **(70, 0)**
> **(80, -13)**
> **(90, -16)**
> **(100, 0)**

Select **OK** to exit the Options dialog box

Press **Enter** to create the spline

The first spline is created as in Figure 14.16.

Figure 14.16

**Step 2.  Create the second spline.**
Select the **Splines** icon
Press RMB, then select **Options**
Sequentially enter the following eight sets of point coordinate values to the dialog box:

       **(0, 0)**
       **(10, 7)**
       **(25, 5)**
       **(40, -13)**
       **(50, -17)**
       **(65, -10)**
       **(85, 3)**
       **(100, 0)**

Select **Apply** then **OK** to exit the options dialog box
Press **Enter** to add the second spline curve as in Figure 14.17

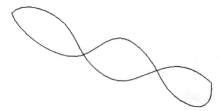

Figure 14.17

**Step 3.  Create the third spline curve.**
Select the **Splines** icon
Press RMB, then select **Options** to open its dialog box
Sequentially enter the following eight sets of point coordinate values:

       **(0, 0)**
       **(25, 10)**
       **(40, 7)**
       **(50, 0)**
       **(65, -15)**
       **(80, -21)**
       **(95, -10)**
       **(100, 0)**

Select **Apply** then **OK** to exit the options dialog box
Press **Enter** to complete the third spline curve as in Figure 14.18

Mastering I-DEAS,
Scholars International Publishing Corp., 1999

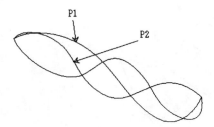

Figure 14.18

**Step 4.** **Move two splines to their new location. Use the pick points in Figure 14.18.**

 Select the **Move** icon

Pick **P1** to select a spline curve then press **Enter**

Enter translation X, Y, Z:   **0,0,-50**

Pick **P2** to select another spline curve then press **Enter**

Enter translation X, Y, Z:   **0,0,-100**

The new drawing becomes Figure 14.19.

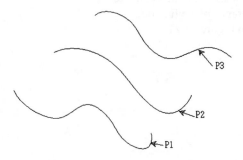

Figure 14.19

**Step 5.** **Create a loft surface. Use the pick points in Figure 14.19.**

 Select the **Loft** icon

Pick **P1** then press **Enter**

Pick **P2** then press **Enter**

Pick **P3** then press **Enter** twice

Set the create surface parameters as below.

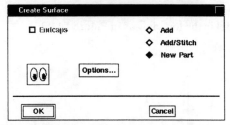

Select **OK** to create the surface as in Figure 14.20

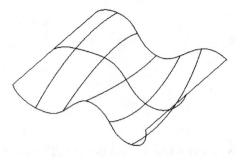

Figure 14.20

**Step 6.  Create a reference plane.**
 Select the **Reference Planes** icon
Press RMB, then select **Axis Planes** from the list
Select the **ZX plane** from the list
Enter distance (0.0): **75**
Pick the **loft surface** as the part to associate this plane to
Press **Enter** again to exit the reference plane function
The reference plane is added as in Figure 14.21.

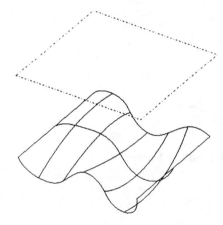

Figure 14.21

 Select the **Top View** icon to display the model in the top view as in Figure 14.22

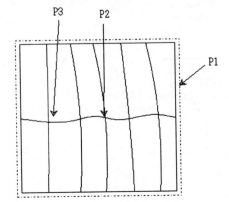

Figure 14.22

14-12

**Step 7.** **Create a circle on the newly created reference plane. Use the pick points in Figure 14.22.**

 Select the **Sketch in place** icon
Pick **P1** to select the reference plane
Select the **Center Edge** icon
Pick **P2** and **P3** to create a circle
Select the **Modify Entity** icon
Change the circle diameter value to **60**
Select the **Isometric View** icon
The circle is added as in Figure 14.23.

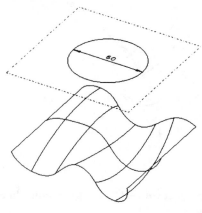

Figure 14.23

**Step 8.** **Create a project curve.**

 Select the **Project Curve** icon
Pick the circle as the entity to project then press **Enter**
Pick the loft surface as the entity to be projected onto
Set the project curve on surface parameters as below.

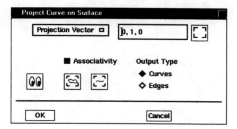

Select **OK** to complete the project curve as in Figure 14.24

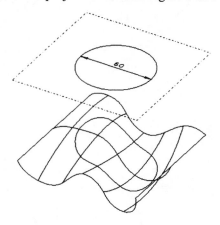

Figure 14.24

**Step 9. Delete the reference plane and the circle.**

 Click the **Delete** icon

Pick the **reference plane** and the **circle** to delete, then press **Enter**

Select **OK** from "I-DEAS Warning" dialog box

Select **Yes** to delete two entities

The new drawing becomes Figure 14.25.

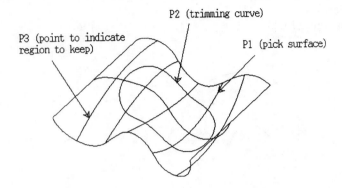

Figure 14.25

**Step 10. Trim the loft surface to the project curve. Use the pick points in Figure 14.25.**

 Select the **Trim at Curve** icon

Pick **P1** to select the surface to trim

Pick **P2** to select the trimming curve, then press **Enter**

Pick **P3** as the point to indicate region to keep, then press **Enter**

The surface is trimmed as in Figure 14.26.

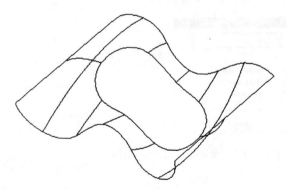

Figure 14.26

14-14

# 14.3 Offsetting Surfaces

The Offset Surface function is used to create new surfaces that are offset from a set of existing surfaces (Figure 14.27). The offset surface dialog box is shown below.

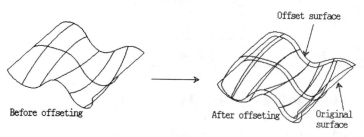

Figure 14.27

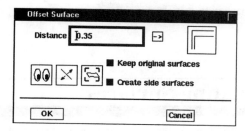

The offset surface parameters are briefly described below:

| | |
|---|---|
| **Offset distance:** | specifies the offset distance in the specified direction. |
| **Individual (Variable) distance:** | specifies the offset distance for each face. |
| **Offset direction:** | toggles to alter the offset direction. |
| **Select face to remove:** | selects a face to remove after offsetting. |
| **Keep original surfaces:** | retains the original surfaces after offsetting. |
| **Create side surfaces:** | adds side surfaces between original surfaces and offset surfaces. |

# 14.4 Extending Surfaces

The Extend Surface function is used to extend a surface along an edge by a given distance. The extension distance is specified by a percentage value (Figure 14.28).

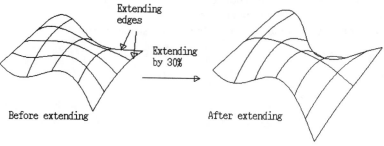

Figure 14.28

The extend options dialog box is shown below.

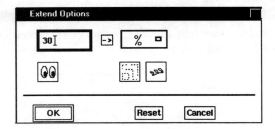

**The procedure for extending a surface is (Figure 14.28):**

1.  Select the Extend Surfaces icon
2.  Pick edge(s) of surface(s) to trim or extend:  Pick two edges as shown
3.  Define the extend parameters as shown above.
4.  Select **OK**

# 14.5  Interpolating Surfaces

The Interpolate Surface function creates a surface between two existing surfaces from the same part. The exact location of the in-between surface is determined by a "Percentage value" which is measured from the first selected surface.

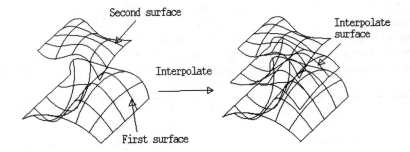

Figure 14.29

**The procedure for creating an interpolating surface is (Figure 14.29):**

1.  Select the Interpolate Surface icon
2.  Pick the first surface to interpolate
3.  Pick the second surface to interpolate
4.  Enter a percentage value (0-100) to locate mid-surface:  50

# 14.6  Show Surface Explode

The Show Surface Explode function explodes the selected surfaces or volumes of a part to help you visualize what each surface looks like (Figure 14.30). This is only a display function. No change is actually done to the part or surfaces.

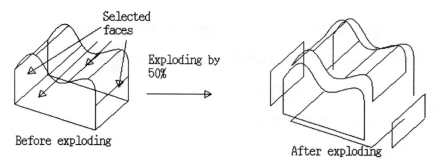

Figure 14.30

**The procedure for using the show surface explode function is ( Figure 14.30 ):**

1. Select the Show Surf Explode icon
2. Pick surfaces/volumes to explode:  pick four faces as shown, then press Enter
3. Enter percentage of explosion (20):   50

# 14.7  Stitch Surfaces

The Stitch function stitches or joins two or more surfaces along shared edges. The system prompts to pick on the overlap of an edge pair to be stitched. The stitched surfaces ensure surfaces are connected to a corresponding or neighboring surface.

# Chapter 14.  Review Questions

1.   What are the derived curves?

2.   List the five types of derived curves and briefly describe what they are.

3.   What are the two ways of specifying the projection direction for creating project curves?

4.   List the nine methods of specifying the projection vectors for creating project curves.

5.   Describe the procedure for creating ISO curves.

6.   Describe the procedure for creating silhouette curves.

7.   Use a drawing to illustrate the principle of trimming surfaces.

Mastering I-DEAS,
Scholars International Publishing Corp., 1999

# Chapter

**15**

# Creating Drawings

## Highlights of the Chapter
- Accessing parts for creating drawings
- Creating a drawing layout
- Creating views
- Clean up the layout
- Adding views
- Modifying views
- Adding dimensions
- Creating annotations
- Modifying dimensions and annotations

## Overview

After a part has been created, it has to be presented in various views with dimensions to communicate with people in design, analysis, and manufacturing. I-DEAS uses the Drawing Setup mode to create various drawing views and modify their cosmetic attributes. The drawing size and sheet format can be specified as one of ANSI or ISO standardized forms. User-defined formats are also possible. I-DEAS provides five view types to create various drawing views including projection view, section view, detail view, auxiliary view, and user-defined view.

The three projection views and an isometric view of the part can be created automatically. They are adequate to present simple parts. Additional views such as detail views, auxiliary views are added to present the details of the local features in rather complicated parts.

Dimensions of part features exist in the part model. They can be shown in the drawing views. I-DEAS automatically shows those key dimensions in the drawing views. It also provides various functions to add dimensions and modify dimensions. This chapter covers the essential concepts of drawing formats, creating various drawing views, showing and adding dimensions, and modifying dimension cosmetics.

# 15.1 Drawing Fundamentals

This section presents essential concepts used in presenting drawing views in the 3-D part model in 2-D settings. The main focuses are in drawing size and view type.

## Drawing Size

ANSI and ISO have standardized drawing sizes for inch and metric systems. Table 15.1 tabulates these ISO and ANSI standard drawing sheet sizes.

## Table 15.1  Drawing sheet sizes

| ISO | | ANSI | |
| Metric Unit | | English Unit | |
| Drawing Size | Dimension | Drawing Size | Dimension |
|---|---|---|---|
| A0 | 841 x 1189 mm | E | 34 x 44 inch |
| A1 | 594 x 841 mm | D | 22 x 34 inch |
| A2 | 420 x 594 mm | C | 17 x 22 inch |
| A3 | 297 x 420 mm | B | 11 x 17 inch |
| A4 | 210 x 297 mm | A | 8.5 x 11 inch |

## View Types

The drawing views of an object can be created in five view types; **projection**, **section**, **detail**, **auxiliary**, and **isometric**. Table 15.2 on the following page, describes these five view types that I-DEAS provided to create various drawing views.

# 15.2  Accessing Parts for Creating Drawings

There are two ways to open a part for creating drawings. The current part in the workstation can be readily used. You can use "Names Part" command to assign a name to the current part. Select the "Drawing Setup" program from the Application list. This active part is then automatically brought in to the Drawing program.

The other way to open an existing part model for creating drawing views is to check out the part to the bin, and then make it active to the Drawing program.

 **The procedure for opening an existing part model for creating drawing views is:**

1. Check the part from the library
2. Get the part from the bin
3. Open the Drawing Setup program

# Table 15.2 View types

| View Type | Description | Illustration |
|-----------|-------------|--------------|
| Projection (Orthographic) | Two-dimensional view of a 3-D object. It is created by projecting a view of an object onto a plane. | |
| Section | The cross-section view on a cutting plane. | |
| Detail | An enlarged view of the selected portion of an existing view. It is used to show the detail of the selected feature. | |
| Auxiliary | They are orthographic views used to present true-shaped views of slanted and oblique surfaces. | |
| Isometric | The isometric view of an object. It shows the object equally in three directions. | |

# 15.3   Creating a Drawing Layout

I-DEAS organizes a group of parameters under Layout to control the layout of drawing views. The Create Layout menu appears as below.

```
Create Layout
  Name    base⌷                              Selected Geometry   [ Get... ]

  Part #  [             ]                              Bin      [ wheel-asse ]
                                             Geometry   [ base   ]
  ◆ Predefined View Layout   [ Four Views ▢ ]
  ◇ Create/Place Each View                  Configuration  [              ]  [?]

  Sheet Format                             Drawing Size   [ A4-H    ▢ ]
    ◆ None                                 Horizontal   [ 297 ]
    ◇ Standard                             Vertical     [ 210 ]
    ◇ Picture File   [                ]  ▣
                                                          [ Options... ]

  [ OK ]          [ Reset ]    [ Cancel ]
```

| | |
|---|---|
| **Name:** | names the layout. |
| **Part #:** | identifies the layout with a part number. |
| **Predefined View Layout:** | selects the type and number of views on the layout. |
| **Sheet Format:** | selects a predefined border and title block. |
| **Selected Geometry:** | identifies the geometry to be used in the layout. |
| **Drawing Size:** | defines the size of the drawing layout. |
| **Options:** | brings up the layout options menu. |

## View Layout

The view layout parameter is used to specify the number of views to create. It has the following two options:

| | |
|---|---|
| **Predefined view layout:** | select one of prearranged view layout. |
| **Create/Place each view:** | select the views one by one. |

### Predefined view layout

The predefined view layout selects one of the following five options to place the views of a part model:

| | |
|---|---|
| **Front:** | creates the front view only (Figure 15.1). |
| **Front/Top:** | creates front view and top view of the model (Figure 15.2). |
| **Front/Rt:** | creates front view and right side view of the model (Figure 15.3). |
| **Front/Top/Rt:** | creates front view, top view, and right side view of the model (Figure 15.4). |
| **Four views:** | creates front view, top view, right side view, and isometric view of the model (Figure 15.5). |

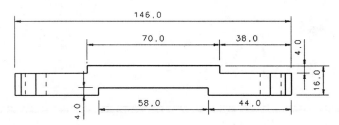

Figure 15.1

Mastering I-DEAS,
Scholars International Publishing Corp., 1999

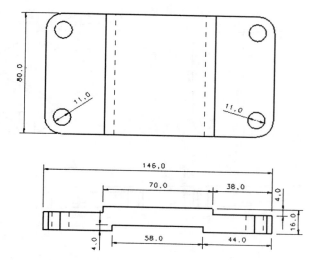

Figure 15.2

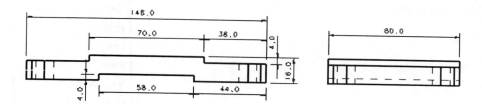

Figure 15.3

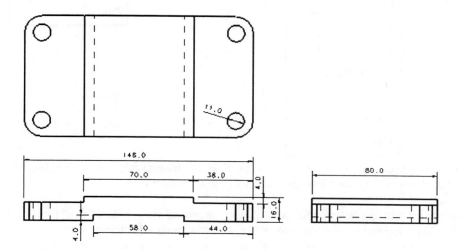

Figure 15.4

Creating Drawings

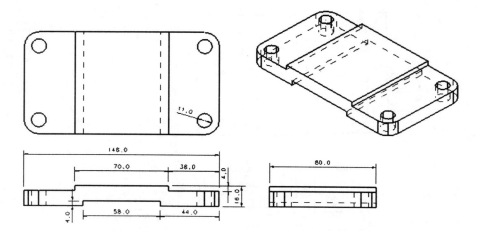

Figure 15.5

## Create/Place each view

This method is used to create drawing views that are added one by one. When this option is selected, the system will prompt an options list for you to select the first view. The Options list appears below.

| Front |
| Top |
| Bottom |
| Right |
| Left |
| Back |
| Isometric |
| User Defined |
| Change Geometry |
| Done |
| Backup |
| Cancel |

The first view normally is the front view. After selecting the first view, the system prompts to "Locate new position". You need to locate a screen location point to place the view. The system prompts other options list below.

| Yes |
| Change scale |
| Change view |
| Rename |
| Backup |
| Cancel |

Very often you need to change the scale of view size. Select "Change scale" from the options list. Enter the desired scale value to scale the view size. Select Yes to accept the view.

The view options list will appear again for you to select the second view. Select "Top" from the list to automatically add the top view to the drawing. You can continuously add "Right" view, "Isometric view", or other view types to the drawing simply by picking the view type from the options list. Select "Done" to exit the view layout function.

Mastering I-DEAS,
Scholars International Publishing Corp., 1999

## Sheet Format

This parameter allows selection of a predefined border and title block of the drawing sheet. It has the following three options:

**None:** no border and title block are included in the drawing sheet.
**Standard:** a predefined format for border and title block is used.
**Picture File:** a picture file format is used.

## Selected Geometry

The part model to be used for creating drawing views can be searched from this area. Click on the "Get..." button to open the "Select Part/Assembly" menu that lists all active part models in the workstation as shown below.

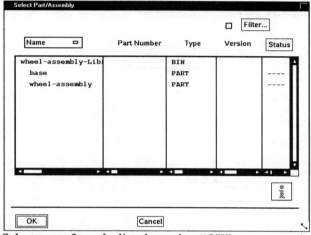

Select a part from the list, then select "OK" to return to the "Create Layout" menu. The part name of your selected part will be automatically reflected on the "Name" parameter.

## Drawing Size

The Drawing Size parameter selects the drawing paper size. The standard paper sizes have been listed in the previous section. Whether the set of metric drawing sizes or inch drawing sizes becomes available for you to choose depends on the unit system your part used.

## Options

Click on the "Options" button to open a "Layout Options" menu as below.

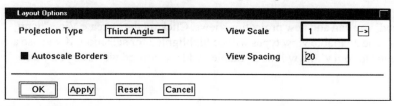

> **Project type:** specifies the projection angle either to be third or first angle (Figure 15.6).
> **Autoscale Borders:** toggles the view auto scaling feature for the borders On or Off.
> **View Scale:** specifies the geometry scale of the view.
> **View Spacing:** sets the distance between geometry in multiple views.

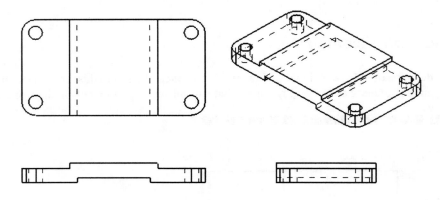

a. Third angle

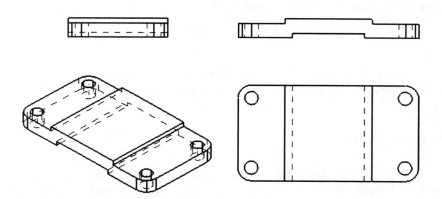

b. First angle
Figure 15.6

# Adding Other Projection Views

After the drawing layout is defined, you can add new projection views. Click on the "Create View" icon to open the Projection Views list. The available view types will be highlighted for selection. If you use a 4-view layout, only Back, Left, and Bottom views will be available. Add the desired views as you want.

# 15.4 Modifying Views

After views are created, we can move any selected view to a new location. Views can also be aligned to match with other views. I-DEAS provides a group of functions to modify views. They are:

**Move:** moves the selected view to a new location.
**Align:** aligns an axis of one view with the axis of another view.
**Resize:** resizes the view border without rescaling the geometry.
**Rename:** changes the name of the selected layout view.
**Delete:** removes the selected view(s) from the layout.

## Moving A View

Views can be moved to any location by using the "Move" command.

**The procedure for moving a view is (Figure 15.7):**
1. Select the Move icon
2. Pick a view to move: pick the front view
3. Locate a new position for the view

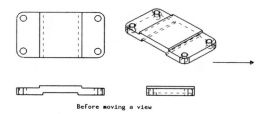

Before moving a view          After moving a view

Figure 15.7

## Aligning Views

Drawing views may not be aligned properly after they are moved. The "Align" function allows views to be aligned in the X or Y direction. You can use the "Align Y" option to align the right-side view with the front view, and the "Align X" option to align the top view with the front view.

**The procedure for aligning a view in Y direction is (Figure 15.8):**
1. Select the Align icon
2. Pick a view to align: pick the front view
3. Pick a view to align to: pick the right-side view
4. The system will open an options list which appears as below.

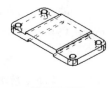

5. Select Align Y from the options list to move the front view in the vertical direction to align with the right-side view.

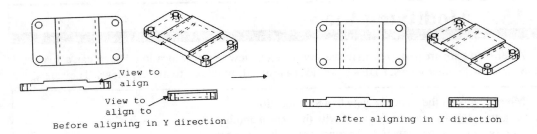

Figure 15.8

**The procedure for aligning a view in X direction is (Figure 15.9):**

1. Pick the top view to align
2. Pick the front view to align to
3. Select "Align X" from the options list to align the top view to front view in the X direction

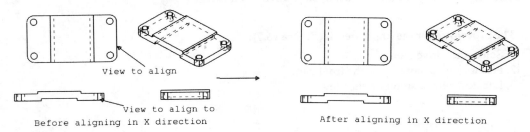

Figure 15.9

# Deleting Views

Drawing views can be deleted from a drawing layout.

**The procedure for deleting views is (Figure 15.10):**

1. Select the "Delete" icon
2. Pick views to delete: pick views to delete one by one,
   then click the middle mouse button to terminate view selection
3. Select Yes from the options list

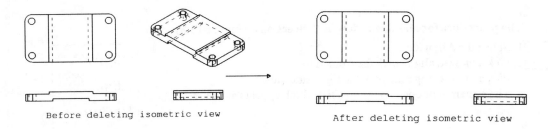

Figure 15.10

15-10

# 15.5 Adding Dimensions

The part created in I-DEAS already has all of the dimensions required to fully define it. No additional dimensional information is required to create the drawing. The dimensions can be derived from the part. These dimensions required to define the part are referred to as feature dimensions. Dimensions that are added to clarify feature characteristics are called reference dimensions. Notes, reference dimensions, and other cosmetic items can be added to the drawing. I-DEAS provides a variety of dimensioning functions to add dimensions. Table 15.3 summarizes these five dimensioning functions.

## Table 15.3 Five dimensioning functions

| Dimensioning Function | Description | Illustration |
|---|---|---|
| Linear dimension between any two entities. | Creating a linear dimension | |
| Angular dimension between two lines. | Creating an angular dimension | |
| Radial/diametral dimension | Creating a radial or diametral dimension of an arc or circle. | |
| Horizontal dimension between two entities. | Creating a horizontal dimension | |
| Vertical dimension between two entities. | Creating a vertical dimension | |

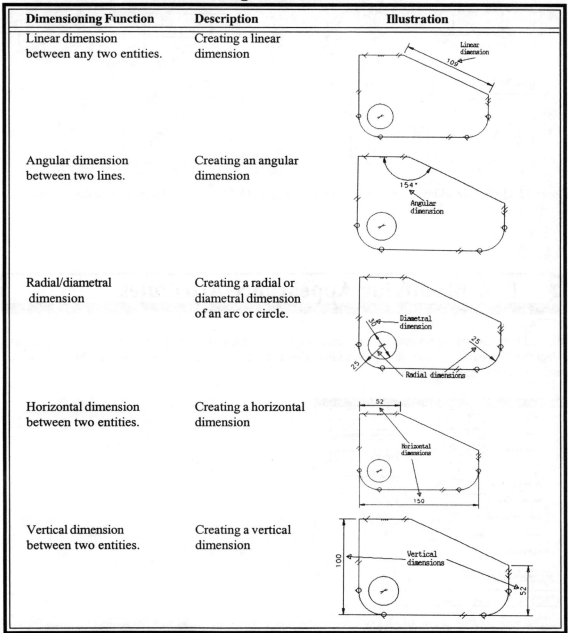

**The procedure for creating reference dimensions is (Figure 15.11):**

1. Select the Linear icon or any other dimension icon
2. Pick the entity as the 1st entity to dimension
3. Pick the entity as the 2nd entity to dimension
4. Drag the mouse to the proper location and click the mouse to place the text
5. Repeat the above steps to add other reference dimensions
   (Note: The reference dimensions are shown in yellow.)

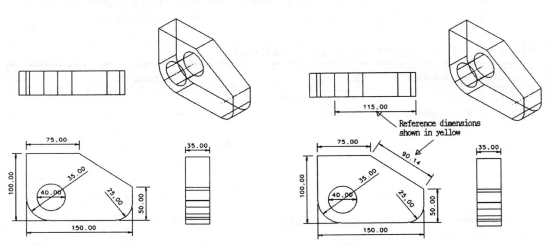

Figure 15.11a Before adding reference dimensions     Figure 15.11b After adding reference dimensions

# 15.6 Modifying Appearance Attributes

Dimensions are regarded as an annotation type. The appearance of annotations can be modified. Select the "Appearance" icon, then pick a dimension to modify its appearance attributes. The appearance attributes menu appears as below.

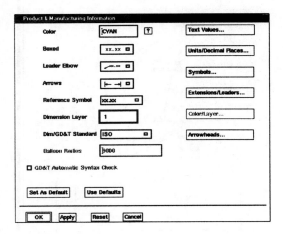

Mastering I-DEAS,
Scholars International Publishing Corp., 1999

Some dimension-related attributes are described below:

| | |
|---|---|
| **Color:** | changes the color of selected dimensions. |
| **Boxed:** | draws box around dimensioned text. |
| **Leader elbow:** | selects placement of leader elbow to text. |
| **Arrows:** | selects the placement of dimension arrows. |
| **Reference symbol:** | selects the symbols used in reference dimensions. |
| **Dimension layer:** | changes the drawing layer of dimensions. |
| **Dim/GD&T Standard:** | sets the standard for a dimension or GD&T symbol. |
| **Text Values:** | specifies the height of dimension text. |
| **Units/Decimal Places:** | specifies units and decimal places for linear and angular dimensions. |
| **Extensions/Leaders:** | sets the gap between the dimension line and text and part outline, as well as the extension distance beyond the dimension line. |
| **Arrowheads:** | selects type, length, and length to width ratio of arrowhead, as well as outside length of arrow leader lines. |

## Changing Decimal Places

The decimal place of dimension values can be set to any place desired. You can change a single dimensions or a group of dimensions. The Unit/Decimal Places dialog box appears on the left below. Click the decimal places button to open the selection list as on the right below.

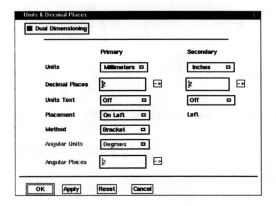

The procedure for changing the decimal place for a single dimension is (Figure 15.12):

1. Select the Appearance icon
2. Pick a dimension to modify (35.00),
   then press Enter key to open Product & Manufacturing Information menu
3. Select the Units/Decimal Places button to open "Units & Decimal Places" menu
4. Enter 0 to "Decimal Places" parameter as below.

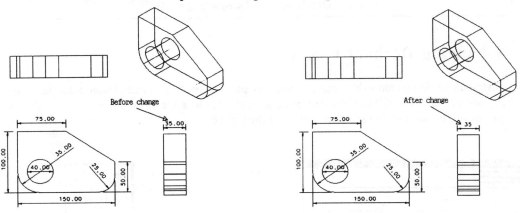

5. Select **OK** → **OK** to complete the change of decimal place

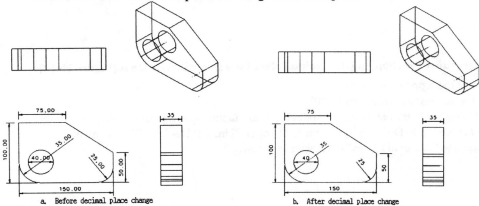

Figure 15.12a

Figure 15.12b

**The procedure for changing the decimal place for all dimensions is (Figure 15.13):**

1. Select the Appearance icon
2. Pick any dimension, then click the right mouse button to open the options list and select All from the list to open Product & Manufacturing Information menu
3. Select theUnits/Decimal button to open "Units & Decimal Places" menu
4. Enter 0 to Decimal places parameter
5. Select **OK** → **OK** to complete the change of decimal place

Figure 15.13

15-14

# Changing the Size of Dimension Texts

The size of dimension texts can be adjusted. Two parameters are used to specify the size of dimension texts; height and width/ratio.

  **The procedure for changing the size of dimension texts is (Figure 15.14):**

1. Select the Appearance icon
2. Pick any dimension to modify then press RMB and select All from the list, then press Enter
3. Select the Text Values button from Product & Manufacturing Information dialog box
4. Set text value parameters as below.

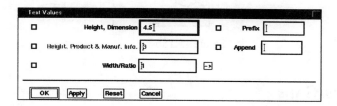

5. Select **OK** → **OK** to complete the change of text size

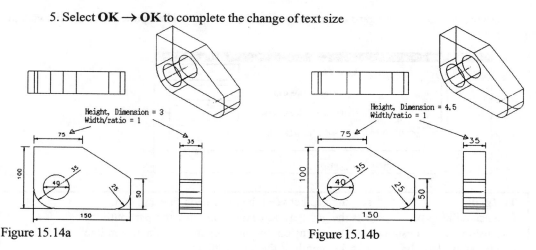

Figure 15.14a                                    Figure 15.14b

# Changing Arrow Direction

The dimension arrows can be placed in two ways; the arrows can be pointing inward (→| |←) and pointing outward (|← →|). Use the pointing inward mode when the dimension space is limited. The default mode is pointing outward.

  **The procedure for changing arrow direction is (Figure 15.15):**

1. Select the Appearance icon
2. Pick the dimension to modify, then press Enter
3. Select the Arrows button from Product & Manufacturing Information dialog box
4. Select the "pointing inward' (→| |←) mode
5. Select **OK** to make the change

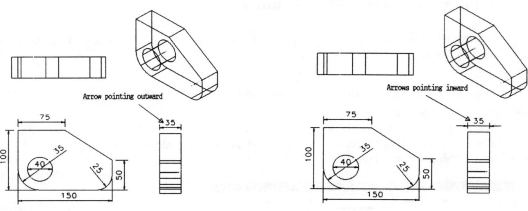

Figure 15.15a                                    Figure 15.15b

## Extensions/Leaders/Gaps

The size of extensions, leaders and gaps in dimensions can be specified. Their parameters are shown and summarized below.

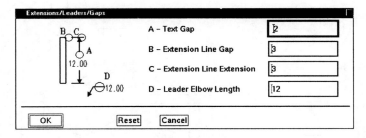

| Text gap: | sets the gap between the dimension line and text. |
| Extension line gap: | sets the gap between extension lines and part outline. |
| Extension line extension: | sets the extension distance beyond the dimension line. |
| Leader elbow length: | sets the length of the leader elbows. |

## Arrowheads Configuration

The type, size and dimension of arrowheads can be specified. Its dialog box appears as below.

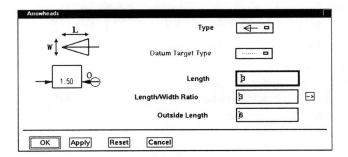

These parameters are briefly summarized below:

| | |
|---|---|
| **Type:** | selects the type of arrowheads. |
| **Length:** | sets the length of the arrowhead. |
| **Length/Width ratio:** | sets the length to width ratio of the arrowhead. |
| **Outside length:** | sets the outside length of the arrow leader lines. |

# 15.7   Show and Hide Dimensions

Dimensions will automatically appear in drawing views when views are created. The locations of the dimensions can be moved. They can be moved to a new location in the same view or moved to a different view. Some dimensions are not required in drawing views. Those unwanted dimensions can be hidden from drawing views.

## Moving Dimensions

The "Move" function can be used to move any dimension to a new location within the same view or another view.

**The procedure for moving a dimension to a new location within the same view is (Figure 15.16):**

1. Select the Move icon
2. Pick the dimension to move
3. Drag to a new location and click the left mouse button to pick the text location

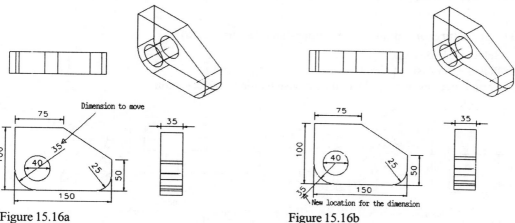

Figure 15.16a                                        Figure 15.16b

**The procedure for moving dimensions to other view is (Figure 15.17):**

1. Select the Move icon
2. Pick the dimension "35" in the right side view to move
3. Click the right mouse button to open the options list, then click "Change view"
4. Pick the top view to place the dimension
5. Pick the text location
6. Repeat the above steps to move the "150" to the top view

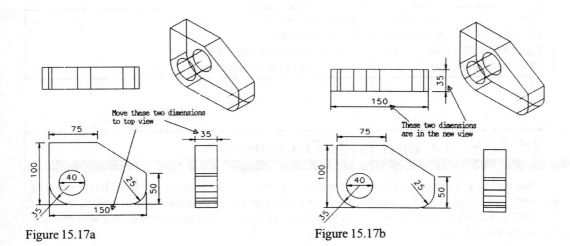

Figure 15.17a                                                Figure 15.17b

## Hiding Dimensions

I-DEAS allows dimensions to be displayed or hidden from drawing views. Displaying dimensions are the default mode. The "Hide" function is used to hide selected dimensions. We can hide dimensions in one of the following three ways:  Hide a single dimension, Hide multiple dimensions and Hide all dimensions.

## Hiding a single dimension

**The procedure for hiding a single dimension is (Figure 15.18):**

1. Select the Hide icon
2. Pick the dimension to hide
3. Press Enter key or click the middle mouse button to end selection

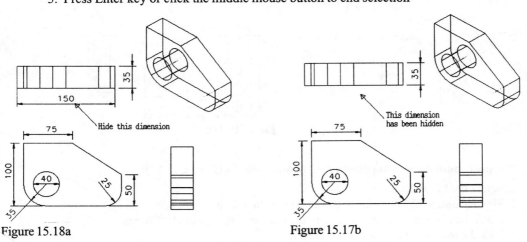

Figure 15.18a                                                Figure 15.17b

Mastering I-DEAS,
Scholars International Publishing Corp., 1999

# Hiding multiple dimensions

**The procedure for hiding multiple dimensions is (Figure 15.19):**

1. Select the Hide icon
2. Pick a dimension (150) from top view to hide
3. Press Shift key and continue to pick another dimension (50) from front view to hide
4. Press Enter key or click the middle mouse button to end selection

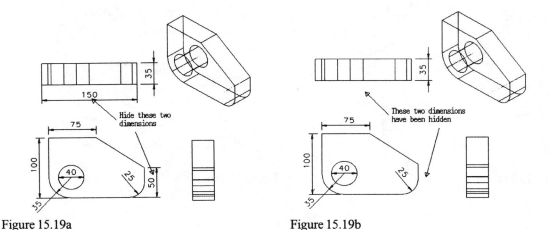

Figure 15.19a                    Figure 15.19b

# Hiding all dimensions

**The procedure for hiding all dimensions from drawing views is (Figure 15.20):**

1. Select the Hide icon
2. Pick a dimension to hide
3. Click the right mouse button to open the options list, then select ALL
4. Press Enter key or click the middle mouse button to end selection

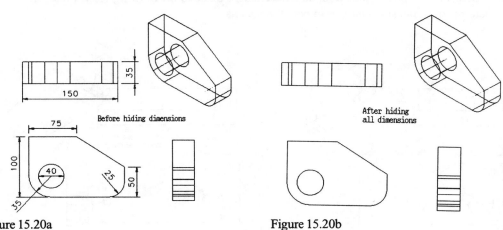

Figure 15.20a                    Figure 15.20b

## Showing Hidden Dimensions

The "Show" function is used to redisplay those hidden dimensions. Click on the "Show" icon to make all hidden dimensions and attributes back to visible. The hidden dimensions are shown in white. Select those dimensions you want to show then press Enter (Figure 15.21).

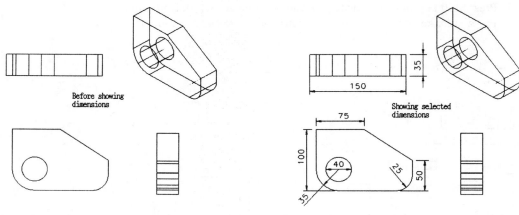

Figure 15.21a                    Figure 15.21b

# 15.8 Modifying Dimension Values

Dimension values of the part model can be modified in the drawing views. The "Modify Entities" function is used for this purpose. Select the "Modify Entities" icon, pick any dimension to be modified then enter a new dimension value. Use the same procedure to make changes to the remaining dimensions. Select the "Update" icon to update the changes made to the drawing view. Figure 15.22 shows an example of dimension changes in two dimensions.

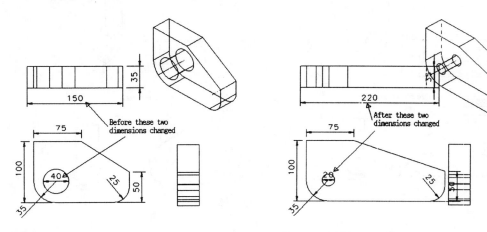

Figure 15.22a                    Figure 15.22b

15-20

# 15.9   Selecting Hidden Line Mode

I-DEAS allows hidden lines to be shown in a variety of ways that are controlled by three parameters; hidden line style, hidden method and hidden line color.

## Hidden Line Style

The hidden line in the model can be shown in one of the three styles; **invisible**, **visible** and **dashed**.

   **The procedure to select the hidden line style is:**

1. Select Options to open the "Line & Hidden Line Options" dialog box as below.

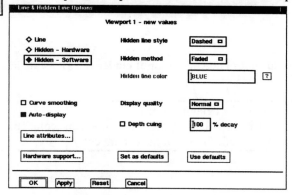

2. Click on the "Hidden – Software" button
3. Click on the "Hidden line style" button to open the three options. Choose one, then select **OK**

| | |
|---|---|
| **Invisible:** | hidden lines are not shown in the model (Figure 15.23). |
| **Visible:** | hidden lines are shown as solid lines (Figure 15.24). |
| **Dashed:** | hidden lines are shown in dashed lines (Figure 15.25). |

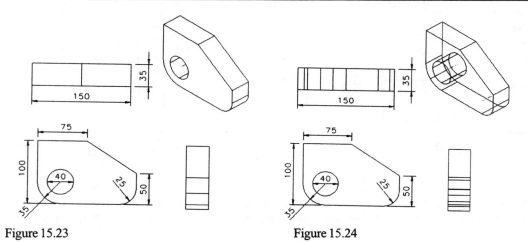

Figure 15.23                                    Figure 15.24

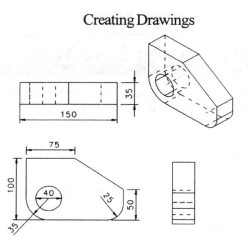

Figure 15.25

# Hidden Method

I-DEAS provides the following three options to control how the color of hidden lines appears in the part model and drawing views:

| | |
|---|---|
| **Normal:** | shows the hidden lines in the default color. |
| **Fixed:** | shows the hidden lines in the color specified in "Hidden line color" parameter. |
| **Faded:** | shows the hidden lines in faded mode of the default color. |

# Line Attributes

The "Line attributes" function allows **selecting line**, **hidden line** or **edge attribute** options. Click on the "Line attributes" button to open its dialog box as below.

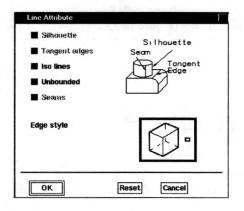

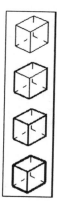

The thickness of edge lines can be specified in one of four thicknesses. To change the line thickness, click the line thickness box to open its list, then select one thickness. Figure 15.26 shows two different thicknesses of the lines.

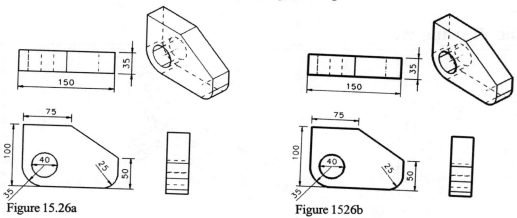

Figure 15.26a

Figure 1526b

# Project 1.
# Creating drawing views

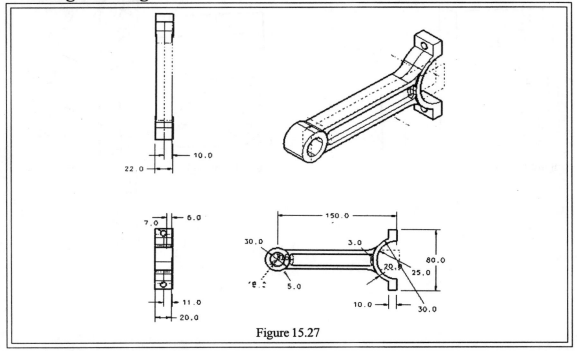

Figure 15.27

**Step 1.  Open Drafting Setup program.**
Select **Drafting Setup** from the task list if necessary

**Step 2.  Check out a copy of "connecting-rod" from the library.**

Select the **Get from Library** icon
Select "**connecting-rod**" from library
Select **Copy** to get a copy of the part
Select **OK** to exit the library

**Step 3.  Crate a drawing layout.**
Select the **Create Layout** icon
Set the layout parameters as below.

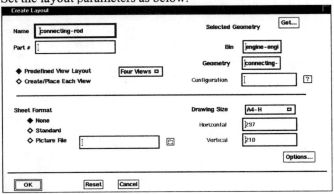

Select **OK**
A tentative front view should appear on the screen
Select **Yes** to "Does front view appear correct?"

Mastering I-DEAS,
Scholars International Publishing Corp., 1999

# Creating Drawings

The four drawing views should initially appear as in Figure 15.28.

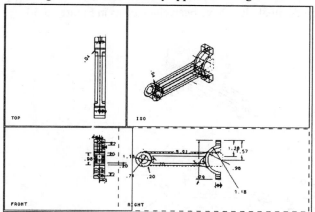

Figure 15.28

**Step 4.  Toggle off view borders and view names.**

Select **View Borders** and **View Names** to toggle them to disappear from the screen
The new drawing views become Figure 15.29.

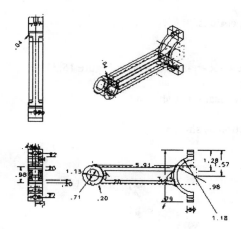

Figure 15.29

**Step 5.  Change unit from inch to mm and decimal places to 1.**

Select the **Appearance** icon
Select any dimension, then press RMB and select **All** from the list
The Product & Manufacturing Information dialog box should appear on the screen
Select the **Units/Decimal Places** button to open its dialog box.  Set the parameters as below.

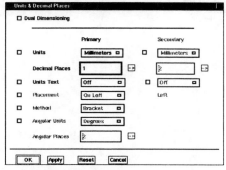

Select **OK → OK**

The dimension unit and decimal place have been changed as in Figure 15.30.

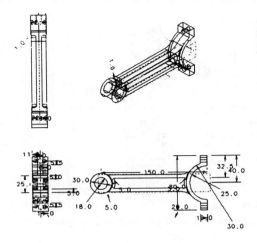

Figure 15.30

**Step 6. Move three views to their new locations.**

 Select the **Move View** icon
Pick the **right side view** to move
Drag the view to the right to a new location as shown in Figure 15.31
Pick the **isometric view** to move
Drag the isometric view to a new location as shown
Pick the **top view** to move
Drag the top view to a new location as shown

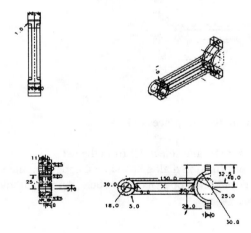

Figure 15.31

**Step 7. Align the drawing views.**

Select the **Align** icon
Pick the **top view** as the view to align
Pick the **front view** as the view to align to
Select **Align X** from the list
Pick the **right side view** as the view to align
Pick the **front view** as the view to align to
Select **Align Y** from the list

Mastering I-DEAS,
Scholars International Publishing Corp., 1999

The three orthographic views have been properly aligned as in Figure 15.32.

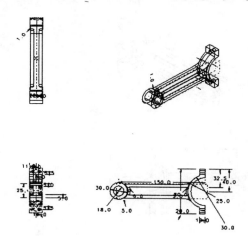

Figure 15.32

**Step 8.  Scale up the isometric view.**

Select the **Scale View** icon
Pick the **isometric view** as the view to scale
Enter view scale (0.5): **0.75**
The new drawing views become Figure 15.33.

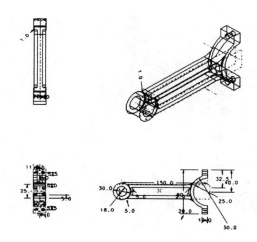

Figure 15.33

**Step 9.  Move dimensions to their proper location.**

Select the **Move** icon
Pick dimensions one by one and drag them to proper locations as shown in Figure 15.34.

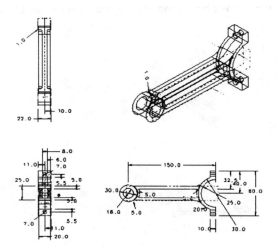

Figure 15.34

## Step 10. Hide unwanted dimensions.

Select the **Hide** icon
Pick those dimensions you don't want to appear on the drawing views
Press **Enter** to complete the selection of dimensions to hide
The new drawing should resemble Figure 15.35.

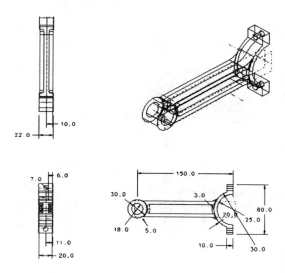

Figure 15.35

## Step 11. Change the arrow directions of some selected dimensions.

Click on the **Appearance** icon
Pick "**10.0**" from the right side view
Pick "**10.0**" from the top view
Pick "**6.0**", "**7.0**" and "**11.0**" from the front view
Select **Enter** to complete the selection
Select the **Arrows** button then select →| |←
Select **OK**

## Creating Drawings

The new drawing becomes Figure 15.36.

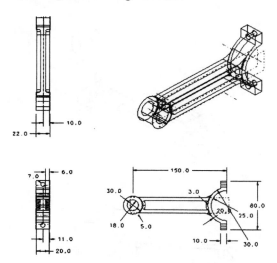

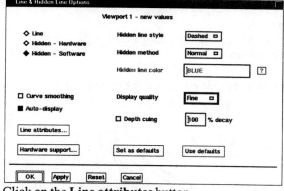

Figure 15.36

**Step 12. Change the hidden lines to dashed mode.**

Select the **Options** icon

Set the Line & Hidden Line Options parameters as below.

**Line & Hidden Line Options**

Viewport 1 - new values

◇ Line
◇ Hidden - Hardware
◆ Hidden - Software

Hidden line style — Dashed
Hidden method — Normal
Hidden line color — BLUE [?]

☐ Curve smoothing
■ Auto-display

Display quality — Fine
☐ Depth cuing — 100 % decay

Line attributes...

Hardware support...     Set as defaults     Use defaults

OK   Apply   Reset   Cancel

Click on the **Line attributes** button

Click on the **Edge Style** button to open its dialog box as here.

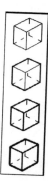

Select **OK** from the Line Attributes dialog box

Select **OK** from the Line & Hidden Line Options dialog box

Hidden lines have been shown on the drawing views as in Figure 15.37.

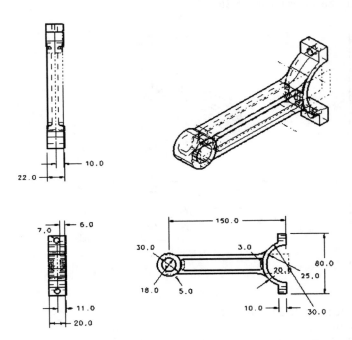

Figure 15.37

## Step 13. Change the hidden lines to invisible mode.

 Select **Options** to open the Line & Hidden Line Options dialog box
Select **Invisible** for "Hidden line style" parameter
Select **OK**

The drawing views with invisible hidden line mode are shown in Figure 15.38.

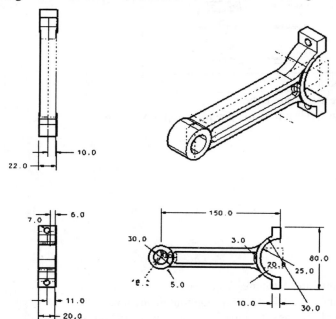

Figure 15.38

15-30

**Step 14. Check in the drawing views to library.**

Select the **Check In** icon

Double click the '**connecting-rod**' name on the list to make the "connecting-rod" drafting setup appear on the list

Click the '**connecting-rod**' drafting setup from the list

Select **OK**

Set the check-in parameters as below.

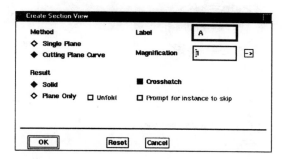

Select **OK**

# 15.10   Creating Section Views

Section views are used to show the internal shape and size of a part. The section view parameters menu appears as below.

## Cutting plane

There are two ways to specify the section cut plane; **single plane** and **cutting plane curve**. In the single plane mode, you need to use an existing plane as the section cut plane (Figure 15.39). This cut plane can be selected from any view. The isometric view can be readily used to select the cut plane. The cut plane option can only be used for creating full section views.

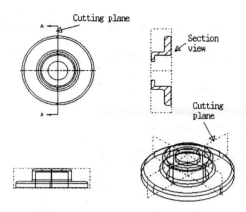

Figure 15.39

The cutting plane curve option allows us to define the cutting plane along a set of lines (Figure 15.40). This option allows creating a cutting plane for partial section views (Figure 15.41).

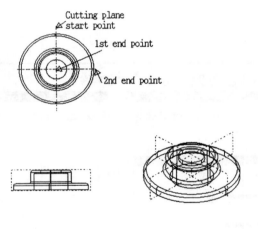

Figure 15.40

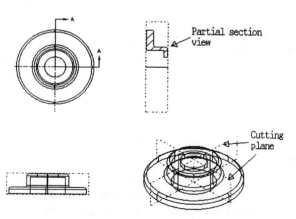

Figure 15.41

# Result parameter

Section views can be shown in 2D or 3D. Selecting the "Solid" option gives a 3D result (Figure 15.42), while the "Plane Only" option provides a 2D view (Figure 15.43).

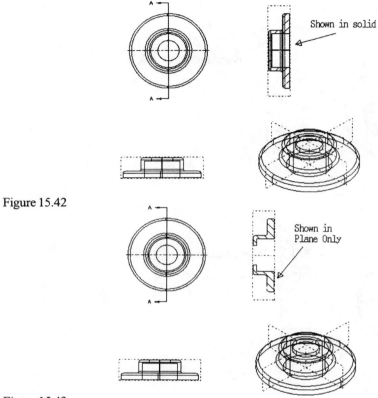

Shown in solid

Figure 15.42

Shown in
Plane Only

Figure 15.43

# Section label

A label is assigned to each section view. Enter the section label into this "Label" field. Typical section labels are A, B, C, etc. The label of "C" in this field will produce the section label C-C with the cutting plane (Figure 15.44).

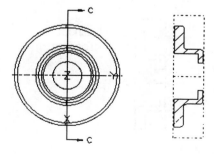

Figure 15.44

# Magnification

This parameter allows us to scale the section view by a given scaling factor. Any scaling value less than unity will reduce the size of the section view (Figure 15.45), and more than unity will enlarge the size of the view (Figure 15.46).

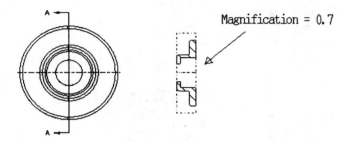

Figure 15.45

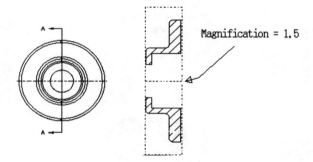

Figure 15.46

# Crosshatch

This parameter toggles to indicate whether to add crosshatching in the section view. Figure 15.47 shows the same section view with and without crosshatch.

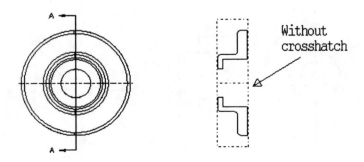

Figure 15.47a

15-34

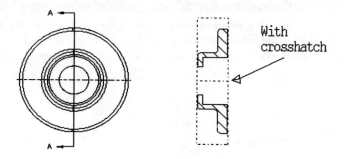

Figure 15.47b

**Procedure for creating a section view (Figure 15.48):**

1. Select the "Section" icon
2. Pick a view for defining a section view
3. Define "Create Section View" parameters
4. Locate cutting plane
5. Locate section view position
6. Select "Yes" from the options list to accept the section view

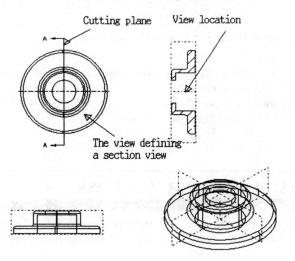

Figure 15.48

# 15.11 Creating Detail Views

A detail view is an enlarged view of a selected portion of the view to illustrate the detail of a local focus (Figure 15.49). You can scale the detail view and place the view in any desired location. The boundary of the detail view is defined by a rectangle that is specified by two corner points.

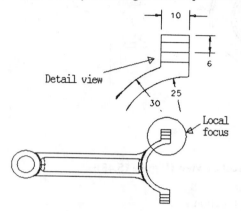

Figure 15.49

The scale value is used to determine the size of the detail view. A larger scale value produces a larger detail view. The default scale value is 2. The system will prompt to enter a new scale value if you do not want to use its default value.

**The procedure for creating a detail view follows (Figure 15.49):**
1. Select the Detail view icon
2. Select the region in existing view: pick two corner points to define a rectangular boundary
3. Locate new position for the detail view
4. Enter detail view magnification factor: 3
5. Select Done from the options list to complete the view

# 15.12 Creating Auxiliary Views

Auxiliary views are normally used to show only the true shape and detail of the inclined surfaces or features. It requires a parent view to create an auxiliary view. The orientation of the auxiliary view is perpendicular to the selected surface (Figure 15.50).

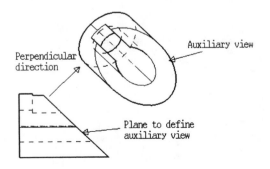

Figure 15.50

Mastering I-DEAS,
Scholars International Publishing Corp., 1999

**The procedure for creating an auxiliary view is (Figure 15.51):**

1. Select the Auxiliary View icon
2. Pick a plane to define auxiliary view
3. Define the projection direction: select Yes to accept the default direction, or select No to reverse the direction, then select Yes
4. Locate a position to locate the auxiliary view (pick the location along the default reference line to align the view to its parent view)

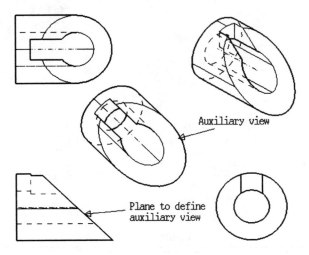

Figure 15.51

# Project 2.
# Adding section, detail, and auxiliary views

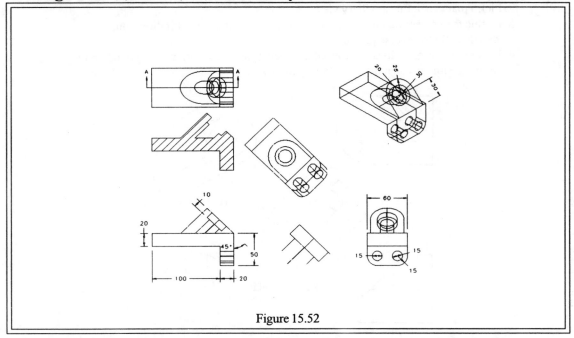

Figure 15.52

This project creates various drawing views for a part that consists of five features. The drawing views include three orthographic views, isometric view, a section view, a detail view, and a auxiliary view as shown in Figure 15.52.

**Step 1.  Create a coordinate system.**

 Select the **Coordinate Systems** icon, then pick the work plane as the entity to reference
Select **Done** to complete the coordinate system

**Step 2.  Create a sketch.**

 Select the **Sketch in place** icon
Pick **XY-plane** as the sketch plane
Use the **Polines** function to create a sketch and apply dimensions as shown in Figure 15.53

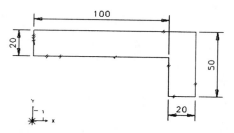

Figure 15.53

**Step 3.  Extrude the sketch by 60-mm.**

Select the **Isometric View** icon
Select the **Extrude** icon then pick the section to extrude

Set the extrude parameters as below.

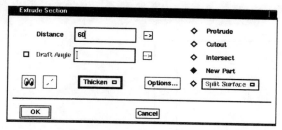

Select **OK** to complete the extrude feature as in Figure 15.54

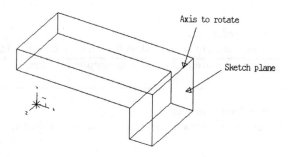

Figure 15.54

**Step 3. Define an angular reference plane. Use Figure 15.54 as reference.**

Select the **Reference plane** icon, then press RMB and select **Angled Surface** from the list
Pick the **right vertical face** as the planar surface
Pick the **right edge** as the rotation axis
Enter theangle between surface (30.0): **45**

Click the **Front View** icon to show the drawing becoming Figure 15.55

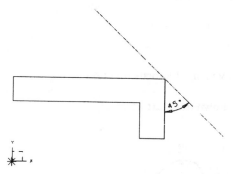

Figure 15.55

**Step 4. Select and show workplane.**

Select the **Sketch in place** icon then pick the **workplane** just created
Select the **View Workplane** icon

# Creating Drawings

The new drawing view should appear as Figure 15.56.

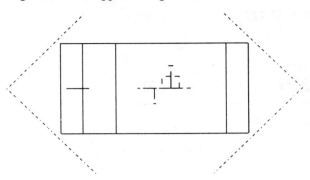

Figure 15.56

**Step 5.   Create a sketch. Use Figure 15.57 as reference.**

Use **Line** and **Start-End-180** arc commands to create a sketch as shown in Figure 15.57

*Note:*   you need to use the Focus function to ensure that entities are applied on the proper locations)

Use the **Center-Edge circle** command to create a circle
Add two dimensions and modify the dimensions to their correct values as shown

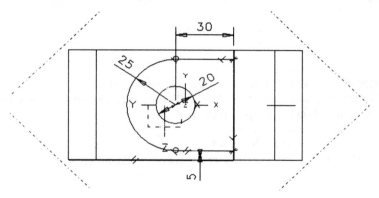

Figure 15.57

**Step 6.   Add an extrude feature to the part.**

Select the **Isometric View** icon
Delete an unwanted line created by using the focus function
Select the **Extrude** icon
Pick entities to create sections as shown in Figure 15.58.

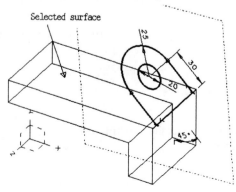

Figure 15.58

15-40

Set the extruding parameters as below.

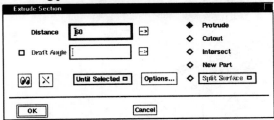

Pick the **top flat surface** as the entity to "extrude until"
Select **OK** to complete the extrude feature as in Figure 15.59

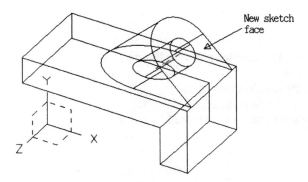

New sketch
face

Figure 15.59

**Step 7.   Add a circle to the sloped face. Use Figure 15.59 as reference.**

 Select the **Sketch in place** icon, then pick the slope face as the sketch plane as shown
Create a concentric circle as shown in Figure 15.60
Modify the circle diameter to **30**

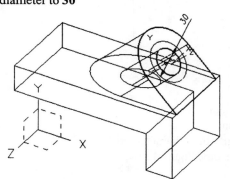

Figure 15.60

**Step 8.   Extrude-cut the circle.**

 Select the **Extrude** icon
Pick the circle just created
Set the extrude parameters
as shown here.

The cut feature is added as in Figure 15.61.

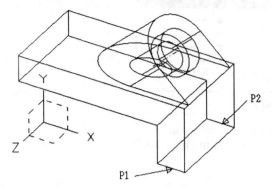

Figure 15.61

**Step 9.** **Add two fillets. Use the pick points in Figure 15.61.**

 Select the **Fillet** icon
Pick **P1** and **P2** to select two edges
Enter the radius for selected edges (3.0): **15**
The two fillets are added as in Figure 15.62.

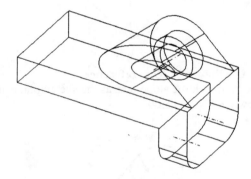

Figure 15.62

**Step 10.** **Create two circles.**

 Select the **Sketch in place** icon
Select the **Center-Edge** icon

 Create two circles and modify their diameter values to **15**
The new drawing should become Figure 15.63.

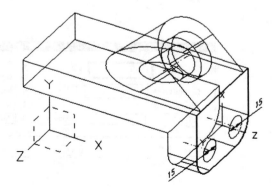

Figure 15.63

15-42

# Creating Drawings

### Step 11. Extrude-cut the two circles.

Select the **Extrude** icon, then pick the two circles just created
Set the extrude parameters as below.

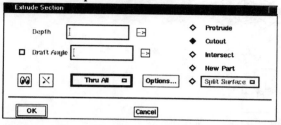

Select **OK** to complete the final model as in Figure 15.64

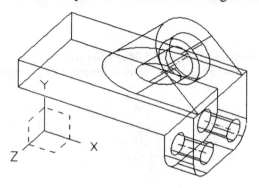

Figure 15.64

### Step 12. Name the part as "L-shape".
Select the **Name Parts** icon, then enter "**L-shape**"

### Step 13. Open the Drafting Setup program.
Select **Drafting Setup** from the task list to open the program

### Step 14. Create four basic views.

Select the **Create Layout** icon
Set create layout parameters as below.

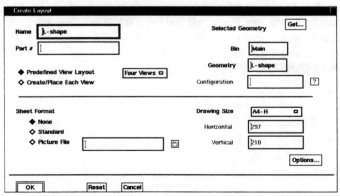

Select **OK**
Select "**Change scale**" from the list
Enter view scale (1.0): **0.5**
Select **Yes** to "Does front view appear correct?"

## Creating Drawings

The four views initially appear as in Figure 15.65.

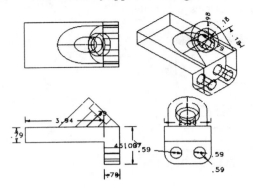

Figure 15.65

**Step 15. Move and align views to proper locations. Use Figure 15.66 as reference.**

 Use the **Move View** and **Align View** icons to adjust the views in their proper location as in Figure 15.66.

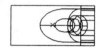

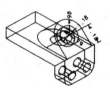

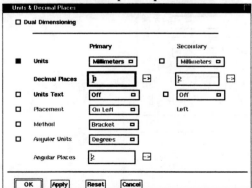

Figure 15.66

**Step 16. Reposition the dimensions. Use Figure 15.67 as reference.**

Select the **Appearance** icon, then pick any dimension and press RMB to select **All**
Click on the "**Units/Decimal Places**" button to open its dialog box
Set units and decimal places parameters as below.

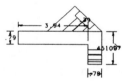

Select **OK → OK** to change the unit and decimal place

15-44

# Creating Drawings

Use the **Move function** to manipulate the dimensions as appearing in Figure 15.67

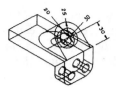

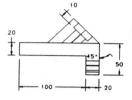

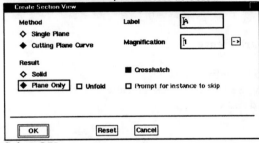

Figure 15.67

## Step 17. Create a section view.

 Select the **Section** icon

Pick the **top view** as the view for defining a section view

Set the section view parameters as below.

**Create Section View**

| | |
|---|---|
| **Method** | **Label** ⟦A⟧ |
| ◇ Single Plane | |
| ◆ Cutting Plane Curve | **Magnification** ⟦1⟧ ⊡ |
| **Result** | |
| ◇ Solid | ■ Crosshatch |
| ◆ Plane Only  ☐ Unfold | ☐ Prompt for instance to skip |

| OK | Reset | Cancel |

Select **OK**

Pick **two points** across the middle section of the top view to define the cutting plane curve

Press **Enter**, then select **Yes** from the list

Drag the view to a proper location below the top view, then click the mouse

The section view is added as in Figure 15.68.

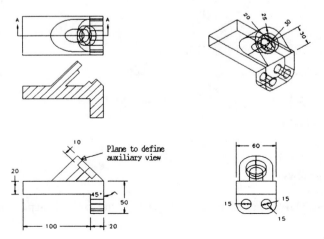

Plane to define
auxiliary view

Figure 15.68

**Step 18. Create an auxiliary view. Use Figure 15.68 as reference.**

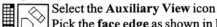 Select the **Auxiliary View** icon

Pick the **face edge** as shown in Figure 15.68 as the plane to define auxiliary view

Select **Yes** from the list to accept the direction

Slide the view along the aligning line to a proper location to place the view

The auxiliary view is added as in Figure 15.69.

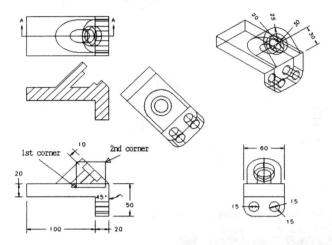

Figure 15.69

**Step 19. Create a detail view. Use Figure 15.69 as reference.**

Select the **Detail** icon

Pick **two corners** as shown in Figure 15.69 to define a box

Drag the view to the location shown in Figure 15.70 to place the view

Select **Done** from the list to complete the detail view

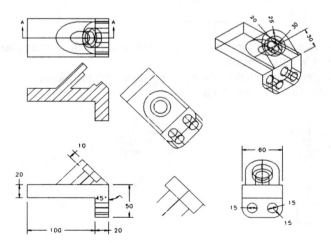

Figure 15.70

**Step 20. Check in the drafting views.**

Select the **Check In** icon

Select **DRAFTING SETUP** of an L-shape from the select entity to check-in parameters as shown next.

15-46

**Line & Hidden Line Options**

Viewport 1 - new values

◇ Line          Hidden line style    Dashed □
◇ Hidden – Hardware    Hidden method    Faded □
◆ Hidden – Software    Hidden line color    BLUE    [?]

☐ Curve smoothing    Display quality    Normal □
■ Auto–display    ☐ Depth cuing    100 % decay

[Line attributes...]
[Hardware support...]    [Set as defaults]    [Use defaults]

[OK] [Apply] [Reset] [Cancel]

Select **OK**

Set the check-in parameters as below.

**Check In**

Project
[exercise]    [Find...]    ◇ Check-in, keep to modify
                            ◇ Check-in, keep as copy
Library                     ◇ Check-in, keep for reference
[exercise]    [Find...]    ◆ Check-in, do not keep

Name:  L-shape       Type:    DRAFTING SETUP
Part #:              Version:  1
Revision [I]

[OK]    [Reset]    [Cancel]

Select **OK**

# 15.13  Creating Notes, Ballon Annotations, and Crosshatch Lines

## Creating Notes

Notes can be added to any location on the drawing layout. The content of the note can come from an existing file or text input. A leader line can be added to the notes. I-DEAS allows for changes to the attributes of the note text. After entering the note text, Select the Appearance icon, then pick the note you want to change to open the "Product & Manufacturing Information" menu as below.

**Product & Manufacturing Information**

Color    [YELLOW]    [?]    [Text Values...]
Boxed    [xx.xx □]           [Units/Decimal Places...]
Leader Elbow    [□]
Arrows    [□]              [Symbols...]
Reference Symbol    [xx.xx □]    [Extensions/Leaders...]
Dimension Layer    [203]    [Color/Layer...]
Dim/GD&T Standard    [ANSI 1982 □]    [Arrowheads...]
Balloon Radius    [9]

☐ GD&T Automatic Syntax Check

[Set As Default]    [Use Defaults]    ☐ Autoscale

[OK] [Apply] [Reset] [Cancel]

## Creating Drawings

Select the "Text Values" button to open the "Text Values" menu as shown below.

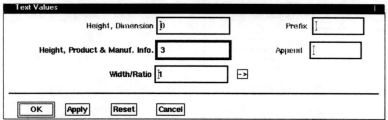

Define the height of the notes and its ratio of width to height. The note text can be slanted by an angle. Figure 15.71 shows notes in various slanted angles.

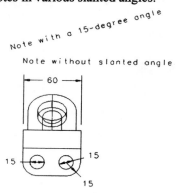

Figure 15.71

  **The procedure for adding notes is (Figure 15.72):**

 1. Select the "Note" icon to open the Note Text dialog box
2. Enter text and define menu parameters as below.

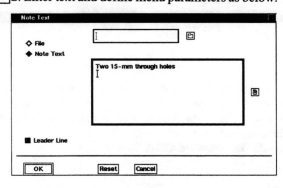

3. Select **OK** to exit the Note Text menu
4. Pick the leader end point location if "Leader" option is used
5. Pick the leader end point
6. The Note Text menu will appear again for adding another note. Select "**OK**" to exit the Note Text menu

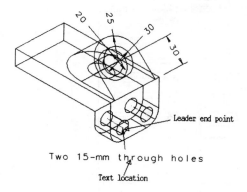

Figure 15.72

## Creating Ballon Annotations

**Follow this procedure to add ballon annotations to the drawing (Figure 15.73):**

1. Select the "Ballon" icon
2. Enter note text to the Note Text menu: enter "Hole A"
3. Select **OK** to exit the Note Text menu
4. Pick a location to place the leader end point
5. Pick a location to place the text

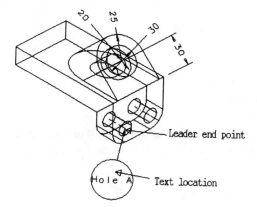

Figure 15.73

It is possible to change the radius of a ballon circle. Use the following procedure to do so (Figure 15.74):

**The procedure for changing the radius of a ballon circle:**

1. Select the Appearance icon
2. Pick the ballon you want to change its size
3. Enter the new radius value to "Ballon Radius" input field as below.

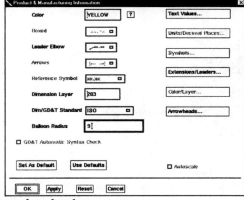

4. Select **OK** to complete the change

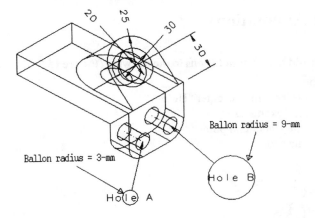

Figure 15.74

## Adding Crosshatch Lines

Crosshatch lines can be added to any selected planar face. The system will prompt "Pick planar face to crosshatch". Figure 15.75 shows crosshatch lines added to a selected planar face.

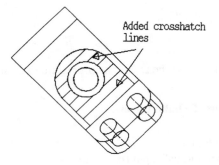

Figure 15.75

You can change the attributes of crosshatch lines.

**Follow this procedure to modify the crosshatch attributes:**

1. Select the Appearance icon
2. Pick at any crosshatch line then press Enter to open Crosshatch Attributes dialog box as below.

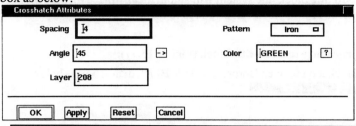

| | |
|---|---|
| **Spacing:** | sets the spacing distance between crosshatch lines. |
| **Angle:** | sets the inclination angle of the crosshatch lines. |
| **Pattern:** | selects the crosshatch pattern. |
| **Color:** | selects the color for crosshatch pattern. |

3. Define the desired value and selection for the crosshatching parameters
4. Select **OK** to change

Figure 15.76 shows an example of crosshatch pattern before and after angle modification.

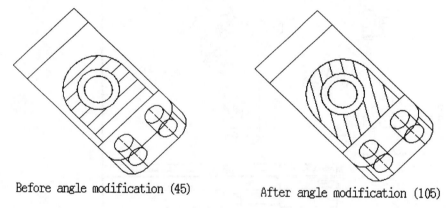

Before angle modification (45)          After angle modification (105)

Figure 15.76a                    Figure 15.76b

# Deleting Dimensions, Notes, and Annotations

Only reference dimensions, notes, and annotations can be deleted from drawing views. Feature dimensions that are required to fully define the part can not be deleted. Feature dimensions are shown in blue and reference dimensions are in yellow. Use the "Delete" command to delete those undesired reference dimensions, notes, and annotations.

# Moving Dimensions, Notes, and Annotations

The "Move" function can be used to move any dimension, note, or annotation to a new location. Dimensions can not be moved to other views in Drafting Setup. I-DEAS allows only moves within the boundary of the view.

# 15.14 Adding Texts and Notes to Title Block

If you use the standard title block, the system will automatically place the title block in the lower-right corner of the drawing sheet. A title block can be added to a drawing sheet.

 **Use the following procedure to add a title block (Figure 15.77):**

1. Select the Title Block icon to open Border and Title Block dialog box as below

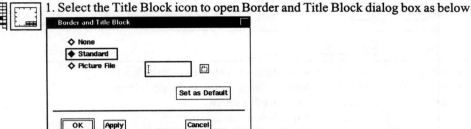

2. Select "Standard" from the list
3. Select **OK**

The title block should be added to the drawing sheet as in Figure 15.77

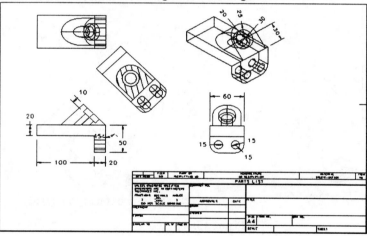

Figure 15.77

You can add notes anywhere in the title block. The procedure for adding notes to the title block is same as adding notes to drawing views. Here we show how to add a text to the title block (Figure 15.78):

  **The procedure for adding text to the title block:**

1. Select the "Note" icon
2. Toggle "Note Text" to On and "Leader Line" to Off
3. Type "Scholars International" to the input field
4. Select **OK** to exit Note menu
5. Click the right mouse button to open an options list
6. Select Attributes to open "Dimensions/Notes/GD&T" menu
7. Select the "Text Values" button to open "Text Values" menu
8. Change "Height,Notes" to 3.5

9. Select **OK → OK**

10. Pick a text location in the title block to place this note as shown in Figure 15.78

11. Repeat the above procedure until other notes are added

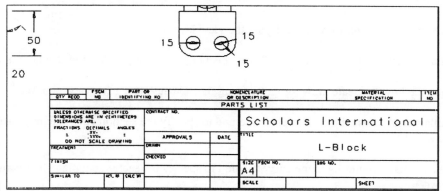

Figure 15.78

After a note is placed in a location, we can use the "Move Entities" function to move it to a new location.

# 15.15   Creating drawing views for assemblies

An assembly is treated as a part model in I-DEAS to create various drawing views. The procedure for creating drawing views for assemblies is the same as those for part model. The assembly needs to be available in the bench to bring into the Drawing Setup program.

# Chapter 15. Review Questions

1.   Give the drawing sheet sizes for the following ISO formats:

A0
A1
A2
A3
A4

2.   Give the drawing sheet sizes for the following ANSI formats:

A
B
C
D
E

3. What are the five drawing view types that can be created using I-DEAS?

4. List the two ways to access the parts for creating drawings and briefly describe how for each method.

5. What are the two options in specifying the view layout?

6. What is the predefined view layout? How many options you can have in this layout options?

7. Describe how to create drawing views using the "Create/place each view" option.

8. Explain how to use the cutting plane method to specify the section cut plane in creating section views.

9. When to use the cutting plane curve method to specify the section cut plane in creating section views.

10. Explain how the two options "solid" and "plane only" of the "Result" parameter affect the section views.

11. What is a detail view?

12. What is an auxiliary view?

13. Explain the procedure for creating an auxiliary view.

14. What command can you use to move a drawing view?

15. Explain how to align drawing views.

16. Explain when to use "Align X" in aligning views.

17. Explain when to use "Align Y" in aligning views.

18. What are feature dimensions?

19. What are reference dimensions?

20. List the five dimensioning functions.

21. List the procedure for adding a note.

22. What are the three styles of showing hidden lines?

23. Explain how to modify dimension values in the Drawing Setup mode.

# Chapter

16

# Simulation Application

---

## Highlights of the Chapter

- Modeling processes for finite element analysis and finite element modeling
- Understanding Simulation Application and its tasks
- Introducing I-DEAS finite element types
- Creating finite element models
- Performing finite element analysis
- Reviewing finite element results

---

## Overview

The intent of this chapter is to provide an overview of finite element analysis using I-DEAS. The finite element modeling concept is introduced. Individual tasks involved with I-DEAS finite element analysis are briefly described. Six projects related to stress analysis are presented to provide an overview and practice of the modeling and analysis processes in I-DEAS. It consists of creating meshes, assigning material properties, applying restraints and loads, performing analysis, and reviewing results. Step-by-step tutorials are provided to guide you through the modeling and analysis processes.

## 16.1 Introduction

Finite Element Analysis (FEA) is a mechanical design engineering process which can, but is not limited to, calculate deflection and stress on a structure. Finite element modeling (FEM) is a modeling method, which divides the structure into a set of "elements" to form a model for finite element analysis. I-DEAS' finite element analysis software is packaged in the Simulation Application and it provides comprehensive capabilities for building finite element models and examining the results. Figure 16.1 shows the fifteen tasks available under Simulation Application.

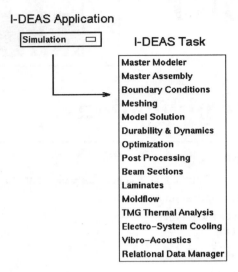

Figure 16.1 I-DEAS Application

In general, finite element modeling consists of three phrases, as shown in Figure 16.2.

Figure 16.2 Phases of finite element modeling

## Pre-processing Phase

This phase includes creating a geometric part, describing material properties, applying boundary conditions and loads, and building a finite element model that divides the part into elements and nodes.

## Solution Phase

The solution phase calculates displacements, strains, and stress that result from the loads and restraints applied to the model. It can be performed either inside I-DEAS Simulation Application, or in an external FEA solver such as NASTRAN, ANSYS, or ABAQUS.

## Post-processing Phase

This phase includes the graphical representations of structural deflection and stress, and the comparison of failure criteria required for the design.

Mastering I-DEAS
Scholars International Publishing Corp., 1999

# 16.2 I-DEAS Simulation Application

There are **five** essential tasks in the Simulation Application used for pre-processing, solution and post-processing. These tasks are categorized into three standard FEA phases and briefly described in Table 16.1.

## Table 16.1 Simulation Tasks

| FEA Phase | Task | Description |
|---|---|---|
| Pre-processing | Master Modeler | Create geometry. |
| | Boundary Conditions | Apply the loads and restraints. |
| | Meshing | Enter material and physical properties, and create finite element nodes and elements |
| Solution | Model Solution | Solve the FEA model and provide the solutions |
| Post-processing | Post Processing | Display the solutions and results |

### Master Model task

Part geometry is created during the Master Modeler task. Finite element models can be created from the parts in the Master Modeler task. These models are stored as parts in the same bins in the model files. A finite element model is associated with a part. If a part is modified, its finite element models can be updated to reflect the changes. If the part is deleted, all the associated drawings and finite element models are also deleted. Before switching to another task, the part must be named using the Name Parts icon command (Figure 16.3).

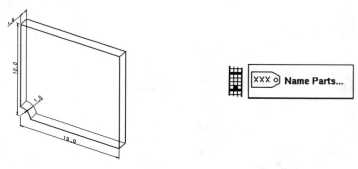

Figure 16.3

### Boundary Conditions task

Boundary conditions are the restraints, loading, and other external effects applied to a model. The boundary conditions that are used in I-DEAS allow any, or all of the six degrees of freedom to be removed. These six degrees of freedom include three translations and three rotations along the X, Y, and Z axis. Removing a degree of freedom means restricting the node or surface from moving in that direction. In addition, a boundary condition can be set up to enforce a displacement at a node.

# Simulation Application

After switching to the Boundary Conditions task, the first thing to do is to create a new finite element model with a given name. This is done by selecting the "Create FE Model" icon command as shown in Figure 16.4 in the Boundary Conditions task. The command will bring up a FE Model Create form to allow you to define a FE Model name.

 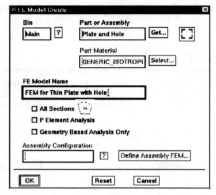

Figure 16.4

Loads and restraints on the finite element model can be applied in the Boundary Conditions task. **Concentrated loads** and **distributed loads** are commonly used in structural analysis. In general, loads can be applied to a **node**, an **edge**, or a **surface**. **Displacement** and **rotation constraints** are generally applied on boundary nodes. The following three icon commands are often used in this task.

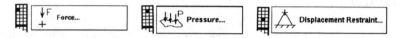

Figure 16.5 shows the boundary conditions applied including two surface displacement restraints and a surface pressure. Detail of the procedure applying these boundary conditions will be illustrated in project 3 in this chapter.

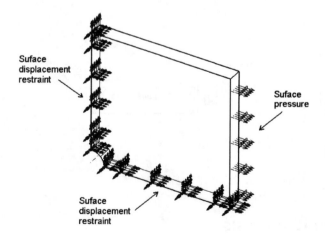

Figure 16.5

After applying the boundary conditions, a **Boundary Condition Case Set** containing a set of restraints and loads should be defined. The following Boundary Condition icon command will bring up a Boundary Condition Set Management form and let you define the load set. Note that more than one boundary condition case set can be created and used for different kinds of boundary conditions. In addition, it is important to save your file before switching to Meshing or Model Solution task.

16-4

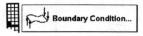

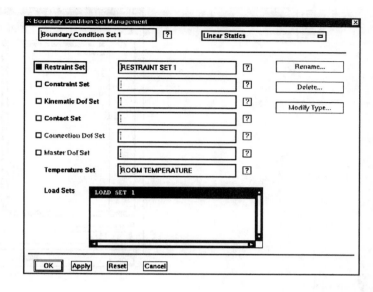

Figure 16.6

## Meshing task

Nodes and elements can be created in the Meshing task. Before generating a finite element model, less significant features can be suppressed to reduce the elements and solution time. Material, physical and cross section property tables should be defined before applying automatic meshing. Each element contains a material property ID that refers to a table of material properties. These material properties can be **isotropic**, **orthotropic**, or **anisotropic**. If not specified, the system will assign the default steel properties to the element. Physical properties includes element thickness and beam cross-section properties. Table 16.2 summarizes element types and their associated properties. More information details regarding these three element types will be shown in section 16.3. Figure 16.7 shows the Material icon command and the associated pop-up used for defining the material properties.

## Table 16.2 Element Types and Properties

| Element Type | Material Property | Physical Property | Cross Section Property |
| --- | --- | --- | --- |
| Thin-shell | Yes | Yes | No |
| Solid | Yes | No | No |
| Beam | Yes | Yes | Yes |

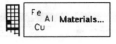

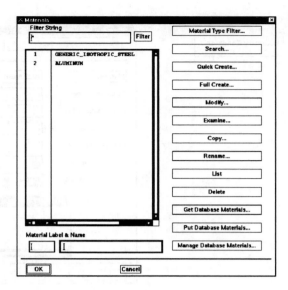

Figure 16.7

Figure 16.8 shows the Physical Property icon command and the associated pop-up for defining the physical properties.

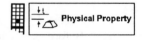

| Lumped Mass |
| Spring |
| Damper |
| Gap |
| Interface |
| Axisymmetric Interface |
| Rigid Surface |
| Axisymm Rigid Surface |
| Constraint |
| Rigid |
| Rod |
| Beam |
| Pipe |
| Plastic |
| Plane Stress |
| Plane Strain |
| Axisymmetric Solid |
| Thin Shell |
| Membrane |
| Plate |
| Axisymmetric Shell |
| Thick Shell |
| Solid |

Figure 16.8

There are **three ways** to generate a finite element mesh: **manual creation, shell mesh** and **solid mesh**. Manual creation does not need an existing part. The other two methods require an existing part with a given name. Manual meshing creates nodes by keying in their coordinates or generating by copying, reflecting, or generating nodes between two sets of existing nodes. Elements can be created by picking nodes or by generating elements from existing elements. This method will be used in the first project of this chapter.

Mastering I-DEAS
Scholars International Publishing Corp., 1999

Automatic meshing is a preferred method for creating nodes and elements. For example, beam elements can be generated on part edges, thin-shell elements on part surfaces, and solid elements on part volumes. Project 3 illustrates the generation of solid elements, project 4 shows the process involved with mesh refinements, project 5 uses two-dimensional thin-shell elements, and project 6 includes two-dimensional plane-stress elements.

There are several ways to generate a mesh using automatic meshing commands. Among those, Define Shell Mesh and Define Solid Mesh commands are commonly used in this task. The element type, element length and material should be specified in the Define Mesh pop-up form before you can preview the mesh. If you are not satisfied with the mesh, you can adjust the parameters in the same form. Select the Keep Mesh button to keep the mesh. Figure 16.9 illustrates the processes to select the icon commands, adjust the parameters in the associated pop-up and show the generated mesh.

Icon command          Pop-up form          Generated mesh

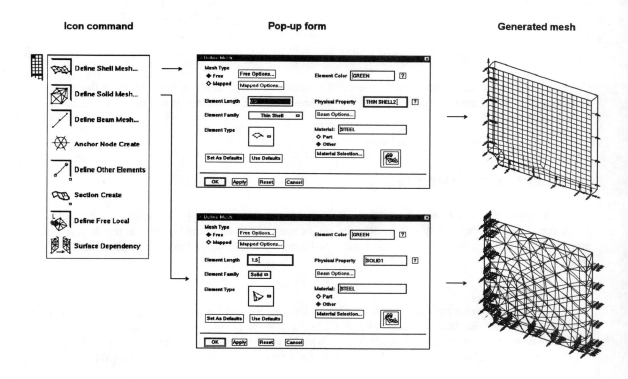

Figure 16.9

Again, saving the finite element model is recommended before switching to the Boundary Condition task or Model Solution task. Note that the saved finite element model is associated with the part, and more than one finite element model (mesh) can be created for a single part.

## Model Solution task

Before the finite element model is solved in this task, a Solution Set defining a requested output such as deflections and stresses should be created. This can be done by selecting the "Solution Set..." icon command to create a solution set with a given name and boundary condition set.

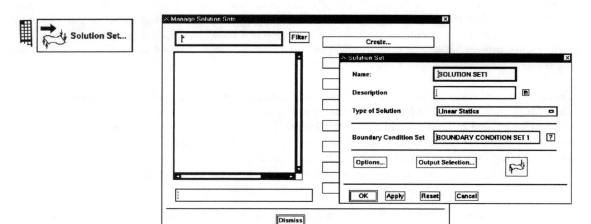

Figure 16.10

Once the solution set is defined, you can select the following Solve icon command to solve the model. Depending on the complexity of the model and the speed of your computer, it will take a while before the answer is solved.

## Post Processing task

This task employs **display**, **shade**, **contour**, and **color** to present the output from a Solution Set defined and solved in the Model Solution task. Results can be viewed and examined to help in the design process through the following three commonly used commands: **Result**, **Display Template**, and **Display**.

### Result

The Result command allows you to choose Display Results for selected stress and Deformation Results for displacement options (Figure 16.11). In the Display Results, you can select the Component option for the stress such as Von Mises, Maximum Principal, Minimum Principal, etc. In the Deformation Results, you can choose the Component option for Magnitude, etc.

Figure 16.11

16-8

## Display Template

The Display Template controls how results will be displayed (Figure 16.12). For example, you can adjust the stress contour display either in Smooth Shaded or in Stepped Shaded mode.

 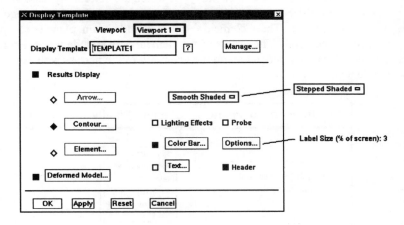

Figure 16.12

## Display

The Display command will display the FEA result defined in Display Template. For example, Figure 16.13 displays the Von Mises stress in a Stepped Shaded mode.

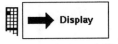 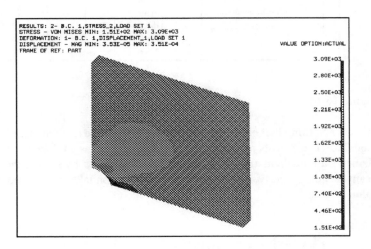

Figure 16.13

# 16.3 I-DEAS Element Types

I-DEAS provides element types which are commonly used in structural analysis. As shown in Figure 16.14, three icon commands are illustrated to define three categories of mesh such as shell, solid, and beam element. These element families include beam, plane stress, plane strain, axisymmetric solid, thin shell, and solid. The orders of the element type include linear, parabolic and cubic. The choice of elements is largely dependent on the geometry of the part, as well as the nature of the analysis to be conducted.

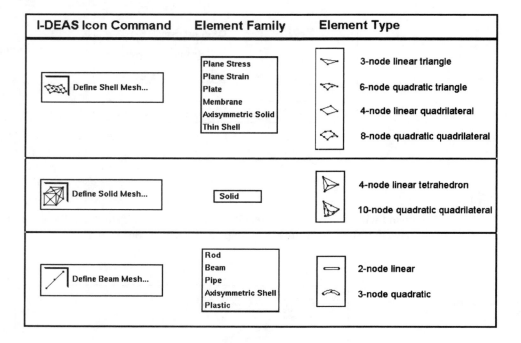

Figure 16.14

In I-DEAS, thin-shell elements and beam elements are mathematically simplified from a 3D physical model to 2D elements by storing the third dimension as a thickness on a physical property table. Beam elements are mathematically simplified to 1D elements by storing the 2D cross-section as a separate beam section property. Each level of simplification takes more preparation time, but reduces the solution time.

## Thin-shell elements

Use shell elements for thin-walled parts. Use these elements to analyze a general two-dimensional model. In addition to thin-shell elements, there are also other two-dimensional elements, such as plane stress, plane strain, and axisymmetric elements. Plane stress is a condition of stress where the out-of-plane stress is zero. Plane strain is a condition of strain where the out-of-plane strain is zero. An axisymmetric element is a two-dimensional element used for problems with axis symmetry. With these two-dimensional elements, you are required to enter a proper physical property to define the thickness.

Mastering I-DEAS
Scholars International Publishing Corp., 1999

## Solid elements

Use solid elements for complex and thick parts. Solid elements are the easiest to create. You don't need to add information with a physical property table. Solid elements give a complete picture of the 3D stress through the part. As a result, it takes longer to solve for the solution.

## Beam elements

Beam elements can be used for finding the deflection in a long, slender beam or truss-type structure. You must define the cross section properties in order to solve for the result.

# 16.4 FEA Projects

This section presents the step-by-step tutorials to create finite element models and perform finite element analysis. The first project determines the nodal displacements and element stresses for a thin plate subject to a uniform tensile traction. The second project uses the finite element model created in project 1 and applies a concentrated load at one free-end. Projects three to six are classical problems in which a thin plate with a small center hole subjected to a uniform tensile traction is analyzed. The major differences among these four projects include project three uses 3-D solid elements, project four involves local mesh refinements, project five applies 2-D thin-shell elements, and project six utilizes 2-D plane stress elements.

# Project 1.
# Uniform Tensile Traction

For a thin aluminum plate subjected to a uniform tensile traction of 1000 lb.shown in Figure 16.15, determine the nodal displacement and element stresses. The plate has the following physical and material properties:

> Plate thickness (t) = 0.5 in
> Young's modulus (E) = 10E06 psi
> Poisson's ratio ($\upsilon$) = 0.30

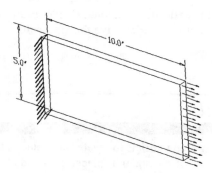

Figure 16.15 Thin plate subjected to a uniform tensile traction

Use the manual method to create the mesh for the finite element model. The plate is discretized into 50 4-node quadrilateral elements, as shown in Figure 16.16.

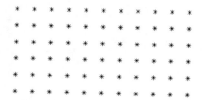

Figure 16.16 Discretized plate

To reduce the stress concentration at the corner, the tensile traction can be converted into nodal forces as follows (Figure 16.17):

> F1 = T A1 = 1000 psi ( (0.5 in ( 0.5 in.) = 250 lb
> F2 = T A2 = 1000 psi ( (1.0 in ( 0.5 in.) = 500 lb

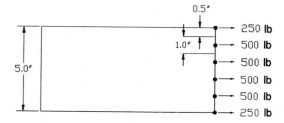

Figure 16.17

After applying the material and physical properties, the model will be solved for the displacements and stresses. And the results will be displayed and examined.

Mastering I-DEAS
Scholars International Publishing Corp., 1999

# Simulation Application

**Step 1.** **Set your I-DEAS Start menu as:**

| | |
|---|---|
| Project Name: | **Your initials (or your account name)** |
| Model file name: | **Project1** |
| Application: | **Simulation** |
| Task: | **Meshing** |

**Step 2.** **Set the unit to inch(pound f).**
Select **Options (pull-down menu) → Units → inch(pound f)**

**Step 3.** **Create a name for the finite element model.**
Select the "**Create FE Model**" icon,
  and enter "**Thin Plate with Traction**" for the FEM Model Name.

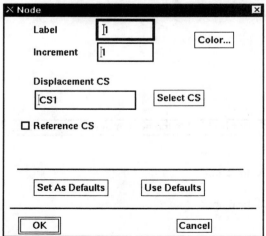

Select **OK** to exit the form.
Select **OK** again to create the new part.

**Step 4.** **Create the first node**
Select the "**Node**" icon, and select **OK** to use the default in the following form.

Enter the node 1 location
Enter **X,Y,Z (0,0,0)**: Press **MMB** to accept the value
Enter the node 2 location
Enter **X,Y,Z (0,0,0)**: Press **MMB** to terminate the Node Command.

The node created is shown in Figure 16.8.

✳

Figure 16.18

**Step 5.   Copy nodes in the Y direction**

 Select the "**Copy**" icon.
Pick **Nodes**: Pick the node just created
Pick **Nodes** (Done): Press **MMB**
Enter number of copies (1): **5**
Enter node start label,inc (**2,1**): Press **MMB**
Enter delta X,Y,Z (0.0,0.0,0.0): **0,1,0**
OK to keep these additions? (**Yes**): Press **MMB**

Adjust your windows to see all the nodes as shown in Figure 16.19.

✳
✳
✳
✳
✳
✳

Figure 16.19

| **Note:** | the Dynamic Navigator highlights the **node number** as you move the mouse across the nodes. |

**Step 6.   Copy nodes in the X direction**
Select the "**Copy**" icon.
Pick Nodes: Pick all the **6** nodes

Mastering I-DEAS
Scholars International Publishing Corp., 1999

| Note: | Drag a rectangular box to include all the nodes. |
|-------|---------------------------------------------------|

Pick Nodes (Done): Press **MMB**
Enter number of copies (1): **10**
Enter node start label,inc (7,1): Press **MMB**
Enter delta X,Y,X (0.0,0.0,0.0): **1,0,0**
OK to keep these additions? (Yes): Press **MMB**

Adjust your windows (**Zoom All**) to see all the nodes as shown in Figure 16.20.

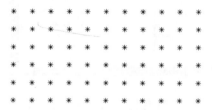

Figure 16.20

### Step 7.   Create a Material Property table for the elements

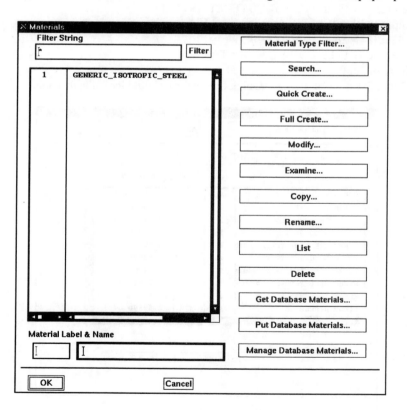

Select the "**Materials...**" icon and the following Materials form pops up.

# Simulation Application

Select the **"Quick Create..."** button in the form and the following Quick Create form pops up.

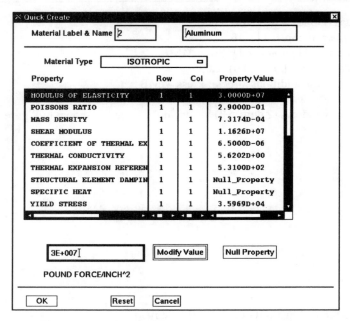

Enter the Material Name field: **Aluminum**
Choose the Property field: **MODULUS OF ELASTICITY**
Enter the Input field: **10E6**
Click the **"Modify Value"** button
Choose the Property field: **POISSONS RATIO**
Enter the Input field: **0.3**
Click the **"Modify Value"** button, the Quick Create form should look like this one:

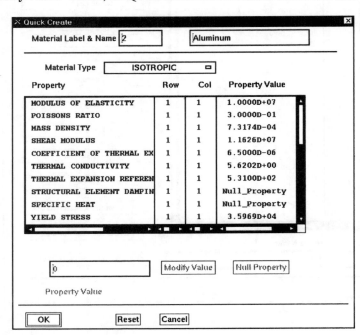

# Simulation Application

Select **OK** to exit the "Quick Create..." form.
Select **OK** to exit the "Materials..." form.
Now the aluminum properties have been properly created.

**Step 8. Create A Physical Property table for the elements**

Select the "**Physical Property**" icon.
Select an element family for properties (Thin_Shell): Press **MMB**
Enter physical prop name or no. (1-Thin Shell1): Press **MMB**
OK to use default values to create table? (Yes): Select **NO**
Enter property name or no.: Select **DIRECTORY**
Enter property name or no.: Select **TK_THICHNESS(4V)**
Enter 1st value for thickness (0.03937...): Enter **0.5**
Enter 2nd value for thickness (0.0): Enter **0.5** (or Press MMB)
Enter 3rd value for thickness (0.0): Enter **0.5** (or Press MMB)
Enter 4th value for thickness (0.0: Enter **0.5** (or Press MMB)
Enter property name or no.: Press **MMB**

**Step 9. Create the first quadrilateral thin-shell element**

Select the "**Element**" icon and the following Element form pops-up.

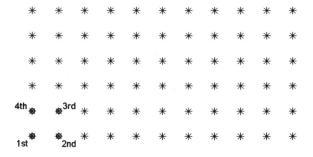

Toggle the "**Other**" option on in the form
Click the "**Material Selection...**" button, choose **ALUMINUM**,
and select **OK** to exit the selection.
Select **OK** to exit the form.
Pick Nodes: Pick the 1st node in Figure 16.21.
Pick Nodes (Done): Shift + Pick the 2nd node
Pick Nodes (Done): Shift + Pick the 3rd node
Pick Nodes (Done): Shift + Pick the 4th node
Pick Nodes: Press **MMB**

Figure 16.21

The element created is shown in Figure 16.22.

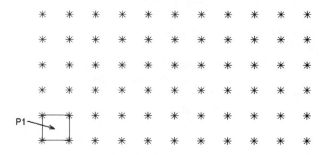

Figure 16.22

**Step 10. Create the rest of quadrilateral thin-shell elements using Copy command**

Select the "**Copy to Existing Nodes**" icon.
Pick Elements: Pick the first element (Pick **P1** in Figure 16.22)
Pick Elements (Done): Press **MMB**
Enter number of copies (1): **4**
Enter a new element start label, inc (2,1): Press **MMB**
Enter node increment between copies: **1**
OK to keep these additions? (Yes): Press **MMB**
The created elements are shown in Figure 16.23

Figure 16.23

**Step 11. Now, we are going to copy these five elements in the X direction.**

Select the "**Copy to Existing Nodes**" icon again.
Pick Elements: Pick all the five elements
 (drag a rectangular box to include all the elements)
Pick Elements (Done): Press **MMB**
Enter number of copies (1): **9**
Enter new element start label, inc (6,1): Press **MMB**
Enter node increment between copies: **6**
OK to keep these additions? (Yes): Press **MMB**

16-18

# Simulation Application

The created elements are shown in Figure 16.24

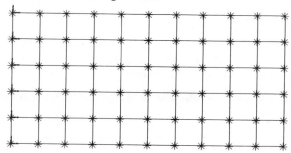

Figure 16.24

Save your file.

## Step 12. Apply the restraints

Switch to the **Boundary Condition** task.

Select the "**Displacement Restraint...**" icon
Pick entities: Pick all the six nodes on the left end.
Pick entities (Done): Press **MMB** and the following form pops up

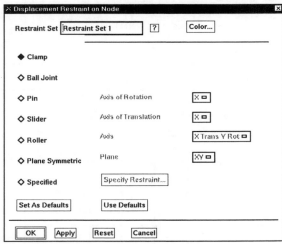

Select **OK** to accept the default "Clamp" option.

The added boundary restraints are shown in Figure 16.25.

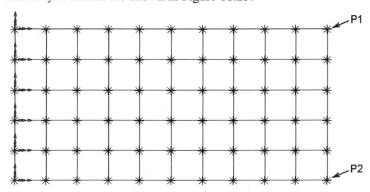

Figure 16.25

## Step 13. Apply the loads

Select the "**Force...**" icon
Pick entities: Pick the top node on the right end. (**P1** in Figure 16.25)
Pick entities (Done): Pick the bottom node on the right end. (**P2** in Figure 16.25)
Pick entities (Done): Press **MMB** and the following form pops up

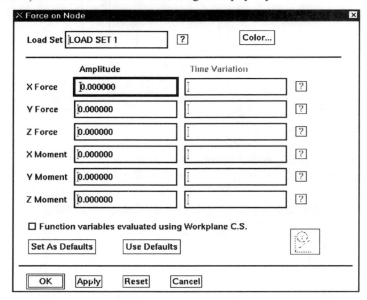

Adjust the X-Force field to **250.00** and select OK. The added forces are shown in Figure 16.26.

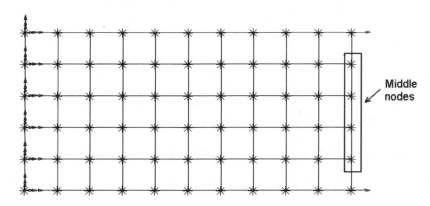

Figure 16.26

## Step 14. Repeat the same process to apply 500lb force on the middle nodes.

Select the "**Force...**" icon
Pick entities: Pick the four middle nodes on the right end.
Pick entities (Done): Press **MMB**

Adjust the X-Force field to **500.00** and select **OK**.
The added forces are shown in Figure 16.27.

Mastering I-DEAS
Scholars International Publishing Corp., 1999

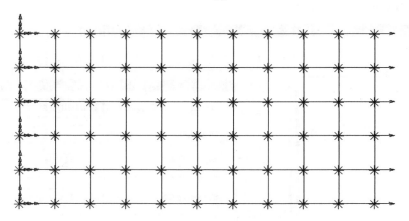

Figure 16.27

**Step 15. Create a boundary condition set for the restraints and forces you just applied.**

Select the "**Boundary Condition...**" icon
In the pop-up, toggle the Restraint Set option **on**, and highlight the **LOAD SET 1**.
The adjusted form is shown here.

Select **OK** to exit the form.
Save your model.

**Step 16. Create a solution set and solve the model**
Switch to the **Model Solution** task.

Select the "**Solution Set...**" icon
In the pop-up, select the **Create...** button.
In the new Solution Set pop-up, select **OK** to accept the default.

# Simulation Application

Select **Dismiss** to exit the "Solution Sets" form.

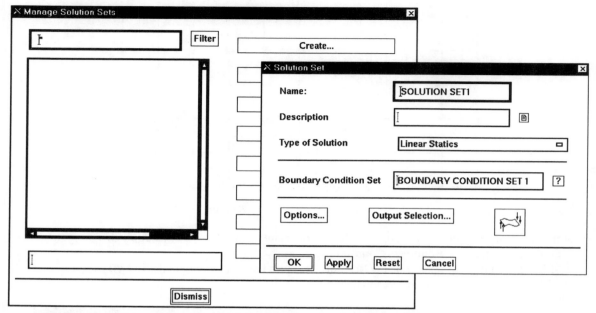

 Select the "**Solve**" icon to solve the model.

**Step 17. Display the results**

Switch to the **Post Processing** task.

Select the "**Display**" icon
Pick elements: Press **RMB** and choose **All**
Pick elements (Done): Press **MMB**

The Von-Mises stress contour is displayed as follow.

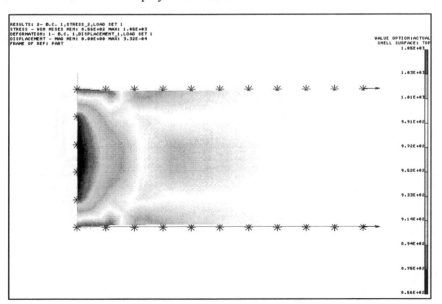

Figure 16.28

# Simulation Application

Select the "**Display Template...**" icon and adjust the following two items.

Change Smooth Shaded to **Stepped Shade**

Select **Options...**, and change Label Size (% of screen) to **3.**

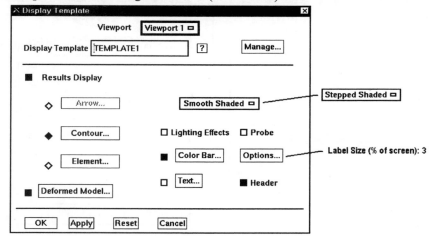

Select **OK** to exit the settings

Select the "**Display**" icon again

Pick elements: Press **RMB** and choose **All**

Pick elements (Done): Press **MMB**

The stress contour is displayed as follows.

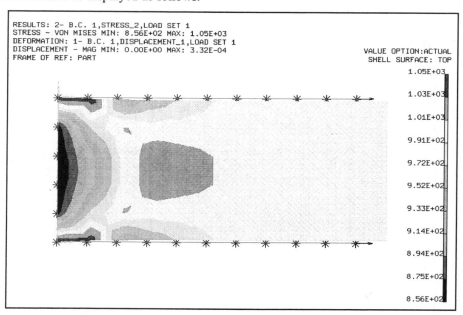

```
RESULTS: 2- B.C. 1,STRESS_2,LOAD SET 1
STRESS - VON MISES MIN: 8.56E+02 MAX: 1.05E+03
DEFORMATION: 1- B.C. 1,DISPLACEMENT_1,LOAD SET 1
DISPLACEMENT - MAG MIN: 0.00E+00 MAX: 3.32E-04
FRAME OF REF: PART
```

```
VALUE OPTION:ACTUAL
SHELL SURFACE: TOP

1.05E+03
1.03E+03
1.01E+03
9.91E+02
9.72E+02
9.52E+02
9.33E+02
9.14E+02
8.94E+02
8.75E+02
8.56E+02
```

Figure 16.29

Select the "**Display Filter...**" icon

Pick the "**FE Model...**" button in the form

Pick the "**All On/Off**" button to toggle all the options off in the FEM Display Filter form

# Simulation Application

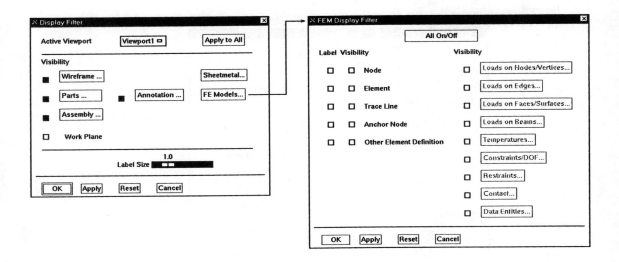

Select **OK** twice to exit the forms
Select the "**Display**" icon again
Pick elements: Press **RMB** and choose **All**
Pick elements (Done): Press **MMB**
The stress contour is displayed as follows.

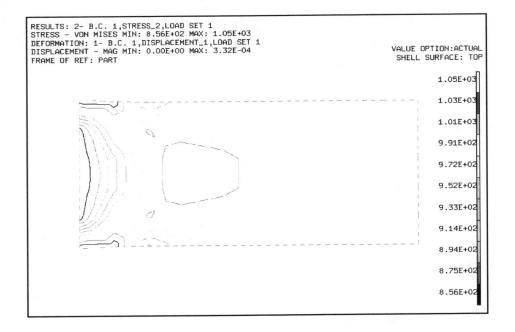

```
RESULTS: 2- B.C. 1,STRESS_2,LOAD SET 1
STRESS - VON MISES MIN: 8.56E+02 MAX: 1.05E+03
DEFORMATION: 1- B.C. 1,DISPLACEMENT_1,LOAD SET 1
DISPLACEMENT - MAG MIN: 0.00E+00 MAX: 3.32E-04
FRAME OF REF: PART
```

VALUE OPTION:ACTUAL
SHELL SURFACE: TOP

| |
|---|
| 1.05E+03 |
| 1.03E+03 |
| 1.01E+03 |
| 9.91E+02 |
| 9.72E+02 |
| 9.52E+02 |
| 9.33E+02 |
| 9.14E+02 |
| 8.94E+02 |
| 8.75E+02 |
| 8.56E+02 |

Figure 16.30

Save the model. You can proceed to Project 2 at this moment. Otherwise, exit I-DEAS.

# Project 2.
# Apply a Concentrated Load

For the finite element model used in Project 1, we now want to apply a concentrated vertical load of 1200lb at the right side (Figure 16.31), and determine the nodal displacement and maximum element stress.

Set the physical property of the plate t = 0.5 in, and the material property E = 10E06 psi, and $\upsilon$ = 0.30.

1200 lb

Figure 16.31 Example of cantilever beam modeled using thin plate elements

We will use the same finite element model and restraint set created in Project 1. Create a new load set (LOAD SET 2) of 200lb on each of the six nodes at the right edge (Figure 16.32). Then, create a new boundary condition set (BOUNDARY CONDITION SET 2) and a new solution set (SELUTION SET 2) and review the result in Display task.

200 lb
200 lb
200 lb
200 lb
200 lb
200 lb

Figure 16.32 Applied 200lb forces at the right edge

**Step 1. Retrieve Project 1 by setting your I-DEAS Start menu as:**

| | |
|---|---|
| Project Name: | **Your initials (or your account name)** |
| Model file name: | **Project1** |
| Application: | **Simulation** |
| Task: | **Boundary Conditions** |

**Step 2. Apply 200lb forces on the six nodes**

Select the "**Force...**" icon

Pick entities: Drag a rectangular box to pick all the six nodes on the right edge

Pick entities (Done): Press **MMB** and the following form pops up

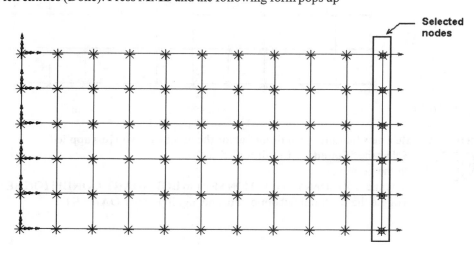

Selected nodes

Figure 16.33

# Simulation Application

In the pop-up form, change

        Load Set: **LOAD SET 2**

        Y Force: **-200.00**

Select **OK** to exit the form

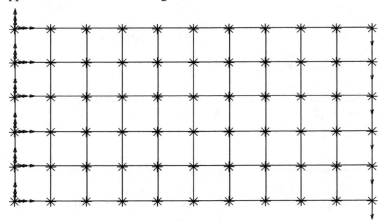

The new applied loads are shown in Figure 16.34.

Figure 16.34

**Step 3.  Create a new boundary condition set for the new forces you just applied.**

 Select the "**Boundary Condition…**" icon

    In the pop-up,

      change BOUNDARY CONDITION SET 1 to **BOUNDARY CONDITION SET 2**.

    Toggle the Restraint Set option **on**, and highlight the **LOAD SET 2**.

# Simulation Application

The adjusted form is shown as follows.

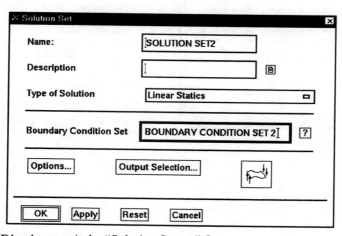

Select **OK** to exit the form.

Save your model.

**Step 4.  Create a new solution set and solve the model**

Switch to the **Model Solution** task.

 Select the "**Solution Set...**" icon

In the pop-up, select the **Create**... button.

In the Solution Set pop-up, select the boxed question mark **?**,
and choose **BOUNDARY CONDTION SET 2**.

Select **OK** to exit the "Solution Set" form.

Select **Dismiss** to exit the "Solution Sets..." form.

 Select the "**Solve**" icon to solve the model.

Select **OK** in the Solve form to accept default settings.

### Step 5. Display the results

Switch to the **Post Processing** task.

> **Note:** There are two solution sets for this finite element model. Follow these procedures to choose the proper set.

 Select the "**Result...**" icon to activate the following form.

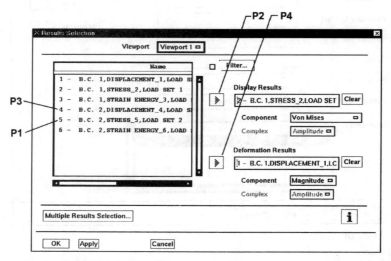

To see the result from LOAD SET 2, follow the pick points P1, P2, P3 and P4 in the form to adjust the result setting.

The adjusted result is shown as follows:

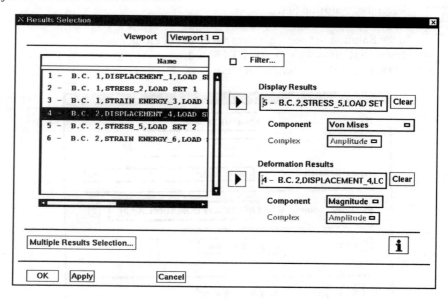

Select **OK** to exit the form.

 Select the "**Display**" icon
Pick elements: Press **RMB** and choose **All**
Pick elements (Done): Press **MMB**

# Simulation Application

The stepped-shaded Von-Mises stress contour is displayed as follows.

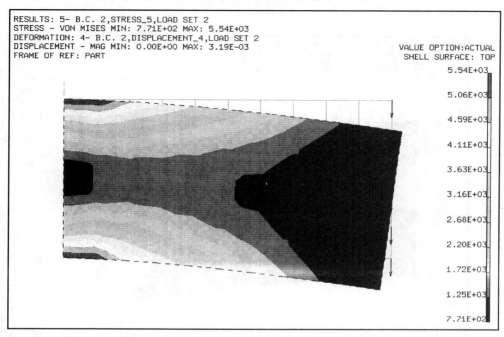

Figure 16.35

 To display the principal stress, Select the "**Result...**" icon
and adjust the Component option to the following settings.

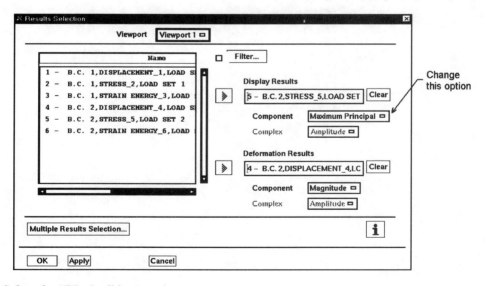

 Select the "**Display**" icon again
Pick elements: Press **RMB** and choose **All**
Pick elements (Done): Press **MMB**

# Simulation Application

The stepped-shaded max principal stress contour is displayed as follows.

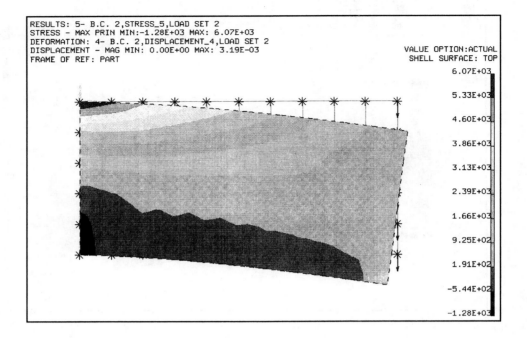

Figure 16.36

Save the model and exit I-DEAS.

# Project 3.
# Thin Plate with Hole

For a thin steel plate with a small center hole subjected to a uniform tensile traction of 1000 lb. shown in Figure 16.37, determine the max. principal stresses. The plate thickness t = 1.0 in. (physical property), E = 30E06 psi, and υ = 0.25 (material property).

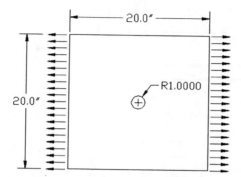

Figure 16.37 A thin plate with a hole

This model illustrates the commands for automatic solid meshing, how to apply surface pressure load and symmetric boundary restraints to the edges. Although we can model the whole plate, one-fourth of the plate could be used as a result of symmetry. The model is shown in Figure 16.38.

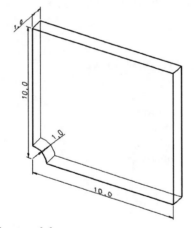

Figure 16.38 One-fourth plate model

**Step 1.   Set your I-DEAS Start menu as:**

Project Name:          **Your initials (or your account name)**
Model file name:       **Project3**
Application:            **Simulation**
Task:                  **Master Modeler**

**Step 2.   Set the unit to inch(pound f).**

**Step 3.   Create the part and the FE Model.**
Create the part as shown in Figure 16.38

Select the **Name Parts** icon
Enter "**Thin Plate with Hole**" for the part name.
Switch to the **Meshing** task
Select the "**Create FE Model**" icon,
and enter "**FEM for Thin Plate with Hole**" for the FEM Model Name.

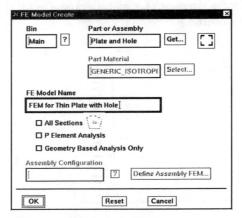

**Step 4.  Create a Material Property table for the elements**

Select the "**Materials...**" icon to bring following Materials form up.
Select the "**Quick Create...**" button in the form to bring Quick Create form up.

In the Material Name field: type **Steel**
In the Property field: Choose **MODULUS OF ELASTICITY**
In the Input field: Enter **30E6**
Click the "**Modify Value**" button

Again, in the Property field: Choose **POISSONS RATIO**
In the Input field: Enter **0.3**
Click the "**Modify Value**" button
Select **OK** to exit the "Quick Create..." form.
Select **OK** to exit the "Materials..." form.

Now the Steel properties have been properly created.

Save your model here.

**Step 5.  Apply the restraints**

Switch to the **Boundary Conditions** task.
Select the "**Displacement Restraint...**" icon
Pick entities: Pick the surface at the left end.

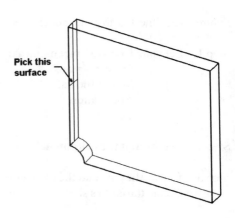

**Pick this surface**

Figure 16.39

Figure 16.39

Pick entities (Done): Press **MMB** and the following form pops up
Adjust the following two translation restraints in form as shown in the following:

Y Translation → Free
Z Translation → Free

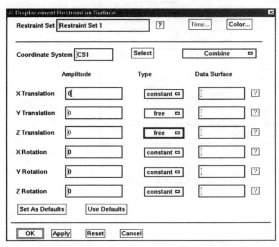

Select **OK** to exit the settings.

The added boundary restraints are shown in Figure 16.40.

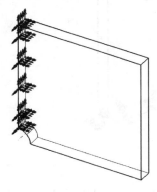

Figure 16.40

Select the "**Displacement Restraint...**" icon again
Pick entities: Pick the button surface
Pick entities (Done): Press **MMB** to bring the following Displacement Restraint form up
Adjust the following two translation restraints in the form:

X Translation → Free
Z Translation → Free

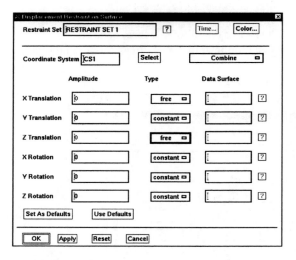

Select **OK** to exit the settings.
The added boundary restraints are shown in Figure 16.41.

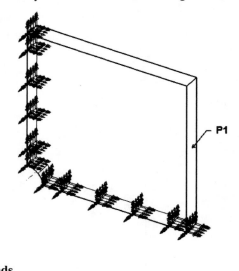

Figure 16.41

**Step 6. Apply the loads**

 Select the "**Pressure...**" icon
Pick Surfaces: Pick the surface on the right end (**P1** in Figure 16.41).
Pick Surfaces (Done): Press **MMB**

In the following form, adjust Pressure = **-1000**

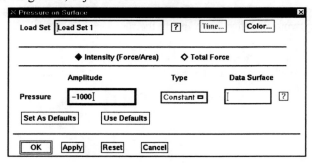

# Simulation Application

Select **OK** and the added forces are shown in Figure 16.42.

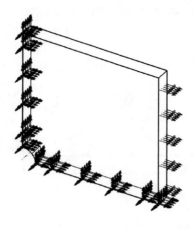

Figure 16.42

**Step 7. Create a boundary condition set for the restraints and loads you just applied.**

 Select the **Boundary Conditions** icon

In the pop-up, toggle the Restraint Set option **on**, and highlight the **LOAD SET 1**. The adjusted form is shown as follows.

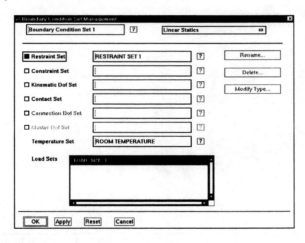

Select **OK** to exit the form.

Save your model.

**Step 8. Create the finite element model**

Switch to the **Meshing** task.

 Select the **"Define Solid Mesh..."** icon.
Pick Volumes: Pick any place on the part
Pick Volumes (Done): Press **MMB**

In the following pop-up, select **Other** → **Material Selection...** → select '**2    Steel**' → **OK**
Adjust element length = **1.5**.

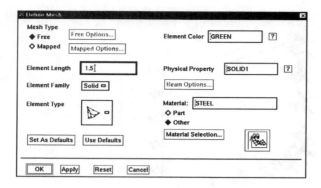

Select the **Preview** button to preview the meshes as follow.

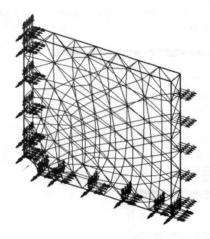

Figure 16.43

**Note:** If you are not satisfied with the meshes, you can adjust other parameters in the pop-up.

Select the **Keep Mesh** button to keep the meshes.

Save your model here.

**Step 9.  Create a solution set and solve the model**
Switch to the **Model Solution** task.

Select the "**Solution Set...**" icon
In the pop-up, select the **Create...** button.
In the new Solution Set pop-up, select **OK** to accept the default.

Mastering  I-DEAS
Scholars International Publishing Corp., 1999

# Simulation Application

Select Dismiss to exit the "**Manage Solution Sets**" form.

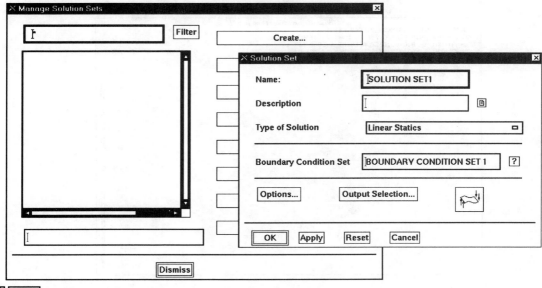

 Select the "**Solve**" icon to solve the model.

## Step 10. Display the results

Switch to the **Post Processing** task.

 To display the principal stress, Select the "**Result…**" icon
Adjust the displayed stress from "**Von Mises**" to "**Max Principal**".
Select **OK** to exit the setting.

 Select the "**Display Template…**" icon and adjust the following two items.

Change from "Smooth Shaded" to "**Stepped Shaded**"
Select **Option**, and change Label Size (% of screen) to **3**.

 Select the "**Display Filter...**" icon
Select the "**FE Models...**" button to display the "FEM Display Filter" form.
Click on the "**All On/Off**" button to turn all FE Models off.
Select **OK → OK** to exit the forms.

 Select the "**Display**" icon.
Pick elements: Press **RMB** and choose **All**
Pick elements (Done): Press **MMB**

# Simulation Application

The stress contour is displayed as follows.

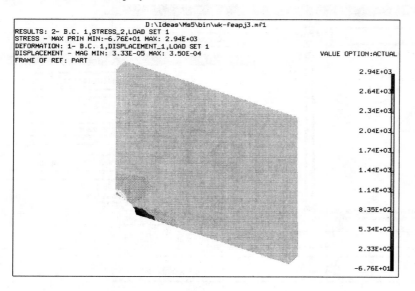

Figure 16.44

Save the model.

You can proceed to Project 4 at this moment. Otherwise, exit I-DEAS.

Mastering I-DEAS
Scholars International Publishing Corp., 1999

# Project 4.
# Refined FEM for Thin Plate with Hole

For the finite element model used in Project 3, we now want to generate a finer mesh around the circular area (Figure 16.45), and perform the same analysis. This can be done by specifying the number of elements around the edges using "Define Free Local" icon command.

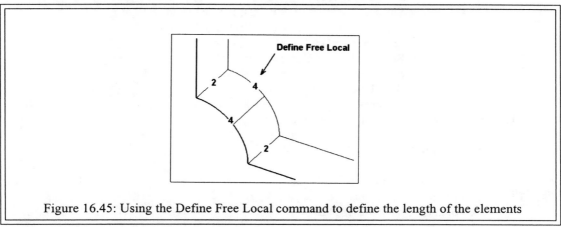

Figure 16.45: Using the Define Free Local command to define the length of the elements

We will use the same finite element model created in Project 3 and create a new finite element model with a given name - Refined FEM for Thin Plate with Hole. Then, apply the "Define Free Local" icon command to refine the mesh.

**Step 1. Apply the restraints**

Switch to the **Boundary Condition** task.

 Select the **"Create FE Model"** icon
Enter the **"Refined FEM for Thin Plate with Hole"** for the FEM Model Name.

Repeat exactly steps 5 through 7 in Project 3 to apply the same restraints and load.

**Step 2. Create the finite element model**

Switch to the **Meshing** task.
Zoom up the lower-left corner.

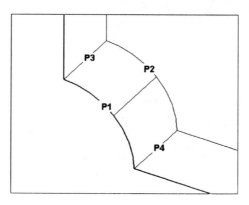

Figure 16.46

Select the "**Define Free Local**" icon.
Pick Vertices/Edges/Surfaces/Curves/Curve Points: Pick **P1** (Figure 16.46)
Pick Vertices/Edges/Surfaces/Curves/Curve Points(Done): Press **MMB**
Enter number of elements on edge(1): **4**
Pick Vertices/Edges/Surfaces/Curves/Curve Points: Pick **P2** (Figure 16.46)
Pick Vertices/Edges/Surfaces/Curves/Curve Points(Done): Press **MMB**
Enter number of elements on edge(1): **4**
Pick Vertices/Edges/Surfaces/Curves/Curve Points: Pick **P3** (Figure 16.46)
Pick Vertices/Edges/Surfaces/Curves/Curve Points(Done): Press **MMB**
Enter number of elements on edge(1): **2**
Pick Vertices/Edges/Surfaces/Curves/Curve Points: Pick **P4** (Figure 16.46)
Pick Vertices/Edges/Surfaces/Curves/Curve Points(Done): Press **MMB**
Enter number of elements on edge(1): **2**
Pick Vertices/Edges/Surfaces/Curves/Curve Points: Press **MMB**
The edges are numbered as shown in Figure 16.45.

Select the "**Zoom All**" icon.

 Select the "**Define Solid Mesh...**" icon.
Pick Volumes: Pick any place on the part
Pick Volumes (Done): Press **MMB**

In the following pop-up, select **Other** → **Material Selection...** → select '**2    Steel**' → **OK**
Adjust element length = **1.5**.

Select the **Preview** button to preview the meshes as follows.

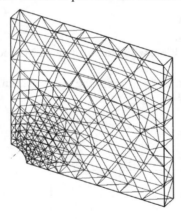

Figure 16.47

Select the **Keep Mesh** button to keep the meshes.

*Note:* If you do not see the mesh, select the "Display Filter..." icon, select the "FE Model..." button
and make sure the "Element" Visibility is turned on.

Save your model here.

**Step 3.** **Create a solution set, solve the model and display the results**
Repeat steps 9 through 10 in Project 3.
The max principal stress contour for the refined mesh is displayed as follows.

Mastering I-DEAS
Scholars International Publishing Corp., 1999

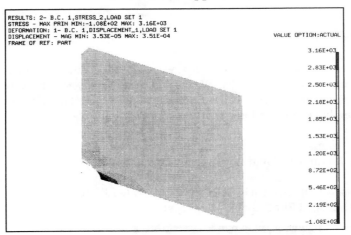

Figure 16.48

The Von Mises stress contour for the refined mesh is displayed as follows.

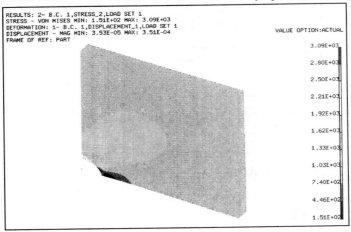

Figure 16.49

 Select the "**Manage Bins...**" icon, and examine the items in the Main bin. These items include one part and two FE Models.

You can "Get" a previous FE Model and review the result.

Select **Dismiss** to exit the form.

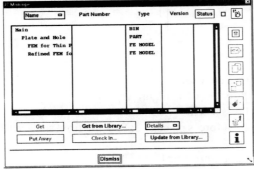

Save the model.

You can proceed to Project 5 at this moment. Otherwise, exit I-DEAS.

> *Note:* As you complete this project, you will be able to analyze the same part using different meshes and boundary conditions. The finite element models and results are saved in the model file.

# Project 5.
# 2-D Thin shell element

For the finite element model used in Projects 3 and 4, we now want to apply 2-D thin shell element, perform the analysis, and examine the results. We need to specify a physical property (thickness of the plate) in a 2-D thin shell analysis. Detail of the procedure can be referred to in Project 1. For a 2-D problem, we need to apply an in-plane force and edge restraints.

**Step 1. Apply the restraints**
Switch to the **Boundary Conditions** task.

Create a new finite element by selecting the **"Create FE Model"** icon
Enter **"Thin Shell FEM"** for the Model Name.

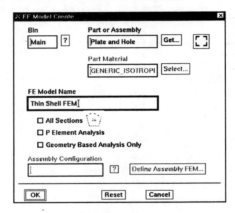

Select **"Redisplay"** to redraw the screen to see the following model.

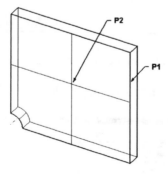

Figure 16.50

Select the **"Force..."** icon command.
Pick entities: Pick at the edge (**P1** in Figure 16.50)
Pick entities (Done): Press **MMB**
Pick surface to set direction of forces on edge 2: Pick the front surface (**P2** in Figure 16.50)

The added force is shown in Figure 16.51.

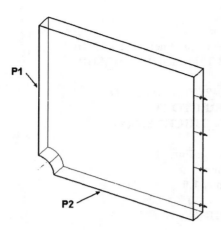

Figure 16.51

 Select the "**Displacement Restraints...**" icon command.
Pick entities: Pick at the left edge (**P1** in Figure 16.51)
Pick entities (Done): Press **MMB**
Adjust the Displacement Restraint on Edge form with: **Y Translation → Free**
Select **OK** to exit the form.

Select the "**Displacement Restraints...**" icon command again.
Pick entities: Pick at the bottom edge (**P2** in Figure 16.51)
Pick entities (Done): Press **MMB**
Adjust the Displacement Restraint on Edge form with: **X Translation → Free**
Select **OK** to exit the form.

The added restraints are shown in Figure 16.52.

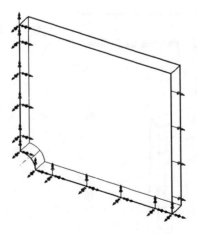

Figure 16.52

Create "**Boundary Condition Set 1**" for the model.  Details can be found in Step 7 of Project 3.

**Step 2. Create the finite element model**

Switch to the **Meshing** task.

Select the "**Physical Property**" icon.
Select element family for properties (Thin_Shell): Press **MMB**
Enter physical prop name or no. (2-Thin Shell2): Press **MMB**

OK to use default values to create table? (Yes): Select **NO**
Enter property name or no.: Select **DIRECTORY**
Enter property name or no.: Select **TK_THICHNESS(4V)**

Enter 1st value for thickness (0.03937...): Enter **1.0**
Enter 2nd value for thickness (0.0): Enter **1.0**
Enter 3rd value for thickness (0.0): Enter **1.0**
Enter 4th value for thickness (0.0: Enter **1.0**
Enter property name or no.: Press **MMB**

Select the "**Define Shell Mesh...**" icon.
Pick Surfaces: Pick the front surface
Pick Surfaces (Done): Press **MMB**

In the following pop-up form, select **Other → Material Selection...→ '2    Steel' → OK**
Adjust **Element Length = 0.5, Element Type → 8-node quadrilateral element.**

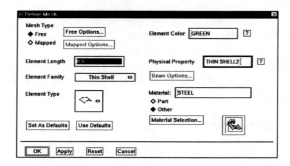

Select the **Preview** button to preview the meshes as follow.

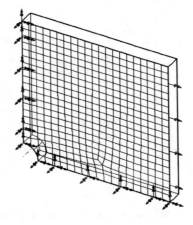

Figure 16.53

16-44

Select the **Keep Mesh** button to keep the meshes.

> *Note:* If you do not see the mesh, select the "Display Filter..." icon, select the "FE Model..." button and make sure the "Element" Visibility is turned on.

Save your model here.

**Step 3.  Create a solution set, solve the model and display the results.**
Repeat the same steps 9 through 10 in Project 3.

The max principal stress contour for the thin-shell model is displayed as follows.

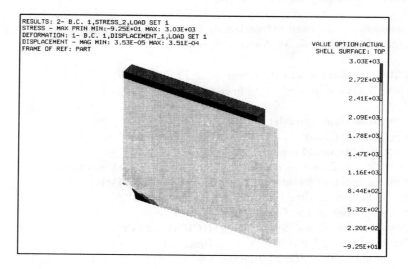

Figure 16.54

Save the model.  You can proceed to Project 6 at this moment.  Otherwise, exit I-DEAS.

# Project 6.
# 2-D Plane Stress Element

For the finite element model used in Project 3, 4, 5, we now want to use a 2-D plane stress element, and perform the same analysis. We need to specify a physical property (thickness of the plate) in a 2-D plane stress analysis. This procedure is very similar to Project 5. Again, for a 2-D problem, we need to apply an in-plane force and edge restraints.

**Step 1.** **Apply the restraints**
Switch to the **Boundary Conditions** task.

Create a new finite element by selecting the "**Create FE Model**" icon
Enter "**Plane Stress FEM**" for the Model Name.

Select "**Redisplay**" to redraw the screen,
and follow the rest of procedure outlined in Step 1 of Project 5.

**Step 2.** **Create the finite element model**
Switch to "**Meshing**" task.

Select the "**Physical Property**" icon.
Select element family for properties (Thin_Shell): Select **Plane Stress**
Enter physical prop name or no. (2-Thin Shell2): Press **MMB**
OK to use default values to create table? (Yes): Select **NO**
Enter property name or no.: Select **DIRECTORY**
Enter property name or no.: Select **TK_THICHNESS(4V)**
Enter 1st value for thickness (0.03937…): Enter **1.0**
Enter 2nd value for thickness (0.0): Enter **1.0**
Enter 3rd value for thickness (0.0): Enter **1.0**
Enter 4th value for thickness (0.0: Enter **1.0**
Enter property name or no.: Press **MMB**

Select the "**Define Shell Mesh...**" icon.
Pick Surfaces: Pick the front surface
Pick Surfaces (Done): Press **MMB**

In the following pop-up form, select **Other → Material Selection... →'2   Steel' → OK**
Adjust **Element Length = 0.5, Element Family → Plane Stress,**
 **Element Type → 8-node quadrilateral element.**

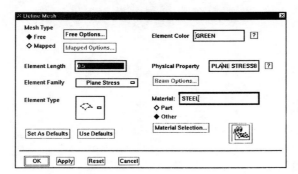

## Simulation Application

Select the **Preview** button to preview the mesh.
Select the **Keep Mesh** button to keep the mesh.

Save your model here.

**Step 3:** **Create a solution set, solve the model and display the results.**
Repeat the same steps 9 through 10 in Project 3.

The max principal stress contour for the plane stress model is displayed as follow.

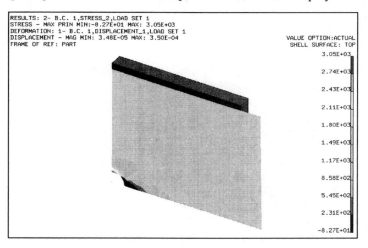

Figure 16.55

Save the model, and exit I-DEAS.

# Chapter 16. Review Questions

1. What is finite element analysis?

2. What is finite element modeling?

3. List and describbe the three phases of finite element modeling.

4. What are boundary conditions?

5. How do we remove degrees of freedom?

6. What are the three types of element properties required in finite element analysis?

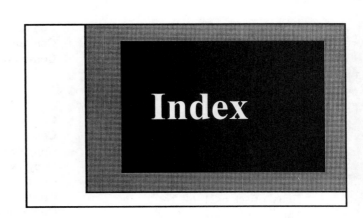

# Index

# Index

**Index**

## -P-

## -Q-

## -R-

**Index**

**Index**

# Mastering I-DEAS

Su-Chen Jonathon Lin, Ph.D.
Professor of Computer-Aided Manufacturing
College of Technology
Eastern Michigan University

F.C. Tony Shiue, Ph.D.
Professor of Computer-Aided Design
College of Technology
Eastern Michigan University

Scholars International Publishing Corp.
Ann Arbor, Michigan, USA

**Warning and Disclaimer**

**Scholars staff:**
Marketing manager: Grace Lin
Chief Editor: Jonathon Lin
Project Editor: Karen L. Sterzik
Illustrators: Samba Chanamolu and Twishampti Dattgupta
Cover artist: Joshua Chen
Printer/Binder: Bookcrafters, Chelsea, Michigan
Printed and bound in the United States of America
99 2000  - - 10 9 8 7 6 5 4 3 2 1

To request more information on this publication, contact:
**Scholars International Publishing Corp.**
**605 Green Road**
**Ann Arbor, Michigan   48105**
**Phone: (734) 930 - 0813  or FAX: (734) 741 - 1927**
**Internet: WWW.Scholarsbook.com**

Lin, SuChen Jonathon, and Shiue, F.C. Tony
Mastering I-DEAS
Includes Index.
ISBN 1-886552-12-6

D
620.0042
LIN

# Preface

I-DEAS is a very powerful high-end parametric based solid modeler. It tightly integrates several modeling and analysis modules together to effectively perform design and analysis tasks. I-DEAS software programs have been widely used in industry and educational institutions all over the world. This is the first text that provides a useful description of important features and functionalities as well as step-by-step tutorials for learning I-DEAS.

The book consists of sixteen chapters. It covers basic parametric modeling concepts, Boolean operations, sketching fundamentals, creating base features and added features, patterning features, creating variables and equations, data management system, creating catalogs and family tables, creating and animating assemblies, creating and editing surfaces, creating drawing views and finite element analysis.

This book is intended to be used by new and experienced I-DEAS users. It can be used in 3D CAD and engineering design courses in various levels of educational institutions as well as training seminars and courses offered by industry.

Experienced I-DEAS users may also find this book useful as a reference resource and may explore new techniques to the problem solving.

We also added the appropriate icons to the tutorial projects. Both the location and symbol of command icons are included. To find those icons, first look for the location to open the icon list and then pick the desired icon. Only those new icons are included in the later chapters.

Jonathon Lin

Mastering I-DEAS
Scholars International Publishing Corp., 1999